PREVIOUS BOOKS BY HAROLD C. SCHONBERG

The Great Pianists
The Great Conductors
Grandmasters of Chess
Lives of the Great Composers
Facing the Music
The Glorious Ones:
    Classical Music's Greatest Performers

H

HAROLD C. SCHONBERG

orowitz

HIS LIFE AND MUSIC

SIMON & SCHUSTER

NEW YORK   LONDON   TORONTO   SYDNEY   TOKYO   SINGAPORE

SIMON & SCHUSTER
Simon & Schuster Building
Rockefeller Center
1230 Avenue of the Americas
New York, New York 10020

10   9   8   7   6   5   4   3   2   1

Library of Congress Cataloging-in-Publication Data

Schonberg, Harold C.
  Horowitz: his life and music / Harold C.
Schonberg.
      p.   cm.
   Discography:
   Includes indexes.
     1. Horowitz, Vladimir, 1904–   .   2. Pianists
—United States—Biography.   I. Title.
ML417.H8S3   1992
786.2'092—dc20   92-24000
[B]   CIP
                                                         MN
   ISBN 0-671-72568-8

Title page photo: Horowitz, 1927. (RCA/BMG)

A leatherbound signed first edition of this book has
been published by The Easton Press.

To my sister: dear, sweet, patient Edith

In 1837 Princess Belgiojoso scored the social coup of the Parisian decade by enticing the two greatest lions of European pianism into giving a "duel" in her salon. Franz Liszt and the celebrated newcomer Sigismond Thalberg, who was amazing audiences wherever he played, met face to face. Each played a solo group and then they came together in a piece for two pianos. After it was over the Countess d'Agoult was asked what she thought.

"Thalberg," she said, "is the first pianist in Europe. Liszt is the only one."

Contents

Preface   13

1   Return of the Native   19
2   Growing Up in Kiev   36
3   Novorossiisk, Taganrog, Gomel, Batumi   50
4   A Greenhorn in Berlin   67
5   Crashing Through   76
6   Parisian Lion   82
7   On the Road   96
8   "The Octaves Race"   105
9   "King of Kings"   114
10   Marriage   131
11   Disappearance   147
12   In Horowitz's Shoes—and Tails   160

13	The Lazy Life	176
14	Uncashed Checks	191
15	Media Blitz	206
16	Still the Master	214
17	The New Horowitz?	221
18	Sonia	232
19	Traveling à la Paderewski	239
20	Anniversaries	247
21	Collapse	258
22	Resurrection	266
23	Globetrotter	276
24	Last Pupil	292
25	Mozart and *Liebestod*	302
26	Artist-As-Hero	310

The Horowitz Recordings — 317

Appendix I	1926–53	319
Appendix II	LP and Stereo	329
Appendix III	1965–82	339
Appendix IV	1985–89 with a Digression on Horowitz and Mozart	346

Discography of Horowitz — 355

Chronological Section	357
Index and Release Section	378
Composer Index	378
Performer Index	405
Index	407

Preface

Near the end of his life Vladimir Horowitz started thinking about writing his memoirs. With his approval, Simon & Schuster engaged me to help him with the project, and we started work in January 1987. He dictated his reminiscences into a tape recorder.

Unfortunately the project broke off about six weeks later. Horowitz was preoccupied with his preparation of the Mozart A major Concerto (K. 488) for his forthcoming recording in Milan with Carlo Maria Giulini and the Scala Orchestra, and he was a little nervous about it. He had never played it in public.

Horowitz left for Milan and I never saw him again. On his return to New York he dropped the project, though in the last months of his life there were indications that he was interested in resuming work on the memoirs. It was not to be. But at least he had passed to me some of the material that would have gone into his memoirs. All of the Horowitz quotations in this book come, unless otherwise specified, from those taped interviews early in 1987.

During most of the 1987 Horowitz sessions his wife, Wanda, the daughter of Arturo Toscanini, was present. She was the moderating force, prompting him, correcting those dates about which he was hazy, and keeping him on line. Horowitz would often tend to digress. Mrs. Horowitz would firmly set him straight. After fifty-four years of married life she knew how to handle him.

I was no stranger to Vladimir and Wanda Horowitz. Since 1954 I had frequently interviewed him for the New York *Times*. Whatever Horowitz did was, after all, news, and through the years I had a journalistic relationship with him. If we were not exactly close friends—critics on the *Times* shunned social relationships with artists they were in a position to review—at least I believe we understood each other, and, as musicians who had grown up with a set of traditions that had all but vanished, we shared and relished a common musical language.

Invariably, when the interviews were over, Horowitz would want to relax, talk, gossip. He never went to many recitals, but his natural curiosity about pianists young and old kept him glued to the three major good-music radio stations of New York. If he did not hear the competition in the concert hall, he could and did hear it broadcast on records.

He did not think too highly of the culture and general musicianship of the pianists he heard ("They don't *sing*"), but the fingerwork of a few virtuosos of the younger generation impressed him. "Some of them," he said in 1987, "have extraordinary techniques. I heard on the radio a Liszt record, the *Faust* Waltz, played by Jean-Yves Thibaudet. It was amazing, such dexterity, such technique, such articulation, such command. I could not do that today." Pause. "But I do certain things they can't do, so that makes us even."

On the whole, though, he liked very little of what he heard, and his brief, dismissive comments could be devastating. Vladimir Ashkenazy? "Ashkenazy was good once. Not now." Glenn Gould? "I heard a recording of the Wagner *Siegfried Idyll* played by Glenn Gould. It was his arrangement. He played like a stupid ass. The tempi were all wrong. He was not normal." The great Josef Hofmann? "A very good pianist but a second-rate musician." The legendary Solomon? "Boring." The equally legendary Arturo Benedetti Michelangeli? Here Horowitz expressed admiration with a qualification: "Interesting pianist, but I think he is just a little bit *meshuga.*" André Watts? "Technically formidable, fantastic fingers, musically horrible." The new Russian school? "Of the Russian pianists I like only one, Richter. Gilels did some things well, but I did not like his mannerisms, the way he moved around while he was playing." Claudio Arrau? "I heard his *Emperor* and it was terrible. He plays so slow, ugh. Also the *Waldstein.* So slow."

He would go to the piano to illustrate a point and, once seated, could remain there for several hours. Often I turned pages for him. He was a fabulous reader, taking in five measures at a glance no matter how difficult the music. He had in his fingers much of the active repertoire. In his entire career, for instance, Horowitz never programmed more than about a half dozen of the Beethoven sonatas, but he knew all thirty-two by heart, and at home he would sit at the piano playing one of the early sonatas, or sections of the *Hammerklavier,* or the beginning of the last movement of Op. 109, wondering why pianists played it merely as chords without getting the melodic line and the chordal balances. Fooling around at the keyboard he might drift from the Saint-Saëns C minor Concerto to sections of Tchaikovsky's *Eugene Onegin,* to the Chopin Etude in Thirds ("I am too old to play this in public"), to the Schumann Concerto, to Mozart's G minor Symphony, to some Moszkowski he had learned as a child, to some completely unfamiliar Liszt.

He had in his fingers many of the Russian operas and would play long sections from Tchaikovsky's *Eugene Onegin* at the slightest prompt. The *Ring* cycle he knew by heart and could still play some of the transcriptions he had made as a youth. He also had a passion for Bizet. "When I go to Père Lachaise I put a flower on Bizet's grave. I think *Carmen* is unsurpassable. I love *Pearl Fishers,* a beautiful opera. I love his Symphony in C." He also loved Saint-Saëns's *Samson and Delilah* (but the piano music of Saint-Saëns did not interest him except for the Fourth Concerto).

He liked jazz or, at least, jazz pianists, some of whom almost came up to his own demanding technical standards. Henry Pleasants, who had covered the jazz beat and written with perspicacity about jazz singers, told the story about Horowitz sneaking in to listen to the jazz pianist Art Tatum. He was terribly impressed with Tatum's technique and his easy, natural way of playing, and on one occasion couldn't understand how Tatum did what he did in "Tea for Two." So he introduced himself. Tatum admitted that yeah, he had heard of Vladimir Horowitz. The two men had a pleasant talk, and then Horowitz asked Tatum how long it had taken him to learn "Tea for Two." Tatum looked at him as though he were crazy. "I just made it up," he said. Horowitz went home and worked up his own arrangement of "Tea for Two," which he played as a party piece.

He was to the piano playing of his day what Jascha Heifetz was to the violin. All of the world's young violinists wanted to be Jascha Heifetz, and all of the world's young pianists wanted to be Vladimir Horowitz. Especially in the period from 1940 to 1960, the young pianists tried. They tried to get his kind of sonority, they aped his physical mannerisms, they played Horowitz-like programs. If Horowitz revived a seldom-played piece—Schumann's *Kreisleriana,* say—almost everybody was programming *Kreisleriana* the following year. They tried to copy the Horowitz phrasings, the Horowitz agogics. Of course it was an impossible quest. Personality cannot be imitated or transferred. The Horowitz personality was accepted by most pianists with awe and even worship. Horowitz once went backstage after a concert by Alicia de Larrocha, whom he had never met. When she saw him in the green room she nearly fainted. Then she dropped to her knees and kissed his hand. Horowitz had that effect upon pianists.

His virtuosity was, of course, integral to his triumph with the public, as it has always been with any amazing virtuoso since the days of Paganini and Liszt. But sheer virtuosity was only part of the Horowitz gestalt. Not many realized how serious a musician he was. Yes, he sometimes could go overboard. Yes, he could miscalculate in concert. Sometimes his dares did not come off; or a listener could legitimately ask why he took a phrase in this or that manner. But never was there a letdown in interest, tension, or drama, his ability to keep an audience at the edge of the seat.

He had that from the very beginning, all through a professional career that started in 1921 and ended in 1989. When he came to international attention in the late 1920s, he was up against a handful of pianists who had set standards for all time: Rachmaninoff, Hofmann, Lhevinne, Friedman, Cortot, Schnabel, and a few others. But almost all had disappeared by 1950, leaving Horowitz pretty much alone, certainly as an exponent of Romantic music. In the public eye, and to most of the professionals too, he was the world's greatest pianist for the entire last half of the twentieth century. And when he died there was nobody to replace him.

The literature on Horowitz is scant. There have been one biography and one volume of reminiscences by a friend. Otherwise information about Horowitz has to be gleaned from interviews and from past magazine and newspaper articles and radio interviews. Under the circumstances, a bibliography would be nonexistent; in the running text of this book I have generally documented the source of quoted material.

The book could not have been written without the help of many individuals and organizations. I owe special, heartfelt thanks to:

Virginia Bach, Herbert Barrett, Coleman Blumfield, Werner Burkhardt, Schuyler Chapin, Robin Commagère, Ivan Davis, Martin Feinstein, Vladimir Feltsman, Rudolf Firkusny, Thomas Frost, Raya Garbousova, Peter Gelb, Alexis Golovin, Gary Graffman, Naomi Graffman, Horacio Gutierrez, Leonid Hambro, Eduardus Halim, Orrin Howard, Lawrence Ingram, Byron Janis, Constance Keene, Dr. Aaron Kellner, Igor Kipnis, Howard Klein, Richard K. Lieberman, Dr. Heinz I. Lippmann, Josephine Mangiaracina, Nikita Magaloff, Vera Michaelson, Nathan Milstein, Franz Mohr, Bryce Morrison, John F. Pfeiffer, Henry Pleasants, Richard Probst, Phillip Ramey, Regula Rapp, Halina Rodzinski, Dr. Albrecht Roeseler, Natasha Saitzoff, Jon M. Samuels, Alexander Schlempp, George Schneider, Rudolf Serkin, Harold Shaw, Mordecai Shehori, Nicolas Slonimsky, Dorle Soria, Christian Steiner, Joseph Stelmach, Hans Vogel, Lev Vlasenko; and also to those who were interviewed but who did not wish their names to be used;

Ileene Smith, my editor at Summit Books, who steered me into the right lane before I veered off into disaster;

My wife, Helene, who contributed valuable ideas about organization;

Lucy Kroll, my literary agent, who analyzed the manuscript and had valuable suggestions to offer;

Caine Alder, who supplied clippings and other material from his vast Horowitz collection, and who read the manuscript, correcting some dates and factual errors;

Max Massei, the French Horowitz specialist, who also read the manuscript, corrected some dates and offered many constructive suggestions. Much of the information on Horowitz's first season in Paris has been derived from M. Massei's memorial article in the March 1990 issue of *Le monde de la musique;*

The Music Division of the New York Public Library at Lincoln Center, with special thanks for its collection of newspaper and periodical clippings;

The morgue of the New York *Times,* that incredible compilation of nearly 150 years of day-by-day history;

Henry Z. Steinway, who generously let me go through the files of Steinway & Sons, and also gave permission to reproduce photographs from the company's archives;

Harold E. Samuel, music librarian of Yale University, and Kenneth Crilly, public services librarian, who guided me through the Horowitz archives at Yale;

The National Sound Institute and the Newspaper Library of the British Library;

And to Marilyn Egol of BMG Classics, Albert Imperato of Deutsche Grammophon, Jennifer Heinlein of PolyGram, and Susan Schiffer of CBS/Sony Classics, who were kind enough to send me Horowitz recordings on compact discs, opened the picture files of their respective companies, and were indefatigable in their efforts to check dates for me.

1

Return of the Native

I got excited. It was my country. I looked through the window
[of the airplane] and I said this is Russia. This is where I was
born. This is where I grew up. I never thought I would have this
kind of thrill, this kind of nostalgia, this remembrance of things
past. All educated Russians have certain things in their blood
that never vanish. We grew up reading Pushkin, Dostoevsky,
Tolstoy, Chekhov. We all, and not only musicians, have Glinka,
Mussorgsky, Rimsky-Korsakov, and Borodin in our ears. This
was what I was going back to, and it evoked memories. Even
pride in old Mother Russia it evoked.
  —*Vladimir Horowitz, 1987, describing his feelings en route to
  Russia in 1986*

On April 20, 1986, the wheel came full circle for Vladimir
Horowitz with an audible click, and he recognized it as such. His
life, as he later said, was "now completely rounded out."

The man generally considered the world's greatest pianist, the
archetype of Romanticism, the most electrifying pianist of his time,
the last great direct descendant of the old Russian school of piano
playing, the virtuoso supreme, on that date appeared on a Russian
stage after an absence of sixty-one years.

But a few days before his appearance at the Great Hall of the
Moscow Conservatory he had gone through another powerful
emotional experience. Shortly after his arrival in Moscow, Horowitz told the authorities that he wanted to visit Scriabin's house.
For that he had deep-rooted reasons. His uncle Alexander from

Kharkov had alerted Scriabin in 1914 about a promising youngster in Kiev who was on his way to becoming a great pianist. So when Scriabin gave a concert in Kiev, Uncle Alexander arranged for his eleven-year-old nephew, Volodya, to meet with the great pianist-composer. They had a short visit. As Horowitz remembered it:

> Scriabin must have hated the experience. He had to listen to me only a few hours before his concert. He was short, elegant, and nervous. He was going to play two of his difficult late sonatas in a few hours, and he could not have been very interested in a little Jewish boy from Kiev. I played for him a Chopin waltz, the *Melodie* by Paderewski, and Borodin's *Au couvent*. Perhaps he was polite and did not want to talk about my playing. Instead he said that I should grow up to be a cultured man. There were many pianists, he said, but very few of them were cultured.

Scriabin's words remained in Horowitz's mind all his life. And Horowitz adored Scriabin's music, recorded a fair amount of it, and played it better than anybody else. So a pilgrimage to the Scriabin Museum, which was also the house in which Scriabin had lived, was high on Horowitz's list of priorities.

The Russians said yes, of course, but wait a day or two. What Horowitz did not know was that the building had been neglected. A crew of painters and workmen was rushed to 11 Vakhtangov Street and two rooms were put into passable shape. When Horowitz arrived at this Potemkin Village the paint was still wet, although he was so thrilled to be in the Scriabin ambience he did not notice it.

He, his wife, Wanda, and Peter Gelb, Horowitz's manager, were greeted by Scriabin's daughter, Yelena, eighty-six years old. On Scriabin's piano Horowitz played the composer's early C sharp minor and D sharp minor Etudes, which he had also scheduled for his Moscow concert. The instrument, a Bechstein concert grand that had been a present from the famous German manufacturer in 1910, was in terrible shape; but nevertheless there were tears in Yelena's eyes as he played. Afterward they reminisced. (She was to die four years later, in August of 1990.)

When Horowitz looked at the contents of the two rooms, what impressed him most was Scriabin's desk. It was a standing desk, which meant that Scriabin composed standing up and not at the piano. Horowitz could not get over it. The visit, said Gelb, left Horowitz "visibly moved." Another segment of his past, one that meant a great deal to him, had activated his memory bank.

Most Russians had no memory bank at all when it came to Vladimir Horowitz. Sixty-one years is a long time. Nevertheless the Russians were in a state close to hysteria when the announcement was made that Horowitz would be giving a concert in the Great Hall of the Moscow Conservatory. If Horowitz was an overwhelming presence in the West, he was sheer myth in Russia. Russian musicians, of course, knew what he represented—Romanticism incarnate, harnessed to incredible fingers—but very few had actually heard him. For decades he had played only in America.

When it was learned that Horowitz was coming to Moscow, there was, as the Russian pianist Vladimir Feltsman described it, "a sort of insanity. I don't ever remember such excitement for any musician who played there." To pianists of Feltsman's generation, Horowitz was "a sort of antique hero, something from mythology." Feltsman's teacher at the Moscow Conservatory, Jacob Flier, was a Horowitz admirer who had managed to collect some of his recordings, and Flier made his class listen to them. Now the antique hero could be heard in person.

There also was something else in the mind of some Russian pianists—a show-me attitude. Russia was not entirely divorced from the intellectual life of the world, and the pianists there had heard that Horowitz had the reputation in certain circles of being all fingers and no brain. Thus there were those Russian musicians prepared in advance to dismiss him as a superficial virtuoso. The others, who desperately *wanted* him to live up to his reputation— after all, he was the legendary Russian pianist Horowitz—were worried. Could an eighty-three-year-old musician possibly do so? And if by now Horowitz had no technique left, what else could he possibly offer? Could he certify his standing as a legend?

So when Horowitz stepped on the stage of the Great Hall of the Moscow Conservatory, the event was much more than a mere piano recital. A mighty figure had returned; and more, a *Russian* who had conquered the world. And he still was one of their own, even after sixty-one years. There was an outpouring of love and pride from the audience, captured eternally on the videocassette made of the concert.

In a way it was a sort of miracle that Horowitz played in

Russia at all. His appearance had been preceded by some high-level negotiations involving the United States and Russia, the State Department and the Politburo, President Reagan and Chairman Mikhail Gorbachev. The two superpowers had not had a cultural exchange since the Soviet invasion of Afghanistan, and there still was considerable tension between them.

And at the beginning of the negotiations there also was Vladimir Horowitz to deal with—the temperamental Horowitz with his demands for all of the amenities when on tour, with his financial arrangements, with his piano, with his entourage. He expected certain niceties and would not travel unless he was sure they would be forthcoming. As things turned out, it took the combined resources of several governments to make him happy.

But as far as Horowitz was concerned, the time was right. He had gone through a terrible period during 1983 and 1984, when he had to overcome psychological and physical ills and the wreck of one of the great techniques in pianistic history. Nobody thought he would ever play again. But he pulled through, started practicing, found that his skills had returned, and he reentered the world. Early in 1985 he had given concerts in London and Milan for the first time in decades. The recitals were a huge success, he was greeted as myth come to life, and he felt that he had played well.

And he was at a point in his life where he was prepared to accept many of the things he had rejected in the previous decades. He had hated traveling, staying in hotels, breaking up his comfortable way of living. Now, in recent years, he had decided that traveling was not so bad. He even enjoyed it. He liked taking the Concorde, staying in the great hotels, going to great restaurants even if he ordered only boiled chicken or Dover sole. He loved playing for audiences who had not heard him for many years or, as was generally the case in Europe, had never heard him.

Thus he was feeling euphoric in 1985, and when his manager, Peter Gelb, proposed the return to Russia, Horowitz did not need much urging. But he immediately set a condition. As on his return to England, where his sponsor had been Prince Charles, he would not go to Russia unless he was invited by the government. The financial aspect was also important. If Horowitz never did things *only* for money, he expected a good return when he did play.

Horowitz had said for many years that he would never go back to Russia. "We all say things, only to live long enough to discover that people and events can make a person change his mind," said Horowitz, discussing his trip in 1987. *Glasnost, perestroika,* the new wave of liberalism sweeping over the Soviet Union, the change in the climate between the two superpowers—all these factors, said Horowitz, entered into his decision to go.

He also thought about his family, the little that was left of it. His mother had died in 1930 and his father in a gulag in the late thirties. Jacob, Horowitz's eldest brother, had died during the Revolution in the early 1920s. He had left a child who had a son, who in turn had a son who attended the Horowitz Moscow concert. George, the other elder brother, had died during World War II. Vladimir's sister, Regina, who was always called Genya and was three years older than he, had died in 1984. It is not generally known that in February 1975, Horowitz tried to get Genya to the United States for a three-month visit. He filled out all the requisite papers and made applications to the State Department, but the Russians would not cooperate. The only way Horowitz could keep in touch with her was by phone. There was a daughter from Genya's first marriage, Yelena Dolberg, who was nine years old when Horowitz left Russia. Now she was seventy.

When Horowitz finally indicated that he would go to Russia, Gelb called Bernard Kalb, a former New York *Times* reporter then an assistant secretary of state in Washington. Could Kalb call Ambassador Arthur A. Hartman in Moscow and ask him if he could accommodate Horowitz and his considerable needs, warning the ambassador that it might involve "turning the house upside down." Within twenty-four hours Gelb was notified that Hartman would do anything possible. Gelb then phoned Gosconcert, the Russian agency that handled tours of foreign artists within the Soviet Union. Indeed, yes, Gosconcert was very interested.

Ambassador Hartman exerted himself on behalf of Horowitz at the White House and State Department, neither of which needed much urging. The political climate was right. Gorbachev and President Reagan had just signed a protocol that, among other things, reintroduced cultural interchange between the Soviet Union and the United States. The feeling was that as a Russian-born musician, even though he had left there over sixty years ago and not been back since, Horowitz would be the ideal American representative to reopen cultural exchange.

In December 1985, Gelb got a visa and left for Moscow. Like

any Horowitz tour managed by Gelb, this one took furious last-minute planning. Gelb met Ambassador Hartman and had a long talk with him about what Horowitz considered basic amenities. Horowitz could live only on certain foods. His bedroom had to have black drapes to shut out all light. He was not to be disturbed until noon. The embassy cook had to be briefed on how the food was to be prepared. A videocassette machine in the Horowitz bedroom was mandatory. The complete list was not as long as the *Encyclopedia Britannica,* but formidable nevertheless. Somewhat dazed but determined to cooperate, Hartman gallantly started mobilizing forces all over Moscow, calling for help from the diplomatic corps in Russia. The Italian ambassador promised to be responsible for bringing in the fresh asparagus demanded by Horowitz. The British ambassador was responsible for the Dover sole, flown in four times a week. (Certain members of the American embassy had T-shirts printed up saying DOVER SOLE AIRLIFT. On the back was printed GROUND CREW. The wearers were the ones responsible for going to the airport to pick up the precious commodities.) Sent from New York were some thirty videocassettes, mostly adventure and science fiction, to keep Horowitz happy during those long Russian nights.

Said one awed diplomat, "It would be easier to prepare for the arrival of a symphony orchestra."

Gelb met with the head of Gosconcert and worked out a deal. Horowitz, he said, had agreed to play for nothing. All Horowitz wanted was cooperation in terms of television. Gosconcert was happy to go along.

Word about the Horowitz return to Russia was of course big news and it received international coverage. The announcement of Horowitz's decision to play in the Soviet Union appeared in the New York *Times* on January 17, 1986. Horowitz told the *Times:* "Before I die I want to see the country in which I was born." He told friends he also was curious about Russia. How much had it changed after all those years?

And of course there was the selection of music to occupy his mind. What programs to play in Russia? Horowitz decided to play old friends for his first concert. There would be Chopin's A flat Polonaise, some Scriabin, Schubert, Liszt, Mozart. One night Horowitz had several people in his living room, talking about the program. Horowitz said one of the pieces would be the Scriabin

Etude in C sharp minor (Op. 2, No. 1), a slow, gorgeous threnody for everything Russian. Wanda said, "But Volodya, you have not practiced it." Horowitz said he did not need to practice it. He had known it all his life. He grew angry. That *he* should not know Scriabin's Op. 2, No. 1! To prove it, he went to the piano and played it beautifully.

But an episode in Moscow almost canceled all of this frantic preparation. Vladimir Feltsman, the dissident Russian pianist who has since come to the United States, was asked by Ambassador Hartman to play in the American embassy. Feltsman had put in for immigration to Israel in 1979, and for the next seven years found himself a nonperson. Ambassador Hartman became interested in him and often invited the young pianist to give recitals at the embassy.

Such a Feltsman recital there was scheduled shortly before the Horowitz arrival. But the embassy piano on which Feltsman was to play was sabotaged before the concert, and when Horowitz read about it he said that he would not go to Russia. Gelb had to pull strings to get a letter from President Reagan assuring Horowitz that he would be under the protection of the U.S. Government, which would put a guard over his piano.

The instrument (his beloved Steinway CD 314 503 in his Ninety-fourth Street living room) was, as promised, removed from Sheremetyevo Airport under the suspicious eyes of a military guard and kept under constant observation by armed marines when it arrived in Moscow well in advance of the concert. Steinway sent the piano over, and also Franz Mohr, its head technician, to tune and regulate it, paying all expenses. Steinway also sent Richard Probst, its director of the Artists and Concerts Department.

Probst was somewhat startled by the Russian way of moving pianos. It was his responsibility to see that the instrument got safely to the stage of the Great Hall of the Moscow Conservatory. When the truck pulled up, he said, about twenty of the hugest men he had ever seen came forth, picked the piano up by its rim and "wafted" it up the many steps leading to the hall "as though they were carrying a briefcase."

Horowitz and Wanda started preparing for the trip early in April. The night before they left for Moscow by way of Paris they went out for a farewell dinner with a few close friends—the Gelbs; Wanda's old friend Sally Horwich; Jack Pfeiffer, for many years

Horowitz's record producer, and two or three others. Champagne toasts were made and everybody kissed the Horowitzes good-bye.

Horowitz was told everything was arranged, including the live television special that Gelb was going to produce. That was how Horowitz would get his compensation. CBS bought the American rights. Other broadcasting companies around the world bought rights for their own countries. It was claimed by CBS that this would be the first time a full piano recital in its entirety would be broadcast live over a commercial network in the United States. Horowitz's 1968 Carnegie Hall concert had been announced as a one-hour television special rather than a concert.

Deutsche Grammophon, at that time Horowitz's recording company, agreed to provide the audio equipment for the telecast, and a crew of about forty-five technicians from Europe and America was selected for Moscow. That caused resentment in Gostel Radio, the Russian television monopoly. But the Westerners had dealt with Russian television previously and considered it medieval. They finally got their own way. Or thought they did.

What happened was that a few days after Horowitz arrived in Moscow, the Americans found out that Gostel was pulling a rearguard action. The imported team of television technicians was not going to be given visas. The Americans immediately told the Soviet leaders that the action of Gostel would break up the Reagan-Gorbachev accord. Ambassador Hartman let the Soviet Presidium know that if a contract were not immediately signed, Horowitz would pull out and the whole deal would be off. The contract was quickly signed. Deutsche Grammophon used state-of-the-art electronic equipment to record the concert. For the video facilities, Gelb engaged a Swiss company named Polivideo. The *Horowitz in Moscow* compact disc and videocassette turned out to be among the biggest-selling items in the history of classical music.

Because of the time difference, the Horowitz concert could be shown in America only on Sunday morning as a CBS special news report. The program was to be broadcast live in the United States and almost every country in Europe. CBS sent Charles Kuralt and a news crew for the broadcast. Kuralt provided a running commentary not only of the concert but also of Horowitz sightseeing in Moscow.

Gelb had to be everywhere at once, and he was a nervous man: not nervous about Horowitz changing his mind, but about international politics. Horowitz had a history of last-second cancellations, but Gelb did not worry about that. As he later explained:

> In my years as Mr. Horowitz's manager, he never cancelled
> a concert at all, and fear of his cancelling in Moscow was the
> last thing from my mind. I *was* concerned about any other
> number of things that might have caused the concert to be
> cancelled, such as last-minute interference by the KGB because
> of the political tension over the bombing of Libya or because
> of the Soviet unhappiness about the television production not
> being under their control. I never thought that Horowitz
> would cancel for any reason except a sudden illness, and he was
> very healthy in Moscow.

On April 14, 1986, Horowitz and Wanda boarded a plane from Paris to Moscow and soon saw the Russian soil. When they arrived, he called himself "an ambassador of peace." He and Wanda were put up at Spaso House, the residence of the American ambassador and hence American ground. So in a way Horowitz felt that he was still in America. He rested and practiced. His way of practicing, as always, was to play a piece through two or three times. He was in full agreement with Nathan Milstein's observation. "If you don't know a piece after having it in your repertoire for fifty years you never will know it," Milstein once told him. When he was not at the piano he was exercising his considerable charm on the ambassador and his wife and on all those who came near him. He also used the embassy car for a bit of sightseeing and was shocked to see how shabby Moscow had become.

Two days before the April 20 recital at the Great Hall of the Moscow Conservatory, which seats about 1,700, he played an open rehearsal there, a tryout to gauge the hall and go through the program. The concert was supposed to be exclusively for students. But many of the tickets were seized by the conservatory faculty, and by bureaucrats and politicians with connections. There was no advertising, no official recognition of the Horowitz presence, but in Russia word of mouth has been refined to a high art and everybody knew about the advance concert. Many students crashed the hall, breaking through the police barriers and invading the premises. Things like that just did not happen in the Soviet Union in those days. Horowitz, when he was later told about it, was pleased and touched, and hoped none of the kids got into trouble.

Probst of Steinway said that the concert for the students, even more than the official concert, was one of the great experiences of his life. Some of the "students" in the audience, Probst said, were older than Horowitz. But there were also many youngsters. Probst, who was in one of the stage seats at the rehearsal, was able to look into the auditorium:

> When Horowitz started the Scriabin C sharp minor Etude, I looked at the faces of the audience, and I still get shivers when I think about it. His playing, and that particular piece of Russian music, was lifting the entire audience out of the weight of their problems, lifting the yoke off their shoulders, transfixing them. To me it was kind of a prayer that Horowitz was making, an offering of some kind. It was a kind of religious experience.

Feltsman was in the audience. The first thing that struck him when Horowitz started to play—it was a Scarlatti sonata—was the Horowitz sound:

> It took me half a minute or a minute to adjust my ears. The sound was very, very soft, very gentle, very piano, very beautiful. I can tell you that I have never heard in that hall, where many major artists played, this sort of sound. Fragile, floating, very sad. It was indescribable. Some of us pianists are good technicians, some of us are good musicians, but very few have this magical touch where the sound is floating. He had it. He had it as probably nobody else. It was physically, almost unbearably beautiful when he played Rachmaninoff's Prelude in G sharp minor. The last section, where there is the theme in the left hand, he crossed over and hit that D sharp, where he kept it floating for about half an hour. It was a real miracle, absolutely a miracle. Technically there were a few little mixups, but that was beside the point. I didn't care how many wrong notes he played—there weren't many—because the playing was so beautiful. Such a unique, magic touch, this unique floating sound, I have never heard from any piano player in my life.

Feltsman came away from the concert with changed ideas about Horowitz. He too had heard from some of his colleagues that Horowitz was nothing but an acrobat with fingers. After this concert he knew they were wrong. "I could not agree with those who had said that Horowitz was a great piano player but a lousy musician."

After the rehearsal Feltsman and many other musicians went backstage. Feltsman introduced himself. Suddenly Horowitz made the connection. "Oh, I know you. You're the guy whose piano got messed up." Feltsman said, "Yes, I'm the guy." Then Horowitz wanted to know where Feltsman sat. Feltsman told him. "Tell me, tell me, how did it sound?" asked Horowitz.

> Of course [Feltsman said] we spoke Russian. He spoke exquisite Russian. He wanted to know if the acoustics were all right. He asked me if I knew how old he was. "Yes, Maestro, I know how old you are. But I can reassure you that your piano playing even at your age is much better than all of us youngsters put together multiplied by ten."

Horowitz beamed.

The next day Donna Hartman, the ambassador's wife, telephoned Feltsman. Could he come right over? Horowitz, she said, wanted to see him. Feltsman said that he never moved so fast in his life. He was at Spaso House "with the speed of a nuclear missile." He and Horowitz spent about three hours talking, mostly about music. Finally Horowitz said that he had to take his nap, but first would Feltsman like to play something? Feltsman said that since there was so little time, perhaps Horowitz would like to play? "With pleasure," Horowitz said, and played Chopin's A minor Mazurka from the Op. 17 set, the Liszt *Consolation* in D flat, and then looked through a pile of music and picked out the Schubert-Liszt *Ständchen*. This he played from the printed notes, Feltsman turning pages for him.

"It was *divine*," Feltsman said. "I was watching his hands. I noticed that he was motionless. His face was serious and tense, like a mask. This was total concentration. His technique was very peculiar, and I don't think that anybody could copy it. He was playing only from elbow to finger. The shoulder never moved. Flat fingers, as we all know."

Feltsman was an accurate observer. Horowitz never used much shoulder motion. "I never take chords from the shoulder," he once told an interviewer. "It's like a boxer. When he boxes from far away, he loses power. Good boxers cut short. When you play like that, the sound is pleasant and full. You can hear every chord and every note equally. It's never hard—just like an organ chord." Horowitz loved to watch prizefights on television and considered himself an authority on boxing.

A single poster on the wall of the Moscow Conservatory was the only announcement of the official concert on April 20, 1986. The poster said, merely, VLADIMIR HOROWITZ, USA. The hall was, of course, packed for Horowitz's first official Russian appearance since 1925. Only about four hundred tickets were put on sale, at eight dollars; the rest of the seats were reserved for dignitaries. But the state box used by Politburo members was empty. Philip Taubman, the Moscow bureau chief of the New York *Times,* covered the concert as a news story. He explained that the box was empty because top government and party leaders would have considered it inappropriate to attend a recital by an American citizen after the United States air strike against Libya, a Soviet ally. At this concert, as at the rehearsal, about two hundred students stormed the hall and managed to get in.

The April 20 program had to be specially arranged because it was being televised by a CBS crew for the program *Vladimir Horowitz in Moscow,* carried in America on the CBS *Sunday Morning* show. It was a rather light program. Horowitz did not play Schumann's *Kreisleriana* (which he did play in Leningrad), because he thought it was "too long and intellectual" for a worldwide television audience. He opened with three Scarlatti sonatas. Instead of the Schumann he had Mozart—the C major Sonata (K. 330)—followed by two Rachmaninoff Preludes, in G and G sharp minor (Op. 32, Nos. 5 and 12); Scriabin's Etudes in C sharp minor (Op. 2, No. 1) and D sharp minor (Op. 8, No. 12); Schubert's B flat Impromptu, the delicious Schubert-Liszt *Soirée de Vienne* No. 6, and Liszt's *Sonetto 104 del Petrarca;* Chopin's Mazurkas in C sharp minor (Op. 30, No. 4) and F minor (Op. 7, No. 3), and, to conclude the concert, the old Horowitz *cheval de bataille,* the A flat Polonaise. For encores there were Schumann's *Träumerei,* Moszkowski's *Etincelles,* and the Rachmaninoff *Polka de W. R.*

The concert was an emotional experience on all sides, to be forever shared by those who own *Horowitz in Moscow,* the videocassette. Horowitz came forth and affectionately patted his piano lid before acknowledging the audience. Then he bowed in his usual courtly manner and sat down. Off he went into Scarlatti. The camera showed an audience in rapt attention. When Horowitz got to the Scriabin C sharp minor Etude, that distillation of Mother Russia, people were seen weeping. At intermission and at the concert's end, bouquets of flowers were brought to the stage. Before starting his first encore, Horowitz played a chord or two and laughed. Then came his "official" encore piece, Schumann's *Träumerei,* which he almost always played. Here too one could see people weeping. *Etincelles* and the Rachmaninoff *Polka* brought down the house. There were six curtain calls.

After the concert Horowitz was visited by his niece, Yelena Dolberg, the daughter of his sister. She told him that the concert was wonderful, and that she also had been at his last recital in Moscow, which was in 1925. Horowitz said that he probably played better now.

Taubman reported the reaction of many musicians to the Moscow concert, among them the well-known composer Alfred Schnittke, who said, "The playing is remarkable. There is infinite contrast and finesse. He plays with total freedom." The Russian pianists in the audience were swept away. All of a sudden they were faced with music making that hit at the roots of their racial and genetic subconscious, and they suddenly realized the glory that Anton Rubinstein and the old Russian pianists must have been.

It was the freedom above all that so amazed them. Lev Vlasenko, a prominent pianist and teacher at the Moscow Conservatory, said that all of them had heard some of the Horowitz records, of course, but those gave little idea of the Horowitz aura in concert —his color, his sound, above all the freedom that he represented. But, said Vlasenko, "It was a controlled freedom."

A few years later he told an American critic that after the concert he had to spend a few days thinking over what Horowitz had done. Then there was more thinking about how to explain this kind of playing to his pupils, who had been brought up on a much stricter philosophy of interpretation. Vlasenko vowed that he would try to get some of that freedom into his pupils' playing— and his own, for that matter. In the last decades, he admitted, the Moscow Conservatory had been like conservatories everywhere: a factory for virtuosos groomed for international competitions. The music world had become internationalized.

Feltsman was at the concert. Horowitz had played the same

program as at the rehearsal, and the thing that most struck Feltsman was that he played it very differently. Some things were better
than at the rehearsal, others he thought not as good. "It was the
same program but a different concert."

Several days later he and Horowitz met at a party. "Now,"
Horowitz said, "tell me the truth. What did you think?"

Feltsman told him he liked it very much but that the second
concert was completely different from the first.

"It's always like that," Horowitz said. "It's *supposed* to be like
that. I cannot play always the same way." Then he went into detail
about why his ideas had changed and how he went about this
particular concert. It became "crystal clear" to Feltsman after this
conversation that the often-expressed opinion about Horowitz,
that he was nothing but a virtuoso, "a kid genius who is playing by
intuition, and has no mental concept about what he is doing," was
all wrong. "Deeply wrong. He knew exactly what he had done
differently, and why. He could analyze his playing. It was not a
matter of his mood. I was very impressed, because this myth which
is very common even now was simply not true."

The Moscow concert, with its accompanying international telecast, received worldwide attention, and the next day Horowitz and
the American embassy were deluged with congratulatory messages.
There was no telegram, however, from Jack Pfeiffer, and that
caused a rupture in the long friendship. The Horowitzes felt insulted: "What kind of friend is that?" They never saw him again.
When he was later told of the incident, Pfeiffer was surprised. He
had never sent a telegram to Horowitz after his European concerts,
or any other concert, for that matter.

Taubman, who followed Horowitz to Leningrad, wrote that
even more than in Moscow "this was clearly an emotional home-
coming for the Russian-born pianist." Horowitz, he thought,
"played with a passion and a flair that seemed inspired in part by a
renewal of affection for the city." He quoted Horowitz as saying,
"For me, Leningrad is like home." Leningrad always had been
Horowitz's favorite Russian city. It was there that he had played a
mammoth series of twenty programs in the 1924–25 season, becoming a hero of the Leningrad music-loving public and an object
of awe to his colleagues. It was also still the most beautiful city in
the Soviet Union, even in its shabby 1986 condition. In addition
Horowitz loved Philharmonic Hall, the concert hall in the Winter

Palace, both for its tradition (nearly every major musician since the early 1800s had performed there) and its acoustics.

As in Moscow, the concert left many in tears. Again as in Moscow, students crashed the hall, and those who could not get in were seen peering through windows and skylights. After the concert, which he played on April 27, an old woman came up to tell him how much she had liked the recital. She was the daughter of Rimsky-Korsakov.

For the Leningrad program Horowitz substituted Schumann's *Kreisleriana* for the Mozart sonata. Otherwise the program was a duplicate of the Moscow one, but it was the lengthy Schumann that made the Leningrad affair much more imposing. Horowitz later said that the Moscow program had been "political," which was his way of saying that it had been put together for television.

Did Horowitz feel a special kind of pressure in the Russian concerts? He said that he did not. In Russia, he said, he suddenly felt like a Russian. It was noted that he started speaking in Russian even to Americans. There was a sixty-one-year retrogression. Suddenly Horowitz was cast back in time and started reliving his youth. He described his feelings on his return to New York:

> What was fantastic was that after sixty years without contact with the Russians, everybody still knew my name. Not only pianists came to the concerts. The public was anxious to hear me. When I walked out I was not nervous at all. I felt as though I was home. It felt like home. I wasn't worried about having a success, not having a success. I was home, and at home everybody loves you. I felt also like an ambassador of peace from America to Russia. In Moscow I was not nervous, no. I was more nervous in Leningrad. Nerves often help you to focus your energy. The program in Leningrad was better—less political, more demanding. Maybe that's why I played better in Leningrad than I had in Moscow. Also the hall in Leningrad has better acoustics than the Great Hall of the Conservatory in Moscow. Leningrad has the best hall in Europe, I think. It is in the Winter Palace, originally the ballroom of Catherine the Great. Everybody was heard there. Berlioz was there, Wagner, Clara Schumann, Anton Rubinstein. I also felt that I had a warmer reception playing there than in Moscow. Moscow is like New York, it has many nationalities in it. People come from everywhere. But Leningrad is more Russian. I would go tomorrow to Leningrad if I was invited.

In Russia I recognized my Russian heritage. I am a Russian pianist, born in the Ukraine and a student at the Kiev Conservatory there. Thus I like to think that my playing and my musicianship reflect a Russian tradition. Once a critic in America said that my playing, my style, was in the Anton Rubinstein tradition. I think he was correct. Josef Hofmann, the most famous of the Rubinstein pupils, heard me play one of the Liszt *Petrarch* Sonnets and said to me, "You know, I think my teacher would have liked your pedaling."

In Leningrad, Horowitz stayed at the residence of the American consul general and showed no inclination to leave. Even after the disaster at Chernobyl he did not want to leave. (If he had any plans of returning to Kiev, his hometown, Chernobyl effectively scotched that.) He was adulated in Leningrad, and it was good for his ego. When he went to a performance of *Eugene Onegin* at the Kirov Opera, the audience stood and applauded when he entered. It was an opera he loved, and after the performance he went back to his hotel room, rushed to the piano and for over an hour played *Onegin* excerpts.

Politically Horowitz never had any love for the Russian system, but he did not find things as bad there as he had been led to believe. When he asked his relatives about conditions in Russia, they told him that they were very well off. One was an engineer, the other a mathematician, so Horowitz figured out that perhaps they enjoyed special privileges. Or perhaps they did not feel free to say all the things that were on their minds, and he did not press them. He knew that it could be dangerous for Soviet citizens at that time to criticize their country.

In Russia, Horowitz went to the opera, to the ballet, to museums, to Tchaikovsky's house in Klin, to Scriabin's house. In Klin he played on Tchaikovsky's piano. "Tchaikovsky composed the *Dumka* on it. I was given a facsimile of Tchaikovsky's *Pathétique* Symphony. In the manuscript score he marked the last movement andante, not adagio the way conductors today play it."

He had been to all of those places before leaving Russia, but did not remember them and was happy to renew acquaintance. "I was too young for it to mean much to me. When you're twenty-two you're not impressed with those things." He met many pianists, conductors, and spent some hours with Dmitri Kabalevsky, whose music Horowitz had played with considerable success in

America in the 1940s. Horowitz was fascinated with the cemetery in Leningrad. "First is Tchaikovsky, then Anton Rubinstein, then there's Borodin, Rimsky-Korsakov, Mussorgsky. Just like that. At the end are Dostoevsky, Pushkin, Stassov. Everybody is there."

Horowitz did not live long enough to follow the amazing weeks of late November 1989, when the Soviet system suddenly went to pieces, much less the staggering events of 1991, when communism died. He would especially have been pleased when Leningrad once again became St. Petersburg. The observation he made on his return home was short and pithy: "People are a bit down, and life is hard, but now Gorbachev is trying to make some better life there for the people. They deserve it. They have suffered very much, the Russians."

2
Growing Up in Kiev

> When I was young I spent much time playing operas. I was in
> love with opera and with singing. I didn't play Bach, I didn't
> play Mozart or Scarlatti at that time. Operas only. When I was
> twelve, thirteen, I was playing operas of Verdi, Puccini, Tchai-
> kovsky, Wagner. By that time I was really a very good sight
> reader. So I could play almost anything. But not scores. That I
> am not so good with. But piano reductions of operas and sym-
> phonies, those were easy for me.
> —*Vladimir Horowitz, about his childhood*

Vladimir Horowitz grew up in Kiev, studied there, and gave his
first recital there.

But was he born there, as all reference works until very recently
have said?

Horowitz insisted that Kiev was his birthplace. But there are
those who claim he was born in Berdichev, an unglamorous city in
the Ukraine about eighty miles southwest of Kiev, with a large
ghetto. Prosperous Russian Jews at the turn of the century regarded it with contempt. Indeed, to all Russians the dismissive
expression, "a Jew from Berdichev," meant a Jew of the lowest
order. No Jew from Berdichev who left and made a success ever
wanted to be reminded of his birthplace.

In the seventh edition of *Baker's Biographical Dictionary of Mu-*

sicians (1977), its editor, Nicolas Slonimsky, leads off the Horowitz entry with "b. Berdichev, Oct. 1, 1904." Slonimsky's authority for Berdichev came, he said, from a sworn document alleged to have been written by a rabbi. In a 1991 interview, however, Slonimsky admitted that he himself had not seen the document. "But," he said, "I was assured by several people who had."

This kind of hearsay evidence would not stand up in any law court.

Horowitz's lifelong friend Nathan Milstein also claimed Berdichev as the Horowitz birthplace because, he said, one of Horowitz's aunts had hinted as much to him. And in his autobiography, published in 1990, Milstein flatly stated that Horowitz was born in Berdichev.

But the hint of an aunt seems as tenuous a piece of evidence as Slonimsky's rabbi.

Yet equally tenuous was Natasha Saitzoff's argument in favor of Kiev.

Natasha was Horowitz's first cousin and they had grown up together in Kiev. In 1991, Mrs. Saitzoff, a sprightly ninety-year-old widow living in Washington, D.C., discussed *l'affaire Berdichev*.

Natasha's father, a lawyer named Alexander Bodick, had a sister, Sophie, who married one Samuel Gorowitz. Among their children was Vladimir Gorowitz. (In Russia, the Horowitz name was and still is Gorowitz. There is no exact equivalent to "h" in the Russian alphabet, and "g" was used for it. A foreigner with the name, say, of Harold will have it pronounced and spelled Garold.)

Mrs. Saitzoff, who was very close to her cousin Volodya (the affectionate Russian diminutive for Vladimir), pooh-poohed the Berdichev theory. Her uncle Samuel, she said, "married my aunt Sophie in Kiev and they immediately went off to Liège, where he completed his engineering studies. When they returned from Liège they lived in Kiev and started having a family. As was customary in those days, my aunt Sophie went to my grandmother for her confinements. My grandmother lived in Kiev. How could any of the children have been born in Berdichev?"

But Natasha admitted that she had come to Kiev from St. Petersburg as a child, and by then all of the Gorowitz children had been born. She would have taken it for granted that they came from Kiev. But that does not necessarily make it true. The Bodick and Horowitz families, consisting of prosperous, educated Jews accepted into Gentile society, would not have wanted to let it be known that some of their family members came from a shtetl in Berdichev. It would have been the deepest of family secrets had it been true.

If indeed Horowitz had been born in Berdichev—and it remains a big "if"—it is a fact that he and his family were living in Kiev when he was a baby, and it is very possible that under the circumstances he grew up without ever having heard "Berdichev" mentioned. Thus he would have genuinely believed that he was born in Kiev. Or, to offer another hypothesis, if Samuel and Sophie Gorowitz did indeed live in Berdichev but went to Kiev and Natasha's grandmother for the birth of their children, then Volodya was really born there, as were his brothers and sister.

If the vital-statistics bureaus of Berdichev and Kiev could produce a birth certificate, there of course would be no problem. Unfortunately no such thing exists. Many records were destroyed in both cities during the aftermath of the 1917 Revolution, and what remained was destroyed during World War II. A 1991 search in Kiev and Berdichev failed to turn up any birth certificates prior to the middle 1920s. The *Russian Encyclopedia* gives the Horowitz birthplace as Berdichev, and most Russian musicologists say that the entry is correct. No definite proof of that attribution, however, has been found.

At least now there can be no doubt about the actual birthdate of Vladimir Horowitz. It was October 1, 1903, and not 1904 as all references have it.

In 1987 Horowitz, reminiscing about his departure from Russia, said that when he applied for a visa in 1925 there could have been trouble if his true birthday was known:

> My birth year was 1903, and all men born in 1903 were considered ready for military service in 1925. So my brother George looked at my identity papers and said there was no problem. He took a little knife, scratched out the 3 in 1903 and made it a 4. With that paper I went to the passport office and was issued one. Now my passport said I was born in 1904 and therefore was still too young to go into the army. Ever since then I have "officially" been born in 1904, and all musical encyclopedias give that as my birth year.

According to Mrs. Saitzoff, the idea of tampering with Volodya's birthdate, she said, came from Horowitz's father, her uncle Samuel.

Kiev, the capital of the Ukraine, was a lovely city in 1903, with an active musical and intellectual life. Legend has it that the city was founded in A.D. 864 by three brothers, Kiy, Shcek, and Khoriv. Prince Vladimir, the first saint of the Russian church, had his subjects baptized in the Dnieper River in 988, after which Kiev became the seat of the first Christian church and of the first library in Russia. In the tenth century it was an important trading and cultural center. Some of the original walls of the city still stand and are memorialized in "The Great Gate of Kiev" from Mussorgsky's *Pictures at an Exhibition*.

Kiev was destroyed by the Tatars in the thirteenth and fourteenth centuries. Then it belonged to the Lithuanian principality (1320–1569), then to Poland, and not until 1686 did it become part of the Russian Empire. When Horowitz was born, the population of Kiev was about 320,000, of whom roughly 12,000 were Jews.

As early as 1704 Kiev had a municipal orchestra. Not much later came a symphony society, a professional choir, an opera company, and, in 1868, a music school that later became the Kiev Conservatory. All the great musicians of Europe, from the early nineteenth-century soprano Angelica Catalani to Franz Liszt and Josef Hofmann, performed in Kiev.

Horowitz's father, Samuel, was an electrical engineer who went into business for himself and represented big American and European electrical firms in Russia. Later, around 1912 as Natasha remembered it, he formed a partnership with his brother-in-law, Alexander Bodick. Natasha remembered her uncle Samuel as a handsome, dignified man, "rather pretentious," accustomed to having his own way. Horowitz remembered his father as being "a cultured man, and he owned a big library. I read all of it while I was growing up—the Russian classics, Dickens in English, Dumas in French, and so on. Even though I could not speak English then, I learned to read it."

Volodya's mother, Sophie, was a great beauty. Natasha called her "a little cuckoo," meaning fey. She had temperament to spare, and she was always jealous of her husband. Natasha said she never knew if Sophie had a reason for her jealousy. "I was too young." But she remembered very well that Sophie and Samuel had many arguments, and that when her family talked about her they called her "impossible."

Sophie had trained as a pianist at the Royal Music School in Kiev. She was adept but never pursued a professional career. The only professional musician in the family was Samuel's brother, Alexander, a pianist who had studied with Scriabin. He lived in Kharkov, about 250 miles west of Kiev. Kharkov was a business center and also a cosmopolitan city with a university, an important library, and a thriving musical life. Volodya's uncle Alexander was prominent there as pianist, teacher, critic—and eccentric. Natasha described him as "quite a character, tall, skinny, with big moustaches like you never saw. He had the big Horowitz nose. Anybody who met him could never forget him."

Samuel and Sophie had four children—Jacob, George, Regina (or, as she was always called, Genya), and Volodya, in that order. All the children had a governess, tutors, and a good private education. Volodya's governess was French, and he grew up speaking the language with as much ease as Russian. And all the Horowitz children had to study music. Their mother saw to that. Jacob was a talented pianist. George took up the violin. Genya became a professional pianist and teacher. And there was Volodya.

Volodya grew up hearing music almost from the moment he was introduced to the world. His mother practiced constantly, and when she was not practicing she would be teaching her children. That was significant. More often than not, musical prodigies come from musical families or are surrounded by music from the beginning. This is also true of most composers. Bach, Mozart, Beethoven, Schubert, Chopin, Liszt, Mendelssohn, Saint-Saëns (perhaps the most remarkable prodigy of all), Brahms, Rachmaninoff—all grew up hearing music. And all were pianists.

By the age of seven or so most prodigies are well into the mysteries of playing and, in some cases, composing. All great performing musicians have to start very early. After the age of six it may be too late; the reflexes for virtuoso piano and violin playing have to be trained in babyhood. In the entire history of piano and violin playing it is hard to think of an important artist whose ability did not reveal itself by the age of six.

Horowitz always maintained that, unlike most of the world's

great pianists from Mozart on, he had never been a child prodigy. Liszt, Anton Rubinstein, Josef Hofmann, Leopold Godowsky, Ferruccio Busoni, and many other of the superpianists, he pointed out, were playing at the age of four, and their styles, in effect, had been fully formed by the time they were fifteen. At that age they were also veterans of the concert stage. Horowitz claimed that he started "late, around five." He conceded that by ten he thought he had "some talent," and that he was "a not so bad sight reader." (From Horowitz, "not so bad" meant mildly stupendous.) He claimed that he never practiced very much, which may or may not have been true. Many pianists like to pretend that they never practice. This is a form of professional machismo. But it is a fact that as a young pianist Horowitz was compulsively reading through the piano literature and opera scores instead of practicing his scales.

Yet in claiming that he had never been a prodigy, Horowitz was being a little disingenuous. The only reason he wasn't immediately recognized as a prodigy was the fact that the public did not know about him. His family was wealthy enough to avoid pushing their brilliant child or exploiting his extraordinary gifts.

The literature on prodigies is small. Psychologists have not been able to explain the phenomenon. But some children are born with an order of musical reflex that sets them apart. They usually have absolute pitch, the ability to name any note or combination of notes on hearing them. When they approach the piano at the age of two, when most children bang around aimlessly, they try to pick out concords and play little tunes. Their hearing is unusually acute. They have a tendency to move ahead faster than their mentors can teach them. They have amazing memories, to the point where they can hear a long piece of music two or three times and reproduce it on their instrument without ever having looked at the printed notes. Then they carry it in their heads for the rest of their lives. Little Volodya was typical of the species.

Not all prodigies develop into great performing artists, but on the other hand one cannot become a great performing artist without having been a prodigy. Horowitz certainly met all of the qualifications, and everybody who came into contact with him as a child or young man knew it. Sergei Tarnowsky, his second teacher at the Kiev Conservatory, said that if Horowitz had not been a child prodigy, "then there never had been such a thing." Horowitz amazed him with the rapidity with which he learned new pieces, with his phenomenal ear and his sight-reading ability. The boy stunned his teacher when he reproduced sections of operas and symphonies by ear, after hearing them performed only once.

But for all of this talent there is usually a price to pay. A by-product of being a child prodigy is often a one-sided attitude toward life. Prodigies, especially musical prodigies, start honing their gifts as little more than babies—sometimes *as* babies—and devote the rest of their lives to a ferocious discipline, a strenuous development of those gifts to the exclusion of almost everything else. The result can be a warped childhood, monomania, and a lack of general education. Prodigies are supremely gifted in their particular discipline but frequently unworldly outside of it. What else can one expect from a pianist or violinist who starts practicing perhaps an hour or so a day at the age of three or four, three hours a day at five or six, five hours a day at nine or ten, and frequently six or more for the rest of his life?

The pronounced talent of the two youngest Horowitz children, Genya and Volodya, was immediately noticed by their mother. That also is one of the advantages of being born into a musical family. Sophie started teaching them the piano when they were about five years old. Volodya's affinity for the instrument was immediately apparent. Many years later, in 1932, Horowitz received a letter from his governess. She wrote that she remembered the day when her charge, age five or six, sat at the piano imitating thunder and inventing a little story to illustrate the music. When Volodya finished and went away, Samuel, who had been listening in another room, came up to the governess and said, "That boy will be a famous pianist." Horowitz kept the letter, which is now in the Horowitz Archives at Yale.

Genya, three years older than her brother, was a very good pianist, and Horowitz claimed that she was better than he was at his age. Volodya would listen to her lessons, automatically memorizing everything he heard. Like most prodigies, he had absolute pitch. He did not especially like practicing and was not taken to many piano recitals as a child. At best, he said, he was an average talent. But "I read through all of the music at home, and there was a great deal of music." He also played four-hand music with his mother or sister, reading through the standard symphonies and chamber music and committing them to memory.

Volodya started composing before he was eight, "and I think

maybe I had some talent there." In later life he constantly kept referring to his urge toward composition, but that need not be taken seriously. Had he really wanted to be a composer, he would have composed, and composition instead of giving concerts would have dominated his life.

As a child his principal love was opera and singing, and that drove his mother to distraction. Here was her promising son, exceptionally gifted, who refused to practice scales and subject himself to the traditional and expected discipline. What would become of him? As Horowitz explained:

> My mother was out of her mind. She thought I was never going to be a real pianist. I was collecting records of singers, never of pianists. I was interested in Battistini and Caruso, and on the piano I would try to imitate the singers. That is still true of me today. The most important thing on the keyboard is color and singing. I would much rather go to the opera than to piano recitals. At piano recitals I was bored. They played good octaves, double notes, so what? They all sounded the same. If you don't have color, you don't have anything. Anton Rubinstein, I later learned, told his pupils the same thing. Try to imitate the sound of the human voice, he kept saying.

Anton Rubinstein. The legendary Anton (1829–94) was a colossus of the piano, in his day considered second only to Franz Liszt, and Volodya grew up hearing the name of Anton Rubinstein spoken in awed voices.

A powerful, dominating, volcanic man, Rubinstein played volcanic piano. He had a gigantic technique, but when he got excited wrong notes spewed forth in every direction. "Strength and lightness, that is the secret of my touch," he said. "I have sat for hours trying to imitate the timbre of Rubini's voice in my playing." He was a veteran of the concert stage by the age of ten and, in the 1840s, part of the Liszt circle, though he never studied with Liszt. He founded the St. Petersburg Conservatory in 1861—it was the first music conservatory in Russia—and his younger brother, Nicholas (also a superb pianist), founded the Moscow Conservatory in 1866. The two brothers created a Russian piano tradition that for several generations was the dominating force in the Russian conservatories.

Thus the name of Anton Rubinstein was in the cultural subconscious of every piano student in Russia in Horowitz's day. They all aspired to be another Anton Rubinstein, just as pianists of the 1950s aspired to be Vladimir Horowitz. Rubinstein died about ten years before Horowitz was born, but he was an integral part of Volodya's life:

> As a student I heard many accounts of his playing from those who studied with him or heard him in concert. Nobody who ever heard him could forget the experience. I have a biography of him in Russian in which Liszt is quoted as telling Rubinstein after Karl Tausig died [in 1871, at the age of thirty], "now there are only two of us in the world." Paderewski once told me about the time he heard Rubinstein. It was in Paris, and Paderewski was nineteen years old. Rubinstein at that time was getting old and sick and he had bad eye trouble, glaucoma. He couldn't see very well. He played the big F sharp minor Sonata of Schumann. Paderewski said that the first movement was terrible. Rubinstein had lost control. But when he came to the second movement with the long melody Paderewski told me, "I never in my life heard such a singing piano. He impressed me more than any pianist I ever heard."

In 1912, not yet nine years old, Horowitz (and also his sister) entered the Kiev Conservatory. There he had his first dose of discipline, and he did not like it very much. He was required to start learning the standard repertoire, and that took away from the time he could spend with his beloved opera scores.

At the conservatory he studied first with Vladimir Puchalsky, a pupil of Theodor Leschetizky's, and then with Sergei Tarnowsky. That provided another Leschetizky connection because Tarnowsky's teacher had been Annette Essipov, who had been a Leschetizky pupil, a great pianist, and one of Leschetizky's many wives. The Polish-born Leschetizky (1830–1915) produced an extraordinary number of pupils who went on to great careers, including Paderewski, Ignaz Friedman, Ossip Gabrilowitsch, Mieczyslaw Horszowski, Benno Moiseiwitsch, and Artur Schnabel. But Horowitz's last teacher was Felix Blumenfeld, who had studied with Anton Rubinstein. Because of the Blumenfeld connection Horowitz liked to call himself a spiritual grandson of Anton Rubinstein, though he could with equal justice have called himself a grandson of Theodor Leschetizky.

Puchalsky was the director of the Kiev Conservatory when

Volodya entered it. Sophie had originally intended that Volodya should start his studies with Marian Dombrowski, and actually enrolled him and Genya in his class. She thought that Puchalsky was too old to take competent care of her children. But when Puchalsky heard about this, he had a fit; and the embarrassed Sophie transferred her children from Dombrowski to Puchalsky. "He was the teacher of my mother, and that's why she sent Genya and me to him," said Horowitz. Dombrowski was so annoyed that he made a point of never listening to any Horowitz performance in the conservatory. When the boy would start to play in one of the student recitals, Natasha said, she would see Dombrowski making a big show of standing up and stalking out. According to Natasha, Dombrowski never heard Horowitz until years later, at a recital in Warsaw. After the concert he came up to Horowitz and apologized, saying that he was sorry he had missed such brilliant playing up to then.

Horowitz claimed that Puchalsky did not give him very much:

> Already I was playing differently from his other students, and he did not like that. I had much more freedom than he liked. He was screaming at me like, I don't know. I couldn't stand him. I hated him. He was anti-Semitic and a very nasty person. He would tell the class to be at the classroom tomorrow at four. So we would get there at four. But he might not turn up until nine-thirty, and we had to wait. He complained about me to my mother. He said to her, "Your son is terrible. He has no discipline, he has no nothing. He plays everything too fast, too loud." Maybe he was right. When I was young I was much less controlled than now. But he wanted conformity. If you are different you cannot be good. That was the way he felt. But I didn't care then, and I don't care now. When I was eight my style in a way was already formed. By the time I was fifteen it already was formed. I had a naturally big sonority and my hands were the same size as they are now. I never had a big hand. I can just take a comfortable tenth. But that was big enough for the Rachmaninoff Third Concerto, which I was playing when I was fifteen or sixteen.

Puchalsky, who was director for about three years after the Horowitz children went there, was fired in 1914 by Rachmaninoff, at that time the inspector general of all the conservatories in Russia. Puchalsky, who was allowed to continue teaching, was replaced as director by the prominent composer Reinhold Glière, who brought Tarnowsky, Volodya's next teacher, to the conservatory. Born in 1882, Tarnowsky was a solid musician and an autocratic teacher. In 1915 Volodya and Genya entered his class.

Horowitz said that Tarnowsky was more flexible than Puchalsky. He assigned the young Horowitz a kind of repertoire that the strict Bach-Beethoven-Chopin Puchalsky probably did not even know. Under Tarnowsky's direction Horowitz learned pieces by Liapounov, Raff, and Saint-Saëns in addition to the works that every piano student has to master. Tarnowsky, an elegant-looking gentleman and a fine musician, was constantly working with Horowitz on his sound. Horacio Gutierrez, who studied with Tarnowsky many years later in Los Angeles, was convinced that his teacher was largely responsible for the Horowitz sound. Tarnowsky was always urging Gutierrez to dig into the notes; and, Gutierrez said, "When you watch Horowitz play, you can see that he is always going into the center of the key, so that the tone is as carrying as it possibly can be. That was something that Tarnowsky harped on very much."

In the 1920s Tarnowsky went to the United States, teaching first in Chicago (where he married one of his pupils, a girl considerably younger than he was) and then in Los Angeles. Two years after Horowitz came to America, he wrote a terse and rather grudging testimonial for his teacher:

> New York City
> March 12, 1930

> From the time I was twelve years old until I was sixteen Sergei Tarnowsky was my teacher. I studied under Professor Tarnowsky at the Kieff Conservatory. I shall always be grateful for all that I learned musically and technically from Professor Tarnowsky.

> Vladimir Horowitz

Puchalsky had complained about Horowitz's approach to the piano, and so did Tarnowsky, who had trouble toning down his young charger. Looking back, Horowitz grudgingly conceded that he would have given any teacher trouble. From the beginning he was going to do things his own way. No wonder they got angry at him, and Horowitz in his old age understood their problems. "I suppose that it was true that I banged a lot," he said some seventy years later.

Horowitz grew up musically in what he considered "the Russian style" as practiced by Rubinstein. "Anton Rubinstein was very free in his style, and his was the tradition I grew up with. The idea was that you were supposed to know everything about your instrument, then everything in music, as much as you could learn, and then form your own personality. Rubinstein was a very free pianist, never mechanical." Horowitz developed along the same lines; he always was the exponent of instinct over mechanical drill. "If you grow up playing only Kalkbrenner, Henselt, and Czerny etudes," Horowitz said, "you will never become a pianist. Never. Impossible. You must know the great music from the beginning, be saturated with it. I never wanted to work only on technique." To the end of his life, he never worked on traditional technique. No scales for him. His technique came out of the great music he played and certain finger exercises, derived from the music itself, that he devised.

It was not only the conservatory that occupied his student days. He also had to go to school. Though the Ukraine was a center of Russian anti-Semitism, Horowitz said,

> I was never touched by it. After my tutoring days and while I was in the conservatory I had to go to school, to the local gymnasium, what in America is called a high school. In the classes of about forty pupils there could be about four or five Jews. That was the normal quota. All Russian schools worked on a quota system for Jews. I was in the quota, and my teachers liked me very much. I will tell you why. Generally the Jewish students were the best in the class, the smartest. They would win all the prizes and everybody hated them for that. But I was never smart. I was interested only in music. Otherwise I was not a good student, I neglected all of my studies, and everybody liked me because of that, because I was not a smart Jew. "Oh, you're wonderful!" they said. I was their friend.

It was not long before Horowitz was recognized as the most promising of the piano students at the Kiev Conservatory. And he knew how good he was. As a teenager Horowitz was handsome, an elegant dresser, suave but something of a loner. Extremely high-strung, he could become irritable and something of a monster when things did not go his way. The child already was father to the man.

After one concert that Horowitz gave at the conservatory, he was unhappy with the way he had played. He went home, threw glass objects on the floor, kicked the furniture, and made everybody miserable for a few days. Tarnowsky, who told this to Gutierrez many years later, said that Horowitz's mother rushed to him and asked for help. "Please come and quiet him down," she pleaded.

Cousin Natasha and Volodya lived in the same house when she and Volodya were teenagers, and were always seeing each other. "We were family, we were very close." As a boy, Natasha said, Volodya was very much what he became as a man. He was intensely interested in himself, "very self-centered," had to be the center of attraction, was rather selfish. "Nobody else was important. He was like his father. The same character. But Volodya had the right to feel proud of himself." Natasha also said that Volodya, unlike his father, could exert a charm that nobody could resist. Horowitz admitted that he had been a reclusive adolescent. "As a young man I was crazy. I had very few friends, was not socially inclined, and did not go out very much. Basically, I didn't like people. This went on for many years."

He was in love with music and the piano, and crazy about vocal records. Often Natasha got records he did not have, and when she told him he would rush to the Bodick apartment, where she and Volodya would listen together. They would try to sing the arias *a due*. "It was lucky he was a pianist," she said when discussing Volodya's singing voice. Then he would drift over to the piano. "You couldn't keep him away."

Although many of the world's major recitalists came to Kiev, Horowitz heard surprisingly few pianists on the concert stage when he was young. But he did go to a few concerts while still a student. Naturally he went to hear Josef Hofmann when the great Polish-born pianist played in Kiev. Hofmann was the idol of the Russian public, and many considered him the greatest living pianist. But Horowitz was disappointed. "Hofmann did not impress me very much. Of course he was a great pianist with incredible facility, but I did not like his interpretations. I was bored. Later on, in America, I heard him many times and had no reason to change my initial impression."

Of the pianists he remembered, Rachmaninoff made the strongest impression. "With Rachmaninoff I had an immediate identification. He gave a concert of his own music that I heard when I was nine or ten. I also was playing his music at that time. He was *singing* on the piano all the time."

While Rachmaninoff was in Kiev, Volodya's mother made an appointment for her son to play for him at his hotel. But when the Horowitz family arrived they were told he had left. "He didn't want to listen to some young pianist he had not heard anything about. I reminded him of this when we became friends," said Horowitz.

But, Horowitz said, the musician who made more of an impression on him than anybody else was not a pianist. He heard one of Fritz Kreisler's violin recitals "and he was fantastic. I did not sleep nights after I heard him, and I wanted to make that kind of sound on the piano."

3

Novorossiisk, Taganrog, Gomel, Batumi

> I worked out my own technique. For some pieces I used a flat
> hand position, for others a curved one. Every piece dictated its
> own approach. I played with the little fingers of both hands
> curled up tight. Nobody ever taught this to me. It was the way
> my fingers worked.
> —*Vladimir Horowitz, discussing his Kiev Conservatory days*

*I*n 1914 Russia went to war, and in 1917 came the proletarian
revolution. To a young piano student named Vladimir Gorowitz
the war did not mean much. Nor, indeed, did the arrival in St.
Petersburg of a man who called himself Lenin. Kiev was far away
from all the turmoil. It was not until the early 1920s that the
proletarian revolution came to Kiev, and then the lives of Volodya
and his family were changed forever.

The only immediate impact of the 1914 war on Volodya's life
was the evacuation of the conservatory to Rostov, a long way from
Kiev, at the outbreak of hostilities. Volodya did not go there, nor
did Tarnowsky, who continued to teach his gifted pupil at the
Horowitz home.

When the 1917 Revolution started, the conservatory returned

to Kiev. New faculty names suddenly turned up. They belonged to professors from the St. Petersburg and Moscow conservatories who had come to Kiev (some taking with them their best students), fleeing from the turmoil in their home cities. Now there were some very distinguished musicians at the Kiev Conservatory. Among them were the pianists Felix Blumenfeld and Heinrich Neuhaus, the violinist Paul Kochanski and the tenor Leonid Sobinov. Blumenfeld was to have a major impact on Horowitz's life; he became the young virtuoso's last, and most important, teacher.

Horowitz got into Blumenfeld's class in 1919 by accident. Tarnowsky had gone on a concert tour and word got back to Kiev that he had died of typhus, whereupon Horowitz was assigned to Blumenfeld, along with Genya and all the other Tarnowsky pupils. There was consternation about six months later when a healthy Tarnowsky turned up at the conservatory. He had indeed contracted typhus, but had survived and taken a convalescence in the Crimea. Tarnowsky was as bitter about losing Horowitz, his best pupil, as Blumenfeld was happy to get him. And Horowitz was happy to get Blumenfeld, who was more glamorous than Tarnowsky, closer to the center of musical Russia, and a more experienced all-around musician. Most important of all, as far as Volodya was concerned, Blumenfeld had been associated with Anton Rubinstein and would thus be able to transmit his teachings at first hand.

Blumenfeld's credentials were imposing. Pianist, composer, conductor, teacher, Blumenfeld knew everybody in the Russian musical establishment. He had studied piano with Rubinstein himself, composition with Rimsky-Korsakov, taught at the St. Petersburg Conservatory, accompanied such singers as Feodor Chaliapin, conducted at the Imperial Opera in St. Petersburg, and was one of the conductors at Diaghilev's famous 1908 season in Paris. Toscanini heard him conduct *Boris Godunov* there and was impressed. Blumenfeld was in Kiev from 1918 to 1922, after which he joined the Moscow Conservatory, where he remained until his death in 1931.

Neuhaus, who was Blumenfeld's nephew, became Horowitz's close friend. Fifteen years older than Volodya, he had been in the West, and to the impressionable student he was a cosmopolite. Horowitz described him as a pianist-musician rather than a virtuoso, and it is clear that Neuhaus meant a great deal to his musical and intellectual development:

> He was very musical, an artist. Technique in a pianist never impressed me. I never in my life heard a pianist whom I liked just because of his technique. The moment they start to play very fast I want to go home. Neuhaus was very musical, so I was interested. We played much four-hand and two-piano music. He was a wonderful musician and he introduced me to a great deal of music I had not heard. He played beautifully some late Scriabin sonatas, all of which were new to me. He also analyzed pieces with me. He had studied with Leopold Godowsky in Berlin. I was a provincial boy and was fascinated to hear him describe how Ferruccio Busoni played, how Godowsky played, how Moriz Rosenthal played, how Ignaz Friedman played, how this player and that player sounded. He liked Alfred Cortot best of all.

Later Neuhaus went to the Moscow Conservatory, where he became a legendary teacher. His pupils included Emil Gilels and Sviatoslav Richter. Judging from his recordings, he was exactly what Horowitz said: more a musician than a pianist.

Horowitz called Blumenfeld his best teacher, although he was handicapped by his inability to illustrate the big pieces at the piano because he had had a stroke. But he and Volodya played four-hand music together and went through a great deal of the classic literature in duet arrangements. He was also able to give Volodya ideas about pedaling. Technique he was not interested in; he took it for granted that anybody in his classes could play anything. How the pupil's fingers got through the notes did not concern him. But he was amazed by Horowitz's unconventional hand positions, which were too *outré* even for him. Said Horowitz:

> He told me if you have a long nose, play with your nose. He said he did not care how a pianist got an effect as long as he got it. But he did not understand my technique. No teacher liked my system, not one. It went against all their rules. They liked what came out, but didn't like the way I made it come out. It was not natural, it didn't look right. Even my colleagues didn't like it.

According to Horowitz, Simon Barere was considered the best pupil in Blumenfeld's class at that time. Barere, who had followed

Blumenfeld from St. Petersburg to Kiev, was about seven years older than Horowitz and was an amazing technician whose fingers sometimes outran his brains. He was, however, capable of ravishing playing. He concertized in Europe and England before moving to New York. Toward the end of his life he suddenly began to attract a wide public and was on his way to stardom when he collapsed and died on the stage of Carnegie Hall in 1951 while playing the Grieg Concerto. Of course his dramatic death gained him more publicity than he ever achieved in his life. Horowitz was half impressed, half amused by this pianistic phenomenon:

> Even when a student with Blumenfeld he had this extraordinary technique. But that was about all he had. He was a very simple man, a nice fellow, not a cultured person or musician, perhaps not very smart. The only thing he knew was to play fast. I remember when he played the Schumann Toccata so fast that I went to him and asked him why that crazy tempo? So he answered me: "I can play it faster than that." The best things he did were the big Liszt transcriptions, things like that. Blumenfeld liked him more than me. I remember I was a little bit jealous.

Under Blumenfeld, Horowitz felt that he was progressing musically. He was also developing a large repertoire. Blumenfeld assigned him the big Liszt transcriptions and major Schumann works, along with the usual Beethoven, Chopin, and Mendelssohn. Most of the time he let Horowitz play what he wanted. And naturally Horowitz continued to read through all the music he could get his hands on.

That included Mozart, whose music Horowitz discovered on his own. He had never been assigned any Mozart sonatas in class. The Mozart sonatas then were regarded in the Kiev Conservatory and probably everywhere else, even in Germany, as simpleminded, something not worth wasting much time on. Horowitz managed to locate a volume of the complete sonatas and played them through for himself. He tried to get acquainted with the concertos, but the music of most of them was impossible to find. He became familiar with whatever was available and loved everything he played. But it was a love not translated into steady action until toward the end of his life.

And, as always, he constantly searched for music he considered "pianistic." That to him meant music with technical ingenuity paired with interesting content. The Liapounov etudes he found interesting: "They are difficult and very beautiful." He even became interested in Alkan and read through some of his music. Charles-Valentin Morhange Alkan (1813–88), sometimes called the Berlioz of the Piano, was an eccentric pianist-composer who wrote pieces of stupendous length and difficulty. As a pianist he was equated with Liszt and Thalberg.

In his later conservatory years, Horowitz developed a passion for Grieg and played many of the *Lyric Pieces* and the Ballade. "I simply loved Grieg. Also Chopin and Schumann, of course. I went through all their music. The Liszt transcriptions went easily. I never had much trouble memorizing music like that. Once the forms and textures were in the mind, the rest was easy. Memorizing the classical composers was much harder." Grieg must have been an adolescent crush. There is no record of Horowitz playing any Grieg during his professional career.

As in later life, Horowitz avoided piano concertos as much as possible. Of course he had to learn many of the standard ones as a student, beginning with the Beethoven Third, which traditionally has been the first concerto students have to learn. It is a masterpiece; it verges on Romanticism and poses no great technical problems. Blumenfeld also assigned him the Tchaikovsky B flat minor, the Rachmaninoff C minor, both Liszt concertos, and Chopin's F minor. (Horowitz never did study the Chopin E minor Concerto.) Blumenfeld also gave him the Arensky F minor Concerto, which he played in public and which is almost never heard outside of Russia. It is a pleasant and technically brilliant work, but an unabashed plagiarism of the Chopin F minor.

When the Revolution finally came to Kiev, the city was in a state of anarchy. The White Russians were in control for a while, and there was also a strong Ukrainian nationalistic movement. Those factions battled each other, and then the Communists sent troops in to impose their new system. Everybody, said Horowitz,

> was fighting with everybody else. I don't want to talk much about when the Bolsheviks came to Kiev in 1920. Don't ask. They stole, they wanted to rape women, they came to our house and threw the piano through the window. The entire house was vandalized, books, music, furniture, everything. My father was wonderful. He had a revolver, I remember, and when the

soldiers threatened to harm us he shot the gun into the air. They ran. It's lucky we didn't get killed. It was a terrible time. My father lost his business—all his money, our apartment, everything.

With the arrival of the Communists, the once-happy and prosperous Horowitz family was shattered. Jacob, Volodya's eldest brother, was drafted into the army and died during the Revolution. George became a drifter who settled for a while in Leningrad. Samuel's business was seized by the state, and he was forced into a dull bureaucratic job.

During all this terror, Volodya was in his last year at the Kiev Conservatory, preparing for his final examinations. For his graduation recital in 1920 Horowitz played the Bach-Busoni Toccata, Adagio, and Fugue in C; the Mozart Gigue in G; a Beethoven sonata (Horowitz forgot whether it was the *Appassionata* or Op. 110); Schumann's *Symphonic Etudes;* the Rachmaninoff B flat minor Sonata; Chopin's F minor Fantasy; "and something modern, I don't remember." He ended with the Mozart-Liszt *Don Juan* and said that after he had finished it the jury stood up to express its approval. That had never happened before in the entire history of the conservatory, Horowitz believed.

For his required concerto he chose the Rachmaninoff Third. For his chamber-music pieces he selected the Schumann Quintet and Schubert's *Winterreise.* The concerts were tremendous successes. An elated Blumenfeld wrote to Rachmaninoff in New York about his talented pupil and the brilliant success he had had with Rachmaninoff's music.

That was the end of Volodya's studies. Now he was on his own.

Or he would have been had he not had his family to worry about. Now, at the age of seventeen, he had to start his professional career if only to become a breadwinner. Filial obligations forced him to face the public perhaps sooner than he would have wished.

"Somebody," he said, "had to support the family. My father had lost everything. So since he had given me an education and taken care of me, now it was my turn to take care of him and the rest of the family. I had to play the piano to bring in money. Or food. In those days people were just as happy to get food instead of money in payment for their services. Food, soap, shoes, clothing, all those were legal tender."

Horowitz gave his first public concert in Kiev on May 30, 1920. At the debut, Horowitz said, there were not many in the hall. That state of affairs would not last long. Vladimir Horowitz had all of the ingredients for stardom. It was not only his pianistic skill. Perhaps equally important, he made a striking appearance on stage. He looked like the kind of pianist a romantic novelist would have invented. He was slim and handsome, with a pale complexion and a profile that suggested Chopin's. He wore his hair long and curly. His hands were beautiful. He dressed impeccably; from the beginning he was a dandy. Many years later Horowitz, looking at one of his photographs from those days, grinned and said, "I was very esthetic."

Word got around about this exciting new pianist, and for his next two recitals in Kiev the hall was filled. Horowitz then played in Kharkov under the auspices of Uncle Alexander, and went to Moscow, Odessa, Baku, and any other city that would have him.

So in 1920 the Horowitz concert career started. Within a few years he would be a presence, the greatest presence among the new pianists. Audiences were going to marvel at his incredible, unerring fingers and his unorthodox approach to the keyboard: wrists turned out and often below the keys; flat fingers, the little fingers of both hands curled in, opening to strike with the rapidity of a cobra, then instantly recoiling. Audiences were going to experience a new kind of sound, a sound unique in its color, sensuousness, and subtlety. (Many years later William Kapell said, "If people understood what Horowitz's tone meant, he would be banned from the keyboard.") Horowitz also had worked out a system of muscular control that enabled him to produce, without banging, without any sign of physical effort, crashing fortissimos that could ride over the loudest orchestra. The Horowitz sonority could well have been unprecedented in pianistic history.

Shortly after the beginning of his career Horowitz made a friend who was to be close to him for the rest of his long life— Nathan Milstein, whom Horowitz met in 1922.

Milstein was then eighteen and a prodigiously gifted violinist. He came from Odessa (a city that spawned an unusual number of musically gifted Jewish children who subsequently went on to great careers as pianists and violinists), had studied with Peter Stolyarsky and then with the great Leopold Auer in St. Petersburg. Auer, a Joachim pupil who had been born in Hungary in 1845, had a successful recital career and then became the most important violin teacher of the late nineteenth and early twentieth centuries; his pupils, among them Jascha Heifetz, Efrem Zimbalist, and Mischa Elman, were the equivalent of the Liszt and Leschetizky pupils on the piano.

Milstein was concertizing throughout Russia in 1922. In Kharkov he met Horowitz's uncle, who raved about his brilliant nephew. When Milstein went to Kiev to play several concerts at the conservatory with Horowitz's former teacher Tarnowsky at the piano, Horowitz and Genya went to all the recitals, visited him backstage after the first one, and invited him home for tea. He stayed for dinner. After his second recital he was invited to stay with the Horowitzes. "You could say," Milstein wrote in his chatty but sometimes inaccurate autobiography, *From Russia to the West,* "I came to tea and stayed three years."

On their very first night together there was, of course, music.

"Genya and Volodya played for me," Milstein remembered many years later. "She played Schumann, Liszt, Chopin ballades. But Volodya played only his own Wagner transcriptions for me. He had never written them down. He played the 'Forging Song' from *Siegfried,* unbelievable. He could play *Götterdämmerung* by heart. He was like a tiger. I was terribly impressed." Thus began a friendship that would continue for the rest of Horowitz's life.

"Volodya was a little wild about music," said Milstein. "He was terribly instinctive, you know. He was a great talent and you cannot judge such a talent by normal measurements. When he was wrong it was also good. He was a genius, unlike anybody else. He always did things his own way. He was at that time, and he always remained, a musical inventor. But certain things he could not or would not do. He could never play all the Chopin etudes. Never played more than a half dozen. He told me learning all the etudes was too much work."

Milstein and Horowitz read through a good deal of the violin literature. They started to give concerts together. Indeed, writes Milstein in his autobiography, they gave a concert in the hall of the Kiev Merchant Guild ten days after they met. They were a great contrast: the shy, introverted, poetic-looking Horowitz with his resplendent coiffure, and the shorter, extroverted, happy-go-lucky, close-cropped Milstein. What they had in common was a supreme command of their instruments. Genya was sometimes part of the team; she would accompany Milstein, and Horowitz would play solo groups. Or Horowitz would accompany and Genya would get her chance as a soloist.

In the days she was part of the Horowitz-Milstein duo, Genya was already married and divorced. She had married a ne'er-do-well in 1916, when she was sixteen, and had a daughter, Lena, the following year. Some years after the divorce she wed a famous Russian economist, Evsei Lieberman. They lived in Kharkov, where she taught at the conservatory and served as accompanist for, among others, David Oistrakh.

Milstein said that Volodya never was an accompanist. "We were equal partners." They also played concertos, the orchestral part played in a piano reduction, as was the custom in those days. It has been decades since concert violinists programmed concertos with piano accompaniment, but until about the beginning of World War II concertos were standard fare in violin recitals. Milstein and Horowitz played the Glazunov A minor Concerto and several others in their concerts. Horowitz also had a solo group.

Looking back, Milstein said that the most remarkable thing about their joint appearances was that they never bothered to rehearse. They were musicians who thought alike and worked together with such rapport that they immediately "synthesized" in concert. "Volodya was absolutely out of this world. Rehearsals were not necessary. We had such spontaneity on stage. We had a contact, a spiritual contact. And he was such a wonderful sight reader, almost as good as Rachmaninoff."

When the Horowitz-Milstein duo found other musicians willing to join them, they played trios or piano quartets. Horowitz sometimes accompanied singers, which he loved to do. One of them was Nina Koshetz, who had toured with Rachmaninoff as an interpreter of his songs. She and Horowitz gave a recital in Moscow. Later she went to America and had a great career. When he accompanied Zoya Lodaya in Schubert's *Winterreise* cycle, he played the entire piano part from memory. Among his favorite singers were Chaliapin, with whom he became friends years later in America, and the tenor Leonid Sobinov, about whom he said in 1987:

> He was a wonderful actor, a beautiful man. He was a real
> musician and sang with Toscanini at La Scala. I once saw him

sing the tenor part in Beethoven's Ninth Symphony without the music in front of him. That is very rare. I accompanied him in one of his recitals. I never met Battistini but I got every record of his I could find. He was the greatest of the bel canto baritones and very free in his style. He once had a terrible argument with Toscanini, who thought he was too free. He was always sliding from one note to another. I never heard a singer with such a portamento. I loved it. I try to do it on the piano. You can do it with the pedals. I do it all the time.

Mattia Battistini was the most famous Italian baritone of his time. Born in 1856, he made his debut in 1878, and was still singing in 1927. His career took him to opera houses from Lisbon to St. Petersburg, and he became known as *La Gloria d'Italia* because of the beauty of his voice and his phenomenal technique. Horowitz was fascinated with his breath control, his ability to execute long cantilena passages, and the freedom of his phrasing; and Battistini was a real influence on the way Horowitz phrased and colored a musical line.

At first Horowitz and Milstein booked their own concerts, in which they were helped by Uncle Alexander in Kharkov. Later the state stepped in. An organization called Muzo-Narkompros, known as MUZO, began to establish full supervision over all of the musical life of the Soviet Union. Artists were required to get MUZO's permission for all concert tours. MUZO also engaged and booked artists on its own.

For two years MUZO sent Horowitz and Milstein all over the country to play for workers and peasants, most of whom could not have cared less about going to concerts. Years later, Horowitz laughed at the recollection. It was obvious that nobody in the audiences had ever been to a concert. They were bored and restless and could not wait to get out of the hall.

"We went to Poltava, Gomel, Kharkov, Ekaterinodar, Simferopol, and Sevastopol. We were in Taganrog, Novorossiisk, and Nakhichevan. We appeared in the Caucasus, in Batumi, Tiflis, and Baku. There were interesting trips to Saratov and the Tatar Republic," wrote Milstein. By this time the Revolution was controlled by the military and there were soldiers and militia in every city. In Kiev, a curfew was enforced because of all the looting and shooting. The Horowitz apartment house was occupied and the family had to move to smaller quarters. It was very dangerous to go out at night. The country was in a state of anarchy. At one point, a bomb went off very near Volodya and he was almost killed.

Horowitz owed his Moscow orchestral debut to his father, who in 1923 went to the Auer pupil Lev Zeitlin, an old friend who was the concertmaster of Persimfans in Moscow. According to Volodya, Samuel said, "I have a son and if you engage him he will be very famous, and you can believe me."

Persimfans, an acronym for First Symphonic Ensemble, was the only orchestra of its kind. It was a full symphony orchestra, more than eighty players, without a conductor—a Communist experiment in collectivism. The players sat in a circle and watched Zeitlin, who gave the downbeat and started them off. Horowitz played the Rachmaninoff Third with them and said it was a very good performance. Milstein shared the program with Horowitz, playing the Glazunov Concerto. When Darius Milhaud visited the Soviet Union he heard the orchestra and said it was very good, but wryly added, "a conductor would have achieved the same results, no doubt a little faster."

Horowitz was the first pianist to feature the Rachmaninoff Piano Concerto No. 3 as a repertoire piece. From the beginning of his studies he had identified with Rachmaninoff's piano music, and it had an influence on his actual playing. Many years later, in a 1971 interview with Phillip Ramey, Horowitz said, "I loved his compositions even as a young man, and playing them somehow developed in me a technique that was in affinity with his."

Horowitz and Milstein stayed in Moscow for a few months in 1923. Among their important concerts was one in which they played the Russian premieres of Karol Szymanowski's Violin Concerto No. 1 and Prokofiev's Violin Concerto No. 1, Horowitz playing the orchestral reduction on the piano. Milstein wrote that if you have a pianist like Horowitz playing with you, you don't need an orchestra. In the Szymanowski, Horowitz played with such fire and brilliance that Milstein could scarcely be heard but, as he noted in his book, "It's quite possible nobody cared." (Of course all violinists are convinced that their partners always play too loud, and Milstein was vociferous on the subject.) The Prokofiev, played at the Moscow Conservatory on November 21, 1923, was a sensation, and the composer Nikolai Miaskovsky wrote to Prokofiev in Paris notifying him that as a result of the premiere his popularity was "almost indecent. You've eclipsed even the Moscow idols, Rachmaninoff and Medtner!"

The Horowitz family came to Moscow for these concerts and also the ones Horowitz and Milstein gave with the young cellist Raya Garbousova. Born in 1906, Garbousova was a remarkable prodigy, and not only as a cellist. She played the piano so well that Heinrich Neuhaus invited her into his class at the Moscow Conservatory. The beautiful seventeen-year-old girl was "adopted" by Samuel Horowitz, who called her "our Raya," and he kept insisting that she was a member of the family. Garbousova occasionally concertized in Kiev, and then she would have stayed with Samuel and Sophie in the big apartment they used to have when she played there. But now Samuel and Sophie were living in a wretched one-room flat.

With Horowitz in Moscow, Garbousova played the Rachmaninoff and Debussy sonatas. With Horowitz and Milstein she played trios by Rachmaninoff, Arensky, and Tchaikovsky. Later she came to the United States and concertized regularly.

"We were very serious," recalled Garbousova in 1990:

> I remember like today the way Volodya played the Wagner *Ring* cycle. In those days Russians knew only *Lohengrin,* and it was Volodya who introduced me to the other Wagner. Volodya at that time was a beautiful man. He used a little makeup on stage, you know. He darkened his eyebrows. He *had* to be pretty. I adored him. He was a king among Russian pianists already then. All of his qualities were there, that sound, that articulation, that unusual way of playing with those flat fingers. It was not normal, and he could not explain it or teach it. Those were the days in Russia of NEP, the New Economic Plan, and there was no food. I remember that we sometimes were paid off in chocolate and we complained. We wanted meat, salami, not chocolates. We never lost touch with each other after we came out of Russia, and I used to see Volodya and Wanda whenever I could.

Horowitz made a tremendous impression wherever he played and was soon being talked about as the most formidable Russian pianist of his generation. It was not only because of the incredible accuracy of his pianistic mechanism but also because the playing far transcended mechanics. Horowitz had the magic, and that cannot be taught. There was something demonic in that tense figure at the keyboard, a suppressed force waiting to be released, a high-voltage charge (even when he played softly) that communicated itself to everybody in the audience. Gregory Ginsburg, for instance, was an admired pianist at that time whose fingers matched those of Horowitz, who was certainly at least as good a musician, who was motivated by the highest ideals. But Ginsburg did not have the magic. Horowitz did. It was a matter of temperament, of daring, of an alliance with the audience, of a new kind of playing and an unmatched degree of personality and tonal imagination.

Horowitz and Milstein went to St. Petersburg in 1923. At that time it was called Petrograd, and it was renamed Leningrad the following year. (Now, of course, it is St. Petersburg again.) They had a wonderful time there. Word of mouth had preceded them, and they lived up to their advance reputation. They played before sold-out houses and were riding high. The famous Alexander Glazunov, head of the St. Petersburg Conservatory, composer, conductor, put his orchestra at their disposal. They had money, were well clothed "and even wore spats, a sure sign we belonged to the elite," said Milstein. Most of the population was desperately striving to survive, but the amenities were there for those who could afford them. Horowitz and Milstein ate at the best restaurants, purchased the most fashionable clothing, even had a fan club. In short, they had arrived.

In Petrograd, Horowitz and Milstein introduced works by new Russian and Polish composers. At one concert, with Glazunov conducting, Milstein played the Glazunov Concerto (the only one of his many compositions that has remained in the active repertoire), and Horowitz did the Liszt E flat and Rachmaninoff Third.

Glazunov was not a very good conductor. His tempos were phlegmatic and slow. When he was drunk ("which was often," said Horowitz) they were even slower. At this performance Horowitz could not stand it. He rushed ahead, letting Glazunov follow him as best he could. Glazunov was considered one of the major Russian composers, but the Glazunov music that Horowitz heard never interested him enough even to take a look at his piano concertos.

The climax of Horowitz's career in the Soviet Union came shortly before he left the country. In one season in Leningrad, 1924–25, he played some twenty concerts with ten programs to wildly enthusiastic audiences.

This was a tribute to Horowitz's popularity, and there had not been anything like it since 1912, when Josef Hofmann gave twenty-one consecutive concerts in St. Petersburg, playing 255 different works. Horowitz's Leningrad recitals were the product of fast and furious labor, he said:

> I still don't know how I prepared those ten programs in so short a time. I certainly could not do it today.
>
> My Leningrad programs have never been published outside of Russia. They are in the archives of the old St. Petersburg Conservatory, now the Lenin Conservatory. Between October 15, 1924, and January 18, 1925, I played those twenty concerts. Altogether there were forty-four big works and sixty-six small works on the programs. The major Liszt works were the B minor Sonata; the *Spanish Rhapsody; Mephisto* Waltz; *Funérailles;* Tarantelle from *Venezia e Napoli;* the *Don Juan, Nozze di Figaro,* and other transcriptions; and the First Piano Concerto. Of Schumann there were the C major Fantasy, *Symphonic Etudes, Carnaval,* and the three *Romances.* Chopin—Ballades in G minor, F, and F minor; the A flat Polonaise; the second and third sonatas; the Barcarolle; the four scherzos; and the F minor Concerto; and of course selected mazurkas, etudes, preludes, and waltzes. I was interested in Ravel in those days and played the Sonatine and *Alborada del gracioso* plus some smaller pieces. Rachmaninoff—piano concertos two and three plus small pieces. I played a good deal of Medtner. I always played Bach-Busoni at that time, and on the programs were toccatas and fugues; the Toccata, Adagio, and Fugue in C; and the Chaconne.

A search in Leningrad turned up only the last program, which was played on January 18, 1925. Devoted to Chopin, it contained the Ballade No. 2, two scherzos, a nocturne, six etudes, six mazurkas, the Sonata in B flat minor, and the A flat Polonaise.

It is interesting that Horowitz claimed to have played the Rachmaninoff Piano Concerto No. 2 in his Leningrad series. If his statement was correct—Horowitz could be unreliable—this would be the only known public performance he ever gave of the work. Horowitz once explained that he had never played it in America because during the climax of the third movement, the piano has only neutral chords instead of a big display involving the famous theme. Horowitz said he once asked Rachmaninoff, "If I play it, can I double the orchestra's theme on the piano?" Rachmaninoff looked at him, shrugged his shoulders, and said, "*Nu*, Horowitz, do what you want." In the 1950s Horowitz was talking with Victor about recording the Second Concerto, but nothing came of it.

Leningrad audiences went wild at the Horowitz concerts, and he was the talk of the town. A fan club of young girls was on hand at every concert to cheer their hero on and follow him in the streets. At his last concert, it was reported, they went backstage, surrounded him and started snipping at his tail coat with scissors. Horowitz was furious but could not withstand the onslaught. The girls emerged triumphantly with black cotton-swatch memorabilia of their beloved.

About this time Horowitz made up his mind to leave Russia. He and Milstein had, during the previous few years, spent hours talking about making careers in the West. Like many musicians, they were less than enchanted with Soviet ideology and the mess it had made of the economy and the lives of the people. Horowitz's father was an ever-present case in point. Even when Horowitz was a student his friends, colleagues, and teachers had suggested that his future lay outside of Russia.

"I talked about Europe with my friends," he said. "As early as 1921, Blumenfeld and Neuhaus were giving me advice. Don't study with Schnabel, don't study with Godowsky, don't go to anybody because you don't need any more training. If you go to anybody, go to Busoni." Horowitz would have been glad to study with Busoni. Ever since childhood he had been fascinated by the man and his music; he had read everything he could find about him and pumped dry all the musicians he had encountered who had heard him play.

Horowitz knew that eventually he was going to leave. He had his passport ready, the passport that had been issued with a falsified date to make him a year younger. Unfortunately there was to be no Busoni in his life. The great Italian-German pianist and composer died shortly before Horowitz left Russia.

Things started to move when Horowitz met an impresario named Alexander Merovitch, a Russian who had started a concert bureau in Moscow. Merovitch was well aware of the potential that Horowitz and Milstein represented. He had met them around 1923, Horowitz said, and he kept following them, cajoling them, promising great things if they played in Berlin and other European capitals under his direction. A smooth talker, Merovitch assured them that they would have a tremendous success. That helped Horowitz, who was more impressionable and innocent than the skeptical and more worldly Milstein, make up his mind. Finally he told Merovitch that he would go. Another thing urging his departure was the dread possibility of his being drafted. (The thought of Vladimir Horowitz as a soldier boggles the imagination.)

Horowitz secured a visa to Germany on the grounds that he needed to complete his studies with Artur Schnabel in Berlin. That was not true, but he had to give some reason and that sounded convincing. Then he went on vacation in the Crimea, where he rested and practiced the Chopin F minor Concerto and the Tchaikovsky B flat minor Concerto. He had studied the Tchaikovsky with Blumenfeld but had never played it in public. Ten days before leaving Russia, Horowitz played both concertos in a single concert. His father came to Leningrad to hear it, and Horowitz remembered his advice: "Never play the Chopin again. Only the Tchaikovsky!" Samuel felt that the grander and more brilliant Tchaikovsky was a much better vehicle for his virtuoso son.

In September 1925 (Horowitz never could remember the exact date), pianist and impresario took the steamship from Leningrad to Bremen, en route to Berlin. Berlin, said Merovitch, was the only city in Germany that really counted artistically or professionally. Merovitch also started arranging for dates in Paris, a city that certainly had equal stature with Berlin as one of the two artistic capitals of Europe. Horowitz had British currency—£1,000, about $5,000—in his shoes. That was the money put aside for his first three concerts in Berlin. Milstein, who had some concert dates in Russia to fulfill, was to follow soon after. Now the Merovitch concert bureau had expanded to all of two musicians—but two such musicians any impresario would commit murder to put under contract.

Horowitz was twenty-two years old. He never thought he would be away from Russia for a long time. Quite the opposite. Deep down he had the feeling that he would not have the success that Merovitch had promised. He had his backup plan figured out. "I had become very popular in Russia, and if I would not have an equal success in Germany or France I would go back to Russia where they liked me and where my family was."

It was a quiet departure. Nobody from the family came to

Leningrad to see him off. If for no other reason, travel was next to impossible those days. Volodya and his father had taken leave of each other when he had played the Tchaikovsky and Chopin concertos ten days before the steamship to Bremen. Natasha had previously managed to leave Russia for studies in Europe. She later heard from the family that her uncle Samuel and Merovitch had a long private session in Moscow. "Uncle Samuel told Merovitch all about Volodya," she said. "How temperamental and difficult he was, and how to handle him." After Volodya arrived in Germany there was little contact between him and his family. It was not that he did not like his parents. "He was as interested in family as much as he could be interested in anybody but himself, and he really adored his mother," Natasha said. "But his career came first. Later on, when he was established, he corresponded with them. He never lost touch."

Horowitz, many years later, told Samuel Chotzinoff that a Soviet guard at the border examined his papers and passport, looked at him and said, "Do not please forget your motherland." It could have happened. It could also have been a romantic invention that Horowitz made up.

4

A Greenhorn in Berlin

I played a virtuoso program in Berlin—Bach-Busoni, Liszt, and so on. Schnabel came backstage and was very enthusiastic. But Schnabel told me he never played that kind of music. "I don't have the time," he said. "I still don't even know all of Bach." I said to him, "You know, Mr. Schnabel, I do just the opposite. First I play these things and then I will have time for Bach."
  —*Vladimir Horowitz, describing an encounter with Artur Schnabel*

*B*erlin in the mid-1920s was a sad, bad, glad, mad city, striving to pull itself out of the terrible inflation that had massacred the economy after World War I. But it had the most intellectually stimulating life of any city in Europe except Paris and, musically, it was more exciting than Paris. In the 1920s Berlin was the city of the Staatsoper, where Erich Kleiber conducted the world premiere of Alban Berg's *Wozzeck* in 1925. It was the city of the Kroll Opera, in which Otto Klemperer conducted many premieres shortly after Horowitz arrived there; and the city of the Städische Oper headed by Bruno Walter. It was the cabaret city of the Kurt Weill–Bertolt Brecht *Dreigroschenoper* and *Mahagonny*. Arnold Schoenberg, Paul Hindemith, Max Planck, Oskar Kokoschka, Vassily Kandinsky, and Thomas Mann lived and worked there. So did many great pianists.

It was a city of superb museums and symphony orchestras. It was an open, decadent city filled with homosexuals, prostitutes, con men, and shady nouveau-riche industrialists. The George Grosz drawings give an idea of the underside of Berlin in those years. To a provincial like Vladimir Horowitz it was a revelation.

Horowitz looked, listened, and started to work. There was one physical change. Merovitch decided that the curly locks Horowitz shook in Russia had to go. They were attracting too much attention and derisory laughter. Horowitz was given a close-cropped businessman's haircut.

He spent three months practicing, learning the language, and going to concerts and opera before making his Berlin debut. For once in his life he was a constant concertgoer. He wanted to understand what German music making was all about, what the German pianists represented, how he stacked up against them and the international keyboard celebrities who were always passing through Berlin.

When Horowitz arrived in Berlin, Wilhelm Backhaus, Walter Gieseking, Artur Schnabel, and Edwin Fischer were the major resident pianists there. The young Rudolf Serkin was beginning to make a name. Horowitz rushed to hear their concerts, to assess them and all the others. There were the Liszt pupils: Emil Sauer and Moriz Rosenthal. There were the Leschetizky products: Paderewski, Ignaz Friedman, Benno Moiseiwitsch, Ossip Gabrilowitsch, Mark Hambourg. There were the Slavic and Hungarian contingents, headed by Mischa Levitzki and Ernö von Dohnányi. The great Alfred Cortot, who often played in Berlin, was the leader of the French school.

Today it is hard to tell the difference between a Juilliard or a Moscow Conservatory graduate. But in Horowitz's early days, all pianists before the public were trained by musicians who had been born in the nineteenth century, and all represented distinct national schools as well as nineteenth-century performance practice. All were individualists; but no matter how different they were from one another, they had several things in common—beautiful sound, big technique, an ability to organize and move the basses, an interest in texture that included the exploitation of inner voices, and a constant use of delicate tempo fluctuations. That was true even of so sober and dedicated an artist as Artur Schnabel. He was the first to record all thirty-two Beethoven sonatas, and his "Romanticisms" of the 1930s bother some of the more austere Beethoven stylists of the 1990s.

There were three main schools. Pianists of the French school played "on top of the keys," which results in a somewhat shallow, percussive tone. (The German-influenced Cortot was an exception.) They strove for clarity rather than sonority. Their fingerwork was sparkling. Their tempos were fast, as French tempos historically have been. They played with alertness and intelligence, with driving rhythm, with effervescence. There is something of the salon in this kind of playing, which reflected a tradition established by Henri Herz, Pierre Zimmerman, and Antoine-François Marmontel, the dominant piano teachers at the Paris Conservatoire for most of the nineteenth century. French pianism to this day is a kind of frozen history.

The German school when Horowitz first experienced it was much more philosophical, serious, and angular than the French, more text centered, and made up of musicians who shared Richard Wagner's belief that the German-speaking nations had invented music. Their repertoire was rather one sided, centering around the German and Austrian classics. Composers like Rachmaninoff were considered frivolous. On the whole the German performers were more interested in the architecture of the music than its color, and they searched deep for the spiritual meaning of that architecture. They were thinking musicians who excelled in the music of their own heritage, sober rather than extroverted, convinced of their rectitude and, it must be said, rather patronizing to outsiders who played German music. Of course they produced some of the finest musicians in history.

As for the Slavic style, it was warm, generous, extroverted, and it represented a different kind of repertoire than did the German school. Very few German pianists, for instance, have ever achieved much fame as Chopin players. That was largely the province of the Poles and Russians, and a surprisingly large percentage of them were Jews. Leschetizky would always ask prospective pupils three questions: Were you a child prodigy? Are you of Slavic descent? Are you a Jew? If all three answers were yes, Leschetizky would rub his hands with glee. (He himself was not Jewish, by the way.)

The Slavic school concentrated more on the Romantics than on Beethoven or Schubert (late in his life, Rachmaninoff was surprised to discover that Schubert wrote piano sonatas), had a healthy respect for pure virtuosity, and were more color conscious than the Germans. They represented the kind of tempo fluctuation that came to life in the middle of the nineteenth century with the conducting of Wagner and Liszt: a fluctuation in which rhythms could vary but never the underlying meter. Liszt's piano playing, which had a great influence on the Russians, exemplified this approach, and he passed it on to his pupils. Color and sensuousness marked the Russian style, and such dissimilar pianists as the classic Hofmann, the volcanic Friedman, the aristocratic Moiseiwitsch and Lhevinne, all shared the same traits. They spoke the same language, even if each pronounced it differently.

Horowitz did not like the German school of music making. He found German piano playing "pedantic, square, boring," heavy, hidebound, thick, too severe, lacking in color, metrically too strict, obsessed with *Seele* (soul) and metaphysics. He hated the kind of programs they often put together—the last three Beethoven sonatas, the last three Schuberts. To Horowitz, this was not program making, and his Russian *Seele* rebelled against it then and until the end of his life.

Shortly after his arrival in Berlin, Horowitz met Rudolf Serkin, and a lifelong friendship began. Serkin was friendly with the cellist Francesco Mendelssohn (a descendant of the composer), and one evening invited him to a party in his house. Mendelssohn came with Horowitz in tow.

Serkin had not heard of Horowitz, and he politely greeted the unexpected guest. There were food and drink, conversation, music. Serkin played. Mendelssohn told Serkin that Horowitz was a very good pianist, and Serkin asked him to play something. Horowitz, who never needed much urging, complied. What Serkin heard galvanized him. It gave him a completely new idea about piano technique and the possibilities of the instrument, and the experience remained vivid with him for the rest of his life. He spoke about it not long before he died in 1991:

> Horowitz played a Liszt transcription and some Chopin. I was completely overwhelmed at this kind of technique, power, intensity, and musicianship. The colors! I never heard anything like it. We liked each other and had a lot to talk about. Later he stayed with me in Basel for three weeks. We played four-hand music together, we played for each other, we discussed everything about the piano. We became very close friends and re-

mained so. I learned so much from him. Never had I seen such concentration at the keyboard. Only a pianist can appreciate what he did. I had never even imagined this kind of playing before, and it opened a new world for me.

Horowitz looked up Artur Schnabel, an atypical product of the Leschetizky school in that he turned almost exclusively to Bach, Beethoven, Mozart, and Schubert in his later years. But the supposedly austere Schnabel continued to play Chopin and Liszt until about 1930. The fact that he became the leading pianist of the Austro-German classics did not inhibit his Romanticism in that kind of music; and, remembering his concert appearances and listening to his recordings, one hears a kind of Romantic rhetoric that has vanished from the playing of Beethoven, Mozart, and Schubert today.

Schnabel had heard Horowitz play in Leningrad and had told Genya that he would take him into his class if he ever came to Berlin. Horowitz, for his part, had heard Schnabel in Leningrad and was impressed, especially with his performance of the Chopin B flat minor Sonata (a work that Schnabel dropped from his repertoire in the 1930s). "In the last movement, every note was there!" enthused Horowitz. (The last movement is a short—about one and a half minutes—sotto voce, prestissimo movement in single notes an octave apart, and it is very difficult to carry off.) He also heard Schnabel play Liszt, and his comment many years later was, "Not bad." From Horowitz that was extraordinary praise.

So Horowitz got in touch with Schnabel, went to his studio, and played the Schumann Fantasy. He claimed to have played only ten bars or so when Schnabel interrupted him, swept him away from the piano, sat down and started to play the piece himself to demonstrate how Schumann really intended it to go. He ended up, said Horowitz, playing the complete work. Horowitz hated every bar of it. A few days later Schnabel sent a bill for £5—$25—to Merovitch for the "lesson." Horowitz was at first stupefied, then outraged, and finally he thought it was funny. He did not know if Schnabel was ever paid. "If he was, Merovitch never told me."

Horowitz had a theory about Schnabel's well-known technical sloppiness in the last part of his career: .

> For ten years he played mostly Beethoven, with a little Schubert. So he lost his technique. When you play nothing but

Beethoven you lose technique. He lost everything; he couldn't even play a scale. Nothing! That's when I decided not to play too much Beethoven. Schnabel was for me an example of what could happen.

Yet Horowitz admitted that he had heard Schnabel and Furt-wängler in the Brahms Second Piano Concerto during those years and was so excited that he started to learn it, though he was more taken with the music than with Schnabel's performance. Horowitz never could understand the hold that Schnabel had on his public. Nor did he think much of his Beethoven editions. He was amused by the fact that Schnabel never played Beethoven according to the strictures of his own editions.

Schnabel took his position as flagship of the German school of piano playing very seriously, and he regarded himself with equal seriousness. In America he could not find a Bechstein, his instrument of choice, and selected a Steinway. Alexander Greiner, the manager of the Concert and Artists Department of Steinway & Sons in New York, was half amused, half irritated by what he considered Schnabel's pompousness. In an unpublished memoir he described Schnabel's didactic speech and deportment:

> Liszt [Schnabel told Greiner] started those atrocious piano transcriptions of orchestral music! Wagner's *Tannhäuser* Overture! The *Ride of the Valkyries!* Isolde's *Love Death!* And, horror of horrors, Liszt even had the temerity to transcribe for piano Beethoven's symphonies. Just think of it! Beethoven! To make those orchestral pieces sound as loud as possible Steinway made their bass in their concert grands ever more powerful, ever louder and louder! But I pity Bee-tho-ven! Bee-tho-ven did not need Mr. Liszt, he knew what to write for orchestra and what for piano! He never intended his symphonies to be played on the piano. And Bee-tho-ven never intended his piano to sound like orchestral symphonies!

Greiner went to Schnabel's Bee-tho-ven concert and wrote that he played beautifully. He was so impressed that he went back-stage to pay his respects and thank him for a "glorious concert," and stopped dead when he heard Schnabel telling his acolytes about the inadequacies of the Steinway piano. "Oh," Schnabel told his admirers, "if only I had at my disposal one of those wonderful Bechsteins. Yes, the Bechsteins understood Bee-tho-ven. They made their marvelous pianos for Bee-tho-ven's music."

Of all the German pianists Horowitz heard, the two he most admired were Walter Gieseking and Wilhelm Backhaus:

> I was impressed mostly by Gieseking [Horowitz said in 1987]. He had a finished style, played with elegance, and had a fine musical mind. Emil Sauer was also a good pianist, good technique, style. Very good fingers. He was a Liszt pupil. He was at his best in salon music—Chopin waltzes, things like that. But I heard him play a very good, very correct Op. 109. Some of the Liszt pupils were horrible. One I never could understand was Siloti. He played very badly. Another Liszt pupil was the famous Moriz Rosenthal, and I hated his playing. He couldn't make one nice phrase. I don't understand how he got his fame. Perhaps when I heard him he was too old to have any control. He had dexterity but he had no real technique, and I don't think he really knew how to play the piano. He didn't make music.
>
> Backhaus was a wonderful pianist, not really representative of the German style. About him I can speak with real enthusiasm. He was more relaxed than most of them. I once heard him play the Chopin etudes and it was remarkable. In the first one in C major not a single note fell under the piano. It was fantastic. He heard me play Liszt's *Feux follets* and came up to me. "Horowitz," he said, "I could never do that." But he was being nice. He could have if he wanted. I have often been asked what I consider the most difficult piece I have ever played. I can answer that quickly. It was *Feux follets*. The Liszt *Don Juan* is not an easy piece, either.
>
> I heard Edwin Fischer, who did not mean much to me. I heard another pianist in Berlin who had a big success and I thought he was awful—Mischa Levitzki. Just fingers, and you cannot listen only to fingers. There is a difference between artist and artisan. Levitzki was an artisan. But Ignaz Friedman, who I admired, was a great artist. He had wonderful fingers and a very personal, individual way of playing, even if some of his ideas were very strange to me. He had no hesitation touching up the music. I got annoyed with him at one concert when he changed the basses in Chopin's F minor Ballade. I didn't like that. For some reason he was happier making records than he was on the stage.

Horowitz went to the three Berlin opera houses as often as he could. His favorite work was Richard Strauss's *Salome*. In Russia he had become familiar with the music and had memorized large sections of it. To the end of his life he played excerpts from the opera at home for his friends, tearing into the "Dance of the Seven Veils" with abandon. In Berlin he heard the composer conduct *Salome*. One thing about the performance Horowitz never forgot. Strauss was constantly looking at his watch.

For the oncoming three recitals scheduled for January, Horowitz and Merovitch put together programs they hoped would demonstrate all aspects of his talent—his sonority, his virtuosity, his musicianship. The first program was built around the Schumann Fantasy. It opened with the Bach-Busoni Toccata, Adagio, and Fugue in C. Then, after the Schumann, there would be Rachmaninoff and the tremendous Mozart-Liszt *Don Juan* paraphrase. The second program contained Chopin's B flat minor Sonata, Ravel (the Sonatine and other pieces), and the Mozart-Liszt *Figaro*. For the third program there was the Liszt B minor Sonata, a work not played very often in those days, especially in Germany. The thunderous Liszt, of course, is one of the monumental piano works of the nineteenth century. Merovitch had also signed a contract with the Berlin Symphony (not to be confused with the Berlin Philharmonic) for a performance of the Tchaikovsky B flat minor Concerto with Horowitz.

Horowitz tried out the pianos of the various manufacturers and settled on a Steinway, which he played for the rest of his life. No other instrument, he felt, could approach its powerful, brilliant bass, the responsiveness of the action and its potential for color. Merovitch scouted around for a manager and finally settled on the Wolff-Sachs agency in Berlin. Wolff-Sachs would handle all of the details of the Horowitz appearances—advertising, choice of hall, responsibility for pulling in audiences, and the press releases to newspapers and critics.

Wolff-Sachs was not particularly lavish in its publicity efforts. The only advertisement one can find appeared January 1, 1926. On that day readers of the *Musik-Zeitung*, Berlin's most important musical weekly, could learn from a small advertisement that one Vladimir Horowitz would be giving three *Klavierabende* in the Beethovensaal on January 2, 4, and 14. Wolff-Sachs had also arranged for an appearance with the Berlin Symphony after the second concert.

A debut recital in a major city is a harrowing, even searing, experience for any musician, especially an unknown one. Weeks before the advertisement appeared, Horowitz and Merovitch started worrying. Terrible, nightmarish things must have gone through their minds. *Item:* Wolff-Sachs was a highly respected agency, but would it be able to attract any kind of audience for a young, unknown Russian pianist? How awful it would be if nobody came. *Item:* Would a critic attend the concert? If there was no press coverage, the recital might be a waste of time and money. *Item:* If a critic did attend, would he understand what the performer was trying to do? *Item:* Would any major musicians attend the recital? For word of mouth in the professional musical community is of supreme importance in furthering a career. *Item:* Would there be the kind of miracle wherein a wealthy music lover would be so impressed with the young Russian genius that he would act as his sponsor?

All one could do was practice, wait, worry, and hope.

5
Crashing Through

> My career was finished forever. I didn't sleep the whole night. I
> was in despair. I called a doctor to give me an injection to calm
> me down. I told him I have to go back to Russia.
> —*Vladimir Horowitz, after his second Berlin concert*

*I*t was a nervous young man of twenty-three who walked on to
the stage of the Beethovensaal on January 2, 1926, bowed to the
audience, and started playing. The high-strung Vladimir Horowitz
was on edge after a sleepless night. He admitted as much many
years later. He also said that perhaps he was not at his best, because
so much was hanging on this concert that nerves got the better of
him.

He also remembered that there were no more than fifty people
in the audience (the hall seated around a thousand) and no critics
at all.

His memory was inaccurate on both counts. The audience was
reported in the press as half full, and there were indeed critics there,
including Heinz Pringsheim of the *Musik-Zeitung*.

Two days after the debut Horowitz played the second recital, and he thought the concert had gone flat. He was hysterical when he got back to his hotel room. He had failed, he told Merovitch. He was a miserable pianist. He had to go back to Russia.

But there was still the Tchaikovsky B flat minor Concerto with the Berlin Symphony under Oskar Fried to be played, and after that the January 14 recital. Merovitch was not going to let Horowitz run back to Russia. He soothed Horowitz, assured him that the recital had been brilliant, swore to him that he had heard nothing but wonderful things about Horowitz's playing. A few days later Horowitz played the Tchaikovsky, as planned, and thought it went well. Fried was a very experienced conductor and, Horowitz said, interested in his conception of the music.

Then Horowitz and Merovitch anxiously awaited the reviews.

One of the first was in the January 8 issue of the *Musik-Zeitung,* which carried an article by Adolf Diesterweg not about the January 2 debut but of the concerto performance. It was the kind of excited review that Horowitz inspired throughout his life. Diesterweg hailed this "hitherto unknown young pianist" as a brilliant newcomer endowed with a dashing bravura technique and yet musical enough to play lyric passages beautifully and with charm, unlike most bravura pianists.

On the same day another review of the Tchaikovsky, written by a critic who signed himself Schliepe, appeared in the *Deutsche Allgemeine Zeitung.* Herr Schliepe was carried away. "Hardly ever has a young pianist had such a rousing success as Vladimir Horowitz on the occasion of a special [i.e., nonsubscription] concert of the Berlin Symphony in Blüthner Hall. Tchaikovsky's B flat minor Concerto is a thriller which should not be brought in unless played with such taut, fiery rhythm, such gleaming octaves, such verve in all details and an explosion in all the dynamics."

The first reviews of Horowitz's Berlin debut recital on January 2 did not start appearing until almost two weeks after the event.

In the January 13 issue of the *Vossische Zeitung* an unsigned critic wrote: "It has been a long time since a young pianist has so spontaneously aroused such interest." In the January 15 issue of the *Musik-Zeitung,* Dr. Pringsheim reported: "From the first note of the Bach-Busoni Toccata in C, which started Vladimir Horowitz off in the first of three piano evenings at the Beethovensaal, one felt: here sits a professional at the piano." He was pleased with

Horowitz's "sense of proportion and individual quality of sounds, precision and elastic rhythm," and was amazed that such playing could come from a twenty-year-old pianist (he made Horowitz three years younger than he actually was). He had a few reservations about the Schumann Fantasy performance, which he thought a bit immature. But he concluded that the new pianist was going to have a great future.

In the March issue of *Die Musik,* Adolf Weissmann had a short entry in his Berlin report: "In recent years rarely has there been a piano recital that, through warmth of tone and identification with the instrument as well as the music, has made so strong an impression as that of the young Vladimir Horowitz."

Horowitz always claimed that Mrs. Sachs of the Wolff-Sachs agency was the one primarily responsible for his success. She had come to his first recital and at its end loudly announced, "This is the second Anton," meaning Rubinstein. She was so excited, Horowitz said, that she personally invited Weissmann to the second concert, and she raved about Horowitz to all of the important members of the Berlin musical establishment.

So the $5,000 that Horowitz had smuggled out of Russia was well spent. The gamble had paid off. Reading the reviews, one paramount thing becomes immediately apparent: everybody realized that Horowitz had something more than fingers. He could communicate. That slim, intense figure on stage simply forced the audience into awed respect. Horowitz had extraordinary personality, a stage presence all but palpable. All of the artists who have gone on to superstar status had this charisma, and it is something that cannot be taught. Toscanini had it. Callas had it. Horowitz had it. Whatever it is, it resides in the performer's psyche, and without it there can be no super career.

The third recital was sold out and Horowitz finally was satisfied with himself. He thought he played as well as he could. The public was enthusiastic, especially about the Liszt Sonata. German critics and audiences of the day had a tendency to regard the Liszt B minor Sonata with distaste; to them it was a large dead animal that was somewhat overripe. But they had not heard Vladimir Horowitz play it. After his performances the Liszt B minor Sonata began to be recognized for what it is—a great, imaginative, monumental piece of music, something far more than a technical stunt.

Offers came in—for concert appearances and also, from Welte-

Mignon, for piano-roll recordings. Horowitz and Merovitch looked at each other. Things were going along very nicely.

Merovitch booked two concert appearances in Hamburg, and he and Horowitz arrived there a few days before the concerts. An advertisement in the Hamburg *Echo* notified the public on January 17, 1926, that Vladimir Horowitz would be giving a recital on Tuesday, January 19, at the Hotel Atlantic.

But no critic from the *Echo* was there to review it. Instead there was a review in the *Fremdenblatt,* which appeared, atypically, on January 20, the day after the concert. It was signed M. Br.-Sch., which stood for Max Broesecke-Schön. He must have been one of the faster writers in the German critical press.

In his review Broesecke-Schön spoke of the talented young Russian who had come to Hamburg "with a big reputation" (word had already gotten around) and played for a well-attended hall. Horowitz, he said, was a player of sparkling temperament, polish and poetry, with steellike strength in forte passages and a virtuoso technique of flawless security and command; with elastic rhythm, youthful sparkle and occasionally a nervous flexibility in his interpretations. He had an attractive, Slavic kind of rubato that gave his playing animation. His emphasis at present was toward virtuosity. The Chopin Barcarolle was on the superficial side; it needed a more mature and soulful player. But some etudes and mazurkas were played with an easy brilliance and elegance, and also with the poetry happily grasped. In Chopin's B minor Etude the breathtaking tempo and octaves were amazing. And in the Liszt B minor Sonata there was a fiery, emotional, well-shaped reading "something in the style of the modern 'Psychologismus' à la Scriabin and Miaskovsky." (Whatever that may mean.) The evening ended with a "strong" performance of the rarely played *Figaro* transcription by Liszt.

This was, on the whole, a review that would have made Horowitz and Merovitch very happy. In the afternoon they left the Atlantic Hotel, where they were staying, and went for a walk. The rest is history. As Horowitz told the story:

> We went out walking, in the zoo. When we came back to the hotel about six-thirty there was waiting for us the manager of the symphony orchestra. He was very nervous. A woman [Helene Zimmermann] who was supposed to play the Tchaikovsky with the orchestra that very evening had fainted during

the rehearsal and was in no condition to play. He asked me to replace her.

It was six-thirty when I received the news. "Can you play in two hours?" On two hours' notice? No rehearsals? I thought a little bit and said yes. I rushed to shave and get into evening clothes. Of course there was no time for rehearsal. Before the concert Eugen Pabst, the conductor, had a little talk with me about tempos. He was not very simpatico. He looked at me as if to say, "Who is this guy coming here to play with me?" He said, "I conduct like this, and this, and this. You have to follow me." I said, "OK, sir. OK, sir. Yes, I will." I didn't even know what kind of piano I was playing. Of course in Hamburg it had to be the Hamburg Steinway, but was it even in tune? How was the action? I knew nothing. It turned out to be a very good piano.

When I came out nobody even applauded. They had never heard of me. Just like if you go to a concert to hear Mr. Smith. Who is Mr. Smith? So Pabst started the concerto, pom, pom, pom, pom, POM. When I played the first three chords he turned from the orchestra, he looked at me like he didn't believe what he was hearing, and he didn't conduct for a while. He came next to the keyboard to listen. He still didn't believe it. He never heard sound like that. When I finished the cadenza and he was back on the podium, he began to follow me. There was no longer any question of me following him. When the concerto was finished, it was bedlam, absolutely bedlam. The audience went wild. I never saw anything like that in my life. In 1986 I returned to Hamburg for the first time since then, and I got a letter from Pabst's daughter. She apologized for being unable to attend the [1986] concert, and then in the letter she told the whole story about the Tchaikovsky again.

M. Br.-Sch. was also at the concerto performance and wrote about it in the *Fremdenblatt* on the following day, January 21. Horowitz, wrote Broesecke-Schön, gave a bravura performance, one with temperament and élan, on the highest level. The way Horowitz, conductor, and orchestra avoided "the hazards and pitfalls" of this difficult concerto and emerged with such fine ensemble was "most impressive."

Curiously, a review signed by one S. Sch. also appeared on January 21, in the Hamburg *Nachrichten,* but it was not of the Tchaikovsky. Instead, S. Sch. reviewed the January 19 Hamburg debut recital. It was a peculiar review—a rave with some astrology in it. After exclaiming over the skill, personality, line, and rhythm of the pianist, he went on to write that the horoscope of this young and accomplished artist was under a good constellation, and he continued with still many more paragraphs of astrologobabble.

The second recital, after the Tchaikovsky furor, was immediately rebooked into a larger hall, and it was also a triumph. Horowitz was told that Hamburg had not reacted so strongly to a musician since the last appearance of Caruso. When he came out of the concert hall after the second recital there were hundreds of people waiting for him. They lifted Horowitz and carried him to his hotel. When they got there they found hundreds of people in the lobby. "But they were not interested in me. There was a man there who had given a lecture and everybody wanted to meet him. His name was Adolf Hitler."

On January 27, the *Echo,* which had not yet taken note of any of the Horowitz appearances, carried a review of the second recital, in which Horowitz had played the music of such dangerous moderns as Medtner and Ravel. As such, wrote S. S. (whoever he was), the Horowitz program represented a fast-dying species of art. But as a pianist Horowitz "deepened the great impression he had previously made."

After the Hamburg concerts, word was flashed all through Germany and Horowitz was famous. Merovitch was now able to book him for about forty European concerts through 1927 at an increased fee.

Germany was conquered. Now it was time for Paris. Merovitch had booked a hall there for an early February concert and, full of elation and anticipation, Horowitz and his manager took the train to the French capital. They traveled third class; they were just about broke.

6

Parisian Lion

I remember once when I was new in Paris a lady I knew who managed concerts asked me to sit for a portrait. She said the artist was very good and one day would be famous. I asked her what I would have to do for that. She said sit for two or three hours twice a week. Never, I said. Never. Good-bye. The painter's name was Bonnard.

—Vladimir Horowitz, about a missed opportunity during his early days in Paris

*H*e made Paris tremble," Arthur Rubinstein once ruefully said, talking about that first Horowitz season early in 1926.

It did not take Horowitz and Merovitch very long to discover that Horowitz's reputation had preceded him in the French capital. Horowitz may have been unknown to the French public, but not to the professionals. Word of mouth in musical circles had traveled with its usual speed. The critics were primed and waiting. This time, Horowitz said, he did not feel edgy. After his German success he was confident that he could handle himself anywhere.

And he could. He simply overwhelmed Paris, and seldom in the musical life of that city did an artist make so explosive an impact. The startled critics and the public were carried away with what they instantly recognized as a new style of playing.

Only one thing bothered Horowitz on his arrival. He had very little money. Although the financial prospects for the coming season looked good, at the point of his arrival in Paris Horowitz had played only seven concerts in Germany at a small fee. So, Horowitz said, he did what many Jews did. He got an introduction to the Baron de Rothschild and asked for a loan:

> I said I had a contract for concerts and would return the money to him. He immediately wrote out a check for me because by that time I was already well known. He said I would not have to give anything back. After a few concerts I made enough to be able to repay what I owed, so I paid him back, and he said that was the first time in his life such a thing had happened to him.

The cellist Francesco Mendelssohn, who had introduced Horowitz to Serkin in Berlin, happened to be in Paris. He introduced Horowitz to Denise Tual, a woman who was active in the arts and held her own salon. She had a Bechstein grand in her home and made it available. Horowitz practiced on it and she fed him sandwiches while he worked.

He had trouble finding a Steinway for his concert. In Paris a pianist was expected to play one of the two major French instruments—a Gaveau or a Pleyel. Steinway & Sons did not even have a bureau in Paris at that time. Horowitz and Merovitch had to search everywhere before managing to locate a Steinway, and it was not a very good one.

The first Horowitz appearance in Paris took place on February 12, 1926, and the locale was the hall of the old Paris Conservatoire, where Chopin had played the premiere of his Andante Spianato and Polonaise in 1835. The Horowitz concert was hastily arranged, without much in the way of publicity. That accounted for the small audience. Many of those present were Russian émigrés, gathered together by Merovitch. The program consisted of the Bach-Busoni Toccata, Adagio, and Fugue in C; the Liszt Sonata; several of Ravel's *Miroirs* (including *Alborada del gracioso*) and *Jeux d'eau;* and a Chopin group consisting of the Barcarolle, some etudes and mazurkas and the A flat Polonaise.

But if the audience was small, the important critics were there, and they realized that they were in the presence of something new. A long review came from Edouard Schneider in *Le monde musical,* who pointed out that "in the person of this pianist, not much more than twenty years old, there is a remarkable master of the piano who is going to be discovered by Paris. He is in the class of the greatest ones who have come out of young Russia." He found interpretations that, far from giving the impression of mere facility and an exceptional technique, "offered an edifying example of insight and probity. . . . Those of you who have a passion for the literature of the piano should make a point of hearing him."

On March 12, Horowitz gave another recital at the Conservatoire, this time to a sold-out house. He played the Bach-Busoni Organ Prelude and Fugue in D, Schumann's *Carnaval,* five Rachmaninoff preludes, Liszt's *Lac de Wallenstadt* and first *Valse oubliée,* the Schubert-Liszt *Liebesbotschaft* and *Erlkönig,* and the Saint-Saëns–Liszt *Danse macabre.* "He has surpassed anything it would have been possible to predict," wrote Arthur Hoërée in *Le menestrel.*

Less than two weeks later, on March 24, Horowitz made a guest appearance in the Salle Gaveau in a program, presented by *La revue musicale,* that consisted mostly of choral works. He played Bach's Toccata in C minor and Liszt's *Sonetto 104 del Petrarca, Funérailles,* and *Mephisto* Waltz. An appearance in a concert like this would not have been booked by Merovitch. Horowitz was asked to play by the *Revue* because all Paris was anxious to hear the new celebrity, and room on the program was hastily made for him.

Henry Prunières wrote about it in *La revue musicale.* He said that Horowitz possessed "the most remarkable technique possible to imagine. . . . Never was there a lapse of taste, never a breach of musicianship." (It was Prunières who alerted America to the new pianist. Prunières was the Paris musical correspondent for the New York *Times,* and the following year, on July 10, 1927, the American public could read that "I question whether we have heard a virtuoso of his stamp since Liszt and Anton Rubinstein.")

May 6, 1926, again saw Horowitz at the Gaveau, playing the Liszt E flat Concerto with an orchestra conducted by Walter Straram (here he used a Gaveau piano). Critics reported that Horowitz played so impetuously that the orchestra was hard pressed to follow him.

On May 30 Horowitz was at the Salle des Agriculteurs, playing the Bach-Busoni Chaconne, the Schumann Fantasy, Liszt's *Vallée d'Obermann, Cloches de Genève, Au bord d'une source,* and two of the Liszt *Paganini* etudes—A minor and E flat. He ended with the Liszt-Busoni *Figaro* paraphrase. (The Salle des Agriculteurs later became a movie house and is no longer in existence.) Finally, to conclude his 1925–26 season, Horowitz played once more at the Gaveau. This time his program consisted of the Vivaldi-Bach D minor Concerto, Schumann's *Novellette* No. 8 and *Arabesque*, Mendelssohn's *Spring Song*, two Chopin mazurkas and the B minor Scherzo, the Ravel Sonatine, and Liszt's *Spanish Rhapsody*. "The perfection and the leggiero quality of his style," wrote Emile Vuillermoz in *Candide*, "surpassed all that it was possible to dream of." So far, in these concerts, Horowitz had not repeated a single piece.

Vuillermoz was one of the most respected critics in Paris, and his words carried considerable weight. Everybody started comparing Horowitz to Liszt and Anton Rubinstein, and he was called the legitimate successor of Busoni. All other pianists playing in Paris in those days were overshadowed, and Russian pianists following Horowitz had a hard time of it. The legendary Vladimir Sofronitzky, who came to Paris a few seasons after Horowitz, did not make anywhere near the impression that Horowitz had made.

Returning to action in the winter season, Horowitz, on December 5, 1926, played the Tchaikovsky B flat minor Concerto at the Conservatoire, with an orchestra conducted by Philippe Gaubert. About this, Schneider wrote in *Le monde musical* that the concerto had never before been heard "phrased with such poetic ardor, imperial and sure attacks, a quality of song more ardent, skill more exalted in color and rhythm." The climax of Horowitz's first year in Paris came with a recital at the Opéra on December 14. This time he repeated some of the pieces he had been playing in his previous series: the Bach-Busoni Toccata, Adagio, and Fugue in C; the Liszt Sonata; six Chopin etudes, three mazurkas, and the A flat Polonaise; the two Paganini-Liszt etudes and the *Spanish Rhapsody*. His encores were Mendelssohn's *Spinning Song*, the Schubert-Liszt *Liebesbotschaft*, and his own *Carmen* Variations. The *Carmen* threw the audience into a frenzy, and the police had to be called in to evacuate the hall.

In the ten following years, until his first retirement, Horowitz gave some thirty concerts in Paris. The city could never get enough of him; he created a sensation every time he played. And, of course, every pianist rushed to hear the fabulous new virtuoso.

Among them was Rudolf Firkusny, a young Czech pianist

who went on to a very distinguished career. Firkusny said that while he lived in Paris he had heard a broadcast of the Tchaikovsky. What he heard electrified him, but he was not able to attend a Horowitz concert in Paris until 1931. "I was walking on clouds after the recital," said Firkusny.

Firkusny made an important point about the impact of the "new" Russian school of piano playing as represented by Horowitz. All Central-European pianists of his own generation, Firkusny said, had been exposed almost exclusively to the German school, as represented by Backhaus, Schnabel, Fischer, and Sauer, and had been taught in that tradition. Not until the mid-1920s did pianists start coming out of Russia. What pianists like Rachmaninoff and Horowitz represented, said Firkusny, was something new and radical to the German-trained ear, something free, colorful, thrilling. "It was a new world, a different approach to the piano," said Firkusny, "and the Horowitz recital made one of the greatest impressions of my life. Horowitz was even more interesting than Rachmaninoff. It was not only the famous Horowitz electricity. There also were all those nuances, and I must say that his playing was always very musical."

The young George F. Kennan, later a distinguished diplomat and authority on Russia, heard Horowitz in Paris, and in his *Sketches from a Life* (1989) he gave a good idea of how a sensitive nonprofessional listener experienced Horowitz in 1926:

> I was so keyed up watching the player (we sat in the third row) that I got very little out of the music, except an impression of exquisite musical taste and incredible technique. I don't think I ever in my life saw anyone who seemed to be under a more excruciating nervous strain. He is a slight boy, with a long black pompadour, ashy gray complexion, handsome, other-worldly face, on which there is a drawn expression, as though he were in continual pain. His mouth and eyes were incredibly sensitive. When he played (it was a Tchaikovsky concerto) it seemed as though he himself were being played upon by some unseen musician—as though every note were being wrung out of him. His nervous, spidery fingers trembled on the keys, his face worked as though he were in agony, perspiration dripped from his forehead, and he groaned with every chord of the crescendo passages. Whenever the accompanying symphony orchestra played a few measures of accompaniment without him, one

could see his whole body, from head to foot, vibrating tensely to every note of the music.

Naturally this brilliant newcomer was automatically admitted to the most exclusive salons of Paris. Chief among them was the home of the Princesse de Polignac, where one would invariably bump into Stravinsky, or members of Les Six, or Nadia Boulanger. It was in the salons that much new music was first heard; composers tried out their pieces there. Horowitz was always welcome chez Polignac, and also at the salons of Vicomtesse de Noailles, or Elsa Maxwell or Misia Sert. About two years later he met the American composer Alexander Steinert at the salon of Prince Rofredo Bassiano, and Steinert became one of his closest friends.

Arthur Rubinstein in his memoirs has given a vivid idea of life and fun in the Parisian salons of his day. He was on close terms with all the right people—Countess Greffulhe, Count Jean de Castellano, Princesse Yourievskaya, Count Potocki, Prince and Princesse de Polignac and Count and Comtesse de Ganay. In one charming passage of his memoirs Rubinstein reports spending a weekend with the Polignacs at Reims. Back in Paris he runs into Jean Cocteau. "Are you going to Misia's?" Cocteau asks. Rubinstein says he has not been invited. "Come with me. She has Diaghilev, Massine, and Eric Satie to hear a ballet by Milhaud which he will play four-hands with Auric." The ballet was Milhaud's wonderful *Le boeuf sur le toit*. Such was the artistic life in Paris in the 1920s. What a time for the young and talented in music—or, of course, in any of the arts—to be there! Picasso and Braque and Vlaminck; Joyce and Hemingway; Cocteau, Honegger, and Massine; Ravel and Poulenc; René Clair, Virgil Thomson, and Diaghilev; Dali, Chagall; the stern goddess known as Nadia Boulanger; Gertrude Stein. . . .

Many Russian refugees were in Paris at the time—intellectuals, musicians, nobility, military men, all waiting for the nonsense in Russia to be over so they could go back. They thought the Revolution was only temporary. Chaliapin, Prokofiev, Stravinsky, and Balanchine were living in Paris. Such Russian critics as Leonid Sabaneyev, Boris de Schloezer, Peter Souvtchinsky, and Arthur Lourié became fixtures of the musical life there. Horowitz and Merovitch were friendly with all of them. Merovitch even talked Prince Alexis Zereteli, the manager of L'Opéra Russe in Paris, into becoming his agent in France. The tight little colony of Russian intellectuals in Paris were constantly in touch with each other and exerted a good deal of influence in the artistic life of the city.

Young, handsome, shy, brilliantly talented, elegant in dress and demeanor, fluent in French, Horowitz became an increasingly popular figure in the salons. There he met all the important musicians, *littérateurs,* and society figures of Paris. Among the composers he socialized with were Roussel, Poulenc, Szymanowski, Honegger, and Respighi.

"One night," he recollected, "I played Ravel's *Jeux d'eau* at a salon and this little man came to me and said that he was Ravel and that I had a great talent. 'But,' he said, 'you should know that in our country we play *Jeux d'eau* differently. We play it more impressionistically, more like Debussy, but you played it in the style of Liszt.' I said I was sorry. What could I say? In the meantime Ravel was thinking. He looked at me and said, 'I think you are right. It is very Lisztian.' " Newspapers later helped Horowitz out by improving on the story. Most versions have Horowitz not knowing who the little man was until Ravel, after the musical talk about the piece was over, introduced himself and left Horowitz with his mouth wide open.

Horowitz met Prokofiev at Steinert's house in the late 1920s, and the two musicians became friendly. Prokofiev had a reputation for being sarcastic, and he was, said Horowitz,

> but I never saw that side of him. Others did. He was a pretty good pianist. He told me the story of a girl who had played one of his sonatas at her recital in a small hall in Paris. Prokofiev was in the audience, and after the performance he went on stage and congratulated her. Later he went to her in private and told her that she was a rotten player, that she had spoiled his sonata, and that it was the worst thing he had ever heard. Fortunately, he added, nobody in the audience was in a position to know about the slaughter that had occurred. He was brassy and athletic, just like his music. He was basically a very simple man. He liked me very much, I think. It was a pity that he and Rachmaninoff never got along. They hated each other.

(The mutual dislike stemmed from the time just after Scriabin's death in 1915, when Rachmaninoff played several concerts of Scriabin's music to honor his memory. His playing was not in the

Scriabin style, and there were those who did not like it. Prokofiev was one. Scriabin's playing, Prokofiev wrote, had been "all allure and suggestion." With Rachmaninoff, the notes "stood firmly and clearly on the ground." Prokofiev went backstage after one of the concerts and in a manner that Rachmaninoff took to be condescending said that he had played "very well." Rachmaninoff was furious. Who was this twenty-four-year-old kid to tell *him* about piano playing?)

Horowitz thought that as a pianist Prokofiev was "not bad," but that his tone was percussive. Prokofiev suggested that Horowitz play his Third Concerto. "Don't play the Second. I don't like it myself." Naturally Prokofiev would have loved it if the brilliant Horowitz had taken up one of his concertos with the ardor he showed for the Rachmaninoff Third. Horowitz got a copy of the Prokofiev Third Concerto, read through it and liked it, but not enough to play it in public:

> It is not my kind of concerto. I like his First Concerto also, but again I would not play it. Prokofiev came to one of my recitals, and his only comment was that he liked *La campanella* the most because the trill was fantastic and I could hold it for five minutes. He asked me several times why I didn't compose more. I told him that I felt too many weaknesses in my technique. I did not know counterpoint, I could not write a good fugue. . . . Prokofiev interrupted me. "I can't write a fugue either," he said. "It makes no difference. You can compose anything. Your *Carmen* is beautiful." Suddenly he disappeared. He went back to Russia without telling anybody.

Prokofiev was not the only one who praised Horowitz's compositions. Rachmaninoff once told Nathan Milstein that Horowitz had more talent for composition than he had for the piano. "Can you believe that? Perhaps," added Milstein, "Rachmaninoff was a little jealous of the big success that Horowitz was having as a pianist?" (But on another occasion Rachmaninoff told Milstein that Horowitz played the Third Concerto better than he did.)

None of Horowitz's music has been published. He composed a number of piano pieces, a violin sonata, a cello work, and some songs. The only work of his own that he ever recorded on flat disc is his *Danse exotique*. It is charming and sophisticated, in the French salon style, influenced by Poulenc and ragtime. Horowitz claimed that he had written it before leaving Russia. He made a Welte piano roll of the piece in 1926 and also a Victor recording in 1930. On the roll its title is *Moment exotique*. For Victor it has two names. First it came out on a ten-inch disc as *Danse exotique* by Horowitz-Demeny. Nobody seems to know who Demeny was. This was followed by the same performance, also on a ten-inch disc, under a different title: *Danse excentrique,* and the composer is listed merely as Horowitz. The reference to Demeny has vanished. Both discs have the same label number—1468.

The ebullient Poulenc and Horowitz were introduced at one of the salons and became very good friends:

> He was wonderful. He would barge into my flat without an appointment, always in a hurry, full of enthusiasm. "Horowitz, I have for you a nocturne! I have come to play it for you!" He would sit down and play it. "Good-bye!" And he would rush away. He knew the piano well and was a very good pianist. For years I played his Toccata in my recitals. I remember once we all had dinner at Charles de Polignac's salon. Poulenc played a new piece for me and I told him the ending was terrible. So he changed it. I sometimes played my own compositions for him, and he enjoyed them very much. The three composers who had the nicest things to say about my pieces were Poulenc, Prokofiev, and Szymanowski.

In Paris the most important French pianist was Alfred Cortot, one of the supreme twentieth-century keyboard artists. Horowitz blew hot and cold about Cortot. It always seemed hard for him to give another pianist unqualified praise. But even so, Horowitz admired Cortot the interpreter even if he did not admire Cortot the technician:

> His Chopin and Schumann were for me the best. His Schumann was fantastic. He had good taste and a good but not great technique, though he lost his technique in the last years of his life. He played a lot on the radio. I remember hearing him in many things. Once I visited Rachmaninoff in Switzerland at his house. When I walked in he was laughing so loud his false teeth were coming out. I asked him what was so funny.
>
> "I have just been listening on the radio to Cortot playing all the Chopin etudes."
>
> "That was so good?" I asked.

"Wonderful. But, you know, the most difficult of the etudes were the ones he played most 'musical.' "

The word "musical" applied by virtuoso pianists to other pianists is often a code word meaning good musician, not so good fingers or, in baseball lingo, good field, no hit. Rachmaninoff was so amused because Cortot covered up his technical deficiencies by playing slowly in the hard passages. Critics and connoisseurs, taken in, automatically hailed the slow passages as "musical." So the more Cortot slowed up, the more everybody would say "How musical!" (When Horowitz told the story a sour look came over his face. "Today," he said, "that has become the thing. Everybody plays slow, pianists, singers, everybody, and that shows how musical they are. It is crazy, I tell you.")

As a matter of fact, Cortot could have a brilliant technique when he put his mind to it, as witness his spectacular recording of the Liszt Hungarian Rhapsody No. 11. But he never worried much about wrong notes or memory lapses in recitals, or even on recordings, for that matter. Cortot carried a tremendous work load and the chances are that he could never find the time to practice very much. He was a splendid all-around musician—pianist, teacher, conductor, author, editor, scholar—with a most idiosyncratic style. Trained in the French method at the Conservatoire, he became a Wagnerian, conducted the first French performance of *Götterdämmerung,* and brought a certain Germanic quality to his piano playing. He was the master of a singing line, a pronounced rubato which (especially in his early recordings) takes some getting used to, a luminous streak of poetry and a tremendous authority. A few wrong notes do not matter in this kind of playing. He was one of the very great pianists of history.

Horowitz played a good deal for Cortot and may have gotten more from him than he was willing to acknowledge. Often Cortot invited him to dinner. His wife, who had been married to the famous novelist, playwright, and musicologist Romain Rolland, threw very glamorous parties. "They were very intellectual, the Cortots," said Horowitz. "He also was one of the worst anti-Semites in Europe, as bad as Karl Muck." Muck, a German conductor, subscribed wholeheartedly to Richard Wagner's poisonous racial theories. "But," continued Horowitz, "Cortot was a fine musician. He had done one of the best editions of Chopin. In the footnotes he worked out exercises based on the technical problems of the music and they were very good. Cortot's Chopin edition is still in use and is very valuable."

Later Horowitz played, with Cortot conducting, the Rachmaninoff Third Concerto (on October 16, 1932) and the *Emperor* Concerto (on December 24, 1933). Horowitz said that after the Beethoven performance Cortot called him the prince of the piano.

> His conducting [said Horowitz] was not bad. Not long before my performance with Cortot I had played the *Emperor* with Toscanini. Toscanini did not like the way I, and every other pianist, played the turn in the slow movement, right after the trills and where the cantabile starts. The tradition was to play all the notes of the turn between the B and the F sharp evenly. This was very classic. But Toscanini insisted that there was to be a little hold after the B. So I played it Toscanini's way and Cortot stopped me. "Why do you play it like that?" I told him it was Toscanini's idea. "Ah. To Toscanini I bow." In the *Emperor* his conducting was very eloquent. He was a terrible person, a *collaborateur* during the war, but a beautiful musician.

Despite his flattering words to Horowitz face to face, Cortot did not have the highest regard for him—at least, if the French critic Bernard Gavoty is to be believed. After the *Emperor,* Gavoty asked Cortot what he thought of the performance. "A great boredom," replied Cortot. "Puny, cramped playing." Cortot went on to say that Horowitz had been described to him as an albatross, but that he could find no wings on the Russian pianist, who was only a first-rate technician. Was Gavoty quoting Cortot accurately? "Puny" is an unusual adjective for Vladimir Horowitz. If Gavoty is to be believed, Cortot even bad-mouthed Horowitz in the Rachmaninoff Third. The composer would have disagreed.

Horowitz said in 1987 that he heard many pianists in Paris but was not impressed with what he encountered. But surely he must have run across Alexander Brailowsky, who had been a fixture in Paris since his wildly acclaimed debut in 1919. Until Horowitz appeared, Brailowsky was the darling of the Parisian audience. In a way his background was much like that of Horowitz. Born in Kiev, he had studied with Puchalsky (Horowitz's first teacher) before going on to Leschetizky and finally Busoni.

Horowitz admitted that he was more interested in going to

Montmartre and having a good time than in attending piano recitals. But, "I heard the young Iturbi. He was a good pianist. In America he was especially popular. In my first years in America there were four young pianists who made the biggest hit with the public—Iturbi, Mischa Levitzki, Gieseking, and me. But Rachmaninoff did not like Iturbi. He went to one of his recitals and walked out. He thought he had nothing to say."

When Horowitz arrived in Paris he had a letter of introduction from Neuhaus to Arthur Rubinstein, who was about twenty years older than Horowitz and a popular pianist in Paris, especially in the salons. They saw a good deal of each other, but Horowitz had the feeling that Rubinstein didn't like him very much. "Something didn't click between us. Maybe he was jealous." Nevertheless they often met in Rubinstein's house in Montmartre. "He once played the orchestral part of the Brahms B flat Concerto for me on the second piano. He hadn't studied it at that time and wanted to be more familiar with it. At least we had one thing in common— neither of us ever worked on technique. We studied only repertoire. Rubinstein never practiced. Like with me, everything with him was spontaneous."

The basic difference between Rubinstein and Horowitz was that where Rubinstein generated love, Horowitz generated awe. In *My Many Years,* the second volume of his autobiography, Rubinstein has a few words to say about his relationship with Horowitz. Even before they met he admits to some jealousy because everybody in Paris was talking about the young Horowitz. Shortly after their first meeting, Rubinstein went to a Horowitz concert and was impressed: "I shall never forget the two Paganini-Liszt etudes, the E flat and E major ones. There was much more than sheer brilliance and technique; there was an easy elegance—the magic which defies description."

After the concert Rubinstein went backstage with many others. Horowitz, "sweating and pale, received the great homage with regal indifference." When Rubinstein went up to him Horowitz said that he had played a wrong note in Chopin's Polonaise-Fantaisie. "I would gladly give ten years of my life," Rubinstein ruefully noted, "to be able to claim only one wrong note after a concert."

The two often played together, four hands or at two pianos. On the surface they were friends, but Rubinstein says that he began to feel "a subtle difference" between them:

His friendship was that of a king for his subject, which means he *befriended* me and, in a way, used me. In short, he did not consider me an equal. It caused me to begin to feel a deep artistic depression. Deep within myself I felt I was the better musician. My conception of the sense of music was more mature, but at the same time I was conscious of my terrible defects —of my negligence for detail, my treatment of some concerts as a pleasant pastime, all due to that devilish facility for grasping and learning the pieces and then playing them lightheartedly in public; with all the conviction of my own musical superiority, I had to concede that Volodya was by far the better pianist.

Incidentally, Rubinstein thought of Jascha Heifetz much as he thought of Horowitz. "I never envied either of them their great success and I took it for granted that Heifetz was the greatest violinist of his time, who never touched my heart with his playing, and Horowitz, the greatest pianist but not a great musician. On this premise our trio got along together quite well."

A pianist Horowitz met in Paris and admired very much was Ignaz Friedman, a Pole born in 1882 who had been a Leschetizky pupil. In recent years piano buffs and young pianists have rediscovered the Friedman recordings, all made before World War II, and have been studying them openmouthed. Friedman was a technician almost in Horowitz's class, with an even bigger, more colorful sound. He played with great generosity of spirit and an abandon that was always emotionally controlled. Nobody has played the Chopin mazurkas with such a rakish quality, such affinity for the rhythms of the Polish dance, such fluency and imagination. He was a very close friend of Rachmaninoff's, and that alone would have endeared him to the young Horowitz, who idolized Rachmaninoff but had not yet met him.

Friedman was one of the few pianists about whom Horowitz, later in life, would talk about with real respect. "Nobody has made a better recording of the E flat Nocturne [Op. 55, No. 2] than Friedman did. It is amazing." But in concert Friedman occasionally bothered Horowitz with "too many eccentric ideas. He played the F minor Ballade rolling all the left-hand chords at the big opening theme. Personally Friedman was a nice man, a darling, an angel. He loved to hear me, came to all my concerts, and he understood my playing."

Horowitz had mixed feelings about another giant, Leopold Godowsky:

> Godowsky had tremendous equipment, but in public he pulled back and was not very exciting. In the studio Godowsky was something else. I used to stand near the piano and watch his fingers. He had incredible leggiero. Such scales! He had been a friend of Saint-Saëns's, and he got that technique from him. He got incredible effects but I did not like his playing. It was not for me. What a pianist can learn is very easy. What you cannot learn is very difficult. Anybody can learn to play fast. When you practice Chopin ten hours a day for years, as Godowsky did, of course it will go like that. That's no real achievement. Godowsky was a very good musician, but he overloaded the music he played. It was too much, all the extra stuff he put into it. In his Chopin he played all the notes but everything else was missing. He played everything mezzo-forte, without dynamics. It all sounded the same.

Horowitz kept a small apartment on the rue Kléber in Paris. It was all that he could afford. Until he went to America in 1928, he was playing a great deal all over Europe but not making much money. Or so he said. It is true that in 1926 and 1927 he was unable to command the fees that his American success in 1928 guaranteed. But even before the days of real affluence, Horowitz had money. His problem was that he spent it almost as fast as he made it. Always the dandy, he bought clothing "and nice things." And the more he made, the more he spent. When he went to England after his American tour, he had enough left over to buy a Rolls. He had $6,000 in the bank and the Rolls cost him $5,000, an enormous sum in those depression days. Horowitz never learned to drive his Rolls and had to engage a chauffeur. Driving a car was too hard for him, he said. Playing the octaves in the Tchaikovsky was much easier.

7

On the Road

We always had to borrow money. When we traveled, it was third
class because we could not afford the best accommodations. I ate
cheese sandwiches, believe me, not truffles or caviar.
— *Vladimir Horowitz, on his early touring days with Merovitch*

Now that the Horowitz career was under way, he started
the traveling routine that is part of the recitalist's life. He went
where his manager sent him. Young artists do not pick and choose;
a career is yet to be solidified. So Horowitz learned to put up with
the drudgery of the routine: into a city after a long train trip, into
a third-class hotel, a concert that evening, bad pianos everywhere,
dull after-concert receptions, inferior food, and then, as often as
not, back on a train the next day. Horowitz discovered, as all the
others have done, that there is nothing very glamorous about a
touring artist's life. As early as the 1850s the American idol Louis
Moreau Gottschalk had expressed it as well as anybody: "Arrived
at half-past eight at the hotel, took in a hurry a cup of bad tea, and
away to business. One herring for dinner! nine hours on the train!

and, in spite of everything, five hundred persons who have paid that you may give them two hours of poesy, of passion, and of inspiration. I confess to you secretly that they certainly will be cheated this evening."

Horowitz found himself playing in most of the European countries, going from Portugal to England to Norway to Sweden to Germany and Italy, and it is hard to find a negative critical response to the young Horowitz. A reviewer might have had reservations about this or that, but every one responded to the high-voltage playing and the powerful musical personality.

When Horowitz left Paris, it was to make a tour of Germany. At least he would find in Germany good Steinway pianos from Hamburg. There is a belief among piano manufacturers that God put pianists on earth for one reason only—to complain about pianos. Horowitz did his share of complaining, especially about the situation in France. As late as 1938, in a letter to Alexander Greiner, head of the Steinway & Sons Artists Department in New York, he complained bitterly about the pianos of Paris. "In all France exist only two or three concert grands Steinway and these instruments are already twelve years old and very bad in quality." Horowitz then hinted that he might be forced to turn to instruments of other manufacturers. The upshot was that the company shipped several "concert grands Steinway" to Paris when Horowitz agreed to split the cost. Steinway did not want to alienate the pianist who by then was the most exciting of the new generation.

German critics continued to search for nouns and adjectives to explain the Horowitz phenomenon. The *Boesen-Courier* of Berlin on October 30, 1926, hailed Horowitz's Liszt playing as brilliant, nimble, transparent, of flawless clarity. In Breslau the *Schlesische Zeitung* of November 10 spoke of piano playing that could not be surpassed. The Hamburg *Correspondent* on November 14 spoke of "extreme stupefaction . . . phenomena . . ." and said that an apparition like this appeared only once in a hundred years. The Berlin *Tageblatt* on November 16, 1926, hailed Horowitz as "a true joy."

In 1927 a major conductor with whom Horowitz played was the legendary Karl Muck in Hamburg, where they did the Rachmaninoff Third. Muck was the emperor of the Bayreuth Festival, the martinet who browbeat the musicians of his orchestras, the ultimate baton technician, the thin man with a big head and a jutting chin who looked like Mr. Punch out of Richard Wagner.

He had come to America as conductor of the Boston Symphony from 1906 to 1908 and returned in 1912. There was a great scandal when Muck refused to conduct *The Star-Spangled Banner* in Boston during World War I, and he was deported as a wartime alien in 1917. After that he did not like America very much.

> He was very tough [Horowitz said]. Mischa Levitzki came to play the Schumann with him in Hamburg, and after the first rehearsal Muck threw him out, calling him a *Schuster,* a shoemaker. He also was one of the biggest anti-Semites in Europe. He liked me very much and invited me for tea. He said to me, confidentially, "If every Jew was like you, it would be a different world." He was the first musician to mention the name of Toscanini to me. He had heard Toscanini at Bayreuth and told me, "He's a good musician. But sugary, all sugar." At that time I had never heard the name of Arturo Toscanini.

With Wilhelm Furtwängler he played the Tchaikovsky. Most musicians of the period would have said that Furtwängler was the only living conductor to challenge the preeminence of the great Arturo Toscanini. They were polar opposites. Toscanini was objective, Furtwängler subjective. Toscanini was the exponent of fast tempos and strict rhythms. Furtwängler inclined toward slow tempos and tremendous fluctuation of tempo. There probably was not a single point where their musical philosophies were in agreement.

Horowitz and Furtwängler did not get along very well:

> Furtwängler was a hysterical conductor. He never could beat two bars the same. He looked on the players as wild animals in a zoo that he had to tame. He trained them to understand his beat. When he had to face a new orchestra he was helpless. He had to spend time training them to follow his beat. I had a disagreeable experience with Furtwängler some years later when I played the Brahms B flat with him. He put the Bruckner Eighth Symphony, without cuts, as the first piece on the program. Then at the rehearsal when I started to play he made nasty remarks about my playing. He had never a big success in America and he resented mine. He hated all the Americans. So he would stop me and say, "We don't play here like that. Only in America they play that way." So I never played with him again and never saw him again.

(Though Horowitz never saw him again there was a sort of collision in 1949, when the Chicago Symphony was negotiating with Furtwängler to bring him there as conductor. A group of prominent musicians, Horowitz included, announced that they would not ever again play in Chicago if the "Nazi" Furtwängler were appointed the head of the orchestra. Furtwängler had remained in Germany during World War II and it was alleged that he had close ties with Joseph Goebbels, the propaganda minister of the Third Reich. After the fall of Hitler he was forbidden to work and he was not de-Nazified by the American Military Government until 1948. In the New York *Times* of May 6, 1949, Horowitz was quoted as saying that Furtwängler's prestige was such that he could have had a career anywhere in the world, but he chose to remain in Germany.)

Incidentally, the first cellist of Furtwängler's Berlin Philharmonic from 1924 to 1928 was a brilliant, amiable, fun-loving Russian giant named Gregor Piatigorsky. Horowitz and Milstein (who by now had established himself as one of the world's supreme violinists) became Piatigorsky's closest friends. It was impossible not to be captivated by the irrepressible Piatigorskian charm, zest for life, sense of humor, and superb musicianship. The three friends remained inseparable for the rest of their lives, and inevitably they were dubbed The Three Musketeers.

When Piatigorsky left the Berlin Philharmonic, it was to pursue a solo career under the Merovitch management. To promote the new addition to the bureau, Merovitch arranged for a concert in Hamburg with the new pianistic star, Vladimir Horowitz, at the piano. They played the Beethoven D major Sonata, the Brahms E minor, and the Chopin. Piatigorsky of course had studied those pieces when he was a student. Horowitz had never seen the music and it took him about two weeks to learn the three sonatas to his satisfaction.

The Hamburg concert in 1927 was one of the few times he played with Piatigorsky. Nor did the three friends ever form a professional trio. There have been stories about the Horowitz-Milstein-Piatigorsky Trio and the wonderful performances they gave. None of them is true. The only time the three ever played together in public was years later in New York during the Great Depression. The occasion was a concert for the Musicians Emergency Fund, set up to aid unemployed musicians, and the March 30, 1932, Carnegie Hall program had three works—the Brahms C major Trio, the Beethoven *Archduke,* and the Rachmaninoff Trio.

Before the concert the three musicians played the Brahms for Rachmaninoff in his home. He wanted to hear the work, which he did not know. He did not like it. Nor were the New York critics carried away. The fact that three supreme instrumentalists had come together for a single performance, the consensus ran, did not necessarily guarantee great chamber-music playing.

Milstein pursued his own career under Merovitch's management, though he did not like him very much. He compared Merovitch to a gigolo who attached himself to women, except in this case he had attached himself to three of the world's most promising musicians and, Milstein thought, was interested only in exploiting them. "The man had no great artistic vision," Milstein flatly said in 1990. "He didn't know anything, he didn't do anything, he spoiled everything. He spoiled everything for Horowitz." And in his autobiography Milstein called Merovitch "an unbalanced person and a lousy manager besides: he didn't plan anything, didn't foresee anything, and made loads of mistakes."

It was Milstein's belief that Merovitch, interested only in making money, pushed Horowitz into a showy repertoire that militated against his artistic growth. He also told Horowitz the most outrageous things, Milstein said, and Horowitz tended to believe him. Milstein remembered being backstage at a Horowitz concert when Merovitch said to the pianist: "You know, Volodya, you have many enemies who will try to spoil the concert. I will hypnotize them." Milstein said that he honestly believed the man was unbalanced. "Can you imagine telling that to a pianist before he goes on stage?"

In 1925 Horowitz had arrived in Germany with $5,000. But at the end of the first German season he had in his pocket "maybe a hundred dollars, and I had to live on that all summer." Agents' fees and living expenses had eaten everything up. "And maybe Merovitch," Horowitz said, "was careless with money?"

It was hard for any musician in the late 1920s to make much money in Germany. The economy was in tatters; inflation had wiped everybody out. "It was a terrible life in Berlin," mused Horowitz. "When I wrote home around 1930 I said that Germany and all of Europe were *Götterdämmerung*. Something was not good in the air. I was not stupid," said the man who in 1926 had peripherally encountered a demagogue named Adolf Hitler in Hamburg.

Horowitz played a great deal in Germany, but he made Paris his headquarters. At one of his recitals there, in 1927, a very sharp, experienced pair of ears listened to the playing with more than usual interest, and then read the reviews with a calculating eye. The result was an offer to go to America under the very highest auspices. Horowitz and Merovitch would, of course, have eventually made their way to New York, but the deus ex machina who was at the 1927 concert made the process that much easier.

He was the American concert manager Arthur Judson. Judson approached Merovitch, offering to represent Horowitz in America and suggesting thirty concerts in the United States for the 1927–28 music season. Merovitch may have known something about the Judson organization, but neither he nor Horowitz could have realized the power that Judson exerted in the musical life of America. They were, after all, still greenhorns from Russia. But to a musician who knew anything about the commercial and managerial side of American classical music, an unsolicited approach from Arthur Judson would be something like a parish priest being summoned by His Holiness the Pope.

At that time Judson was already the strongest manager in America, and that was nothing compared to what he became a few years after he took Horowitz under his wing. His very presence carried an aura of power. A big, handsome, dignified, imposing, even imperious man, a trained musician (violinist and conductor), he took over a good part of the American musical establishment.

Between 1930 and 1935 he was, simultaneously, the manager of the New York Philharmonic and its summer concerts at Lewisohn Stadium; the manager of the Philadelphia Orchestra and its Robin Hood Dell summer concerts since 1915; the president of Columbia Concerts (the largest music managerial office in the world) and Community Concerts (which he had set up to book musicians into cities all over the United States); the second largest stockholder of the Columbia Broadcasting System, and the sole owner of Columbia Records. Most of the world's leading conductors were under contract to him, and many of the greatest instrumentalists and singers. Thus when a Columbia Concerts artist appeared with an orchestra or was booked around the country, Judson shared the artists' fee.

Such power as Judson wielded caused much grumbling in the music world, but few musicians or people connected with the business of music dared stand up to him. Not until 1941 were accusations publicly leveled against the all-powerful Judson. The one who first brought the Judson monopoly to the public's attention was Artur Rodzinski, the New York Philharmonic's conductor, who called Judson a "czar" and demanded that his power be curtailed.

Suddenly *l'affaire Judson* was in the newspapers, and critics discussed the issues pro and con. There was talk of a federal antitrust investigation. Statistical tables were prepared showing how many Judson artists appeared with leading orchestras and opera houses as against the artists of other managers. It was true that Judson artists had the edge. But, as was pointed out, Judson had cornered many of the world's leading musicians and therefore it was inevitable that they lead the pack. Slowly Judson's power eroded, though until the day of his death on January 28, 1975, at the age of ninety-three, he still exerted considerable influence. The company that he built, Columbia Concerts, still thrives as Columbia Artists Management, Inc. (CAMI), the biggest musical management company in the world.

Judson's influence up to World War II extended into the press, which was not then as concerned about conflict of interest as it is today. Two great New York newspapers had critics who were in effect on Judson's payroll. Olin Downes of the *Times* was intermission commentator for the New York Philharmonic broadcasts, and that stately figure of Yankee probity, Lawrence Gilman of the *Herald Tribune,* wrote the program notes. Nobody raised an eyebrow; it was common practice. Today, on the New York *Times,* such extracurricular activity would be unthinkable.

Judson and Merovitch worked out the schedule for the first Horowitz appearances in America. His debut was scheduled for January 12, 1928, with the New York Philharmonic conducted by Sir Thomas Beecham in Carnegie Hall. It also was to be Beecham's debut. Then there would be a concert tour of the United States, first in concerto appearances, then in solo recitals.

Horowitz was thrilled with the prospect and also, as he said, frightened a little. Could he conquer America as he had Europe? And there was something on his mind that compulsively overrode everything else, including even his American debut, important as that was.

Now was his chance to meet Sergei Rachmaninoff, who was living in New York.

Horowitz and Merovitch sailed to New York on the ship with Judson, who briefed them on what to expect in America. "He and

I got along very well," said Horowitz. "I liked him. He was a very nice man, even if some of the people around him were not very ethical."

Horowitz arrived barely able to speak a word of English. On the way to the hotel Merovitch tried to put a blindfold on him so he would not feel frightened by the great buildings or think they would fall on him. Fifty years later, Horowitz still recalled Merovitch's actions with amazement. "He was not normal."

At first, Horowitz did not pay much attention to New York. He had only one thing on his mind—a meeting with Rachmaninoff. It was a desperate need that took priority over everything else. Later there would be time enough to explore the city and get ready for the debut. After all, he knew the Tchaikovsky Concerto.

So on his second day in New York Horowitz got Alexander (known to all as Sascha) Greiner, the concert and artists manager of Steinway & Sons, to telephone Rachmaninoff and make an appointment. "Greiner was a nice man and all the Steinway pianists liked him," said Horowitz. "But he had some strange politics. He told me that Hitler was a great man who would save Germany. I don't know if Greiner ever changed his mind in later years."

Greiner, Russian-born and a graduate of the Moscow Conservatory, left an unpublished memoir, finished in 1957, the year before he died. The twenty-five-year-old Horowitz made a big impression on him at their initial meeting. "He appeared," wrote Greiner, "in a perfectly fitted suit of the latest fashion, made by the finest London tailors. His hair was sleek and smoothly kempt. He looked like a young man ready to exhibit with a beautiful partner in an exquisite ballroom dance." He listened to Horowitz trying out a few pianos in the Steinway basement. Greiner found Horowitz a "fantastic" pianist, all the more unbelievable "coming from the polished, frail-looking, drawing-room lion."

On the designated afternoon, Horowitz went to visit his hero. Rachmaninoff, then fifty-five years old and thus more than twice the age of Horowitz, had an apartment on West End Avenue. Horowitz was trembling when he rang the doorbell:

> I was scared to death. Would my idol like me? He was a little bit anti-Semitic, you know. He was terribly anti-Communist, and he thought it was the Jews who had made the Communist revolution. He opened the door and was very polite. We started to talk about music and especially about his Third

Concerto, which I had to play. He asked me what cadenza I played, and this and that. He said, "When you are free I would like to hear you and I will accompany you." Then he went to the piano and played pieces by Medtner. He never had a good instrument in his house. It was a small apartment. The piano, a Steinway Model L, was in his bedroom. We both liked Medtner's music very much, though I had not played it in public for a long time. Rachmaninoff and I immediately had a rapport, right away. Like electricity. I don't know how it happened.

Horowitz also played some Medtner. Rachmaninoff listened, not saying much. The two men were sizing each other up. They chatted pleasantly; they discussed the forthcoming Horowitz performances of the D minor Piano Concerto; they talked about Blumenfeld, Prokofiev, and other musicians they knew and the musical scene in Russia. Horowitz felt that they were going to be friends despite the thirty-year difference in their age.

The next day Rachmaninoff reported back to Greiner by telephone and discussed Horowitz's playing. "I don't know how Horowitz does it," Rachmaninoff said. "He plays against all the rules and regulations of piano playing as we were taught—but with him it works."

About Rachmaninoff's anti-Semitism: perhaps Horowitz was reading things into a few offhand remarks that Rachmaninoff made. In the Rachmaninoff biography by Sergei Bertensson and Jay Leyda, an episode is cited that suggests Rachmaninoff's strong aversion to racism. In 1912 he was a vice president of the Russian Musical Society, and when "he learned that a very good musician in an administrative post in one of the Society's schools was to be dismissed on the ground that he was Jewish, Rachmaninoff promptly submitted his resignation."

Now Horowitz, thrilled that he and Rachmaninoff had hit it off, was in an elated frame of mind for Tchaikovsky, Beecham, and the Philharmonic.

He could not have known what was about to happen.

8

"The Octaves Race"

> I was less controlled in those days and there was sometimes a
> show-off quality to my playing. Beecham tried to keep up but
> couldn't, and he and I did not end together, but the important
> thing was that I played my way, not his.
> —*Vladimir Horowitz, on his American debut with Beecham*

Ｎew York had never seen a debut appearance like the collaboration between Vladimir Horowitz and Sir Thomas Beecham. Horowitz was to describe it as "crazy."

Beecham undoubtedly had heard of Horowitz, but had not heard him and certainly did not know how he was going to approach the concerto. Anyway, Horowitz believed that Beecham was much more interested in making a good impression in his New York debut than in paying much attention to "me, a little Jewish boy from Kiev."

At the rehearsals of the Tchaikovsky, Beecham conducted without music but, Horowitz claimed, he did not know the concerto *that* well. His tempos were the slowest that Horowitz ever encountered, and the disgusted pianist considered them positively plodding. Beecham went his own way, apparently not even bothering to listen to the soloist. So the ensemble was terrible. Conductor and soloist were not together at the rehearsals, and Horowitz had the feeling that they would not be together at the performance. He said he did not sleep at all the night before the big moment, and he arrived at Carnegie Hall on the evening of January 12 in an apprehensive state. Rachmaninoff was in the audience, and that alone would have been enough to unnerve Horowitz. Many other musicians were there; word of mouth about a brilliant newcomer was operating as usual. In Horowitz's own words:

> We walked on stage. His opening tempo was very slow. I still believe he did this on purpose, to play me down. I am told that he broke his suspenders during the first piece and had to conduct with one hand, holding up his pants with the other. [True.] So he was not in a good mood when we came out for the concerto. When the performance started, for a little bit I followed him. Then I felt I could hear people snoring in the audience, it was so slow. I could see that my American career already was over. So I said to myself, "He can go to hell." So I played my own tempos. I wanted to show my octaves, everything. I had to do this because I wanted to have the greatest success of my life. I kept thinking that if I did not have a success I would have to go back to Russia. In the last movement Beecham started slow and when I came in I took my own tempo. I ran away. I played the octaves the loudest, the fastest, they ever heard in their life. I was too fast, I admit it. It was not artistic. It was show-off, *pour épater le bourgeois*.
>
> After the concerto I was greeted by people in the artists' room. One of the visitors was Olin Downes, the critic of the New York *Times*. He was all excited. Then I left for home, saying nothing to Beecham. But we were not enemies or anything like that. He did not dislike me, the way Furtwängler disliked me. A few years later I had to play the Tchaikovsky in London with Beecham. When I walked into the hall for the first rehearsal, Beecham said, "Mr. Horowitz, I have the score." And it was a wonderful performance. This time he was darling.

The octaves Horowitz refers to is the passage near the end of the finale, and it is the climax of the concerto. Horowitz, excited, nervous, took off like a sprinter from the blocks, and he created a whirlwind that simply blew the audience out of its seats. At the end there was an animal roar from the thrilled listeners. Whatever the musical merits or demerits of the Horowitz explosion, New York had never heard anything like it.

There must have been at least twenty-five daily newspapers in New York in those days, including foreign-language papers, and most of them had music critics. Horowitz got some bad reviews— the critic of the *Evening World,* for instance, called the Tchaikovsky "an exhibition of piano playing in its most degraded estate"—but the important critics jumped on the Horowitz bandwagon.

Then, as now, the most powerful arbiter of musical taste was the New York *Times,* and from 1924 to his death in 1955 Olin Downes was its music critic. A stout, extroverted Viking of a man, Downes wrote in flamboyant prose influenced by James Huneker. Himself a bit of a pianist, Downes was basically a fan who empathized with all pianists, mentally playing along and dissolving with excitement when something especially wonderful happened.

Downes called Horowitz "a young virtuoso of brilliant technic and overwhelming temperament . . . sensational if by no means impeccable." He said that it had been years since a pianist created such a formidable impression in New York City. Downes noted that Beecham had not used a score and mildly said that "if he had had a score before him there might have been smoother cooperation with the pianist. . . . It was quickly evident either that conductor and pianist had not sufficiently rehearsed . . . or that there were differences of conception." It was clear to Downes that Horowitz wanted a faster tempo at the beginning of the concerto, "and there were many pages where the two see-sawed in their ideas." Nevertheless Horowitz "made a tremendous impression. . . . His treatment of the work was a whirlwind of virtuoso interpretation. Mr. Horowitz has amazing technic, amazing strength, irresistible youth and temperament." And in the slow movement the pianist showed that he could evoke beautiful colors. Thus despite the lack of coordination with the orchestra and a sometimes overstressed tone in forte passages, the performance triumphed because of the pianist's "electrical temperament, physical capacity for tremendous climax of sonority and lightning speed." The occasion marked "the appearance of a new pianistic talent which cannot be ignored or minimized." In his last paragraph, Downes hedged, as experienced critics are wont to do: "As has before been said in these columns, one concert does not make a conductor or a virtuoso either. Half a dozen barely suffice to test a new leader. But within the limits of a single concert, there was no question of this triumph."

A few weeks later Downes, still brooding about the concert, returned to it in his Sunday column of January 21, 1928. He said that the performance had been a mess, "ragged, superficial and frequently inartistic in character." But it was also a performance that "stampeded the audience as an audience has seldom been stampeded of late years." Why? Because of "the terrific swoop and roar of the octave passage that swept up the keyboard just before the peroration of the last movement. It was like a tiger let loose." The daring brilliance of it reduced the audience to a hysterical mob, and "a mob is a mob; blood is blood; the call of the wild is heard whether it is a savage beating a drum or a young Russian, mad with excitement, physical speed and power, pounding on a keyboard."

(It should be added that Beecham, too, got rave notices from the New York press. He conducted, in addition to the concerto, three Handel pieces, Delius's *The Walk to the Paradise Garden,* Mozart's C major Symphony [K. 338], the "Royal Hunt and Storm" music from Berlioz's *Troyens,* and Wagner's *Meistersinger* Prelude—a strange program but typical of Beecham.)

Downes was one of the few American critics with whom Horowitz became friendly. "I liked him. He always was so enthusiastic about music. Later on he wrote program notes for my concerts." Now Downes was, in effect, on the Horowitz payroll. This was still another example of what today would be considered a most grievous conflict of interest.

Downes was not the only one fascinated by the young Horowitz. Pitts Sanborn of the *Evening Telegram* called the Tchaikovsky a performance of "magnificent muscularity," one with "headlong and undaunted speed . . . breathtaking elements of a mighty technique . . . heaven-storming octaves." The prevailing impression, wrote Sanborn, was that of power and rapidity, even if the opening chords were "unashamedly banged." He noted that pianist and orchestra were far apart: "Rarely in the experience of this present writer have accompanist and accompanied proceeded through a long composition with such a divergent notion of their common pace as Sir Thomas and Mr. Horowitz exhibited yesterday." This was not the Tchaikovsky Concerto, he wrote, but a free fantasia on it.

W. J. Henderson of the *Sun,* the dean of American critics, called Horowitz "a volcano."

A day or two after the performance Horowitz received a letter from Rachmaninoff. It said: "Mr. Horowitz, you have won the octaves race. Nobody has ever played them like you. But I will not congratulate you because it was not musical." Rachmaninoff was disturbed by the undisciplined impulsiveness that Horowitz showed. If ever a pianist represented ultimate technical and emotional control it was Rachmaninoff, and he would not have responded happily to the show-off octaves and extroverted bravura that marked this performance. Horowitz said that he was "disturbed, a little" by the letter, but he felt that it would not harm their relationship. In any event, Rachmaninoff had, of course, known perfectly well what had happened and, seated in the audience, must have sweated out the desperate pianist's problems with his conductor.

As for Merovitch, he was happy. Horowitz's name was in all the papers, and that was all that mattered.

Then Horowitz started his American tour, playing a series of orchestral dates in the big cities. He made his American recital debut in Carnegie Hall on February 20, 1928, playing the Bach-Busoni Toccata, Adagio, and Fugue in C; some Scarlatti; and Chopin etudes and mazurkas and the A flat Polonaise. His *pièce de résistance* was the Liszt Sonata.

Again every pianist who was in New York, or could make it to New York, came to hear the highly touted newcomer. As Horowitz remembered it, there were, seated in the audience with arms crossed and a show-me attitude, "Rachmaninoff, Hofmann, Lhevinne, Gabrilowitsch, Moiseiwitsch, Bauer, Friedman, Levitzki, and I don't know who else." Horowitz said that "after the booboo I made of the Tchaikovsky, they wanted to see if I really could play."

The critics responded to the excitement and virtuosity Horowitz brought to the music, but the consensus was that he still had to grow into it. Downes wrote that Horowitz was a phenomenal technician who "promises to be one of the great figures among the pianists of his day." The Liszt was "noble and powerful from first to last . . . broad and dramatic." Downes had some reservations about the Chopin. But, summing up, Horowitz was "an artist of exceptional intellect, taste and virtuoso quality."

Horowitz gave another Carnegie Hall concert about a week later. On his program were the four Chopin ballades in reverse order. What Horowitz remembered most about the recital was an incident that occurred backstage:

> Merovitch gave orders nobody was to come to the artist's room. He said I would be too nervous. But at the concert he came to me at intermission and said there was a friend, an old pianist named Rabinovich, Heifetz's accompanist, who begged to see me and would I say a few words to him. So the old pianist came and started to rave. Horowitz, he told me, you are sublime. New York has never heard piano playing like this. And please don't pay attention to what the people are saying. Because I heard Hofmann and Rachmaninoff talking, and Hofmann said that he didn't like the Third Ballade and Rachmaninoff said the Second Ballade was not so good, and Gabrilowitsch didn't like this and Friedman didn't like that. Don't listen to what they say.

Perhaps Mr. Rabinovich really was quoting accurately. Rachmaninoff discussed the concert with Horowitz shortly afterward. "He liked only the G minor Ballade," Horowitz remembered. "The other three he didn't like. In later years he seemed to like everything I played. Maybe he changed his mind. Or maybe I matured."

From Ernst Urchs, manager of the Wholesale and Concert Department of Steinway & Sons, came a confidential report to the chief Steinway executives dated February 23, 1928:

> *Re: Vladimir Horowitz.* Concert on Feb. 20, 1928, first piano recital in America. Good house, over $1,400 in box-office sales for first appearance. Great enthusiasm. Some excellent criticisms. Evidently will make great popular favorite. Marvellous technician and best critics count him excellent musician as well. Is only 24 years of age and will undoubtedly improve. Personally a very modest, retiring nature. Amiable and easy to get along with. Has had 12 or 13 orchestra appearances in the United States since arrival beginning of January, chiefly with N.Y. Philharmonic, Philadelphia, New York Symphony, St. Louis, etc. Average fee during season 1927–28 about $500. Reappears United States October to end of December 1928, at

fee of $1,000 less 20% commission to Concert Management Arthur Judson.

His recital dates took him throughout the eastern and middle United States, with thirty-five appearances in eighty-eight days. When he played in the New York area he was usually escorted by somebody from the Judson office. Dorle Jarmel, in charge of publicity for the New York Philharmonic (managed by Judson), remembered his dry sense of humor. She was driving with Horowitz and Merovitch to Long Island, where Horowitz was giving a concert. Darkness was coming on as the limousine proceeded, and the barking of dogs could be heard.

"Wolves?" Horowitz asked, poker-faced.

Wherever he played, Horowitz was anxious to get back to New York and Rachmaninoff. They continued to cement their relationship. Whenever Horowitz returned to the city after playing somewhere he immediately got in touch with his friend, and vice versa.

Perhaps the greatest thrill of Horowitz's life occurred when he played the Third Concerto with Rachmaninoff playing the orchestral part at the second piano in the Steinway basement. Horowitz later said he was so nervous he thought he would die. Also, "He scolded me again for the octaves in the Tchaikovsky." Rachmaninoff was impressed with the way Horowitz took on the Third Concerto and told Greiner so. Rachmaninoff never had the success with it that Horowitz had, and it could even be that the Horowitz performances in America made Rachmaninoff rethink the way he himself played it. At least, in an interview with Phillip Ramey in 1977, Horowitz said that when Rachmaninoff recorded the Third with Ormandy, around 1940, he kept asking the conductor during the rehearsals, "Does Horowitz do that? How does he play this— faster, slower?" Horowitz claimed that Ormandy told him this. "Imagine!" And Rachmaninoff, when anybody would talk to him about the concerto, would say, "That's Horowitz's."

To Horowitz, Rachmaninoff was the greatest of all pianists, "because his playing had such individuality. And such sound. If you want to get an idea of his sound go to the second movement of his recording of his First Piano Concerto. I always thought his Beethoven was the best thing he played, and his Chopin the worst. Rachmaninoff once showed me a letter from Schnabel, who had heard him play a Beethoven sonata. Schnabel said it was the best Beethoven playing he had ever heard."

Rachmaninoff, said Horowitz, was the eternal refugee, unhappy wherever he was. He remained a Russian, his friends were Russians, he preferred to speak Russian. Soon he and Horowitz became more than friends; in many respects Rachmaninoff was a surrogate father, and Horowitz humbly took his advice and suggestions. Their greatest pleasure was in playing four-hand and two-piano music:

> In his homes in Switzerland and Los Angeles we played two-piano music together, his suites and *Symphonic Dances,* the Mozart sonata, and other things. He wanted to give a two-piano recital with me. There is a recording of Ashkenazy and Previn in the two suites. It's a caricature, absolutely a caricature, terrible.
>
> I have said that to me he was the greatest pianist, but that does not mean I liked everything he played. Then again, he did not always like everything I played. I remember once hearing him in the *Moonlight* Sonata. When the melody came, he hit the G-sharps boom, boom-BOOM. Like a trombone, instead of piano or pianissimo. I heard him in his last years play the Beethoven First Piano Concerto. He made the slow movement sound like a Chopin nocturne. This was not Beethoven, although I heard him play other Beethoven things wonderfully, like Op. 111. He had a sense of humor sometimes. He once learned a few Debussy pieces. Debussy was a composer he never had any sympathy for, and I asked him why he put the Debussy on his program. "I want to prove to the public that this is not good music." Rachmaninoff had to wait a long time before his Third Concerto became popular. He grew to dislike the Second Concerto almost as much as the famous C sharp minor Prelude. A lady once came up to him after a concert, raved over the Second Concerto, and asked him what inspired him to compose his Second Concerto with those wonderful, wonderful, wonderful melodies. Rachmaninoff answered her, "Twenty-five rubles."

Rachmaninoff told Horowitz that he had technical difficulties all his life. "This is hard to believe, but that is what he said." He told Horowitz that every morning for three hours he worked on scales. "He went to Godowsky to ask for special exercises. He was a gloomy man. He told me that all his life he had tried to succeed

in three things—composition, piano playing, and conducting—
and had succeeded in none."

Rachmaninoff shunned publicity and gave very few interviews.
Robert Croan of the Pittsburgh *Post-Gazette* told Horowitz in a
1979 interview that he once asked Rachmaninoff why? Rachmaninoff said, "Well, you know, Mr. Croan, I was brought up never to
lie. But I cannot tell the truth."

Horowitz once asked Rachmaninoff what his most memorable
musical experience had been. This, said Horowitz, was a man who
had known Anton Rubinstein, had known Tchaikovsky, had played
everywhere and with everybody.

"I was on tour in Russia with Fedya," Rachmaninoff said.
Fedya was Feodor Chaliapin. "I was his pianist and we gave a
concert in the Crimea. Fedya sang a group of my songs on this
program. After the concert a little man with a beard came backstage
and said to Chaliapin, 'You are fantastic.' Then he came to me and
said, 'Mr. Rachmaninoff, nobody knows you but you will be a
great man one day.' The little man was Chekhov."

After his first season in America Horowitz realized that he
probably would never have to worry about money again. "I could
trace the course of my career by my summers. Every summer I took
a vacation in Antibes. The first summer I walked around on foot.
The second summer I could afford a bicycle. The third I went
around in an automobile—a Studebaker, which I had purchased in
America and shipped back to Europe."

9

"King of Kings"

In the United States I played private concerts at the homes of the
very rich people. In Chicago, for instance, I was engaged by
Cyrus McCormick. I played half an hour, everybody was drunk,
and I got my $5,000, over twice as much as for my concerts. The
millionaires those days could afford it. Today that kind of thing
has disappeared.
— *Vladimir Horowitz, 1987, on his early years in America*

Now Horowitz had achieved his dream. He was interna-
tionally famous, he was regarded with awe by his peers, and he got
reviews that were the envy of the profession. Constantly being
interviewed, he impressed journalists as a happy, well-adjusted
man, always nattily dressed and color coordinated. No matter how
stupid or stereotyped the questions, he answered them patiently,
generally saying much the same things in different cities: how he
played for Scriabin, how much he liked America, what he thought
of American orchestras, and the like. Never did he have anything
provocative to say, yet he always was good copy because he so
obviously enjoyed the attention he was getting and was so willing
to cooperate with the musical press. From his earliest years Horowitz understood the value of publicity.

He watched his fees go up. That was particularly gratifying. Horowitz equated success with his fees, and he was getting big ones. In the days of the Great Depression, when a family man was thrilled to be making $1,000 a year, Horowitz was earning $1,500 a concert, and he was giving many concerts. Between 1928 and 1935 he played nearly 350 times in America alone. He would also crisscross Europe every year, generally in the autumn and spring, finishing off his season with a May or June recital in Paris.

In America the excitement about Horowitz was such that it even penetrated a not very musical White House. Horowitz was invited to play there for President Hoover on January 8, 1931. Over half a century later his memory failed him on that event:

> I seem to have drawn a complete blank on that concert. I remember that I played a white piano, not a good one, and that when I was received by the president I said, "I'm delightful," not, "I'm delighted."

On his program were Bach-Busoni, the Hummel Rondo, Dohnányi, Chopin, and the *Carmen* Variations.

One index to an artist is the kind of audience he draws. Horowitz always attracted the professionals as well as a general audience. It was noted that, especially when he played in New York or a cosmopolitan European city, his concert drew in every musician in the vicinity. In the audience for his Carnegie Hall concert of January 22, 1931, was a musical Who's Who including Rachmaninoff, Hofmann, Milstein, Carl Friedberg, Benno Moiseiwitsch, Egon Petri, Walter Gieseking, Mieczyslaw Munz, Mischa Elman, Jacques Thibaud, Paul Kochanski, and Felix Salmond. Horowitz said that so distinguished and ultracritical an audience never frightened him. He welcomed the challenge.

In his first American tour he had played only the Tchaikovsky, Rachmaninoff Third and Brahms Second with orchestra. Then he added both Liszt concertos, the Beethoven *Emperor,* and the Brahms D minor. Of course he appeared with all the important conductors. He thought that Serge Koussevitzky in Boston was the worst when it came to accompanying soloists:

> He knew his Russian and French repertoire very well but not concertos. That was because he was not a good score reader and somebody had to do it for him. Toscanini knew this and used to laugh about it. Rachmaninoff couldn't stand him.

It was all on account of Rachmaninoff's famous Prelude in C sharp minor. The Gutheil publishing house in Russia bought it from Rachmaninoff at a small flat fee. Later Koussevitzky purchased the Gutheil company and made a fortune out of the C sharp minor Prelude. Rachmaninoff got sick every time he thought about it and could never forgive Koussevitzky.

Wherever Horowitz played, he created a furor. His special kind of electricity paralyzed audiences and most critics. Henry Pleasants, soon to be a music critic in Philadelphia, who had just graduated from the Curtis Institute of Music, never forgot the impression of a 1929 Horowitz recital at the Academy of Music in Philadelphia. He said that the audience was packed with pianists. From the Curtis Institute were Hofmann, David Saperton, and Isabelle Vengerova, who came with their pupils. Olga Samaroff, then teaching in Philadelphia but not on the Curtis faculty, was there. With her pupils, of course. The audience seemed to be wall-to-wall pianists.

"We were knocked flat," said Pleasants. "I never have experienced anything like it. And I never heard a reaction like it. You heard young pianists say, 'I'm going to go home and throw my piano out of the window.' They were simply stunned."

Even the staid Boston audience kicked up its heels when Horowitz appeared. The Boston *Globe* of March 3, 1928, reported that after the Rachmaninoff Third with Koussevitzky the "polite" Saturday night audience acted like "a Fenway Park bleachers crowd. Not satisfied with the usual decorous hand-clapping, the audience cheered, yelled and pounded the seats in enthusiasm." Similar reports came from Cincinnati and Chicago.

From the veteran American critics came a reaction to Horowitz that no previous pianist within memory had achieved. Glenn Dillard Gunn of the Chicago *Herald-Examiner* reviewed a Horowitz concert on January 22, 1934. Gunn, born in Topeka, Kansas, in 1874, was a graduate of the Leipzig Conservatory and had studied piano there with Karl Reinecke. "As a boy," Gunn wrote, "I heard the aged Rubinstein. As a young man I gained knowledge and imagination from Busoni. I am glad that Horowitz has come within the range of my experience with great piano art." There were a few technicians around who could come near to approaching the Horowitz fingers, Gunn wrote. But, "No one of the three or four who today might challenge this young man's supremacy has a like command of the instrument's capacities for contrasts of quality and of power, or is equally gifted with the imagination to exploit such effects." On the Horowitz program were, incidentally, pieces that he seldom or never later played—the Liszt *Dante* Sonata and Beethoven's *Les adieux* Sonata, as well as the "Russian Dance" from Stravinsky's *Petrushka*.

When it came to musical name-dropping, Herman Devries in the March 11, 1935, Chicago *American* went Gunn one better, with an absolutely breathless name-drop—Liszt. Devries, born in New York in 1858, was trained as a singer at the Paris Conservatoire and had a professional career (including appearances at the Metropolitan Opera) before becoming a critic.

"I do not hesitate," wrote Devries, "to proclaim him [Horowitz] one of the greatest pianists that ever existed. Were I an adolescent, or even a middle-aged man, I should not set myself up as a judge, but having heard both Liszt and Rubinstein in my youth, I make free to declare this genius—Horowitz—King of Kings among pianists that are and have been." (In 1946 there was another reference to Rubinstein when the respected pianist Carl Friedberg wrote a fan letter to Horowitz in which he stated that "since Anton Rubinstein I have not heard such master-playing.")

Naturally, Horowitz met all of the musicians active in Europe and America, and once in a while shared the program with them. A concert that one would like to have heard took place on April 20, 1931, at the Pent House in New York. At this society event, held in a hotel, Horowitz and Jascha Heifetz played the Brahms D minor and Grieg C minor sonatas, and each had a solo group.

In Chicago Horowitz met Paderewski for the first time. Paderewski (1860–1941) came to hear the brilliant newcomer play the Rachmaninoff Third Concerto and promptly called Horowitz the best of the young generation of pianists. They became friends, and Horowitz frequently visited him at his home in Switzerland. He had great admiration for the celebrated veteran:

> They say he didn't have a big technique, but he did before World War I. Then he lost it. He liked loud playing. Everything had to be in the grand style. My father told me that Paderewski was the best pianist he ever heard. Toscanini always said he was the best pianist, and that he played the *Emperor* better than anybody else. There is a letter of Tchaikovsky saying that he went to hear a new pianist in Paris called Paderewski and that

he was the greatest pianist of all. You can't judge him on his records, which are not very good. On the stage he played in a very musical manner. You don't get such a reputation as he had for nothing.

Horowitz was correct about most of the Paderewski recordings, but there are some—such as the Liszt Rhapsody No. 10, the Wagner-Liszt *Spinning Song,* and Liszt's *La leggierezza*—that support Horowitz's observation about the glorious sound and nobility of conception Paderewski must have had in his great days. As a technician, however, Paderewski never was in the class of Horowitz, Rachmaninoff, Hofmann, or Lhevinne. Moriz Rosenthal, a Liszt pupil with a phenomenal technique, was once asked what he thought of the glamorous Pole. "Oh, he plays very well, I suppose," said Rosenthal, "but he's no Paderewski."

(In Horowitz's living room in the last years of his life were only three pictures of musicians, all on the piano. One was of Paderewski. The others were Toscanini and Rachmaninoff.)

It did not take Horowitz very long to like America very much. But, as a newcomer to the West and, especially, capitalistic America, one thing at that time he could not understand was business. After his first touring years in the United States and Europe, and with the help of a recording contract, he said, he cleared $100,000. A friend who was a financial adviser took him to a broker so that he could invest in stocks. "What does this mean, invest?" Horowitz wanted to know. "I didn't know what it meant. You make money, you spend it, like in Russia. But in America you had to invest. So the money was invested. So I lost $70,000 in the famous crash of 1929. I had to start all over again. I said I would never buy a stock again, and I never have."

After that, Horowitz put whatever he made into a savings account. Much of that money he used to buy art. Horowitz, Milstein (who painted in his spare time and was a connoisseur), and the conductor Vladimir Golschmann (who had a collection of Picasso and Braque) often went to galleries together. Horowitz also picked the brains of other experts and dealers. The pieces he bought, Horowitz said, ended up a much better investment than the stock market.

"I bought fantastic pictures through the years," he said. "Always I went to the major galleries and spent hours looking. I had a big Picasso from the White Period, a Manet, a Monet, a Renoir, a

Modigliani, a Degas pastel, a Rouault. It was much harder to find them than to buy them, and then it had to be proved they were authentic. Some paintings I bought against the advice of dealers. I paid $5,000 for them. Suddenly they were worth $100,000, and I sold them." The Picasso was a large painting that dominated the living room. When Horowitz bought it, Toscanini came to look at it and wanted to know how much it cost. Horowitz said $23,000. Toscanini said, "All artists are crazy." In the sixties, when Horowitz sold most of his collection, the Picasso alone brought $750,000.

Owning a large and important collection, Horowitz and Wanda discovered, was also a great deal of work. Every summer Horowitz and Wanda had to take the paintings off the walls and put them into storage. Every autumn, when they returned from vacation, they had to put them back. The insurance was fabulously expensive. A good part of their capital was on the walls of their house.

As Judson took over more and more of Horowitz's bookings, Merovitch began to disappear from his former protégé's life. In 1930 Judson gave Merovitch a job as vice president of Columbia Concerts, a job he held for only a few months. After leaving Judson, Merovitch opened his own musical agency, which never was a very successful operation. Horowitz broke off his association with Merovitch in 1933, feeling that he was no longer needed. Judson was taking good care of him, and Horowitz saw no need to pay Merovitch a fee on top of what Judson exacted.

Merovitch did not have a very good reputation. Alexander Greiner of Steinway & Sons kept a top-secret "black book" of all the musicians—not only pianists—his company serviced, with confidential notes about them. Here is his entry on Merovitch:

> MEROVITCH, Alexander: Manager of Horowitz and other artists. When in Paris, summer of 1929, Merovitch told me that he was in very bad financial straits so I spoke to Mr. Paul Schmidt who advanced him $1,000. This money was advanced with a view to helping him out, firstly, and secondly in order to insure his cooperation with us, stopping further demands with regard to the artists under his management. In 1930 joined Concert Management Arthur Judson as Vice President and Director but his attitude toward other gentlemen in the office became so overbearing that he was asked to resign. Refused and withheld $6,000 worth of checks belonging to

Judson. Latter took legal action and Merovitch turned the checks over to them in court. Notified us officially of his resignation April 25, 1930. One should be careful in dealing with him.

He died on August 8, 1965.

(Merovitch, incidentally, had a pianist brother who played in the United States under the name Alfred Mirovitch. He was a good pianist and made a few records in the 1940s for the smaller companies. On one Royale ten-inch disc he played an altogether dashing *Malagueña* and *Seguidillas* by Albéniz. Around 1935, Merovitch, using the clout he had at Steinway because of Horowitz, got the great piano company to service his brother for the few American tours he managed to get. Horowitz never mentioned his name.)

Among the attractions America had to offer Horowitz were films—not art films, but good old American cowboy and gangster pictures. Horowitz liked action in his films. He became a buff, and remained so. A 1934 profile of Horowitz in *Esquire* commented on the pianist's passion: "His favorite diversion is going to the movies; he will go to any movie, no matter how terrible it is, and sit comfortably through it: doesn't even look to see what the picture is, just buys his ticket and walks in." Many years later the appearance of videocassettes was the greatest thing that ever happened to Vladimir Horowitz. Now he could watch his favorite cowboy films as much as he liked without ever setting foot outside his home. He also watched television constantly, concentrating on old films, the news broadcasts, and game shows, of which his favorites were *Jeopardy* and *Wheel of Fortune*.

It took Horowitz a little time to learn about American audiences and tastes. The two big concert agencies, Community and Civic, had virtually a managerial monopoly, and they booked artists (and also what they called "special attractions") to perform around the country only on subscription series. It was not possible to purchase tickets for a single concert; it was all or nothing. That meant the audience had to take what was given to it. A typical series could have included Chinese acrobats (the "special attraction") as well as Vladimir Horowitz. Horowitz didn't like that very much. "But in following years, when I began to get single-admission audiences, it was *my* audience. They came to hear Horowitz."

The New York managers thought they knew everything about

American musical tastes. They discouraged their artists from presenting what they in their infinite wisdom considered "difficult" music, or problematic music, or anything except the well-tried, popular classics. Before World War II, when Horowitz was on the Community Concerts series, he was constantly being asked to change his programs. "In one city they asked me not to play Chopin's G minor Ballade. They thought it was too difficult for their audience. I played it anyway." During the war, Horowitz had a concert in Jacksonville. He was learning the newly composed Prokofiev Eighth Sonata, which he was going to introduce to New York, and he wanted to try it out:

> I didn't like the music so much, but it was a political event. But when I went to Jacksonville with my program, the people from Community Concerts looked at it and said, "Impossible!" They said the Prokofiev would be a dead duck. Thirty-five minutes! Everybody would go to sleep. What else could I play? I said the *Waldstein*. They said fine. But the program, containing the Prokofiev, was already printed. So it was decided to make an announcement from the stage. The man came out and said that instead of the Prokofiev, Mr. Horowitz would play Beethoven's Sonata in Waltz Time. That was the way he heard "Waldstein." Frankly, I do not think it would have made any difference to the audience if I had played the Prokofiev. My best concerts, the ones I remember with happiness, were given in colleges. The young audiences were attentive and appreciative and wanted to know everything.

Audiences constantly demanded from Horowitz the electrifying arrangements he made. Usually he ended the program with one of them, or they were his last encore. The first big one he played was the *Carmen* Fantasy. This came about in "a funny way," Horowitz said:

> Milstein and I were playing concerts in Russia and he often played Sarasate's *Carmen* Fantasy. After a while I got bored with the oom-pah-pah accompaniment so at one concert I improvised variations. Nathan was surprised, then amused. I developed this into my own *Carmen* Fantasy for solo piano. I made variations on Mendelssohn's *Wedding March*, I arranged the Saint-Saëns–Liszt *Danse macabre*, and of course there was my piano version of Sousa's *Stars and Stripes Forever*, which I have not played since 1953. But *Stars and Stripes* was not the

most difficult of my arrangements. The additions I put into Liszt's Second Hungarian Rhapsody, where I brought two themes together, are more difficult by far.

Horowitz never had a wildly adventurous repertoire, but he defied his managers and played such composers as Prokofiev and Medtner. Even the Brahms *Paganini* Variations were suspect by the all-knowing managers. Horowitz had the piece in his repertoire and played it anyway, up to 1943, then dropped it permanently. Later audiences would have given a great deal to hear Horowitz play this brilliant test of a pianist's technique and musicianship. Incidentally, like many pianists of the day—Claudio Arrau, for example—Horowitz did not always play all of the variations; and when he did, they were not in Brahms's order: he generally started with Book II up to the last variation, then went to Book I, and then returned to Book II for the final variation. (He never played the Brahms *Handel* Variations, by the way.)

In 1931 he had Stravinsky's *Petrushka*, seven Brahms waltzes, the Hummel E flat Rondo (an effective, charming piece he probably picked up after hearing Friedman play it), and the Prokofiev Piano Sonata No. 3 on his programs. In those days he was also playing Liszt's E major Polonaise and music by Szymanowski. He played the Liszt *Dante* Sonata in 1934, and that was a virtually unknown piece in those days. He had some Ravel in his repertoire. In 1943 and 1944 he came up with a piece *nobody* knew—the *Ricordanza* Variations by Czerny. He introduced to America three Prokofiev sonatas, he played the world premiere of the Barber Sonata in E flat minor, and he played music by Kabalevsky and Jelobinsky. Horowitz stood up to the managers very well. But after 1945, as a matter of choice and not managerial *Diktat*, his programs began to be more and more conservative.

When Horowitz first came to America music was mostly being made by Europeans. There was no such thing as an American conductor of international stature. Not many famous singers were American. There were no American-born pianists of international fame except Olga Samaroff (née Lucy Hickenlooper in Texas), but Horowitz never heard her play. The great Fannie Bloomfield Zeisler had died in 1927.

One of the most talented American pianists at that time was Gitta Gradova. She had studied in Chicago and New York and also had a few lessons with Horowitz. But she was happily married and never tried to make a big career. Gradova became one of Horowitz's closest friends, and she and her husband used to spend a great deal of time with him, Milstein, and Piatigorsky. Often they all took their summer vacation together in the south of France or Switzerland.

Not until after World War II did an important group of American pianists emerge. Among them was William Kapell. He died at the age of thirty-one in an airplane crash on his way back from an Australian tour in 1953. Horowitz was fascinated with this brash young man. "Kapell lived only a short distance from me, and he was coming to my house all the time. He played for me, but I never even tried to teach him. He had a very tough character and was against all the pianists. He once quarreled with Rubinstein and there was a *scandale* in Chicago." Horowitz received a letter from Kapell dated a few days before he died. In it he tried to express his admiration for Horowitz. The letter arrived ten days after his funeral. Kapell and the Romanian pianist Dinu Lipatti, who died of leukemia at the age of thirty-three in 1950, were two of the most promising pianists of their generation.

Until the outbreak of World War II Horowitz retained his Paris apartment and went back there whenever a tour was finished. Horowitz loved Paris and Paris loved him. He continued to be a favorite in Germany and gave many concerts there. He remembered one in Dortmund,

a little town, where I had an engagement with the orchestra for the Brahms B flat. I was with Merovitch, and after the rehearsal we went back to the hotel with the concertmaster. In our room he said, "Do you want to have a good time? We have a fantastic bordello here." So they decided that since we had nothing to do we would go. I hesitated, because I had to play the Brahms the next night and I did not know the concerto very well. But I went anyway.

The madam let us in, and down the stairs came the girls, all naked. So finally the violinist took one and Merovitch took one, but I said I cannot take one because it is the day before the concert. I said I would wait. Just give me a glass of beer. So I sat there and I saw an upright piano and went to it and started practicing the Brahms. I worked on the octaves of the second movement. Very difficult, you know. The madam came to me and said, "You play the piano quite well." I told her that I was playing with the orchestra the next night. When the concert-master and Merovitch came back they told her all about me and asked her if she wanted to go to the concert. "No," she said, "I never go to concerts." So we went home. But when I gave the concert I looked up at a box and there were sitting six prosti-tutes with the madam in the middle. They were the best-dressed women in the audience. Everybody was looking at them. Every-body knew exactly who they were. It was in all the papers.

When Hitler started coming into power, Horowitz after 1932 refused to play in Germany.

England remained unconquered by Horowitz until 1930. He had played there once previously, in 1927. The 1927 concerts did not go very well. Horowitz appeared twice, once in Albert Hall, which he said was too big, and once in Aeolian Hall, which he said was too small. Albert Hall, which seated about seven thousand, had terrible acoustics and an echo. It was said of this hall that you could hear two concerts there for the price of one.

When Horowitz went back to England in 1930, it was to play the Rachmaninoff Third with Willem Mengelberg and then record it with Albert Coates. It was Horowitz's first concerto recording. The performance and recording startled the British critics and pub-lic, who made a major revaluation of not only Horowitz but also of the Rachmaninoff work.

Two years later, when Horowitz made a tour of England, he sold out everywhere and gained one of his most ardent critical supporters, the celebrated Neville Cardus of the Manchester *Guard-ian*. Cardus, who was held to be the one critic *sans peur et sans reproche,* went his American colleagues Gunn and Devries one bet-ter. He wrote a review flatly calling Horowitz the greatest pianist "alive or dead." He was promptly deluged by mail from fans of Backhaus, Petri, Rosenthal, Cortot, and Rachmaninoff. Others asked him if he had heard Liszt. In a long article written some years later, Cardus defended his statement.

If anything, he wrote, his initial reaction had been an under-statement. "Horowitz must be regarded as the perfect pianist." He had everything—tone, technique, rhythm, sensitivity. "The *ensem-ble* of these attributes has convinced me not once but often that as a pianist pure and undefiled he has had no peer in his time, to say the least. There has never been a romantic pianist of more than

Horowitz's purity of style and pride of carriage." Cardus followed this with about a thousand words of analysis, concluding with, "He brings no portentous message to us from the high gods of music— only rare musical pleasure, beautiful colors, patterns that engage the mind and pulsations that delight the senses."

Cardus was also responsible for passing on a delightful anecdote about a Horowitz rehearsal with Beecham. They were working on the Tchaikovsky for a performance due to be performed on November 10, 1932. At one point Beecham stopped his players and said, "Mr. Horowitz, really, you cannot play like that. It is incredible, not permissible. My orchestra cannot live up to it."

Horowitz played many times with the great Willem Mengelberg and his Amsterdam Concertgebouw, and he remembered especially a rehearsal with them that took place in Berlin on May 3, 1929. Horowitz was to play the Rachmaninoff Third. The orchestra was coming from Amsterdam. But there was a snowstorm, the train was delayed, and the orchestra could not get to the hall until just before the evening concert. "We had to rehearse at 6 P.M. for a concert that night. I told Merovitch that I could not play the whole work through. To play it twice within three hours would kill me. Like Rachmaninoff himself said, it was written for elephants. At rehearsal I said to Mengelberg that I would play at half volume. So we started to play. He always played everything loud. Loud, loud, loud. So I played softer and softer. He turned to me and said, 'Can you play a little louder?' I said, 'If you play softer.'" Four days later Horowitz was in Paris playing still another Rachmaninoff Third, this one at the Salle Pleyel with Monteux.

Horowitz was proud of the system he had with conductors. He would ask them to let him play the first movement without interruption. After the movement was finished, he would say, "Wonderful! Wonderful!" even if it was terrible. Then he would go to the podium and talk to the conductor, who would invariably say that Horowitz was amazing, and then ask the pianist if any refinements were needed:

> I would then talk to the orchestra: the first horn, a little more of this and that; the strings, a little lower in this spot; a little faster here, a little slower there; and so on. All this I would do sincerely, as gracefully as I could, with a happy smile. Each movement went this way. At the end I would tell the conductor that I never had such a good accompaniment, and would be

very careful to say it loud enough for the orchestra to hear. That was my diplomacy. There were only two conductors I never used this technique on. One was Toscanini. The other was Pierre Monteux, and with him I never had to use it because everything always was there. He was one of the greatest, most musical of all conductors, and Toscanini thought so also. Monteux was wonderful, the best after Toscanini. The conductor I preferred for concertos after those two was Eugene Ormandy.

Like all pianists, Horowitz spent a good deal of time at the Steinway showrooms on West Fifty-seventh Street when he was in New York. Nearly all of the major pianists were Steinway artists and that was their headquarters. In the basement was the big selection of concert grands, and Steinway pianists passing through New York all but lived there. It was a place where they could meet, talk, and play for one another. Horowitz was there often because he was living in a small hotel and did not have a room big enough for a concert grand. So he would practice on the grands in the Steinway basement. It was at one of those occasions that he met Josef Lhevinne. "When I walked in, Mr. Greiner said that Lhevinne was there and wanted to meet me, so we were introduced and spoke for half an hour. He was one of the greatest pianists, a tremendous technician and a musical aristocrat."

Josef Hofmann, now living in America, was another pianist who could often be found in the Steinway basement, and he helped Horowitz with his pianos. In Europe Horowitz had been using the Hamburg Steinway and he was always complaining to Greiner about the action of the American Steinway. It was too stiff for him. Hofmann told Horowitz that he had recently invented something that made the instrument easier to play. He called it "accelerated action."

Hofmann was mechanically minded. As a boy of fifteen he had been in communication with Thomas Edison, offering suggestions about improvements in the spring mechanism of the newly invented phonograph. Indeed, Hofmann was probably the first pianist ever to record. When Hofmann played his famous series of concerts at the Metropolitan Opera in 1886 as a boy of ten, Edison was so impressed with the child's genius that he took him to his laboratory and (so legend has it) put him on his lap in front of a piano while the boy played and recorded a few cylinders. Hofmann said that the cylinders were destroyed when a bomb hit his house in Berlin during World War I.

In the Steinway basement Hofmann told Horowitz to try out one of his accelerated-action instruments. "It will be good for you," he said. Horowitz remembered that he laughed. "But when I tried it out, it was wonderful, much better for repeated notes than the standard instruments." Hofmann, said Horowitz, was already having personal troubles:

> He was bitter, he was drinking too much. We became very friendly. I was of a generation where we paid great respect to our elder colleagues. We wanted to learn something from them. It could be that we did not particularly like the playing of this or that famous pianist, but whatever we thought, we kept our opinions to ourselves. Now, at my age, I am entitled to say what I think about my colleagues. But I never would have done it when I was young. It's not like now, when the young pianists laugh at the old ones.

Horowitz went several times to the Steinway factory in Long Island City to study the way pianos were made. On one occasion he startled Henry Z. Steinway, then the manager of the plant, with the accuracy of his ear and touch. Horowitz sat down and tried some of the new instruments. "He knew instantly," said Steinway, "how they were regulated and would say that the touch was not right on this instrument, that the action was a little out of line. The technician would say, 'Oh, no, no, he doesn't know what he is talking about.' So the technician would get out his tools and measure the offending keys, and Horowitz was always right, to the thickness of a sheet of paper. I could see that this guy had it in his fingers. He had the feel."

Steinway & Sons was wonderful to pianists in the days before the depression. Acknowledged to produce the best pianos in the world, the company was making a great deal of money. Thus Steinway & Sons could afford to service their major artists in royal fashion. Concert grands were shipped all over the country at no expense to the pianist. Tuners were thrown into the deal; they accompanied the pianos and took care of them. The pianist could expect to find an instrument in his or her hotel room upon arrival. Horowitz traveled with three, and sometimes four, pianos in his first years in America.

At that time the four most favored pianists on the Steinway roster, designated as Class A, were Paderewski, Hofmann, Mischa Levitzki, and Yolanda Merö. Under them were Class B pianists, who got the same treatment as the four Class A pianists—with one difference: the latter were the only ones who rejoiced in a subsidy of $100 a concert from Steinway.

Levitzki, who died young, was a very popular pianist of the time. His facile elegance charmed a generation of music lovers. Merö was no longer playing after the middle 1920s. She was a Hungarian with extraordinary technique and temperament, if her one recording—a coupling of Liszt's Fourth Rhapsody and Max Vogrich's *Staccato-Caprice*—is any indication. The only reason she was retained in Class A in the 1930s, even though she had retired, was because her husband, Hermann Irion, was a Steinway executive.

Rachmaninoff, like Horowitz a Class B pianist, did not get the $100 subsidy and that rankled. He complained to Greiner, explaining it was not the money. His ego was suffering. Greiner tried to smooth things over by saying that it was done as a tradition. "It is really by the law of inertia that Paderewski and Hofmann still receive this subvention," Greiner said. Whereupon Rachmaninoff growled, in his rumbling bass voice, "Too bad that I am not favored by this law of inertia."

The other Class B pianists, in addition to Horowitz and Rachmaninoff, were Alfred Cortot, Myra Hess, Rudolf Ganz, and Olga Samaroff. Class C artists also included violinists and conductors who needed pianos. They were serviced with Steinway pianos kept by local dealers around the country or, indeed, anywhere in the world. If no piano was in the immediate vicinity, Steinway sent to the nearest city to locate one. Among the Class C group were Ignaz Friedman, Guiomar Novaes, Percy Grainger, George Gershwin, and nearly all of the famous violinists and singers of the day. Then there was the Class D group, which, wrote Greiner, "included more artists of all kinds than could be listed in the Manhattan Telephone Directory." They were furnished pianos free of charge in all cities where Steinways were available, but they did not get one in their hotel room.

As the depression deepened, Steinway & Sons had to retrench. This was done in stages over a period of years. First the subsidy was taken away. Then the artists had to pay part of the transportation charges for their instruments. Then they had to pay the tuners' traveling expenses. Then they had to pay the entire cost of transporting their pianos. Then they had to pay the tuner. Greiner was amused. "Curiously the famous pianists who had always claimed that they simply could not give a concert without a piano tuner accompanying them suddenly realized that the accompanying tuner was really not so necessary."

Rachmaninoff went along with the Steinway decrease in services but had only one question: "Will Horowitz also pay for concert services?" He was assured that Horowitz would indeed have to pay, like everybody else. "Mr. Rachmaninoff," Greiner said to him, "you really don't think that Steinway & Sons will do for Horowitz what they are not doing for you, Hofmann, and Paderewski?"

"Of course, of course, I understand and believe you, but I just wondered . . ."

Horowitz went down fighting. He asked to see Greiner and made an appearance with his new wife, Wanda. Horowitz took the position that as a major pianist who used the Steinway, perhaps Steinway should pay *him* for playing, and thus advertising, the instrument. Greiner quietly pointed out the amount of money Steinway & Sons had paid out for Horowitz advertisements, which meant a bigger box office for Horowitz, which . . . At this point Wanda broke in. "Shut up, Volodya! Mr. Greiner is right!" And she took Horowitz away.

Then there was the matter of the piano stool. Horowitz told Greiner he wanted an upholstered bench exactly 48 inches long and 17 inches high. He could be comfortable on the stage with nothing else. Greiner had four such seats made up for him, "though Steinway & Sons are by no means makers of furniture." In those years —1927 to 1934—Horowitz was playing between thirty-five and fifty concerts a season in America. Steinway sent out four pianos for him, and one of the new benches with each instrument, to strategic points around the country.

But soon Greiner got a long-distance call from Wanda. She told him that Horowitz could not play on those benches. They were ruining his concerts.

On their return to New York, Horowitz and Wanda met with Greiner, and it was agreed that Horowitz would have to order his own benches from a specialist. Greiner suggested Schmieg and Kotzian, escorted Horowitz and Wanda to that venerable firm, and

were waited on by no less than old Mr. Schmieg himself. The
minutest details were discussed, down to an adjustable mechanism
that would work in increments of a thousandth of an inch. The
price came to $500 per bench. At that time many people in America
were not earning that much in a year. Horowitz gulped, but ordered two.

10
Marriage

After we were married Wanda told me that she had made up her mind that I was the man for her. She discussed it with her father, who listened sympathetically and said only, "You will have a difficult life. You will be marrying an artist. Marrying an artist is very difficult." Wanda knew that. Her mother's life was a good example. She had to put up with all of Toscanini's rages, stubbornness, schedules, intolerance, egoism, and infidelities.
—*Vladimir Horowitz, discussing his marriage*

In 1933 Vladimir Horowitz, at the age of thirty, surprised everybody, perhaps even himself. He married Wanda Toscanini, the daughter of the most celebrated of all conductors. The public was delighted. It seemed to be a marriage that was Hollywood come to life: the union of the most admired young pianist of his generation—handsome, athletic-looking, elegant—and the striking, sultry daughter of the man most musicians at that time would unhesitatingly have called the greatest conductor who ever lived.

But there were those who were dumbfounded.

If ever a man seemed destined for bachelorhood it was Vladimir Horowitz. He always had lived a carefree life, relishing his freedom. And, of course, his sexual preferences were no secret to the musical world. Horowitz preferred men. Thus there was a cer-

tain amount of know-it-all smiles when the engagement was announced. Was it a marriage of convenience? Or, perhaps, was it a
desire to be a member of the Toscanini family and sit at the feet of
Maestro? There were those who honestly believed that Horowitz
was more interested in having Toscanini as his father-in-law than
in having Wanda as a wife. Horowitz had played under the old
man's baton and, like all musicians, had been swept away by his
authority, his ear, his understanding of musical form, his personal
and musical dynamism. And Horowitz knew that Toscanini had a
high opinion of his piano playing; the conductor had made no
secret of his admiration for the brilliant virtuoso.

Thus, when Wanda showed interest in Horowitz, he was ripe
for capture. He did want to settle down and, as it turned out, he
did develop a strong emotional attachment to Wanda, a woman
who had been trained to take care of another brilliant and temperamental musician, one Arturo Toscanini.

In 1933, the year Horowitz married his daughter, Toscanini,
born in 1867, had been conducting for more than forty years and
was a firmly established legend. The first of the modern, objective,
the-notes-come-first conductors, he exerted authoritarian control
over his orchestras, demanding a kind of precision and intensity
previously unknown.

He broke away from the German school of Wagner, Bülow,
Mahler, and Furtwängler, with their constant fluctuation of tempo.
They put themselves into their music making. Toscanini tried to
remove himself, believing in nothing but the notes before him. He
felt that it was his sacred duty to realize those notes exactly as they
were printed on the page. (But like all conductors he could make
discreet changes in the orchestration, even of Beethoven symphonies, when he thought they were needed.) He said of Beethoven's
Eroica Symphony, "Some say this is Napoleon, some Hitler, some
Mussolini. For me it is simply Allegro con brio."

But since he was a musician of sensibility, his performances
never suffered from metronomic stagnation. He may have been a
literalist but he was never a purist. "Sing! Sing!" he was constantly
exhorting his players, as he shaped melodies with a patrician line.
"Music must breathe," he said. His explosive rages during rehearsals have become part of the folklore of the performing arts. In his
private life he was insufferable. He was constantly unfaithful to his
long-suffering wife. At home he was prone to terrifying fits of

temper. He was a difficult man to play for and to live with, the kind of man who, when his wife or children said yes, would automatically say no. So if there was not much fun in the Toscanini household, there were always games. Wanda learned early on to state the reverse of what she really wanted.

There were four children in the Toscanini family: Walter, Wally, Giorgio (who died of diphtheria as a child), and Wanda, the youngest, born in Milan in 1908. Wanda grew up in a family dominated by a selfish genius who had little feeling for human relationships, who was accustomed to instant obedience from his orchestras and his family, and Wanda had to bow to his will.

She grew up in the shadow not only of her father but also of her sister, Wally, who matured into a quiet, sensitive, beautiful, extremely feminine young woman. Wally was eight years older than Wanda and, like her mother, Carla, was always the mediator in family disputes. Wanda, who bore a striking resemblance to her father, grew up hearing everybody talking about "La belle Wally, la belle Wally." That was not good for her ego. The young Wanda considered herself a nobody, a little nothing.

She was a volatile girl, and she also had a temper that could get out of control. But she was careful to curb her temper when Father was around. As a child she considered him a scary figure. All of his children walked in fear. Toscanini was the kind of father who was always telling them what was wrong, never what was right. Wanda remembered lunch after lunch, dinner after dinner, at the Toscanini table where her father would eat in black, glowering silence. Nobody dared open his or her mouth. And during the day, when Toscanini was in his study, the children were constantly being admonished: "Don't disturb Father. Don't disturb Father." Sometimes, however, Toscanini could be in a good mood, and there was conversation. Toscanini's idea about entertaining his children at dinner was to explain the *Ring* cycle to them, or discuss Italian poetry.

Wanda had piano lessons. She stopped at fourteen because her father was furious with her for what he considered her lack of talent, and he would scream at her when she made a mistake, which meant that he was always screaming at her. Some years later Wanda secretly took voice lessons, hoping her father would never find out. But he did, and there were thunder and lightning *chez* Toscanini.

He screamed that he would not have a second-rate singer as part of his family. That was the end of Wanda as a singer.

When Wanda grew old enough to be invited to cocktail parties, she would enter the room with real trepidation. She was convinced that nobody would even see her, that she would be completely ignored. To outsiders, Wanda appeared tough. But the toughness was a defense mechanism, and underneath it she was insecure and even timid. That was true even after her marriage. She was surprised when a friend remarked that people were afraid of her. "Afraid of what?" Wanda wanted to know. "Well, you are the daughter of Toscanini, the wife of Horowitz. You seldom smile and you intimidate people. That is why you do not get many invitations for parties. They are afraid you will say no." Wanda suggested to the friend that people try her out. Perhaps she would surprise them and say yes.

Before her marriage Wanda often traveled with Toscanini when her mother had to stay in Milan. At those times she had to subdue her own personality to his, take care of his needs, bow to his every wish. But there were compensations. She also grew up in the aura of her father's fame, partaking of it, relishing it. She was the daughter of Arturo Toscanini, and as such she was royalty, especially in Italy. And one thing she got growing up in the Toscanini household and traveling with Papà was a solid knowledge of the symphonic and operatic repertoire. Wanda was not a trained musician, but her ear and her instincts were very good, and after a while she got to know exactly what went into a performance. It was a knowledge that would be invaluable when she would eventually meet Vladimir Horowitz.

The first time Horowitz and Wanda came face to face was at a party in New York. The year was 1932, and the occasion was a reception given by Columbia Concerts for the Italian pianist Carlo Zecchi. At the party Horowitz wandered over to the piano and started to play Chopin mazurkas. Wanda and he talked "a little bit." That was all. But Wanda went home with the Horowitz sound in her ears, and she told friends that she had never heard anything like it.

Horowitz had not yet met Toscanini, although he had attended some of his concerts. The very first time Horowitz heard him was in Carnegie Hall with the New York Philharmonic in 1928. This was two years after Toscanini had taken over the or-

chestra, sharing the podium with Willem Mengelberg.) Horowitz
was struck by Toscanini's restraint on the podium. Most of the
great conductors he had heard or worked with were always making
big gestures or exaggerated body movements. Toscanini just stood
there and conducted. "I couldn't understand that. But I was a
youngster, you know."

Toscanini did not like soloists and used them as little as possible. But in 1933 he had programmed a Beethoven cycle and
needed a pianist. His assistant conductor, Hans Lange, and the
violinist Adolf Busch told Toscanini that there was one pianist he
would like because he didn't exaggerate. His name was Vladimir
Horowitz, and they said they could vouch for him. The violinist
Louis Krasner, whom Toscanini respected, also put in a good word
for him. So Horowitz was engaged.

When Toscanini told Wanda that he had engaged a pianist
named Vladimir Horowitz for the *Emperor* Concerto, Wanda let
out a shriek. Toscanini knitted his brows and said, "What's the
matter with you?" Wanda said only, "I have heard him and I think
he is very good." Wanda was being smart. She knew her father. If
she had said, "He is wonderful," he would have said Horowitz was
not so good.

Horowitz studied the *Emperor* furiously. He had never played
it in public and he was very nervous about it. He practiced it but,
as he later said, had no real conception of how the work should go.
In Paris, while he was working on the concerto, he met the conductor Issay Dobrowen, who told him that Toscanini took slow
tempos. *"Everything* he conducts is too slow!" So Horowitz believed him and practiced very slow tempos to impress Toscanini.
But he did not like them. The music felt faster.

Before the New York performance he played a tryout *Emperor*
with the Chicago Symphony, under Frederick Stock. It went well,
Horowitz thought, but there was something missing, and the Chicago critics pointed that out. Finally he went to New York and
played it for Toscanini at the Astor Hotel, where Toscanini was
then living. Horowitz remembered that Toscanini was not in a
happy mood because he had bursitis. Nor was Horowitz happy;
the piano was not very good and Horowitz told Toscanini so:

> "Maestro, I am playing on a terrible piano. But I will do
> the best I can." I started to play—the Dobrowen tempo. "No,

no," said Maestro. "It should go faster, like this." And he sang
the theme fast, the way I had felt it should go. "That's right!" I
nearly yelled. I was so happy. We went through it and he liked
it very much right away. We did the performance on April 23,
1933, with only one rehearsal. After that I played the concerto
many times and recorded it with Fritz Reiner, who liked my
playing. He said that this was an aristocratic *Emperor;* that
everybody else pounded it out.

The New York critics were generally pleased with this *Emperor,*
though some did not think it was anything special. Oscar Thompson of the *Sun* called it "a chaste interpretation, unmarred by sen-
suous musical speech." He and Pitts Sanborn both found it rather
cool and lacking in depth. Lawrence Gilman of the *Herald Tribune,*
however, found in this performance fire, a vigorous and poised
style, and "poetic sensibilities unmarred by exaggeration." (The
word "unmarred" seems to have been a popular locution among
the New York critics of the day.)

It was in Milan later in 1933 that Horowitz and Wanda got
to know each other. At La Scala he had played both the Brahms B
flat and the Rachmaninoff D minor in one evening, an endurance
contest he would never think of doing later on. Wanda was there
with a friend. She listened to Horowitz, looked at her friend, and
said, "This is a modern pianist. He combines the styles of a Paderewski and a Friedman, and I have never heard such pedaling." She
began to see Horowitz on a regular basis. They spent several days
together, and on one occasion Horowitz reached into a pocket,
took out a box, opened it and put a gold chain around her neck.
Things were obviously getting serious. On October 8, 1933, their
engagement was announced, and the next day newspapers carried
the story.

Those close to Horowitz and the Toscanini family at that time
thought that Wanda was the dominating force. She was a determined twenty-five-year-old young woman and she appears to have
been very much in love with Horowitz. Of course she had heard
about his sexual tastes, but she thought she could reform him. She
was much prouder of being the wife of Vladimir Horowitz than
she was of being the daughter of Arturo Toscanini. The latter, she
said, and repeated many times in newspaper interviews, was merely
an accident of birth.

For a time there were engagement parties, and Horowitz,

never averse to publicity, played up the forthcoming marriage. "It will be a sensation," Halina Rodzinski, wife of the conductor, overheard Horowitz saying. "It will be in all the newspapers."

Wanda went with Horowitz on his English tour in 1933, with her sister, Wally, as chaperone. Wally, who had married Count Emanuele Castelbarco in 1930, was amused. She said that Horowitz was charming, like a mischievous child. The marriage took place in Milan on December 21, 1933. The Toscaninis were there, and so was Gregor Piatigorsky (Milstein was on a concert tour and could not attend).

There was the question of religion. An Italian priest could not join a Catholic and a Jew. It was suggested to Wanda that she or Horowitz change religion. Wanda laughed it off. "He keeps his and I keep mine." Anyway Wanda, strongly anticlerical, did not want to be married in church. So a civil ceremony in Milan's city hall was arranged.

Wanda refused to wear white. She had on a black gown made by Lucien Lelong and a hat borrowed from Wally. In the excitement of the moment she put on the wrong pair of shoes, a size too small. In the car going to the town hall she exchanged shoes with Wally. As for Horowitz, he had planned to wear a light-colored suit, but a horrified Piatigorsky ordered him into a more respectable black. Toscanini was Horowitz's witness, and Wanda's uncle Enrico Paolo (Toscanini's brother-in-law) represented Wanda. Horowitz, who did not speak Italian, had a translator who put the service into Russian for him. Horowitz answered in Russian, which the translator had to put back into Italian for the authorities. The translator was so nervous that he stammered his way through the entire ceremony. "My friends and I were laughing all the way through," Wanda recalled.

Wanda did not want a big reception after the ceremony, so her mother had a tea party at which the wedding presents were displayed. For one of his presents, Toscanini gave the couple an ivory carving of Saint Francis with his birds. It had belonged to Franz Liszt and then to Wagner's wife, Cosima (Liszt's daughter). Horowitz kept it at his bedside for the rest of his life. Another present came from Steinway & Sons. When Horowitz returned to America, the company notified him and Wanda, a grand piano would be waiting for them. It was No. 314 503, later exchanged for No. 279 503, and Horowitz lived happily with it ever after.

There was no honeymoon. Two days after the ceremony the newlyweds were in Paris, where Horowitz played the Beethoven *Emperor* with Cortot on the podium. Then the couple embarked on the *Rex* (the flagship of the Italian fleet) to America and the Horowitz tour. Also on board to meet their American engagements were the Toscanini entourage, Piatigorsky and Milstein, and the conductor Bernardino Molinari. Under the circumstances Wanda and Volodya did not have much time with each other.

Soon it became apparent to Wanda that Horowitz was something of a hypochondriac. When he had free time he would often go to a spa, with or without her, to purge himself of imaginary ailments. There he would get up at seven, an hour anathema to him, to take the waters and follow the prescribed diet and exercise regimen. He always had a fixation on his health.

Early on, Wanda found a pet name for her husband. In his barbaric Italian he was trying to say something about Respighi's *Pini di Roma (Pines of Rome)*. Instead of saying "Pini," he kept saying "Pinci," pronounced Pinchy. Wanda thought this "adorable," and in affectionate moments her Volodya was forever after Pinci.

Whenever he was in New York, Horowitz tried to spend as much time with Toscanini as possible. Toscanini lived in a mansion overlooking the Hudson River in Riverdale, just north of Manhattan. Horowitz and his bride were constant visitors. "He and I got along all right," said Horowitz:

> We constantly talked about music. Mozart was a special subject. At that time he did not conduct many Mozart concertos, mostly because pianists those days played at best only two or three of them—generally the D minor or the A major [K. 488]. I had not played any in public. But both of us knew all of the major Mozart concertos and loved them. I own scores of the concertos with Maestro's markings and metronome indications. Of course we discussed Beethoven. I remember him saying to me, "Horowitz, I know you don't like to play many of the Beethoven sonatas, especially the last ones, because you think they are badly written for the piano by a deaf man. Why don't you make changes? What is wrong if you make the changes in good taste? We conductors always change Beethoven's scoring in the symphonies and nobody, the critics, the

audience, nobody hears the changes." I told Maestro that conductors could make those slight changes, but in a Beethoven
sonata if the pianist changed one little note everybody would
scream "This is not in the text!" But Toscanini kept on asking
me to make changes for better pianistic solutions of the text.
"What do you care about what they say?" he would ask. But I
never had the nerve.

Another thing they talked about was pianists of the past who
had played with Toscanini or whom Toscanini had personally
known. Horowitz especially wanted to hear about Busoni, and was
pleased to learn that Toscanini had a high opinion of him. Toscanini, said Horowitz,

> was crazy about him as a person and as a musical thinker. But
> Wanda tells me that Toscanini once heard Busoni play the
> *Waldstein* and at the opening measures walked out of the hall.
> There were too many tempo changes. Yet Busoni visited Tos
> canini at the Ansonia Hotel before World War I and played
> Liszt for several hours, until three o'clock in the morning, and
> Toscanini, who did not like Liszt, said it was divine. He said
> he never heard anything better. And Toscanini was difficult,
> very, on pianists.
>
> Another thing that Busoni did that impressed Toscanini
> was at one of the Sunday evening concerts at the Metropolitan
> Opera. The official piano there was a Knabe, and it was an old,
> decrepit instrument used by several pianists and accompanists
> who preceded Busoni on the program. Toscanini said that
> when it was Busoni's turn to play, everybody thought he would
> have the instrument changed. But no. Busoni played the Knabe
> and Toscanini said that he made it sound like the greatest of all
> pianos. Busoni could be very eccentric. In Berlin he once played
> an *Emperor* that was piano and pianissimo from beginning to
> end. He explained that he was curious to hear how it would
> sound that way.

Toscanini was the first great Italian conductor. Up to him, the
German conductors were supposed to be the quintessence of music.
Toscanini felt that the German conductors played too slow, just as
Horowitz felt that the German pianists played too slow. "Everything adagio," said Horowitz. "So Toscanini reacted against that,
perhaps a little too much. He wanted to show how the music

should really sound, and sometimes he overdid it, playing too fast. Now everybody is too slow. They all want to show what profound musicians they are. If you play slow, you are profound."

Tempo, said Horowitz,

is such a funny thing. It can depend on how you feel, or the acoustics of the hall, or anything. There is no one tempo. Rubinstein once told me a story about Brahms and Joachim. It was the first rehearsal of the Violin Concerto and Joachim was playing from manuscript with Brahms conducting. Brahms started at such a slow tempo that Joachim went crazy. But he was not going to say anything. Brahms was the composer and also a close friend. Joachim went home almost crying. The next day at the rehearsal Brahms started the concerto with a much faster tempo. Joachim loved it and asked Brahms why yesterday was so slow and today so fast. Brahms said, "Touch my pulse. It is much faster today."

Toscanini did not have a very high opinion of most conductors. Horowitz thought the only one he admired without reservation was Pierre Monteux, though he had good things to say about Bruno Walter, Erich Kleiber, and Fritz Reiner. He admired Stokowski's ear, and so did Horowitz the time he played Beethoven's *Emperor* with the Philadelphia Orchestra in 1934. It was a concert Horowitz remembered vividly. Wanda and he had recently been married. They were staying at the Plaza, and one night they went to the movies. The next morning the telephone rang and woke them up. "Where are you?" screamed the manager of the orchestra. "You were supposed to be at the Academy of Music at 10 A.M. for the rehearsal." Horowitz rushed to Philadelphia and played without a rehearsal. "The performance went well. Stokowski knew the score."

Horowitz was struck by Toscanini's rehearsal technique. "One thing Toscanini couldn't stand was conductors who were constantly stopping the orchestra during rehearsals, every five bars, explaining, explaining, explaining, trying things over and over and over. The first time Toscanini conducted any orchestra he would go through an entire movement without stopping in order to see how they played, what their ensemble was, and so on. Once he got into an argument with George Szell about this. Szell came to America as a refugee and Maestro invited him to conduct the NBC

Symphony. Maestro was there at the first rehearsal and couldn't stand Szell's constant starting and stopping. He yelled at Szell and there was a terrific scene. It was terrible. He insulted Szell."

Still, Horowitz always said that Toscanini was not as hard to work with as many people thought. If an artist really knew the music, there never were problems. When Horowitz played with Toscanini they almost always went straight through because even when Horowitz thought of stopping and asking for some kind of adjustment he hesitated to interpose. "Toscanini always had the music in front of him, but his eyesight was too bad for him to see the notes and there might have been trouble if he did not know how to tell the orchestra the exact bars. Perhaps he did know them —he had everything memorized, to the last note—but still I felt a little uncomfortable. So I discussed things with him before or after rehearsals. It was not difficult. He could do anything he wanted in front of an orchestra."

Rubinstein told Horowitz about the time he played the Beethoven Third with Toscanini. A few days before the performance Rubinstein was asked to dinner, after which he was supposed to go to the piano to discuss tempos and interpretation. At dinner Rubinstein started telling anecdotes until he looked at his watch and it was one o'clock in the morning. He apologized for forgetting about the discussion of the concerto. Toscanini said it was not important. "We'll do it at rehearsal tomorrow."

At the rehearsal, Rubinstein told Horowitz, "I played my way and it was a disaster. Not one bar together. At least I comforted myself with the thought that I had played with the great Toscanini and it was something to remember. After we went through the entire concerto Toscanini asked me if I had any suggestions, any wishes. I said, 'No, Maestro. It was very good.' Toscanini said, 'Let's go again.' Then came a miracle. He followed me exactly, every rubato, everything was there. While I had been playing he was listening, memorizing everything I was doing."

Often Toscanini and Horowitz disagreed on composers. "I think I was right, because after he stopped conducting he told me he was sorry he had not conducted more music by certain composers, Rachmaninoff, for instance. He never wanted to play his music. He was maybe a little jealous of Rachmaninoff, I think so. Toscanini told me, 'I was so stupid. I heard Rachmaninoff's Second Symphony. Such beautiful music!' He also said that he should have conducted more Tchaikovsky. The only Tchaikovsky symphony he ever conducted was the Sixth." (Tchaikovsky's *Manfred* was in the Toscanini repertoire, but it is not really a symphony.)

Everyone who knew Toscanini and Horowitz at that time were agreed that Horowitz was overawed. Toscanini was the master, Horowitz the disciple, and the disciple would never think of contradicting the master. In any case, one did not argue with Toscanini, who always knew he was right. Horowitz was face to face with unalterable law, and he was swamped. He admitted as much. In 1975 he told John Gruen in a New York *Times* interview, "I had to be rather passive with him, because he needed to be the strong one. He was a very stubborn man. Even when I was not in accord about a certain interpretation, I would have to give in to him." Perhaps that was one reason Horowitz allowed his recording of the Brahms B flat Concerto with Toscanini to be released. "I didn't like anything about it," Horowitz said. "It was too fast, too metronomic, boring."

By the middle 1930s Horowitz was one of the busiest pianists on the international circuit, with annual tours of America and Europe, recording sessions, and the obligation to work on new repertoire during the summer months. In those days musicians really had summer vacations. Serious music came to a halt in May and did not resume until mid-September. Air conditioning had not yet been perfected, and in the United States serious music just was not performed during the summer except for the outdoor concerts at Lewisohn Stadium in New York, Robin Hood Dell in Philadelphia, the Hollywood Bowl, and one or two other places. The idea seemed to be that one would develop brain fever or something equally startling while listening to a Beethoven symphony during the summer months.

To oblige Toscanini, Horowitz learned the Brahms D minor Concerto for the Brahms cycle he was conducting with the New York Philharmonic in the 1934–35 season. He had a tryout performance with Pierre Monteux and the Orchestre Symphonique de Paris on November 25, 1934. With the New York Philharmonic under Toscanini, Horowitz played the work on March 14, 15, and 17, 1935.

W. J. Henderson of the *Sun,* the dean of New York critics, called the performance "finely conceived and beautifully executed." Lawrence Gilman of the *Herald Tribune* was very impressed: "Dazzling virtuosity . . . devoted strictly to a publication of the music's essential traits. . . . Continence and purity of style." Olin Downes in the *Times* found the performance "deeply moving," with "splendor of tone, firmness of grasp and outline, awareness of the composer's requirements."

In those early days of home recording a set of acetates was made from the 1935 radio broadcast, and there was also one from a 1936 broadcast with the Amsterdam Concertgebouw under Bruno Walter. A short section of the first movement of the latter was missing and, when the performance was pirated in America by a small company many years later, the Toscanini broadcast was used to fill in the missing measures.

Through the bad sound in both recordings comes a blazing, even blistering, conception. Without ignoring the musical elements, Horowitz makes a lithe, athletic virtuoso piece out of the concerto. This is an exciting and impulsive Brahms, fast and brilliant, a damn-the-torpedoes performance that is quite likely the only one of its kind. It is even—rare for Horowitz—not entirely clean; the first-movement octaves are smudged and overpedaled. But Horowitz, for better or worse, makes the Brahms D minor sound like a new experience, and it is hard not to respond to the visceral excitement he generates. No pianist who has played this notoriously difficult work has displayed such rhythmic impetus, fantastically clear articulation (forget about the octaves), and sheer power.

The Walter performance is more relaxed than the Toscanini, who did not give his soloist much, if any, breathing space. Walter, in the Adagio movement, let Horowitz bring out some of the inner voices that Brahms so carefully marked and that so many of today's pianists so carefully ignore. Milstein heard one of the Walter performances and Horowitz was pleased that his friend, who always spoke his mind and could criticize him severely, said that it was one of the greatest performances of the concerto he had ever heard.

These two performances of the Brahms D minor Piano Concerto point up the differences between tempos then and tempos now. The last five decades have seen tempos becoming slower and slower. Toscanini and Horowitz perform the concerto in 38 minutes, 56 seconds. The Walter/Horowitz performance comes in at 40 minutes, 42 seconds. By today's (1992) standards, those tempos are not only alarmingly fast; they also will be considered unmusical in many quarters. Toscanini set the tempos for all of his performances. Walter could be more flexible when working with a soloist.

It is hard to come by accurate timings of concert performances in the 1930s, but the fact that neither Downes nor Gilman complained about the tempo of the Brahms in their reviews, or even mentioned it, suggests that in the mid-1930s the Toscanini and Walter approaches were the norm. Three decades later, in the mid-1960s, such pianists as Rudolf Firkusny, Arthur Rubinstein, Van Cliburn, and John Ogdon were timed at between 44 and 46 minutes. In the 1980s Krystian Zimerman, Daniel Barenboim, and Claudio Arrau were running from 48 to over 50 minutes. At those tempos the Brahms D minor Concerto sounds like a different piece from the one that Horowitz with Toscanini and Walter had played fifty years earlier.

Horowitz said he played the Brahms D minor Concerto no more than a dozen times between 1934 and 1936, and he forgot it as soon as he could. "As with the late Beethoven sonatas," he said, "I admit its great message, but it is not my kind of music. Rachmaninoff heard the New York performance on the radio and telephoned me, asking how I could ever play this awful music. It is poorly orchestrated and poorly written for the piano, he said. Myself, I enjoyed playing the B flat Brahms much more. It is a better concerto."

If Horowitz was not happy with the Brahms D minor Concerto in 1934, two events occurred later in the year that took his mind off that work. The fall of that year saw a reunion. Horowitz's father managed to get out of the Soviet Union to visit his famous son. And on October 2 a child, Sonia, was born to Wanda and Volodya.

Horowitz had never lost touch with his family, and had been in communication with his father and mother ever since he had left for the West in 1925. Indeed, he was sending them money on a regular basis. In 1930 Sophie, his mother, had died from peritonitis. Shortly before the reunion with his son Samuel had remarried, but the Russians, as was then their charming custom, kept his wife hostage in Moscow, where they lived. One of the first things that Samuel did after embracing his son in Paris was proudly to show him a photograph of his new wife, a woman considerably younger than he. Horowitz had been very close to his mother, and that action hurt him very much.

Samuel accompanied Horowitz and Wanda on a tour that took in France, Italy, Belgium, and Switzerland before he had to return to Russia. He basked in his son's successes. Wanda thought he was a wonderful person, "very distinguished, very talented, very cultured." She also thought him somewhat anti-Semitic. Many Jews are. German Jews have a tendency to sneer at Russian Jews. Well-to-do Russian Jews sneer at ghetto Jews. Samuel Horowitz sneered at Polish Jews. Vladimir Horowitz himself had his share of this Jewish kind of anti-Semitism. He had, some said, no great liking for "Jewish" Jews.

Shortly after his return to Russia, Samuel Horowitz was arrested during one of Stalin's purges. Nobody knew the reason for his arrest. Nobody ever did in Stalin's day. Perhaps it was felt that by visiting his son, Samuel had been contaminated by capitalism. The poor man was put through hell. Natasha Saitzoff said that when Horowitz's sister, Regina, got permission to visit her father in the gulag, he was in so deplorable a condition that he did not recognize her. He died in the prison camp.

As for Sonia, she was raised in a manner guaranteed to create problems when she grew up. As a busy touring pianist, Horowitz was away from home for long periods. He was also developing emotional and psychosomatic problems that within a short time would result in a disappearance from the stage. Wanda had to be with him in those desperate times. For the first year or so after the birth, Wanda stayed in Milan, taking care of her baby. Then she joined Horowitz in Switzerland, leaving the child with a nanny. Wally, the Countess Castelbarco, then living in Milan, would supervise the nanny. Then Wanda went to America with her husband. She saw Sonia only intermittently during the child's first few years. When Toscanini was at his home in Milan, he too would keep an eye on the child. Or Sonia and her nanny might stay with Aunt Wally at the Castelbarco estate in Crema, near Venice; or at the Toscanini summer home in Isolino on Lake Maggiore. "She was passed around like a package," Wanda recalled. Under those circumstances, Sonia could not put down any roots, and her education was hit and miss. Toscanini loved her—more, it was said by many in the Horowitz circle, than her parents did. To almost everybody, Toscanini could be a monster. But to Sonia he was the doting grandfather, doing everything he could to spoil her.

In retrospect, Wanda thought that Toscanini had a bad influence on Sonia. When she was eight years old he would keep on telling her how brilliant she was, how wonderful, a real genius who could do anything. "If you want to play the piano, you will play the piano. If you want to write music, you will write music. If you want to paint, you will paint." Later Wanda was to realize not only how much damage her father had caused but also how negligent she and Volodya had been as parents.

And during those years of Sonia's childhood, her father was going through his own kind of mental anguish. The result was a physical and emotional breakdown that kept him away from the public for two years.

11

Disappearance

> Up to that point in my life I had never thought much about
> myself. I just played the piano. But when you spend so much
> time sick in bed it changes you a little bit, and sometimes you
> change without realizing it. When I started to practice again I
> think I found something different in my playing. I read through
> much music and started to get interested in modern composers,
> which I never had been except of course for Rachmaninoff, and
> he was really a nineteenth-century composer. I became familiar
> with many composers I had never played, such as Hindemith and
> Respighi.
>   —*Vladimir Horowitz, about his first retirement in 1936*

*I*t did not take Horowitz many years to slide from the top of
his world into a private hell. In the early 1930s Horowitz seemed
to be blessed with everything—fame, money, looks, health, an
adoring international public, the respect of his peers. Yet Horowitz
after 1933, the year of his marriage (which might be more than
coincidence), slid deeper and deeper into a depression to the point
where he could not play at all. The outwardly happy, pleasant,
relaxed public figure that the journalists had been describing started
to slither in quicksands of self-doubt and self-loathing. The years
from 1936 to 1938 that saw him away from the public were a
desperate attempt to find himself and save himself.

   This first Horowitz disappearance from the stage—there
would be three more in the years to come—started with an opera-

tion in 1936, but that was only the physical part of his problems. The psychological part was more debilitating. Horowitz was physically and intellectually drained, and he felt he had played certain works so often "that I couldn't hear them anymore, even while my fingers were performing them."

Occupational fatigue had hit him. He began to hate the concert routine and even his piano. He was dissatisfied with his progress as an artist, and he took it out on the music. His formerly impeccable technique began to sound a bit slipshod, and he did not seem interested in what he was playing. Perhaps, too, his responsibilities as a married man with a child were more than he could face. It was a classic what-did-I-get-myself-into reaction from a free-wheeling bachelor new to matrimony and fatherhood.

Then in 1936 he decided to have his appendix out.

There was nothing wrong with the appendix, as the operation showed. But his mother had died six years previously, at the age of fifty-seven, from peritonitis. There were no antibiotics in those days. After Horowitz received the letter about his mother's death he started brooding and developed intestinal pains. "Of course this was all psychosomatic, absolutely. But you never know," said Horowitz in 1987. "Maybe my appendix was really bad. I was convinced of it." The chances are that Horowitz was having his first attack of the colitis that began to plague him in the 1950s. But he made up his mind that his trouble was appendicitis, and he wanted the offending organ removed.

That was easier said than done. It was no simple matter to find a surgeon who would operate for no clear medical reason. Finally he found a doctor in Paris who would cooperate, and the operation took place in September 1936. "The appendix was clean but the operation wasn't. I developed phlebitis, became really sick and was in the hospital for three months. For almost a year I couldn't walk and during all that time I didn't touch the piano."

This time his illness was physical, and there was a great deal of pain, so much so that Horowitz began to wonder if he would ever be able to play the piano again. He also was still depressed because of his mother's death. "So I was a very nervous man at that time. Then when I started to walk it took months before I felt comfortable again. The muscles were gone."

At the beginning of 1937, Horowitz was still depressed and

actually in the mood of throwing in the towel. He and Wanda discussed the future. He told her that he had the feeling that he would never play in public again, that they could live a quiet life while he taught and composed. Money was no problem. By that time the Horowitzes had more than enough to spend the rest of their lives in relative luxury.

Horowitz convalesced in Bertenstein, Switzerland, in a house overlooking Lake Lucerne. Wanda and Sonia were there as well. Horowitz took the cures at several spas. At one point he and Wanda visited Toscanini in Salzburg, where Toscanini was conducting several operas. Horowitz would sit in the garden with his leg on a stool because of the phlebitis. Toscanini would look at him unbelievingly. "He's crazy," he kept on saying. "There's nothing wrong with him."

But there was, although it was something out of Toscanini's experience.

After almost a year Horowitz recovered his mental balance enough to start working. He had new ideas, he said:

> I started looking at music that was less flashy than the music I had concentrated on. I needed new pieces very badly. Before I came out of Russia I had perhaps twelve recital programs in my fingers. As I continued playing in the West, my repertoire began to shrink, shrink, shrink, until I had only three. In the period I was not playing in public I started to get a repertoire back—four programs, six programs, seven programs. Many of the pieces I had played in Russia, but now I had to rethink them, play them differently, because I was older. I heard the music differently. Being almost forty years old is a big difference from being twenty-one. Today I sometimes hear records that I made around 1930, 1940, and I hardly like one note that I play. I am very critical about myself. I think that during my first sabbatical I must have felt, even if I was not conscious about it, that my playing lacked something and had to be reconsidered.

In this period he spent a good deal of time with Rachmaninoff, who was living near him in Switzerland. Rachmaninoff had cancer and only a few years to live, but still was playing the piano like the giant he always was. In many respects Rachmaninoff was the perfect pianist. His fingers were infallible, he had a technique that could match Horowitz's note for note, his sound was the music of the spheres, and his interpretations were animated by the most aristocratic of musical minds. The man had everything.

In Switzerland, Horowitz and Rachmaninoff talked endlessly about music, they played four-hand music—everything they could get their hands on—and he listened to Horowitz and encouraged him. Horowitz knew that Rachmaninoff was not in good health at the time, and appreciated his help and advice all the more. "He fussed over me and he begged me to practice. At least an hour a day," he said. Rachmaninoff was the stabilizing force in Horowitz's life during this period. He calmed Horowitz down, tried to rebuild his confidence and kept urging him to resume his career.

It could also be that Rachmaninoff saw something new in Horowitz's playing, a maturity, a musical deepening, that interested him. Rachmaninoff never had any doubts about Horowitz as a technician. But "the octaves race" that he had disparagingly cited at the Horowitz debut with Beecham had bothered him throughout the years. Now, perhaps, Horowitz was going to achieve an even higher degree of artistry and dedication to his already imposing arsenal.

It seems clear that between 1936 and 1938 Horowitz was suffering from the first of a series of guilt feelings that afflicted him during his entire professional life and even during his student days. All his life except for his last five years he was torn two ways: between being an artist and being an entertainer. He knew how good he was pianistically, but he had nagging doubts about the way he was employing his gift. He may have been considered by many the world's greatest pianist, but had he prostituted his art? Was he merely pandering to the public by playing his virtuoso stunts instead of devoting his life to the highest artistic ideals? He desperately wanted to be recognized as a great musician as well as a great pianist, but he knew that some of his colleagues and some important critics had reservations about his ultimate artistry. When he began to have doubts about himself as a musician, as opposed to a "mere" pianist, the result was a breakdown that resulted in real and imaginary illness and retirement from the stage.

"When you are away from the public and don't play," said Horowitz, referring to his 1936 retirement, "you have time to think." Horowitz came to the conclusion that he was dissatisfied

with the flashiness that had too often, he felt, become a characteristic of his playing.

A Serkin concert in Switzerland that Horowitz attended gave
Horowitz a traumatic experience that proved to be a turning point.
Horowitz wrote to Wanda, who had returned to Italy for a short
time, saying that he cried when it was over. "What I told Wanda in
the letter," Horowitz said,

> was that I cried because *there* was an artist's artist, and I felt
> that for the last few years I had sold my art for easy success, for
> money. Perhaps my feeling of doubt and inadequacy can be
> traced back to my desire to get out of Russia. I had desperately
> wanted to emigrate, and if I had not had a big success in the
> West, I would have been forced to return. So it could be that I
> tried for success a little too hard, and one sure way to success
> was to play octaves faster than anybody else could play them.
> Anything, so that I would not have to go back to Russia.

Others had noticed this push and pull in 1936. His playing
was lacking in its previous verve and had become stylized and
mechanical. Dinu Lipatti, in a review of a Horowitz concert,
quoted La Bruyère's remark that "People always want to appear as
they would wish to be and not as they are." Horowitz, said Lipatti,
"will be the most extraordinary pianist of all time the day he is
content to accept himself as he is." It was a paradox. Here was
Vladimir Horowitz, the world's supreme piano virtuoso, now a
man of sorrows, afflicted with grief. In a peculiar kind of way he
had brainwashed himself. He had come to the conclusion that great
musicians had to play only the severest kind of music, à la Schnabel
or Serkin, and that he had failed the ultimate test. It simply did not
occur to him that a pianist who could play Liszt rhapsodics, Schumann, Scriabin, Rachmaninoff, and others with such panache,
style, and grace, had as much right to be called an artist as the
pianist who could deliver Beethoven's Op. 110 or Brahms-Handel
with skill and dedication.

His protracted absence from the stage inevitably started the
rumor factory working overtime. Horowitz was fatally ill. Horowitz was in a sanatorium. Horowitz was in an insane asylum. The
climax came with the announcement of Horowitz's death. On vacation in Gstaad in 1938, Milstein and Horowitz one night were

listening to the radio. Suddenly they heard: "Now you will hear music in memory of the pianist Vladimir Horowitz. News of his untimely death just came in from Paris." Horowitz said, unnecessarily, "That's not true!" Then he said, "But what good publicity!" Papers all over Europe carried the news, and Horowitz was one of the few people ever to read his own obituary notices. For days Wanda was on the phone to wire services, newspapers, and friends, correcting the false report. Horowitz was then deluged with congratulatory telegrams on his resurrection.

Gradually he worked himself out of his problems. Rachmaninoff was not his only prop. Horowitz spent some time with Serkin and the violinist Adolf Busch, who was his father-in-law. They lived in Basel, and whenever Horowitz dropped in for short visits they would encourage him, urge him to play, try to build up his ego. Serkin and Horowitz played four-hand music and discussed pianistic problems. Once Serkin listened to Horowitz read through the fugue of Beethoven's *Hammerklavier* Sonata. "It was amazing," said Serkin, "but Horowitz just took it for granted. I think that at that time he did not have a high opinion of himself. We tried to tell him how good he was and he seemed embarrassed."

Early in 1938 Horowitz started feeling that he, the keyboard, and the music were as one again. He was making peace with himself.

Serkin and Busch provided the jumping-off point. They suggested that a quiet return would be best; that instead of returning with a blare of trumpets to a major concert hall, Horowitz should test himself at a benefit concert in Zurich on September 26, 1938, sharing the program with the Busch Quartet. Horowitz agreed. He chose a Chopin group—the Polonaise-Fantasy, Barcarolle, and several etudes. Everything went well. Serkin and Busch told him that he was again in top form, and even Horowitz agreed that it had not been bad. There followed a few concerts in France, and soon Horowitz was once again playing everywhere in Europe except Germany and Italy. Germany was out because of Hitler. Italy was out because Toscanini's son-in-law would not have been welcome in the land of Mussolini. Toscanini, who was a fervent opponent of the regime, was on the Fascist blacklist.

The Horowitz tour culminated in 1939 with pairs of concerts in Paris and London, and his public enthusiastically welcomed him back. Some critics had reservations, but the consensus was that his playing seemed more relaxed, more colorful, more serious. But, then again, critics were always saying that when Horowitz returned after an absence from the stage.

Horowitz agreed with the critics on his return in 1938. He was constantly interviewed and said again and again that his two-year sabbatical had given him a new outlook on music. He said much the same in a letter to Sasha Greiner, telling him that he felt a great change in himself, and that the time he spent away from the concert stage was not lost. Rather it went "to the profit of my art." Horowitz also cut down his work load. "My attitude about concerts had changed," he later said. "I told Wanda that no matter what, we could live comfortably if we were careful. I said that there was no need for me to kill myself playing sixty, seventy concerts a year when twenty or thirty were all that were necessary."

Horowitz played his last European concert for many years on August 29, 1939. Wanda and he were summering in Deauville and Scheveningen when Hitler and Stalin signed their pact. Horowitz looked at Wanda and said, "This means war." Three days later war broke out.

All the experts had told Horowitz there would never be a war. Inconceivable! they said. But Horowitz said he knew war was coming, "and so did Rachmaninoff and Friedman when I had dinner with them in Paris in 1938." Artists have more delicate antennae than politicians, and they recognized the threat from Germany long before the Chamberlains and Lavals and industrialists of Europe. The European establishment seemed to think that accommodation could always be made with Hitler, that there would always be "peace in our time." But time finally ran out and a stand had to be taken. Nobody was more surprised than the German leaders when France and England declared war after Hitler went into Poland. War? Over *Poland?*

Horowitz and Wanda had taken an apartment in Paris in August 1938. When the war started the problem was how the family could get to America. Horowitz was traveling on his Nansen passport. After World War I, the League of Nations devised what came to be known as a Nansen passport, issued to people who had fled their country and could get citizenship nowhere else.

The French consul in Lucerne, where Horowitz gave a concert in 1939, refused to issue him an American visa; he would not honor Horowitz's Nansen passport. He and Wanda, who traveled with an Italian passport, turned to the Italian consul, and Wanda exerted her charm on him in her idiomatic Italian. He gave them a laissez-passer to Genoa, where they managed to get an American visa. It was not easy to get one. When war broke out refugees wanted to go to America, many more than the quota permitted. But Wanda, after all, was a Toscanini, and her sister was a contessa, and no matter what the official feeling in Italy about Toscanini's loud opposition to the Fascist regime, his name was still magic there. And in America, too. State Department officials in Genoa were happy to be of help.

In Genoa, Horowitz, Wanda, and Sonia boarded a ship to New York. Wally went to Paris to take care of the apartment, seeing to it that all the possessions were put into storage.

On his arrival in New York, Horowitz, at the urging of Toscanini, rented a house in Riverdale, close to where Maestro lived. Toscanini wanted all the members of his family close to him. The Judson management started working on a Horowitz tour of America. It would begin on January 7, 1940, in Newark, and there would be a few other recitals to prepare Horowitz for Carnegie Hall on January 31.

His programs were no different from those of the past. They concentrated on the Romantics and ended with a virtuoso tour de force. At the January 31 concert the concluding showpiece was the *Carmen* Variations. His audience gave him a wild welcome-back ovation, to be repeated all over the country. Many critics and colleagues felt that something new had entered Horowitz's playing after his two-year sabbatical and, looking back at his return to America many years later, he agreed:

> I have never analyzed myself very much and I was in no position to say whether or not I was different. I think I was listening to myself more carefully—but from the beginning I always listened to myself carefully. I now tried to control the purely virtuoso elements of my playing and to achieve even more color. In music, however, there always is a place for virtuosity, and I see no need to apologize for ending my programs with one of my big transcriptions. The public expected them and I enjoyed playing them.

On May 6, 1940, Horowitz played the Brahms Second Piano Concerto with Toscanini and the NBC Symphony to universal praise (though years later Horowitz said that he had hated the performance because of its strictness). In his review of the Brahms, Downes in the *Times* found a significant new quality: "Nothing Mr. Horowitz has done here has indicated more impressively his growth as interpreter as well as virtuoso of his instrument."

Everything was going along splendidly until six months after the Brahms performance. Horowitz caught his finger in a door and had to cancel his tour. The physician who brought the injured digit back to health was Maurice Cottle in Chicago, the husband of one of Horowitz's best friends, the pianist Gitta Gradova. Horowitz remained in Chicago for several months. Wanda remained in New York aside from hurried trips to Chicago. Somebody had to look after Sonia.

In 1941 Horowitz rented a house in Los Angeles. He claimed that he had a persistent sore throat, and the California climate would make him more comfortable. Another unstated reason, most likely the real one, was to be near the ailing Rachmaninoff. Once again Wanda and Sonia were uprooted. They joined Horowitz in Los Angeles.

Horowitz and Rachmaninoff resumed their close friendship and also the two-piano playing they had left off in Switzerland in 1937. Their performances went so well that they started inviting small audiences to listen to them. On June 15, 1942, one member of the audience at Rachmaninoff's house was Sergei Bertensson, who later (with Jay Leyda) wrote a well-researched biography of Rachmaninoff. An expatriate Russian who had been an arts administrator in St. Petersburg, Bertensson was friendly with Rachmaninoff and had heard him rave about Horowitz. He never forgot the concert, which he described in the biography:

> Except for members of both families, I was the sole auditor. The program included the Mozart sonata and Rachmaninoff's Second Suite for Two Pianos. It is impossible to word my impression of this event. "Power" and "joy" are the two words that first come to mind—expressive power, and joy experienced by two players, each fully aware of the other's greatness. After the last note no one spoke—time seemed to have stopped.

At another such evening, Bertensson heard the two pianists in Rachmaninoff's own transcription of his orchestral work the *Sym-*

phonic Dances. "The brilliance of this performance was such that for the first time I guessed what an experience it must have been to hear Liszt and Chopin playing together, or Anton and Nikolai Rubinstein."

Rachmaninoff talked very seriously about the two of them giving a two-piano recital in Carnegie Hall, but because of his illness, nothing came of the plan. At least Rachmaninoff could hear Horowitz play the Third Concerto one last time, on August 7, 1942. "One of the greatest moments I ever experienced on the stage came after I played the Rachmaninoff Third Piano Concerto in the Hollywood Bowl," said Horowitz. "William Steinberg conducted. Over 23,000 people came, and when I finished the concerto Rachmaninoff came to the stage and said that I played it the way he had always dreamed it should go." Horowitz was thrilled. But he told friends that Rachmaninoff was merely being nice. "Of course," Horowitz said, "he plays the Third better than I do."

The Horowitz/Steinberg was never recorded, but a few happy collectors have a copy of the May 4, 1941, performance of the Rachmaninoff Third, taken from a New York Philharmonic broadcast performance with Barbirolli. Presumably it would not have been substantially different in conception and execution from the "dream" performance that Rachmaninoff saluted some fifteen months later. It goes at an exceptionally fast clip, much faster than anybody today would dare to play it. Nor is it possible to think of a pianist who could, at that tempo, articulate with the precision that Horowitz brought to it. Yet, with all the speed, Horowitz has time to dwell lovingly on the lyric elements and shape them with a master hand. The dash and élan of the finale are breathtaking. If a performance like this impresses modern listeners as too fast, too virtuosic, it cannot be emphasized often enough that tempos were prevailingly much faster half a century ago, and today's slow tempos actually misrepresent the music.

When Horowitz was notified that Rachmaninoff was dying—he died of cancer on March 28, 1943, at the age of seventy—he canceled over a month of concerts except for an appearance with Toscanini on April 25, and rushed back to Los Angeles to see his friend and mentor for the last time. Rachmaninoff's last words to Horowitz, a few days before his death, were "Good-bye. Good-bye. I will not see you again."

Horowitz was brokenhearted and never really got over it.

Later, when Toscanini died in 1957, Horowitz was shattered, but not even Toscanini's passing left the hole in his life that Rachmaninoff's death did. Toscanini was a sort of Jehovah to Horowitz, a divine presence who could be approached only with awe and reverence, fear and trembling. Rachmaninoff was a friend, a pillar, a surrogate father—and also a colossal pianist who could talk to Horowitz on equal terms. It was Rachmaninoff who was Horowitz's first inspiration when he was a student. It was Rachmaninoff who had been instrumental in pulling him out of his black depression between 1936 and 1938.

"He was like a father to me," Horowitz later said. "He would never let me do anything bad. He always wanted me to play better than anybody else. When Rachmaninoff died I was left without a guide."

After a few months Horowitz picked up his concert life once again. He went at it with a particular kind of fervor because of America's entry into World War II. Horowitz was determined to do what he could for the war effort. After all, America was *his* country. For now he was a United States citizen. He had put in for citizenship shortly after America entered the war, had received his final papers in 1945, and went around telling everybody in his heavy Russian accent how proud he was to be an American.

The Russians were Western allies, and Horowitz started playing contemporary Russian music. He introduced Prokofiev's Sixth, Seventh, and Eighth sonatas to New York in his Carnegie Hall recitals of January 30, 1942, March 14, 1944, and April 23, 1945. (He had previously tried them out on the road.) The Sixth was known as the *War* Sonata because it is supposed to reflect the sufferings of the Russian people during Hitler's invasion of Russia. The Seventh has become one of the more popular pieces in the piano repertoire. Prior to his Carnegie Hall performance, Horowitz played it on January 11 at the Soviet consulate before an audience of about 150. Among the listeners were Toscanini, Bruno Walter, Stokowski, Koussevitzky, the young Leonard Bernstein, and Edgard Varèse. Even for a Horowitz an audience like that must have been daunting.

Prokofiev was not the only contemporary Russian composer programmed by Horowitz. On March 19, 1941, he played Valérie Jelobinsky's *Six Short Studies,* which stayed in his repertoire for just one season and were never again heard, from Horowitz or anybody else. Three works by Dmitri Kabalevsky followed: the Preludes (Op. 38), played on March 4, 1946; the Sonata No. 2 on February 3, 1947; and the Sonata No. 3 on February 2, 1948. (He had recorded the Third Sonata two months previously.) Kabalevsky was then taken much more seriously than he is today. Even in Russia his music is seldom heard anymore. It is skillful but has no individuality, sounding like a combination of Prokofiev and Shostakovich.

The most publicized wartime activity of Horowitz was a concert with Toscanini and the NBC Symphony for the war-bond drive in Carnegie Hall on April 25, 1943. They were heard in the Tchaikovsky Concerto, and the concert brought in an incredible sum for those days—$10,190,045. The concerto was recorded live from the stage. After the concert, Toscanini went to Horowitz's dressing room and kissed his hands. Horowitz also played for such charities as the National Foundation for Infantile Paralysis, the American Red Cross, and Russian War Relief. He even went to naval and military bases and played for the troops—the A flat Polonaise, *Träumerei,* and other short pieces he thought appropriate.

In addition, he maintained a busy touring schedule and worked on a new knock-'em-dead ending for a program. He unveiled it at his Carnegie Hall concert of March 28, 1945, when an astonished audience heard his transcription of Sousa's *The Stars and Stripes Forever.* In this piece, the greatest of all American marches (the greatest of *all* marches?), Horowitz closely followed the score. As he played it, one could hear fifes, trombones, horns. Horowitz made the piano sound like a brass band. It was by far the most popular transcription he ever made. At the premiere, Carnegie Hall all but collapsed from the enormous Horowitz sonorities and the resulting yells, cheers, and general hysteria. Horowitz later said that the Sousa arrangement was a precelebration for the oncoming end of the war. A little more than a month later he played it in Central Park for I Am an American Day.

Travel in wartime could be difficult, but Horowitz stoically accepted the hazards of late trains, inferior food, and sometimes makeshift accommodations. He made one last stab at interesting the American public in a composer he admired. During the 1942–43 season the Horowitz programs contained the Medtner

Piano Sonata (Op. 22). But the music got unvaryingly bad reviews, and this was the last time Horowitz tried to push Medtner.

In 1942 Horowitz made some changes in his management, leaving Judson and going to Annie Friedberg. The veteran Friedberg gave Horowitz more personalized service than the huge Columbia agency did, and she took a smaller cut of his earnings. On the other hand, everybody in the music business knew that Wanda Toscanini Horowitz was the brains behind her husband's business affairs and, indeed, of Annie Friedberg's. Later, Horowitz left Friedberg for David Libidins. He was a Russian-born manager, an extroverted giant of a man with an enormous bass voice. It was said of him that when he whispered in Times Square he could be heard at Battery Park and all the ships at sea. Horowitz felt comfortable with this likable leviathan, all the more because the two could converse in Russian. Horowitz, of course, was the star of the Libidins roster and could be assured of deference and special attention to his demands.

Then Byron Janis entered his life.

12

In Horowitz's Shoes
—and Tails

> But you see, my dear, I get so nervous that I must be able to play
> even if the house should catch on fire. I must be able to play in
> my sleep. I must play it over and over so many times that it must
> be automatic.
> —*Vladimir Horowitz, 1951, to Leonid Hambro*

*B*yron Janis became Horowitz's first pupil. Now Horowitz
was a maestro. Pupils always address their respected mentors as
"Maestro." Of course, all Horowitz pupils were going to be already
finished artists. Horowitz made it clear that he was not going to
teach technique. Anybody who played for him was long past the
stage where a teacher has to do the counting: "ONE and two and
three . . ."

Horowitz later explained that he turned to teaching during the
war years "mostly because I was bored with the kind of music
making I was hearing all around the country. The way performance
was heading did not please me. Everything was beginning to be
dry, metronomic, uninteresting. I missed the panache of the great
pianists, violinists, and singers of the past. I never in my life went

Horowitz at thirteen. At this time he had been at the Kiev Conservatory for four years.

Horowitz's mother, Sophie Horowitz, c. 1915.

Horowitz's uncle Alexander from Kharkov, c. 1910. He was a pupil of Scriabin, a teacher and a critic.

Horowitz's father Samuel, sister Regina (Genya), and brother George. Moscow 1932.

OPPOSITE:
Above, Horowitz, Alexander Glazunov, and Nathan Milstein. The inscription reads: "To dear Vladimir Horowitz in memory of our joint appearance in the concert of December 12, 1923. A devoted admirer of his talent. A. Glazunov, Petrograd 16 Dec. 1923." On this occasion, Horowitz played the Rachmaninoff Third Concerto and the Liszt E flat. Milstein played the Glazunov A minor Concerto.

Below left, Horowitz, c. 1920. The profile bears a slight resemblance to that of Chopin, a fact of which Horowitz was not unaware.

Below right, Horowitz on the occasion of his debut in Berlin, 1926.

The Rubinstein brothers: Nicholas *(left)* and Anton, 1868. Anton, considered the greatest pianist after Liszt, shaped the Russian school of piano playing of which Horowitz was the last direct representative. Nicholas was also a brilliant pianist.

Дорогому Владимиру Горовицу в память совместного выступления в концертѣ 12 Dек. 1923 г.

Искренно преданный почитатель ея таланта

Andante. А. Глазунов.

Петроградъ 16 дек. 1923.

Horowitz, 1928, at the time of his American debut.

Paris, 1929. *From left to right,* Alexander Merovitch, Horowitz, Sascha Greiner.

Horowitz arriving in New York on the *Mauretania* in 1929.

Below left, Vladimir and Wanda Horowitz aboard the SS *Rex* from Italy to New York on the occasion of their honeymoon.

Below right, Horowitz with Mrs. Greiner in New York City, c. 1930.

NEW YORK *TIMES*

Left, Ignaz Paderewski. Horowitz had great respect for the celebrated veteran.

Below, Sergei Rachmaninoff. In many respects he was Horowitz's surrogate father.

Bottom left, Josef Hofmann, considered to be, with Rachmaninoff, one of the two top-ranked pianists of the world.

Bottom right, Ignaz Friedman. Horowitz considered some of his Chopin recordings the finest ever made.

FOUR PHOTOS: STEINWAY & SONS

Above, Artur Schnabel, the leader of the German school. Horowitz had one disastrous lesson with him.

Right, Walter Gieseking, one of the few German pianists Horowitz admired.

Bottom left, Arthur Rubinstein, c. 1930, when he and Horowitz were friends in Paris.

Bottom right, Ferruccio Busoni, who died the year before Horowitz left Russia. Horowitz never met him but constantly played his transcriptions and considered him one of the greatest of all pianists.

Arturo Toscanini, Horowitz, Bruno Walter, 1939. With Walter, Horowitz played the Tchaikovsky and both Brahms concertos.

Below left, Horowitz taking the Oath of Allegiance in Los Angeles, 1942.

Below right, Horowitz with Nathan Milstein in 1950 rehearsing the Brahms D minor Violin Sonata for their only recorded performance together.

Sonia, Wanda, and Vladimir Horowitz at home, c. 1950. On the wall is Picasso's *Acrobat en repos*.

The hands of Vladimir Horowitz.

Left, Mischa Mischakoff, concertmaster, Horowitz, and Fritz Reiner at rehearsal for Rachmaninoff D minor Concerto, 1951.

Below, Wanda Horowitz with Schuyler Chapin and Goddard Lieberson of Columbia Records, 1962. Horowitz had just signed a contract with Columbia.

From left to right, John Steinway, Wanda and Vladimir Horowitz, and Henry Z. Steinway, at that time president of Steinway & Sons, 1965.

Horowitz practicing in Carnegie Hall for his return concert in 1965.
Note the famous flat-fingered technique.

May 9, 1965, arriving at the stage entrance of Carnegie Hall for his
return concert after twelve years away from the stage.

Horowitz at end of his 1967 concert, on the stage of Carnegie Hall.

Below left, Horowitz and Ron Swoboda, outfielder of the New York Mets, on the occasion of Horowitz's first and only baseball game in 1969.

Below right, Sergei Tarnowsky, Horowitz's teacher in Kiev, at the age of ninety in Los Angeles. Four years later he and Horowitz had a pleasant reunion in Pasadena.

Horowitz being greeted by President Carter in the East Room of the White House on February 26, 1978.

Horowitz at his first studio recording in ten years. Thomas Frost, his producer, looks on at this session on September 30, 1985.

Triumphant in Milan, 1985.

Horowitz at the end of the Amsterdam concert in 1986.

In Hamburg, 1986.

Celebrating with Wanda after receiving an honorary medal from the
Mayor of Hamburg in 1986.

Horowitz receiving the Presidential Medal of Freedom from Nancy
Reagan after the 1988 White House concert, as President Reagan looks
on. Wanda Horowitz is at left.

Horowitz signing his records at a New York City record store on October 11, 1989, less than a month before he died. Standing are his business manager, Peter Gelb, and Giuliana Lopes, who worked for the Horowitz family.

The pianist Mordecai Shehori, a friend of Horowitz, took these photos of Horowitz about three weeks before he died.

to many concerts, and now I went to even fewer. Concerts became very boring for me." So Horowitz was "perhaps a little receptive" when he was approached to teach. Perhaps he could give students something of his own methods and philosophy.

In 1944, the sixteen-year-old Janis, a slim, short, nervous-looking boy, played the Rachmaninoff Piano Concerto No. 2 with the Pittsburgh Symphony. His conductor was Lorin Maazel, age fifteen. Horowitz had played in Pittsburgh the previous night and was urged to hear the young pianist. Janis was the protégé of Samuel Chotzinoff, and that carried some weight. Horowitz knew Chotzinoff; he was almost part of the family. Chotzie—everybody called him that—was a pianist who had accompanied Heifetz and Zimbalist and had also been the music critic of the New York *Post*. He had been instrumental in bringing Toscanini to the NBC Symphony in 1937, and as a reward had been given a big job with the radio network. Toscanini was also interested in Janis, who had played the previous year with his orchestra.

Horowitz went to the concert and was impressed. Many years later he told Janis that when he first heard him in Pittsburgh "you reminded me of me as a young man." He went backstage and told Janis to see him in New York, at the Waldorf Towers, where he and Wanda were then living. Janis and Chotzinoff visited Horowitz there, and Horowitz told them he would like to work with the young man as soon as possible. Certain conditions were attached. Janis would have no other teacher. The lessons would have to be paid for, at $100 a session, because Horowitz felt that free lessons were denigrating for him. Teachers should be paid for their services. But the money would be put aside to help the pupil when the time came for a Carnegie Hall debut.

Chotzinoff urged Janis to take advantage of this extraordinary opportunity and Janis went along, "knowing," he later said, "that it would be difficult for me."

His teacher, Adele Marcus at the Juilliard School, could not very well refuse to relinquish her gifted pupil. After all, it was Vladimir Horowitz who was taking over. But she was not happy about it and warned Janis that the Horowitz influence might be too strong for him. She was even less happy after a year or so, when Janis played for her. "She was really upset," Janis said. "She thought I was on the wrong track. She was right in her assessment.

I soon became very disturbed." Marcus had been emphasizing musical sobriety in her work with Janis. Now here was Horowitz teaching him to be a *virtuoso*. Janis was being given a different orientation, and no teacher likes to see that happen to a talented musician he or she had formed.

Horowitz concentrated on certain areas—tone, pedaling, metrical freedom. Janis had never thought much about pedaling, and Horowitz introduced him to an entirely new philosophy, demonstrating how the pedals—left and right working together—could provide color. He showed Janis the polyphony of the pieces he was studying and how the inner voices could be brought out. He wanted Janis to have a big sweep to his playing. "Let's exaggerate," he would say. "On the stage you have to exaggerate. Otherwise it is not very interesting." But he would never illustrate at the keyboard. His theory was that if he played, his pupil would try to copy him. Janis, who had received much stricter, more orthodox training under Marcus, felt "schizophrenic," as he explained in a 1990 interview:

> I understood what he was saying, but I could not control myself and went into strong exaggerations. I overdid it. The interesting thing was that he never, ever, played one note for me during a lesson. Never, ever, ever! But I constantly was hearing him play when it was not lesson time. I was one of the family and I went on tour with him so that I should not miss a lesson. At home he would sit down and play for hours for me, going through the whole piano repertoire. So whatever was gained by his not playing for me during the lesson was undone by my hearing him so much. I knew exactly how he phrased, how he felt about a piece, and it all got into my ear. At that time—I was only seventeen—I did not realize what was happening. Not until later on did I realize I was becoming a copy of Horowitz.

When Janis said he was one of the family, that was literally true. Almost every night he would have dinner with Horowitz and Wanda. Often lessons would be given in the Toscanini house in Riverdale. Janis even accompanied him on tour, the only one of Horowitz's pupils who ever did so, because Horowitz said that he did not want him to miss any lessons. Janis said he felt that Horowitz regarded him as a son. Of course it was inevitable that—gossip in the music world being what it is—there were those who kept hinting that the relationship was maybe a little bit more than paternal.

Janis considered Horowitz a gentle, understanding teacher. He never insisted on anything. He would only suggest. Why not try it this way? That way? Janis remained with Horowitz for about four years, imbibing the big Romantic repertoire that Horowitz assigned him. With Marcus the concentration had been on the Classic repertoire.

After a year or so Horowitz arranged a private recital for Janis at the Ninety-second Street Y. He wanted to see how he would handle himself on the stage. He even presented Janis with a gift of a full-dress suit, one that he had worn in Berlin and had outgrown. Janis played the Bach-Busoni Toccata, Adagio, and Fugue in C; Beethoven's Sonata in A flat (Op. 110); and a Chopin group. Horowitz was pleased and gave him a $500 fee for the concert.

They continued working together until Janis made his Carnegie Hall debut. By this time Janis had an agent, the legendary Sol Hurok. But Horowitz would not allow Hurok to present his protégé until the young man had more experience. He had seen what happened to pianists when they came to Carnegie Hall without having several frequently played programs under their belt. Horowitz insisted that Janis play at least fifty out-of-town concerts before appearing in New York. So Janis toured South America and played in many American cities before the great moment. "Of course Horowitz was absolutely right," Janis said.

Horowitz also cautioned Hurok, Chotzinoff, and Janis, rather naïvely, not to let the young pianist be publicized as the only pupil of Vladimir Horowitz. This was naïve because everybody in music knew that Janis had studied with Horowitz. But Horowitz was worried. "It will kill you," he said. "You will be called a second Horowitz, and that is something you do not want to be." Horowitz added one other thing. "You will make mistakes," Horowitz said, "but they will be *your* mistakes."

On October 30, 1948, Carnegie Hall was packed for Janis's debut. Downes wrote a rave review, and the Janis career was launched. Immediately, Horowitz set him free, telling him that he was now on his own. Janis got married and went on to a brilliant career until arthritis of the hands developed in the 1980s, ending his concert life. He continued to remain close to Horowitz. And never was he accused of being a Horowitz clone.

Looking back on their association, Janis admitted that he had great difficulty escaping Horowitz's influence. "I got confused. It became too hard for me to handle. I had my own way of doing things, and yet what Horowitz taught me made such sense, was so overpowering, that I was torn between the two. I found myself phrasing his way. At one period I kept away from him. He asked me why I stopped playing for him, and I told him that it was because I was becoming too influenced." Janis figured it took him over five years after leaving Horowitz to get out from under Horowitz's spell. He nevertheless concluded that the time spent with Maestro was worth it:

> Definitely. With all the difficulties, with all the struggle to break free of his power, to become Byron Janis, I eventually did find my own style. He was very happy about that. When I would play for him later on he would grin and say, "You are pretty good, you know." We never lost contact, though we did not see each other as much as we used to. I was a pretty busy touring pianist. I remember that when I went to Russia, I telephoned him from Kiev. Horowitz picked up the phone. "Where are you?" I told him I was calling from Russia, from the city where he had grown up. There was a long pause. Then Horowitz said, "From Kiev he calls me. From New York he doesn't." The last five or six years of his life we had a pretty good relationship. It was no longer parent and child. He accepted me as an equal. The last time I saw him we had fun playing two-piano pieces together.

Not long after Janis started working with Horowitz he was no longer playing for him at his hotel. A significant change in Horowitz's life-style occurred in September 1945, when he bought a town house on East Ninety-fourth Street near Central Park in New York. To pay for the house, which cost about $35,000 (when he died in 1989 it would have been worth about $2.5 million), he sold his collection of Fabergé pieces and Russian painted lacquer boxes. Now, for the first time, the Horowitz family had a permanent residence.

But Sonia was not a regular member of the family. She spent most of her time away from home. First she attended a convent school, where she was allowed home only on weekends. Then she was sent to the George Junior Republic School, near Ithaca, where, Wanda said, there were many disturbed children, although she did not realize it at the time. Sonia would come home for vacations, a young rebel, smoking, using foul and abusive language. She was a most unhappy adolescent, and her parents looked at her with dismay. They did not know how to handle the problem, and the girl was permitted to go her own way. She played the piano a bit, painted a bit, wrote poetry. She had talent but never concentrated on anything. In desperation, Wanda sent Sonia to a psychologist, who was unable to do anything for her.

Wanda, at least, tried to do something about her daughter. Horowitz, not an understanding father, ran the other way, retreating into his music.

There was another thing on his mind that nagged at him. The thin-skinned Horowitz was, for the first time, encountering a breed of music critics who despised the Horowitz approach to music.

During the 1940s there was a pronounced change in the nature of the New York music critics—and then of critics around the country, many of whom took their intellectual guidance from the New York critics. There also was an equally pronounced change in the way these new Fauves listened to music.

The older critics in the major cities started to fade away and then disappear after 1940. These were critics who had been born in the nineteenth century, were trained in that tradition, and were thus inherently sympathetic to the Romantic kind of music making that Horowitz represented.

The new school of critics that replaced them was trained differently. To them, Romanticism and virtuosity were dirty words. In the 1940s Mozart and the piano music of Schubert were starting to be rediscovered, atonalism and serialism began to be the new musical language, and new values started to shape musical and critical thinking. To this new age virtuosity was considered vulgar, and any kind of Romanticism was suspect. The musical text started to become more important than the musical meaning. Literalism swept the international musical community. It was the architecture of music that now mattered, not its emotional content.

When Virgil Thomson came to the *Herald Tribune* in 1940 a new critical age was inaugurated. Almost to a man the previous generation of important American music critics had been trained in Germany or were influenced by German Romantic thought. But Thomson's milieu was the chic intellectual and artistic world of Paris in the 1920s. He had been trained not by Rheinberger or

Reinecke but by Nadia Boulanger. His was the age of Poulenc and Stravinsky, not Wagner and Strauss.

Formidably brilliant, he brought to criticism a trenchant, witty style and a large dose of healthy cynicism about what he called "the fifty pieces"—the standard repertoire pieces that were played over and over season after season—and "the business of music." He had relatively little experience with concert life, he frequently reviewed music that he was hearing for the first time (*Die Meistersinger,* say, and a good part of the standard repertoire), and thus he had no icons to worship. In a short time he shook up the American musical establishment, striking out at such sacred cows as Toscanini (an example of the "wow" technique), Sibelius ("vulgar, self-indulgent, and provincial beyond all description"), Heifetz ("silk-underwear music"), and, above all, Vladimir Horowitz.

Yet Thomson could respond to the Horowitz kind of *diablerie.* After Horowitz's performance with Toscanini of the Tchaikovsky Concerto, Thomson wrote in his review of April 26, 1943:

> No pianist since Paderewski in his great days has possessed the incandescent temperament of Mr. Horowitz; and certainly no living virtuoso can approach his mastery of keyboard brilliance. His speed, accuracy, power, control and flamelike musicality are the definition, indeed, today of virtuosity.

But Thomson followed this with a disclaimer: "Applied to music of sober mien they [virtuosos] often overreach themselves and fall short of ultimate musical distinction. Vehicled in Romantic works of passionate *envergure* [scope], they go places."

The fact is that Horowitz represented everything Thomson did not like about Romantic performance practice. Obviously he considered the pianist an intellectual lightweight, and in review after review from 1942 onward he called Horowitz such things as "a master of distortion and exaggeration" interested only in "wowing" the public.

On April 9, 1946, Thomson wrote a critique taken as gospel by many of the new generation of music critics.

In this article Thomson conceded the pianist's technical mastery and the real excitement that he provided. Despite all that, "Horowitz's playing is monotonous and more often than not musically false. He never states a simple melody frankly. He teases it by accenting unimportant notes and diminishing his volume on all the climactic ones. The only contrast to brio that he knows is the affettuoso [affected] style." In the *New Grove Dictionary of Music and Musicians,* Michael Steinberg cribbed Thomson in his Horowitz entry with the statement, "It is nearly impossible for him to play simply, and where simplicity is wanted, he is apt to offer a teasing, *affettuoso* manner or to steamroll the line into perfect flatness."

The *New Grove* was published in 1980, and Steinberg could have backed up his Thomson-based assessment with some of the Horowitz performances of the late 1970s. Horowitz was going through a bad period at that time. But it is difficult to find in Horowitz's playing during the 1940s the kind of "distortion" that Thomson heard. There could be tension verging on neuroticism; there could be a few liberties; there could be fluctuations of tempo not specifically marked in the music. But the liberties and fluctuations were common nineteenth-century practice, and one can only conclude that Thomson did not know much about nineteenth-century Romantic style, and probably would not have responded to it if he did. Always a Francophile, he was oriented toward the clear, objective, lucid French style rather than the generous, colorful Slavic style. His ideal of a fine pianist was E. Robert Schmitz, a French musician completely forgotten today. Another Horowitz basher, B. H. Haggin, took a minor pianist named Webster Aitken as his ideal of music making.

Thus Horowitz started to get bad reviews. The respected pianist Sidney Harrison, writing in the London *Times* in 1951, said that Horowitz was a superpianist—in everything but his Chopin, which was "willful and eccentric." A reviewer in the November 10, 1951, issue of the *New Statesman* called the recording of the Chopin B flat minor Sonata terrible. He complained about "tricks, distortion of rhythm and misplaced bravura." Some critics in Europe and the United States objected strenuously to Horowitz's musical approach when he played the German classics (which were, in any case, only a fragment of his repertoire).

The irony is that the charges critics brought against the Horowitz approach to Beethoven would have disqualified Beethoven himself as a pianist. Beethoven's own way of playing was described by Anton Schindler and Carl Czerny, two of Beethoven's associates who went into great detail about his style—about his metrical freedom, his constant fluctuation of tempo, his rubato, his extreme dynamics. Horowitz, incidentally, had read Schindler and Czerny. One wonders if Thomson had.

Then there was the element of cultural snobbism that swept the international musical life. One heard such comments about any musician as, "Oh, yes, it's all very well that he plays Rachmaninoff, Liszt, and Scriabin. But how can we tell how good a musician he is until we hear him play Mozart and Schubert?" Anybody who timidly suggested the reverse—"Oh, yes, he plays Mozart and Schubert very well, but how good a musician can we tell he is until we hear him play Rachmaninoff, Liszt, and Scriabin?"—would have been branded a musical yahoo. Yet it takes just as much imagination, skill, and inner resource to play Liszt well as to play Mozart well. Perhaps more, considering how few great Liszt pianists we have today compared with the large number of Mozart pianists (though a strong case can be made that today's celebrated Mozart specialists are stylistically wrong in their rigid, literal approach).

But whatever the critics wrote, Horowitz in the 1940s was still a legend to the younger generation of pianists. He remained so as long as he lived, and will remain so after his death. As Claudio Arrau noted in Joseph Horowitz's *Conversations with Arrau,* "There is in the life of every piano-mad youngster a time of absolute Horowitz-worship." In the same book Garrick Ohlsson, winner of the Chopin Competition in Warsaw, 1970, said of his days at Juilliard: "I was a little bundle of energy and very much a Vladimir Horowitz imitator, like so many pianists are." Julius Katchen, considered one of the best young American pianists, spoke about Horowitz in a BBC interview on February 27, 1968 (a year before his death at the age of forty-three). "My generation," he said, "is a continuation of the Russian virtuoso tradition, largely because of the presence of Horowitz in America." The wiser of the young pianists resisted the impulse to ape the Horowitz mannerisms, realizing that Horowitz had a style that was too idiosyncratic for them. Trying to copy him was an impossible quest; and Horowitz, who constantly discouraged his pupils from copying him, knew it. "They think they sound like me but they don't."

The pianists after the Katchen-Ohlsson generation also came under the Horowitz spell. "He touched every musician who ever heard him," said Murray Perahia. "He brought the idea of excitement in piano playing to a higher pitch than anyone I've ever heard," said Emanuel Ax. "He was like a demon barely under control out there on stage," said André Watts.

And, of course, Horowitz could do no wrong as far as the public was concerned. The announcement of a Horowitz concert automatically meant a sold-out house. His popularity was reflected in his fee. Every year the Horowitz fee went up, and he became the highest-paid instrumentalist in the world. In 1950 he was in the $5,000 range. Then his fee ascended to $8,000, then higher. He was playing about thirty-five concerts a year. He could have played more but, remembering his problems in 1934 when he was playing seventy and eighty a season, thought that was enough.

Horowitz and Wanda became a legend in the business; they knew to a penny what was going in and coming out of the box office, and woe to anybody who tried to cheat them. On April 20, 1951, the *Times* carried a story about a suit Horowitz had brought against Heck Brothers, who ran the Carnegie Hall box office. Ever since the hall had opened in 1891 the box office had been run as a concession by the Heck family. Horowitz accused the company of a false accounting of his concerts. When the Heck books were examined, it was found that the company had defrauded not only Horowitz; it also had defrauded the U.S. Government of nearly $150,000 in entertainment taxes. Box-office managers around the country were very careful with the Horowitz account after that.

Though Horowitz and Wanda continued to operate as a business team, their private life started getting into a mess. For a few years, from 1949 to 1953, Horowitz separated from Wanda. Friends said that they were at each other's throats mostly because of the problems with Sonia. There were violent arguments and finally Horowitz moved out. He lived alone in New York, first at the Elysée Hotel, then the Volney. Yet Horowitz and Wanda continued to be in constant touch, spending hours with each other on the phone.

One of his good friends at that time was Oscar Levant, a skillful pianist, wit, film star, and man-about-town. Levant amused Horowitz. They would do outrageous things at the piano, each trying to outprank the other, improvising jazz pieces into which classical themes were inserted, even to playing with their backsides. Both liked jazz piano (Levant often toured the country playing the Gershwin *Rhapsody in Blue* and Concerto in F), and they would work up arrangements of popular tunes.

Levant, a self-destructive talent, had all kinds of psychological hang-ups, enough to make Horowitz seem a picture of mental health. The playwright Sam Behrman said that "there's nothing wrong with Oscar that a really first-class miracle couldn't cure." Levant described himself as "a neurotic basket case" and spent a good part of his life in psychiatric treatment and in asylums. He drove managers crazy by canceling concerts at whim. There were those who claimed that Levant would spend hours dreaming up ways to cancel concerts. Horowitz did his share of canceling in those days. Levant was amused that where he would give two weeks' notice before canceling, Horowitz would cancel at the very last minute. He told Horowitz they should take a joint ad in the trade publication *Musical America:* VLADIMIR HOROWITZ AND OSCAR LEVANT AVAILABLE FOR A LIMITED NUMBER OF CANCELLATIONS.

In his search for contemporary music that he liked, Horowitz found only one important work aside from the three Prokofiev sonatas he had introduced. It was the Piano Sonata by Samuel Barber. The world premiere took place in Havana on December 9, 1949, and then Horowitz tried it out in several American cities before taking it to Carnegie Hall on January 23, 1950. But a short time before, on January 4, Horowitz gave a private performance in the music store of G. Schirmer (the firm that published the sonata) for a small, distinguished audience of composers and critics. He dazzled everybody with the new work.

One of the critics asked Horowitz if it was as difficult as it sounded. Horowitz thought a bit.

"Not very," he said. "About like the Chopin B minor Sonata."

Most pianists approach the Chopin B minor Sonata with fear and dread.

It was around that time that Horowitz first encountered John F. Pfeiffer, known to everybody as Jack. Pfeiffer was to become his record producer and one of his closest friends for many years. He had studied music in Kansas and Arizona (piano and oboe), had spent the war years working on secret electronic projects, mostly radar research, and after the war got a degree in electrical engineering from Columbia University. He also did some composing, especially in the new medium of electronic music.

He joined RCA in 1949 as a design and development engineer. But because of his solid knowledge of classical music, he soon became a producer of the Red Seal Records for RCA Victor. He was a handsome, bright, articulate young man who knew everything about recording—the electronic part of it (he was one of the engineers who developed the Dynagroove LP disc for RCA), the acoustical, the mechanical and, later, the new digital recording process. As a producer he worked with nearly all of the eminent musicians under contract to RCA, including Toscanini, Heifetz, Rubinstein, Reiner, Landowska, Cliburn, Stokowski, and Ormandy. Widely respected in the industry, he eventually became the executive producer of Red Seal Records, Artists and Repertoire.

His first encounter with Horowitz came in 1950. In December Horowitz made a recording at Hunter College, and Pfeiffer was the producer. Was Pfeiffer nervous?

> Oh, good Lord, yes! I was petrified. And at that period Horowitz was nervous, too. He seemed jittery and uncomfortable. He would play a couple of takes all the way through and walk out. He arrived well prepared and knew exactly what he wanted to do. There was no nonsense about it. We had to get the acetates of the session to his house that evening, so we could both go through them. He would indicate which of the takes he preferred. Or if he didn't like any of them, he would go back and redo it. We would sit there listening to the acetates and he would ask me what I thought. Me! My God! It was all very straightforward but for me very traumatic. I had such respect for him. He was one of the giants of all time.

In 1951 Horowitz rented a vacation house in Fire Island, New York, a popular summer resort on the south shore of Long Island. There he made friends with Leonid Hambro, who at that time was a staff pianist at WQXR, the classical-music station of the New York *Times*. Horowitz's summer house was behind the tennis courts, and Hambro made a point of wandering there every day to eavesdrop on his practicing.

"One day," Hambro said, "I walked down the boardwalk, and there he was sitting and looking at the passersby." Hambro introduced himself. Horowitz got excited. "Your recording of Prokofiev's Sixth Sonata is the best I ever heard. In the last movement, that passage, how do you do the fingering?" Hambro told Horowitz that he had, literally, dreamt that fingering. "Very frequently," he told Horowitz, "I dream fingerings. In my business I have to play about two hours of new music every week, so I try to find fingerings for accuracy."

Horowitz was enchanted.

"That's very interesting," he said. "You know, I dream fingerings too. I thought I was the only one." Horowitz went on to say that he spent a great deal of time on fingerings, especially fingerings that would give the best sound and facilitate the execution of the piece—even if it meant cheating.

Horowitz and Hambro had fun talking about cheating. All pianists cheat, and they gleefully tell each other about their ways of simplifying hard passages so that nobody realizes what is being done. Horowitz's attitude, said Hambro, was, "You know how hard it is to play the piano? Why should you make it harder? Better to make it easier." Thus in octave passages he demonstrated to Hambro how he might play only a single note, or rearrange a difficult right-hand episode so that the left hand carried some of the weight. "He understood the sound of the piano," said Hambro. "He understood density, he understood registration, he understood overtones. He put them all to use and was always after simplifications. 'When can I take a note in the right hand that is written for the left?' Or the other way around."

Hambro once got up enough nerve to ask Horowitz why he played the piano "so wrong." He was referring to Horowitz's unconventional hand positions. Horowitz grinned and said, "Bad habit. I have been playing this way all my life and I cannot change now. Anyway, though I know many think it is wrong, for me it works." Said Hambro:

> He had a sound in his ear, and whatever means he used to get the result was fine with him. He would play phrases over and over again, making minute changes in dynamics or color. He was always after amounts of sound. His sense of balancing the various voices, the bass notes against the treble, the tenor voices, whatever it was, amounted to quanta of sound. Perhaps he was too interested in minutiae. In certain pieces that needed a sweep he might stumble and lose the long line because he was too preoccupied with detail. The flow of the music was subservient to the pianism. Horowitz was primarily a *pianist*. Perhaps *too* much a pianist. I asked him why he did not play more simply in small cantabile pieces, such as the *Träumerei*, which in some performances he overplayed and sounded artificial. Horowitz

seriously considered the question. "I keep saying to myself I should do that," he said, "but then I get on stage and I can't do it."

Hambro once heard him practicing a difficult section of a piece, one that ran up and down the keyboard. "After a while I started counting how many times he repeated it, and I stopped at ninety-nine." Horowitz told Hambro that at one time he had *really* practiced very hard. But, he said, luck enters into stage appearances. "You can take a difficult piece and master it at home, but when you get on stage and play it, if it really comes off the way you want it to come off, you are lucky." Horowitz went to the piano and played a tricky spot in Schumann's *Etudes symphoniques,* which, incidentally, he never played in America. "I practiced this passage, and I practiced, and when I would go to play I could never guarantee that I would play it right. When it came out right I was just lucky." He said that the success of a concert was a mixture of hard work and luck. "That's what he said. But," said Hambro, "it was not luck. I heard him practice, and his success came from the fact that he was willing to pay the dues."

Later that year Horowitz went to England, playing the Rachmaninoff Third with the Royal Philharmonic under Walter Susskind on October 8, and followed it with two solo recitals. The concerto was enthusiastically received by the British daily press, as were the recitals. Some critics in the weekly publications, however, had tart words for Horowitz's Chopin, which was too "eccentric" for them. From London, Horowitz went to Paris, conquering the Parisian audience as always but not, this time, all of the critics. Bernard Gavoty in particular wrote a nasty review.

One of the biggest musical events of 1953 was the Horowitz Silver Jubilee Concert on January 12, twenty-five years to the day after his Carnegie Hall debut in the Tchaikovsky with Beecham. The celebration was given as a Pension Fund concert of the New York Philharmonic, which netted $21,000—a considerable sum in those days. George Szell conducted, replacing an indisposed Dmitri Mitropoulos. Downes compared the concerto performance with the 1928 debut. He claimed to see "a ripening of the pianist's perception" and cited Horowitz's greater authority and freedom:

> The power and sweep of it took the audience completely
> by storm. We do not remember any single concert in the

twenty-five years [since the Horowitz debut] when an audience remained so long after the program, splitting its palms and remaining on its feet, cheering wildly. But this power—not merely astounding physical strength and, when necessary, speed, but inherent power—was by no means the sum of it. Mr. Horowitz achieved a wealth of color and nuance, and command of the subtlest shades as well as the broadest brush strokes, which were not his in nearly equal measure twenty-five years ago. . . .

One feels sure that not everything went exactly as it had been decided in rehearsal, that the torrent of the music carried the interpreter, too, on its crest. And that released the irresistible forces of the interpretation, and by the very fact of this excitement and grandeur made the performance gigantic, unpolished, imprudent and overwhelming.

The concerto appearance was followed by a Carnegie Hall recital on February 25. The program contained two works Horowitz had never played in public—Schubert's posthumous B flat Sonata and the Scriabin Ninth. The Schubert and Scriabin pieces had been tried out in recitals around the country but were really programmed with New York in mind. The Schubert was a deliberate challenge. Horowitz was going to show the public that Serkin and the younger generation (who adored the last three Schubert sonatas) had no monopoly on the B flat Sonata.

The attempt misfired. The audience loved it, but the Schubert was not well received by critics and many of Horowitz's colleagues. It ran counter to everything learned musicians understood as correct Schubert playing. It was full of nuances that were considered excessively Romantic, and Horowitz was in effect advised by his critics to stick to music he knew something about.

The reviews came as a shock to him. Horowitz had put a great deal of thought and work into this interpretation and believed he had something legitimate to say about the music—as indeed he did. Some years from now, when performance practice of the 1820s has been more thoroughly analyzed, the Horowitz recording of the posthumous Schubert B flat may well stand out as the poetic, imaginative performance it is.

Horowitz at that time was on one of his manic-depressive swings. Despite the animal excitement he could still bring to his music, he was tired, bored, and, as Pfeiffer had noticed, nervous.

He became prone to tantrums. He also thought he was starting to suffer from colitis, and that terrified him. An attack during a performance would have been too embarrassing for him to bear. He became moody and depressed. His repertoire shrunk. Horowitz-watchers noticed that the same pieces were turning up year after year with distressing regularity. One wondered how many times he could play the Chopin G minor Ballade or A flat Polonaise without going through them as a boring, mechanical exercise.

Horowitz took care of the problem his own way. Not very long after the Silver Jubilee concerts he disappeared, not to be seen on the concert stage for another twelve years.

13

The Lazy Life

They always listened to how fast I could play octaves but they didn't listen to music anymore. It was boring. I played for two hours but they only remembered the last three minutes of the concert. I felt dissatisfied with what I was doing and what I felt I had to do to fulfill my own identity as a musician.
—*Vladimir Horowitz, giving one reason for his retirement*

*T*welve years: 1953 to 1965. For twelve years the most popular pianist since Paderewski hid, in effect, behind closed doors. The public knew that he was alive because occasionally a new recording appeared, but after a while the name of Vladimir Horowitz began to mean less and less. The feeling in musical circles was that he would never again play. His friend Abram Chasins told all within hearing that Horowitz was finished, dead in the water. To everybody, it was a mystery. What tremendous force was it that could paralyze so great a pianist at the height of his career?

Eventually Horowitz gave reasons for his long retirement, but those were long after the fact and nowhere near the full story. During his years away from the public he lived quietly, seldom leaving his house, and not until he was ready to play again did he give the world an idea of what had gone through his mind.

The official Horowitz explanation was given in an interview twelve years later with Howard Klein of the New York *Times,* which appeared on May 9, 1965. "For thirty-three years," Horowitz told Klein, "I traveled—thirty-three years of sitting on trains and going to some small towns. I can't read on trains because the movement bothers my vision. I get there early for the concert and go to a movie. Believe me, I was tired of all this." Many busy touring artists go through a similar experience. They begin to feel like trained monkeys on a treadmill, performing the same tricks over and over again, unable to relax or find pleasure in what they are doing. After a while they just go through the motions, to the detriment of their art.

Thus Horowitz was talking honestly to Klein, and his rationale was true enough as far as it went. In 1953 he was bored: bored with music, bored with the routine of travel-hotel-concert-travel-hotel-concert, bored with himself and with his audiences.

But more. The pattern of 1936–38 was repeating itself. Again there was a search for identity. Again there was self-loathing mixed with self-pity. The bad reviews he received for his Schubert B flat had shaken his self-confidence, with perhaps a childish automatic reaction: "They don't like me? I'll show them! They'll be sorry when I'm dead."

So again there was the chasm between what Horowitz was and what he secretly wanted to be. He was torn two ways, and the result was a severe emotional disturbance.

It was the Serkin syndrome once again, though this time Serkin's name did not come up. What Horowitz wanted more than anything was to be accepted as a great musician rather than a flashy virtuoso. Yet, he found, he was not strong enough to keep away from the flashy kind of music his public demanded as the last piece in his recitals. So, as always, he gave his public what it wanted.

Horowitz blew his dilemma all out of proportion. Romantic pianists of his generation (and of today for that matter) nearly always ended a recital with a piece of pyrotechnical splendor. It was not a law writ on tablets, however, and Horowitz could have played whatever he pleased. But for some reason he refused to realize that his public would gladly take whatever he offered it, anything from Scarlatti to Rachmaninoff, *anything*, as proved when he dropped the virtuoso stunts from his repertoire.

But instead of scrapping the kind of music that had become offensive to him, he simply quit altogether.

There was one other deep-seated reason for the retirement that he did not publicly discuss. In the early 1950s he began having intestinal spasms, which were diagnosed as colitis. That would be enough to scare any public figure. Horowitz's problem was known to his friends, and some shrugged it off as psychosomatic. But Jack Pfeiffer sometimes saw Horowitz double up in pain. "It was real. There was no nonsense about it," said Pfeiffer. "He was sick and he was afraid he was going to get sicker." Giving concerts with that ailment was an impossibility for Horowitz. Suppose he had an attack on stage? Even worse, suppose he cramped up while he was playing a concerto?

Yet Wanda—they were living together again in 1953—believed there was nothing wrong with Horowitz. He was simply the victim of doctors, she thought, and she insisted that the colitis was all autosuggestion and that his psychiatrist was to blame. Horowitz had been seeing a psychiatrist since 1945. In those days everybody seemed to be going through Freudian analysis. It was the fashionable thing to do, and the intellectual buzzwords at that time were id, ego, superego, anal fixation, and the rest of the psychoanalytic jargon.

Wanda developed an abiding hatred for psychiatrists and other members of the medical profession. They had not helped Sonia, they were not helping her husband, they were costing a fortune, and Wanda cursed them with all the fervor of her Toscanini blood. She believed that Horowitz was taken in, and she was voluble on the subject. Everybody was being analyzed in 1945, she said. "If you had a cold, why do you have a cold? Because your grandmother had an affair when you were a child and it stuck in your subconscious." In New York, Horowitz was with the same psychiatrist, Dr. Lawrence Kubie, for many years, and Wanda thought he was crazier than his patients. He never did one thing for Volodya, she fervently insisted. "Not one thing!"

Wanda believed that the colitis attacks claimed by Horowitz were in the nature of grandmother's love affair. But whether they were or were not psychosomatic, Horowitz suffered. It took about five years for the colitis to be cleared up. Horowitz's friends, who followed the progress of his treatments, were half amused, half frightened. They felt that Horowitz was putting himself into the hands of quacks. One of his physicians, for instance, recommended a diet of nothing but mashed potatoes. Horowitz stuck with that for a while. Finally a saner diet and the avoidance of stress associated with the concert life helped him back to health.

But still he showed no signs of resuming his career. If anybody suggested that Horowitz return to the stage he would say: "One more year. Give me one more year." That "one more year" kept stretching on and on.

For the first six months or so he sat at home, sulking and brooding, not even touching the piano. Wanda did her best to give him the peace of mind he so obviously needed. Then friends started to visit. Among them was the ever-faithful Milstein, who would drop in and try to cheer Horowitz up whenever he was in New York.

"People say I was Horowitz's closest friend," said Milstein. "That is not exactly true. Horowitz was like a brother to me, and that is a different thing. Friends give and take from each other. Volodya took but did not give. That was the way he was made, and I accepted it, the way a man accepts the faults of a brother he loves."

It was an observation that others in the Horowitz circle would endorse. You had to accept Horowitz for what he was. He was entirely self-centered, in love only with himself and the piano. Pfeiffer, always in constant attendance on Horowitz, said, "I don't think he had feeling for anyone." Much the same could be said about Wanda's relations with people. "In all the years I knew her," a woman in the Horowitz circle said, "she never once asked me how I was. There was never any concern. All she wanted to talk about were *her* problems."

If nothing else, Horowitz's retirement brought him closer to Wanda than they had ever been, and they never again were to be separated. The relationship between Horowitz and his wife was a continuing topic of conversation among Horowitz-watchers. Most of the people interviewed for this book would not, however, let their names be used when the topic of Volodya and Wanda came up. "Don't you dare mention my name!" Wanda evoked strong reactions. Some considered her a saint, others a monster. One person called the Volodya-Wanda union "a marriage made in hell."

Wanda was not everybody's favorite woman. She was tough and smart and could be abrasive and abusive. She was highly emotional and excitable. She also could be sweet, and there were those who liked her very much. But even those approached her with care. "A dangerous woman," said one of the pro-Wanda group. "She could chop your head off. She could drop you for no good reason that you ever found out. She had a flaming temper, a sharp tongue. A strong-minded woman, very. And mercurial. You never knew where you stood with her. But she was intelligent and amusing. In a funny kind of way I was fond of her. Really fond. I loved her when she was talking about somebody she did not like. When she was at her bitchiest, she knew how bitchy she was being, and a glint of amusement would come into her eyes. She knew that I knew, and we would break into laughter."

Wanda was always very conscious of being the daughter of Arturo Toscanini and the wife of Vladimir Horowitz. She expected to be treated accordingly. The proprieties had to be observed. One did not visit the Horowitz home in sweatpants or blue jeans. Proper attire and manners were demanded. Wanda expected to be deferred to. "When you visited the Horowitz home," said a member of the circle, "you were expected to feel that you were on Mount Olympus with the gods—two gods, Volodya and Wanda. And you were expected to worship."

Yet Wanda was, despite her toughness, insecure. Some of the outrageous things she sometimes said to Horowitz in public (such as: "As a person I do not think much of you, but as a pianist you are pretty good") may have resulted from the necessity of asserting her own ego, of not being swamped by the Horowitz ego.

One of her major concerns was the constant worry about people using the two of them. She was especially wary of the Horowitz pupils. That went for Volodya too, but more for Wanda. She hated the idea of pianists who played only a few times for Horowitz going around calling themselves pupils.

They fought a great deal, always in French. "The more he yelled, the calmer she got, and vice versa," one observer said. "The more she yelled the calmer he got, cool and quiet. Horowitz was used to it. 'Her father was like that too,' he would say." Horowitz and Wanda sometimes fought even in the presence of relative strangers. "She drives me crazy," he told one of his pupils. But, then again, he drove her crazy. "They both had a temper that could explode," said another of Horowitz's pupils. "Once they had a violent argument. She stormed out of the room and Horowitz looked at me and said, 'Not an easy life. She's not as bad as you hear her right now. Not as bad.'"

There were periods when she was not on speaking terms with him. Once Horowitz was trying a piano on the stage of Carnegie Hall before a small invited audience. He started playing, stopped and asked Wanda how it sounded. Wanda, talking with somebody, did not answer. Horowitz asked her again, more loudly. Wanda never stopped talking. Horowitz resignedly said, "I guess she's not speaking to me today." In the last few years of his life they achieved a more tranquil relationship, though even then there could be wild outbursts, mostly from Wanda. Horowitz would shrug his shoulders. "I am too old to fight," he told a friend.

She always spoke her mind. Here are some random Wanda-isms. In the 1940s she invited her father for dinner. Toscanini was feeling sorry for himself and kept saying "Vecchio uomo, vecchio uomo"—"Old man, old man." Said Wanda, "Papa, don't advertise it. We know it anyway." During the Russian trip in 1986 there was a party at the ambassador's residence, and some pretty heavyweight Americans and Russians, eighty or ninety of them, including the grandson of Tolstoi, were present. Speeches were made. Wanda rose, demanded silence and made her little speech. "I want everybody to know," she said, "that these people here in the Soviet Union, these poor people, they had nothing under the czar." Pause. "Now they have even less." There was a sudden hush in the room. Ambassador Hartman blanched. She went to a recital played by Nathan Milstein. He did not have his usual pianist. Wanda rose from her box after listening to an accompaniment she thought disgraceful and loudly said to the stage: "Get yourself a different accompanist." In 1987 in Milan, at a press conference where Horowitz was surrounded by European journalists, Wanda said disgustedly, "Always the same questions," and advised Horowitz to take the Fifth Amendment. At a Horowitz press conference in Cleveland she commented: "*He's* in top form and *we're* all nervous wrecks." On the videotape of the Emmy-award–winning film, *The Last Romantic,* made in the Horowitz living room in 1985, she and Jack Pfeiffer are onscreen. From the rear is heard an anonymous voice: "Jack, what do you think people mean when they say Mr.

Horowitz is at home with Schumann?" Before Pfeiffer could answer Wanda blurted out: "They were both crazy," and then looked
very pleased with herself. No harm intended; she had just released
a Wandaism.

Yes, Wanda was a handful. Yet all are agreed that Horowitz
was lost without her. Theirs was a symbiotic relationship. He relied
very much on her judgment, on the position of the piano in a
concert hall, on the way he played, on the smooth operation of his
home, everything. And she gloried in the aura of being the wife of
Vladimir Horowitz. She needed to take care of him and was fiercely
protective. Horowitz was not easy to live with. Yet she catered to
him, mothered him, and, said one friend, "was his slave. She never
stopped pampering him. Her whole life seemed to be spent in
getting the right kind of help in the house. She *needed* to be en-
slaved. It was a carryover from Papà, who expected everybody to
heed his slightest wish. She was brought up to take care of a genius."

"I admired her tremendously," said a woman who had known
her for several decades. "She had a terrific sense of humor and could
be totally unpretentious. Look what she put up with! First her
father and then this *creature*. She found relaxation with her dogs,
mostly French poodles. What she did to sustain life was nothing
short of amazing. They say she was bitchy. Is that bad? She had
enough on her mind to be bitchy. And her suspicious mind? Why
not? People were always trying to get things from her and Volodya.
She had a right to be eternally suspicious. And it was so frustrating
for her, this long retirement of her husband. Would he ever get his
act together? Here was Volodya, brilliant, amusing, the world's
greatest pianist, wasting his life, stretched out on a sofa and not
doing anything. Yes, he was brilliant. Yes, yes, yes! I think he
pretended sometimes to be a little dense, but always there was this
thing clicking away, remembering everything and filing away
things."

Some family friends said that they really were very fond of
each other. Others said that maybe they liked each other—at a
distance. Another theory was that Wanda was not in love with him
but with his piano playing. Nevertheless, the consensus was that
they were lost without each other. Said one musician who had been
part of their circle for a long time:

It is true that they had a lot of problems with each other, as so many married couples do after so many years. There could be anger in their relationship, but there also could be genuine affection. Both were very strong-minded characters, and there were bound to be clashes. She was very good; she was always there. She was the one he trusted and relied upon. During that twelve-year absence she felt she was more needed than ever before, and that in a way was good for her, no matter how much he drove her crazy. She was extremely protective, perhaps overprotective. You got the feeling she was constantly hovering over him. That upset Volodya. He wanted her to be there when he needed her, but he didn't want her to be there when he didn't want her there. It was an impossible situation and I don't see how she could ever live with it. Her own experiences with her father had been traumatic, and after that in a way all men were problematic for her.

One intimate of the family insisted that Wanda was much more neurotic than Horowitz. At the beginning of their marriage, he said, "certainly they were interested in each other. They once took a bicycling trip through Italy, not long after they were married, bicycling all day. They did things like that together, and you don't do that if you have a marriage for show or for convenience. There must have been a genuine romantic involvement."

Then, he postulates, the marriage developed into a neurotic need on both their parts. Horowitz was well aware of Wanda's makeup and personality, her quirks and needs. He analyzed her behavior very accurately, his friend thought. Horowitz appreciated the fact that she was not getting enough attention; she was "only" the daughter of the great Toscanini, "only" the wife of the great Horowitz. When she put on that stern face and started demanding things and throwing her weight around, Horowitz understood that meant she needed attention. As one friend explained:

The people who knew her only slightly regarded her as this tough bitch, witch or whatever. In actuality she was insecure, soft, and she pulled out the big guns when she couldn't assert her own individuality the way he could. Horowitz was accustomed to being obeyed. "We do it this way," and it would be done this way. She couldn't do that and it built up inside. Then the Toscanini in her came out. She's also shy. She's not good with people, not good at parties, she feels that she's there only because she is married to Vladimir Horowitz. Her self-esteem is low and always has been. That is her basic problem. She was beaten down by her father; hardly anything she did pleased him. Horowitz really knew her problems. She was sometimes very cruel to him. She could be self-destructive and she needed to make herself unhappy. This manifested itself in the way she found fault with everything, and in her screaming tantrums.

Yet there was a side of Wanda that few people knew anything about. "She impresses as hard as granite," said one longtime intimate, "and yet I know that she anonymously helped many deserving people with money. She also donated her services to institutions that she believed in, as when she spent some time at the Harlem School of the Arts when Dorothy Maynor was running it." Maynor was a black soprano who had a brilliant recital career before founding the Harlem school in 1963 and devoting the rest of her life to it.

Wanda expected to be obeyed without question. When Horowitz played in Chicago in the 1982–83 season—a disastrous tour, when he was under medication—she did not feel up to going with him and asked Jack Pfeiffer, as a personal favor, to go in her stead. "And call me after the concert." Going to Horowitz's hotel room after the concert, in the elevator, Horowitz said, "Don't call Wanda. I will call her." Which he did. The next day Wanda called Pfeiffer. "Why didn't you call me up after the concert?" Pfeiffer explained that Volodya had asked him not to. "Oh! You think more of him than you do of me? Obviously you are a better friend of his than you are of mine. Good-bye." She didn't talk to Pfeiffer for months.

On the whole it was not a happy home. The grim presence of Wanda, with her unpredictable temper, inspired fear. People who worked there had to tread very cautiously. "What I noticed," said a woman who was engaged by the Horowitzes, "was the constant tension in the house. But when Wanda went away, to Italy or to her summer place, all of a sudden there was laughter on Ninety-fourth Street. Horowitz suddenly became relaxed, all of us from the kitchen up were relaxed, and Horowitz would giggle at us or make jokes. When Wanda returned the gloom descended. Yet they were complementary in many ways, and Horowitz relied a great deal on her musical judgment."

Immediately after his 1953 retirement Horowitz did nothing. But after a while a way of life developed. His daily routine consisted of getting up around 11, having breakfast around 11:30, going back to his room for a rest, then coming downstairs in the early afternoon in his robe and pajamas to spend an hour or two at the piano or play vocal records. His favorite singer was the Italian baritone Mattia Battistini (1856–1928), who specialized in bel canto roles. That meant incredible breath control and the agility of a coloratura soprano. Battistini was by far the greatest of his kind. By modern standards he took musical liberties, and Horowitz loved them. When he began seeing people he would play "A tanto amor" from Donizetti's *La Favorita* to pupils and other musicians and point out why Battistini did such and so. It did not in the least disturb Horowitz that Battistini took liberties because what he did had an exquisite rightness of its own. The ornate fioritura passages had a virtuoso's ease but, explained Horowitz, were always in good taste. Horowitz would marvel at the felicity of expression and say that any instrumentalist would envy the delicacy of the phrasing. Horowitz loved bel canto operas, and it was not for nothing that many considered him a bel canto pianist.

After the piano or the sessions with old singers Horowitz would go upstairs to have another rest. Lunch was served at 2:30. Then still another rest. At 4:30 he would get dressed and go out for a walk. He thought that walking an hour a day was good for him. When he returned, he took another rest before dinner. After dinner, around 9:30, he was ready for social activities, often involving a canasta game. He seldom went to bed before 1 or 2 A.M.

Cards were a part of his life. Horowitz loved to play canasta, and he played a highly determined, competitive game. It was one of the few outlets he had to rid himself of aggressions. Regular evenings were set aside for the sessions. Players generally included Wanda, Sally Horwich, a close friend of Wanda's who lived down the block, and the pianist Constance Keene.

Keene and her husband, the pianist Abram Chasins, were at that time part of the Horowitz circle. A virtuoso pianist, at the age of twenty-three she substituted for an indisposed Horowitz at a recital in Springfield, Massachusetts. She got very favorable reviews, and a lengthy interview in the New York *Herald Tribune,* all of which gave her career a big boost. She admitted to being a good canasta player, and she said that Horowitz was not bad. He was cagey, and would sometimes try to talk her out of a play that would be unfavorable for him. He simply hated to lose.

The thing she liked most about the canasta sessions was the post–cards routine. The game started around 9:30. Around midnight, after it had broken up, Horowitz and Keene would go to the piano. She might play, and he would offer suggestions. He wanted people to think that he never practiced, but many times he showed Keene exercises he had devised for himself: exercises for the little finger, or for chords, or double notes, or whatever, and he would demonstrate them to Keene for twenty minutes or so. Then he would play. "Connie, you would like to hear my new Clementi sonata?" He would play it, pointing out its beauties and anticipations of Beethoven and other composers.

After Horowitz got over his initial depressive period visitors would drop in—Russian musicians who were passing through New York, young people to play for him who had been recommended by musicians Horowitz trusted, veterans who interested Horowitz. One such veteran was Isidor Philipp, then in his nineties. Philipp, born in 1863, was a famous pianist and teacher who had been a professor at the Paris Conservatoire for some forty years. Among his pupils were Guiomar Novaes and Jeanne-Marie Darré. Philipp died in 1958 after falling down a metro staircase in Paris. Horowitz was charmed with the old man and the stories he told about legendary musical figures. Philipp, who had heard Horowitz play the Tchaikovsky B flat minor Concerto, said to him: "You know, when I worked with Peter on this concerto in the Champs-Elysées he told me to play the cadenza very brilliantly." Horowitz said, "Peter who?" Philipp said, "Tchaikovsky."

Royalty met royalty when Arthur Rubinstein and his wife, Aniela, visited the Horowitzes off and on during the retirement years. Horowitz and Rubinstein had grown cool toward each other during their Paris years and had not seen each other for a long time. Meanwhile Rubinstein had returned to America in 1937 and created a sensation. All of a sudden he was alongside Horowitz in popularity. When they made peace, Horowitz said, "Rubinstein told me that he had been jealous of me for fifteen years, because I had a natural technique which he didn't have."

If Horowitz is quoting Rubinstein accurately, it was a strange statement, because if there was one thing the young Rubinstein had it was a natural technique, as his recording of the Liszt Tenth Rhapsody and other works amply testify. He made those from 1928 to 1937, before he was the great Arthur Rubinstein. Rubinstein always claimed that he had been a sloppy pianist before he married; that not until then did he buckle down and really practice. Nonsense. The fact is that in later life he never had the technique that he displayed in his early recordings. He was always capable of finger slips in his playing because he never practiced very much; but there was never a doubt about Rubinstein being a natural technician.

There was inevitably going to be friction between the two men who developed into the greatest and most popular Romantic pianists of their time after the disappearance of the previous generation of Romantic giants—Rachmaninoff, Hofmann, Friedman, Lhevinne, Godowsky, and the others. Each of the two men wanted the throne occupied by the world's greatest pianist, but thrones are built for one person and in the public eye it was Horowitz who was king.

The two men did not like each other very much, as Rubinstein made clear in his autobiography. On the surface they were friends and observed the usual courtesies, but their personalities clashed and there could never be a real meeting of minds. John Steinway warned Franz Mohr, the first time he went to the Horowitz home, "Never mention Rubinstein." Mohr was Horowitz's piano technician. Said Mohr: "And in all my life I never did. Horowitz would talk about other pianists. He would ask me, 'How is Rudi [Serkin]?' But he never once mentioned Rubinstein's name."

Wanda, so fiercely protective of her husband and his place in the pianistic hierarchy, had all kinds of reservations about Rubinstein. She thought that he was more interested in the good life than in playing the piano; that he mostly wanted to be the great raconteur, to be admitted into the best society, to drink the best wines. Horowitz quoted Wanda as saying: "Music was secondary to him. The piano to him was only a passport to fame. He was a complicated man. Of course he loved music, but he loved music also for the success it would give him."

Horowitz was very familiar with Rubinstein's playing; they had, after all, been friends and partners in the Parisian salons. But he claimed that he never heard Rubinstein in concert until the 1940s, in Carnegie Hall. (That is hard to believe. Surely he must have attended a Rubinstein recital in Paris during the years they were on good terms there.) He also listened to his records. On the whole, said Horowitz,

> I liked him as a pianist. He was a good musician and had a fantastic repertoire. He never had a great technique, but certain things he played well. I heard him play some of the Chopin etudes, the easier ones, with great panache and I told him I had never heard them played better. He said, "Do you mean it?" and I said, "Yes, I do mean it."
>
> Rubinstein was jealous of anybody who had a great success. He was jealous of the Beatles and kept on talking about their tremendous success. When Toscanini died there was a big service in St. Patrick's Cathedral presided over by Cardinal Spellman. Then after a month the body was sent to Milan where there was another big funeral. Rubinstein could not get over it. "Like a king!" he told me and Wanda. "He had *two* funerals!" He didn't like Paderewski, he didn't like Rachmaninoff, he was always criticizing everybody. After 1965, when I returned to the concert stage, he sent me a telegram of congratulations. But he never again visited me.

There was one lovely incident, however, that occurred during Horowitz's absence from the stage. Horowitz went to one of Rubinstein's Carnegie Hall concerts and arranged to be taken backstage at intermission. Martin Feinstein of the Hurok organization, which represented Rubinstein, escorted Horowitz to greet his old acquaintance. Horowitz congratulated Rubinstein, who was surprised and delighted to see Horowitz on one of his rare excursions away from Ninety-fourth Street. Then, to the astonishment of Horowitz and Feinstein, Rubinstein impulsively said, "You know, I'm not really feeling very well, and going on with the second half of the concert will be a big effort. I know the audience will be thrilled if you go out and play the second half for me." Horowitz was speechless and looked at Rubinstein unbelievingly. "He was really startled," said Feinstein. "His eyebrows shot up to the ceiling before he shook his head no."

Rubinstein was in a win position on this one. He knew he had, in poker parlance, a locked hand. The chances overwhelmingly were that Horowitz would say no, but Rubinstein had made his typical grand seigneur gesture and knew that word would get around. Had Horowitz said yes, it would have been on Page 1 of every paper in the world and would have created a billion dollars' worth of publicity for Rubinstein.

Not much later an incident occurred that soured the relationship between them. Rubinstein gave an interview to Milton Bracker of the *Times,* and was quoted as saying something about Toscanini and the demands he made on his orchestras that could be construed as a disparaging remark. Bracker quoted Rubinstein accurately according to Feinstein, who was present at the interview. But Rubinstein was furious and claimed he had been misquoted. Then Wanda called Aniela, Rubinstein's wife, and, said Feinstein, "raised holy hell. Then Nela raised holy hell with Arthur." It was an unpleasant episode that reinforced the underlying bad feelings each couple had about the other.

Even after Horowitz's death Aniela refused to talk about her relationship with the Horowitzes, except to say, "We were not very good friends. Arthur said it all in his book." Milstein had a different theory about the falling-out between Horowitz and Rubinstein. Maybe it was not their fault, he suggested. Maybe it stemmed from the tensions and mutual dislike between their strong-minded wives.

The two women had a great deal in common, different as they were physically. Where the dark-skinned Wanda could be a glowering presence (though not without sex appeal), the effervescent, fair-skinned Aniela was the eternal feminine. But both women had immense strength of character and were accustomed to having their own way. Aniela, who had been a great beauty, came—like Wanda —from a father who had been a conductor. He was Emil Mlynarski, considered one of Poland's most important musicians. She had married a pianist named Mieczyslaw Munz but divorced him to marry Rubinstein in 1932. (Was it more than coincidence that Munz, a brilliant virtuoso, shortly afterward lost control of his right hand and had to abandon his concert career?) Both Aniela and Wanda spent their lives administering to the whims of a pampered idol. Rubinstein was a notoriously unfaithful husband and even left his wife toward the end of his long life to live with his secretary.

The lazy life of the first year of the Horowitz retirement could not last forever. Canasta was fun, and so was watching television and fooling around at the piano. But eventually Horowitz got bored with doing nothing, and he began to work himself into the mood for serious playing and teaching. Gary Graffman arrived to sit at the feet of Maestro. And there was Muzio Clementi to occupy the Horowitz mind and fingers. Horowitz showed no indication of resuming his public career, but at least he started to be a serious musician once again.

14
Uncashed Checks

I can play you a beautiful tone with my knuckle. No, really. A
beautiful tone! What does it mean? Nothing. Meaning comes
from the way one, two, three, four, five tones are connected with
one another. And this is the melodic line, what the pianist must
achieve on a percussive instrument. Not easy!
    —*Vladimir Horowitz to Tom Frost, his record producer, and to
all of his pupils*

G ary Graffman had entered Horowitz's life about two years
before his retirement, and he continued as a pupil when Horowitz
left the stage. Graffman, born in 1928 and a pupil in New York of
Horowitz's friend Isabelle Vengerova, at that time was just beginning a career that would make him one of the major postwar American pianists. Like all youngsters of his generation he had been
hypnotized the first time he heard Horowitz. That would have
been, Graffman figured, in the early 1940s.

"Of course I was aware of his technique," Graffman said.
"Vengerova had told me about that. Her idol was Josef Hofmann,
but Horowitz was her favorite among the new pianists. What I
remember most about the Horowitz recital I heard was his massive
sound and his variety of sounds."

Graffman's father, a Russian-born violinist, was constantly talking about two musicians—Heifetz and Horowitz. In those days, the late forties, Graffman palled around with Eugene Istomin, Leon Fleisher, and Jacob Lateiner, young pianists who went on to distinguished careers, and the pianist they discussed more than anybody else was Vladimir Horowitz, even though Fleisher had studied with Schnabel and Istomin with Serkin. Lateiner was a Vengerova pupil.

Horowitz first heard Graffman play in 1946, when the eighteen-year-old pianist won the regional award of the Rachmaninoff Competition. One of the jurors was Horowitz, and he told Vengerova he liked what the boy had done. The Rachmaninoff Competition turned out to be a one-shot affair. It had been set up to honor the memory of the great pianist-composer, and it was supposed to become an ongoing event, but it collapsed after the first time around. The winner, in 1948, was Seymour Lipkin. Horowitz was also on the jury of the 1948 finals, and he was impressed by Graffman's playing. He voted for him, but Lipkin edged Graffman out by a five to four vote.

Horowitz, through Vengerova, invited Graffman to come and play for him. Which Graffman did. But he was not to become a Horowitz pupil until about five years later. In 1952 Graffman, already a veteran of the concert stage, started playing occasionally for Horowitz, and when Horowitz retired the following year Graffman began to get a weekly lesson. That went on for about a year, until Graffman's career started to take off. Then there would be a lesson every three or four weeks. But during those years Graffman and Horowitz were on the phone with each other almost every day, even when Graffman was playing in Europe. Graffman figured that in all he must have had a hundred sessions with Horowitz.

Unlike Janis, Graffman did not pay for lessons, though at one point the subject did come up. Horowitz, after a year or so with Graffman, began to think that perhaps the young man was not applying himself as thoroughly as he might have. He said to Graffman, "Maybe if you pay for something you might take it a little more seriously?" They settled on $25 a lesson, and Graffman paid by check. His wife, Naomi, noticed that the checks were never cashed, and she told Horowitz that he was messing up her bank statements. At that point the whole business of paying for lessons was dropped.

Initially, Graffman, a confident and well-adjusted young man, moved with care. He did not know what to expect. "Would Horowitz tell me that the way I had been taught was all wrong? Would he try to impose his will on me?" As the weeks went by, Graffman stopped worrying. Horowitz, he decided,

> was for me an extremely good teacher. He taught me things that I used later when I myself began to teach. He played a lot for me but never played what I was studying. He would lie on the couch 95 percent of the time and he would ask me to replay a certain part of the piece I had just played for him, and would ask me why I was phrasing in a certain way, and how would a singer do it? Where would you breathe? How would you shape the line? What is the most important note or notes in that phrase? Why? Is there another way of phrasing it? Very often the conclusion I would reach, with his encouragement, would be completely different from what Horowitz would have done. I was impressed by that. He was very gentle. The worst thing he ever said about my playing was that I had a misconception about a Chopin mazurka I played for him.

Horowitz played his Battistini records for Graffman and even complete operas. "He kept on talking about the human voice and how the piano should sound like that." Graffman heard something along the same lines when he went to Rudolf Serkin's summer school at Marlboro, except that where Horowitz spoke about the voice, Serkin always spoke about instruments. "Make a woodwind sound, a clarinet sound, a viola sound."

Horowitz spent a great deal of time with Graffman on legato playing. The secret, as Horowitz explained it, was to play briefly, very briefly, *through* the preceding note. Most pianists are taught to release the finger before striking the following note. As Horowitz explained it, teachers work in small studios or living rooms, and what is heard from a big piano in that kind of acoustic has nothing to do with the sound coming off the stage of a concert hall. In a concert hall, Horowitz insisted, the tiny finger overlap was necessary. There also had to be a tiny, simultaneous overlap with the pedal.

Horowitz called this "legato pedaling." He thought that Graffman did not use enough pedal, but he was very careful to avoid criticizing the way he had been taught. He approached the subject gingerly. "Look," he said. "You underpedal. I don't want to criticize Vengerova. She is a very great teacher. But she listened to you in a living room and I am thinking how it would be in Carnegie Hall. If you do in Carnegie Hall what you would do in a living room it would sound ugly." Horowitz, said Graffman, was correct. In his own living room Horowitz would combine harmonies that sounded as though they clashed, but in Carnegie Hall it worked.

Unlike Janis, Graffman never allowed Horowitz to dominate his musical thought. Graffman took all of Horowitz's suggestions under advisement, using only those ideas he thought would work for him, discarding others. That included pedaling. He experimented along the lines Horowitz had suggested, but they were not in his nature. He remained his own man, developing into a powerful pianist who still underpedaled—at least, by Horowitz's standard. He was primarily interested in clarity and, despite his Russian-Jewish background, never developed into the kind of Slavic colorist that Horowitz was. Nor did he try. He got from Horowitz other valuable things—ideas about technique, practice habits, about breathing life into a phrase. Perhaps most important, said Graffman, "He taught me a way of listening to myself."

There was one lesson that Graffman vividly remembered. He was working on Rachmaninoff's A minor Prelude, a very difficult piece. Horowitz asked him to repeat a section, which Graffman did, looking at him rather than at the keyboard, "so if I had to play five notes, six of them were wrong. So as I played this complete mess there was a crash, and the photograph of Rachmaninoff on the piano fell down and the glass broke. At that time there were many other photos on the piano, but only the Rachmaninoff fell down. Horowitz turned pale. So did I."

The great experience shared by all of the Horowitz pupils came after the lesson, when Horowitz would seat himself before the piano and play for a couple of hours. He was discovering the music of Clementi at the time, and would play sonata after sonata for Graffman. Or he would pull out Scarlatti volumes and exclaim over the ones he particularly admired.

All of this was an education for any young pianist who was not familiar with the music. He played Scriabin's Sixth Sonata, a piece that Graffman had never heard. He exposed Graffman to the music of Medtner, playing attractive small pieces and large sections of the three concertos. Of course there also were Chopin, Liszt, Schumann. Horowitz invariably prefaced all this varied repertoire with great apologies, saying he was an old man, that his fingers were no longer any good, that he could not play the piano anymore. But he would try. And then, of course, he would tear through a piece in typical Horowitz fashion.

Horowitz and Graffman became so close that they even discussed a scenario for Horowitz's return to the stage. Graffman proposed that at one of his concerts in a small town—Scranton or Bridgeport or wherever—Horowitz should secretly send his own piano ahead. Graffman, on the evening of his recital, would suddenly become "sick," and who would take his place but Vladimir Horowitz? Horowitz was intrigued and, Graffman said, brought the subject up several times. But of course it was, like the offer Rubinstein made in Carnegie Hall, a great idea that never came to pass.

Another pupil, whom Horowitz took on shortly after Graffman, was Coleman Blumfield, who was in his early twenties when he first played for Horowitz in 1956. He had studied in Chicago with no less than Horowitz's old teacher Sergei Tarnowsky, and he was a protégé of Gitta Gradova's, Horowitz's friend from Chicago and herself a stunning pianist. "She kind of oversaw my musical development," Blumfield said. He was accepted at the Curtis Institute, where he worked with Vengerova, who lived up to her reputation as a taskmaster. "She could reduce adult men to tears," said Blumfield in 1991, still shuddering.

Like most young pianists in those days, Blumfield had a Horowitz complex. He admitted that he was "obsessed" with Horowitz. When, thanks to introductions from Gradova and Vengerova, he played for him and was accepted as a student, he left the house and in an agony of exhilaration ran all the way from East Ninety-fourth Street to Times Square. Then he called his parents to tell them the good news.

For the two years he was with Horowitz, Blumfield found himself concentrating on sound and the shaping of phrases, "the point of tension and then the relaxation afterward." Horowitz did not assign him big virtuoso pieces. He felt those were not necessary in this case because Blumfield already had an imposing technique. Instead the concentration was on quiet music, such as the Chopin nocturnes. As usual, Horowitz played vocal records to illustrate his points. And, as always, Horowitz demanded individuality and imagination. "Get behind the notes. *Behind* the notes," he kept

urging. It was the eternal problem of the interpreter: how to translate the notes into a personal message that still respects the composer's intentions.

What did Blumfield get from Horowitz? "He was not a mentor," Blumfield said. "He was a sympathetic adviser. He would
make you think and listen. He brought out the best from within
me. He knew what buttons to press to start pulling it out. I think
I emerged very strong, as my own person with my own ideas."

After two years Blumfield called Columbia Artists and asked
for an audition. He was getting married and felt it was time for
him to stand on his own two feet. He was accepted by Columbia
for its Community series, and was sent around the country. Columbia knew, of course, that Blumfield was a Horowitz pupil. When a
young pianist started to work with Horowitz, everybody in the
music world knew about it. But Blumfield's contract with Columbia brought relations between him and Horowitz to an abrupt end.
Blumfield had gone to Columbia on his own, without notifying his
teacher. Horowitz and Wanda, eternally suspicious, may have felt
that Blumfield was capitalizing on the Horowitz name.

During the early years of Horowitz's retirement, Jack Pfeiffer
became Horowitz's confidant, and they would generally have dinner once a week. After a while Horowitz began to talk with Pfeiffer
about making records, but only if the recording technicians would
come to him. There was precedent for this kind of action. As early
as 1905, in the Paleolithic age of recording, the HMV engineers
packed up their equipment and brought it from London to Adelina
Patti's castle in Wales, where the great soprano made her records.
But an artist needs extraordinary clout for this kind of high-hand-
edness. Patti had that clout. So did Vladimir Horowitz. To RCA
he still was (at that time, anyway), in the jargon of the trade, a
valuable property.

Thus started the series of Horowitz recordings at home.

Horowitz had been looking around for interesting things to
play. In a 1965 radio interview with Abram Chasins, Horowitz
said that in a way the period of his long retirement was like going
back to his childhood. Now he had the time to take a fresh look at
literature he had played when young, including much of the Classic
repertoire that he had neglected.

And then, through Wanda, he rediscovered Clementi. She had

found a volume of Clementi sonatas while on a trip to Italy and brought it home.

Horowitz was not unfamiliar with Clementi's music, but he had never made a serious study of the composer. This time it was a revelation. He had his European contacts get in touch with music dealers everywhere, and before long he had a complete set of all the Clementi sonatas, many in first editions. "He would sit there evening after evening and go through all the Clementi sonatas," said Pfeiffer, who was his page turner. Pfeiffer found this most unusual. Many supervirtuosos had probably never even looked at the music of Clementi, unless they had been assigned the *Gradus ad Parnassum* exercises when they were children.

Muzio Clementi (1752–1832) was an Italian-born pianist, composer and teacher—and piano manufacturer, too—who lived in England most of his life. He was one of the first of the tribe of international piano virtuosos, and he astounded audiences with his dexterity, his double notes, and his singing style. In 1781 he and Mozart met face to face in a "duel" at the court of Joseph II in Vienna. Mozart won the competition; at least the emperor thought so. Perhaps Mozart himself was not so sure. He wrote a violent letter back to his folks in Salzburg, condemning Clementi's playing, calling him a charlatan. Usually Mozart loftily dismissed other pianists. This time he was disturbed.

In a way, Clementi was the Vladimir Horowitz of his day. And to Horowitz's delight there was a taxonomical connection between him and Clementi. One of Clementi's most famous pupils was John Field, the Irish pianist who settled in St. Petersburg. There he taught a pianist named Alexander Villoing. Villoing taught Anton Rubinstein, who in turn taught Horowitz's teacher Felix Blumenfeld. So there was a Clementi connection with Horowitz and he boasted about it. Horowitz would cite Beethoven's interest in Clementi, and would play sections from the sonatas that anticipated not only Beethoven but also Mendelssohn, Chopin, and other Romantics. He became fixated on Clementi and made up his mind to record a group of the sonatas.

When news of the projected Clementi record came out, Howard Taubman, then the music editor of the *Times*, sent a staff critic to interview Horowitz about it. It was felt by the *Times* that the championship of a virtually forgotten composer by the world's greatest virtuoso was a legitimate news story. It was also the first interview since Horowitz's retirement. The recording was issued in 1955. It was not a best-seller, but nobody had expected it to be.

Later that year Victor released a disc that contained, among other things, Horowitz's arrangement of Sousa's *Stars and Stripes Forever*, which elicited the following comments from the New York *Times*. First the critic quoted Saint-Saëns: "In art, a difficulty overcome is a thing of beauty." A requisite in art, the critic said, is craft. The greater the craft, the better the result. Then:

> In music where pianistic craft is the *raison d'être*, Horowitz rises to a level that no living pianist can match. His *Stars and Stripes* is sheer pianistic prestidigitation and, as such, can arouse a sharp esthetic response. Of course it is a stunt, just as running a mile under four minutes is a stunt, or flipping from one trapeze to another doing a triple somersault in mid-air.
>
> But it is a stunt on a transcendental level, and anybody who cannot enjoy it, admire it for what it is, has little sympathy for craft as such. You don't laugh at things like *The Stars and Stripes Forever* when it receives a performance like this; you laugh with it, and at the end you are a little limp from an empathic alliance with the performer: Will he falter? break down? But Horowitz never does.

The longer Horowitz remained in retirement, the more determined he seemed to be to show the world that he could still play. And, starting with the Clementi disc, he began to record material he had never before played in America. In 1956 he came forth with a Scriabin disc that contained the Sonata No. 3 and sixteen preludes, all new to his repertoire. With this disc he leaped into the top echelon of Scriabin performers.

Horowitz was in high spirits at this time, according to Lawrence Ingram, a psychologist who had been sent to him by Dr. Kubie, Horowitz's psychiatrist. Horowitz often had a hired companion around him, to whom he could talk and even exchange confidences, especially when Wanda was away. Ingram filled in for six months during 1956, while Wanda was out of town most of that time, vacationing in the Hamptons or going to Italy.

Dr. Kubie had told Ingram that Horowitz was depressed, but Ingram found no evidence of depression at all. "He was not the neurotic I had expected," Ingram recalled in 1991. "What I found was a total normality in this eccentric human being." He immediately discovered that Horowitz was a very private person, and he never attempted to push him. Ingram also found what others had noted, that Horowitz was a different person when Wanda was away. Then he was gossipy, amusing, fully adjusted to his specialized way of life. When he spoke to Ingram, "there was a lot of free association. He would reach into his past, telling stories about his boyhood, and then relating them to the present." He even talked about going back to the concert stage. "If I wanted to play in Carnegie Hall," he told Ingram, "it would only take me a couple of days to get ready." Ingram did not consider this an idle boast.

Every once in a while Wanda would appear, in town for a few days. She bustled in and bustled out, hardly saying a word. To Ingram, their marriage was "a classic codependentship." It was clear to him that they had reached some sort of understanding that they were inseparable even if they went their separate ways.

Ingram thought that Horowitz had made Dr. Kubie his prop. "An analyst," said Ingram, "becomes your surrogate father and mother." From what Horowitz told him, Ingram deduced that Horowitz's mother, Sophie, was a very strong woman and that Horowitz had never been able to break free of that influence. So he transferred it to Dr. Kubie.

But if Horowitz was euphoric in 1956, there was a setback the following year. When Toscanini died on January 16, 1957, at the age of eighty-nine, Horowitz entered a period of depression. "Horowitz placed him on a pedestal," said Milstein. "All other musicians—not only conductors—were held up against the technical and artistic ideal of Toscanini. It took Horowitz a long time to get over the death. Toscanini frightened Horowitz, maybe even held him back a little bit. Horowitz was like a scared little boy when Toscanini was around. He was intimidated." Intimidated or not, Horowitz had always found his father-in-law a musical prop on which he could lean. Now the prop had been removed, and Horowitz collapsed. He felt much as he had when Rachmaninoff died. The two mentors who had helped shape his ideas of musicianship were gone, and Horowitz felt desperately, irrevocably alone. Wanda, always more realistic than her husband, could cope. Horowitz was shattered.

Then, shortly after Toscanini's death, the Horowitz family was hit by another blow. Sonia had been critically injured in a motorbike accident near San Remo on the Riviera.

Sonia, at that time a young woman of twenty-three, had been living in Italy, spending much time with her aunt Wally, who recently had been divorced from Count Castelbarco. Sonia was much closer to Wally than to her own mother, and it was Wally who probably saved her life. They were vacationing in the Riviera. Wally and she decided to go to a restaurant for lunch. Sonia preceded her on her motorbike while Wally went in her own car. On returning, with Wally in her automobile directly behind her, Sonia tried to pass a bus on a curve. She went out of control and into a lamppost, was thrown and suffered a fractured skull. Wally phoned for help, and Sonia was taken to a hospital. A specialist was called in, and he said that Sonia had to be transferred to specialists in a hospital in Milan. Wally, exerting her considerable influence, arranged to get Sonia to Milan on a U.S. Army helicopter on the grounds that an American citizen had been injured.

In Milan, the specialists found brain damage. Sonia underwent surgery and pulled through. Wanda, as soon as Wally notified her of the accident, took the next plane to Milan. Horowitz stayed home. He may have rationalized that there was nothing he could do, and that he even would be in the way. But his behavior during such a family crisis caused friends to wonder just what kind of man he was. Wanda stoutly defended him, pointing out that at the time he was very sick. Sonia recovered, but Horowitz thought that she was never the same again. The accident, he firmly believed, had impaired her mental capacities.

After recovering from the dual shock of Toscanini's death and Sonia's injury, Horowitz began to see friends and resume his canasta sessions. He also started working again with talented young pianists: in addition to Graffman and Blumfield, there were Alexander Fiorillo, Ronald Turini, Ivan Davis, and several others who played for him a few times and disappeared. Of these post-Graffman pupils, Davis was the only one who went on to a respectable career. Fiorillo, who in 1991 was teaching at Temple University, remembered his studies with Horowitz as "a wonderment and a disappointment." Horowitz, he said, could be generous and also selfish. He gave Fiorillo valuable ideas about technique and tone production, but the young pianist found it difficult to cope with Horowitz's puzzling (to him) "inconsistencies of interpretation." Horowitz began to pay less and less attention to Fiorillo. The result was that the twenty-year-old Fiorillo dropped the piano entirely and did not return to it for several years.

When Horowitz felt ready to record again, he went to Hunter College and Carnegie Hall instead of using his home as a studio. But his relations with RCA were not to last much longer.

Horowitz had been friendly with George Marek, the vice president and general manager of the RCA Record Division. Their friendship cooled in 1955, shortly after the Clementi record. Horowitz had put a great deal of time and effort into it. It had been a labor of love, and he proudly played the disc for Marek. Marek said, "Oh, yes. Wonderful, wonderful. But commercially it doesn't mean anything." Horowitz found this remark condescending and insulting. Pfeiffer, who was there, said that "it was like a pail of cold water in Horowitz's face." Marek may not have been tactful, but he was correct about the merchandising aspects of the discs Horowitz was making. Neither the Clementi nor the Scriabin records sold very well—certainly not enough to take care of Horowitz's $40,000 annual guarantee. And by the early 1960s, Horowitz had not played in public for about ten years and his very name was being forgotten. Sales of all of his records had severely fallen off. The bottom-line men at RCA were not happy.

Then RCA did something very stupid. The company told Horowitz that he should make some records that had "popular appeal." Horowitz asked RCA to suggest repertoire ideas. RCA came up with some remarkable recommendations: the *William Tell* Overture, the *1812* Overture, waltzes. Cocktail pianists could have played this pop stuff just as well as Vladimir Horowitz. Horowitz said, "Is that all they think of me?" Wanda was livid.

Horowitz made up his mind to leave RCA. But before that happened, he was fired. RCA dropped him around 1960, along with a group of musicians that included Gary Graffman. The Horowitz records simply were not selling. Graffman did not get the news about Horowitz until he called him to discuss his own predicament. When Horowitz said that he too had been dropped, Graffman was stunned. Horowitz suggested that the two of them open a whorehouse.

Soon after that, Graffman signed with Columbia and suggested to Horowitz that he get in touch with record executives there. "Do you really think they would be interested in me?" asked

Horowitz, playing the innocent. Graffman laughed. He called Schuyler Chapin, the head of CBS Masterworks. "Would you like to have Vladimir Horowitz on your list?" Chapin instantly got in touch with Horowitz.

Pfeiffer was in Florida on sabbatical at the time and did not know what was going on. He might have been able to smooth things over between Horowitz and RCA. But by the time he returned it was too late. Horowitz had become friendly with Goddard Lieberson, the suave, imaginative head of Columbia Records, and Lieberson offered him every kind of inducement to sign with Columbia, which he finally did.

Chapin negotiated a contract with Horowitz in 1961. Horowitz asked for surprisingly little in the way of an advance or an annual guarantee. He was content to work largely on royalties from the sale of individual records. Wanda was in on all the discussions, and Chapin, as he later said, "rapidly learned that if she had chosen to do so she could have outmerchandised R. H. Macy himself." Throughout the negotiations Chapin had the feeling that Horowitz was "a very shy man, someone who wanted to know that he was going to be loved, admired, and cared for." When the contract was signed, Horowitz turned to Chapin and asked, "Will you take care of me?" Chapin assured Horowitz that he would.

Thomas Frost was appointed by Chapin to be Horowitz's producer. Frost was born in Vienna and came with his family to the United States at the time of the Anschluss in 1938. He had studied the violin as a child. In America he studied theory with Paul Hindemith at Yale. Frost was a thoroughly trained musician, and he and Horowitz became close friends.

Frost worked on Horowitz's first Columbia record, *Columbia Records Presents Vladimir Horowitz,* and was the producer for almost all of his subsequent Columbia recordings. The first record, released on September 24, 1962, contained the Chopin B flat minor Sonata, two of Rachmaninoff's *Etudes-tableaux,* the Schumann *Arabesque,* and Liszt's Rhapsody No. 19 (arranged by Horowitz). It was a typical Horowitz program. He had previously recorded the Chopin and Schumann for Victor. Now, with a new company, he could start rerecording some of the major items in his repertoire. The other pieces on the disc were first Horowitz recordings. Columbia advertised it heavily, and the record became a best-seller.

Frost and Horowitz spoke a great deal about music, and Frost put some of the conversations into his program notes for the first Columbia record. Horowitz told Frost that

> our playing stems from the voice. . . . The meaning must come from the melodic line. There must be some kind of vocal approach, inevitably. If a pianist imitates the voices of the past or the present, then his playing has a logic. You can like it or not, but it is "I, singing at the piano." Even a C major scale has a melodic line.

To Horowitz, the grand manner was not playing loud and fast. Rather it consisted of broad, introspective phrases within a large framework of conception. Technique had nothing to do with the grand manner. "So frequently I am asked about this so-called phenomenal technique which I have," Horowitz told Elyse Mach in an interview, "but I have no phenomenal technique. To be able to produce many varieties of sound, now that is what I call technique, and that is what I try to do." The full gamut of emotions, Horowitz said, must be projected directly and simply. "In simplicity there is wisdom." (It must be noted that Horowitz did not achieve that ideal of simplicity as often as he might have wished. Intellectually he always knew what he was after. But once he was on the stage intellect sometimes might take second place to the emotion of the moment or the demands of the audience.)

According to Frost, Horowitz was no different at the Columbia recording sessions than he had been at RCA. He would record on alternate days—Monday, Wednesday, and Friday, starting at 4 P.M.—and seldom worked more than two hours. He used Columbia's Thirtieth Street studio. His piano was brought there from the Steinway basement. A couch was provided so that Horowitz could rest between takes. After the first session he never listened to playbacks. While recording he almost always played the entire piece through. To Horowitz, Frost said,

> recording was like giving a concert. He did not play for the microphones. He would always look through the window of the control room, smile, see if he was being appreciated. He was communicating to the audio engineers. That evening, at home, he expected Columbia to deliver to him acetates of the afternoon's work. Those he and I listened to very carefully. Horowitz had no tape equipment. He and Wanda were hopeless with electronic gadgets. They had absolutely no aptitude

and were frustrated by all the buttons on the preamplifier. If they pushed a button and nothing happened they would start frantically pushing all the buttons. But Horowitz did know how to put a record on and play it.

While they listened to, and discussed, the acetates after the day's session, Horowitz would plan the next session. Generally Wanda was present at those occasions, and she had her own pointed contributions to offer. Horowitz, Frost said, "was never capricious. He was as demanding of himself as he was of others." The key word was "demanding." Horowitz could drive Frost and all the engineers and Columbia executives crazy, constantly changing his mind. There must have been eyes lifted to heaven at Columbia Records when Horowitz and Wanda were trying to make a decision about a particular take. But all went along, grudgingly or otherwise, as they had to. They were dealing with Vladimir Horowitz.

Frost would edit the record-to-be. Since Horowitz often played the piece all the way through, he and Frost might end up with, say, four performances. Horowitz might want a certain section from the first take, another from the third, and so on. A splice might be as little as one bar. "Even Horowitz could hit a few clinkers," said Frost. "But there never was a huge editing job. It wasn't necessary."

(But other engineers told a different story. They said it *was* a huge editing job, made even harder because Horowitz had such trouble making up his mind which of the takes he preferred. Sometimes, they said, Horowitz records were little more than an assemblage of splices; and they wondered why a pianist so technically formidable and spontaneous in the concert hall should so tie himself into knots in the recording studio.)

Horowitz was greatly concerned about the relative loudness of the sounds he created on disc. In recording, the psychoacoustic effect from loudspeakers is different from actual concert-hall sound. So sometimes it would be necessary to reduce the volume or add volume to give continuity to the relationships Horowitz had in mind. "For instance," said Frost, "if you go from a Scarlatti sonata to a Liszt piece, you have to find the correct dynamic relationship. Horowitz was very particular about volume levels. He was also concerned about the quality of the pressing—were there clicks? tape hiss? surface noise?—and in his contract he had a clause that said he had the right to approve a test pressing. If it did not meet his criteria, he would reject it."

Jack Pfeiffer of RCA thought that under the circumstances the move to Columbia was the right thing for Horowitz. It brought some excitement into his life, a sense of purpose, the desire to work again. Horowitz and Pfeiffer remained the best of friends, and the two of them would listen to the Columbia records as they came out. Pfeiffer thought that Columbia was doing a very good job for him, and it was true. On the Columbia discs the Horowitz sound was less clangorous than the close-up sound Victor had only too often provided. When they listened to the Horowitz performance of Schumann's *Kreisleriana,* Pfeiffer remembered that his reaction was one of acute jealousy. "Why couldn't he have done that for us?"

Chapin was dying to record Horowitz in the Rachmaninoff D minor Concerto with Ormandy and the Philadelphia Orchestra, but Horowitz would have none of that; he felt he was not ready. His second disc featured Schumann's *Kinderscenen,* along with pieces by Scarlatti, Scriabin, and Schubert. It was released on April 15, 1963. Then came a record with the Beethoven *Pathétique,* the Chopin B minor Scherzo, and short pieces by Chopin and Debussy. After that came a disc devoted solely to Scarlatti sonatas. All of the records were best-sellers. Columbia and Horowitz were very happy.

But still there was no indication that Horowitz was ready to give concerts.

15

Media Blitz

That did it. Suddenly it came to me that the younger generation
did not know me at all. I knew that I must play again.
—*Vladimir Horowitz in 1965 after being interviewed by
Howard Klein of the* Times

*I*t was not until 1962 that Horowitz began indicating that
maybe, *maybe,* he would resume his career. When Wanda was asked
what she thought, she would shrug her shoulders and look despair-
ingly at Volodya, who was doing what he seemed to do best—
lying comfortably on his divan.

It was a long hibernation, and Horowitz could not be pushed.
Pushing made him stubbornly react in the opposite direction. What
finally set him moving again was a combination of factors: his
improved physical and mental health, the knowledge that his pianistic skills had not deserted him, and the appearance of such new
Russian heroes as Richter, Gilels, and Ashkenazy. Pride was involved. Who were these upstarts to challenge the only one?

And there was a financial reason for Horowitz to return to

work. After twelve years a good part of his savings had evaporated. He lived as he always had lived—expensively and even lavishly, with all of his needs taken care of. Toward the end of his retirement some financial pressure began to be felt, and one year he actually found himself in debt. So he quietly started selling off his art collection. The Modigliani, Matisse, and Picasso disappeared from his walls, as did the Degas, Renoir, and all of the others.

Ivan Davis was one of the persons indirectly responsible for the return of Vladimir Horowitz to the concert stage.

Davis started working with Horowitz in 1961. He was twenty-eight, the oldest of Horowitz's pupils and already a mature artist with considerable experience. Texas-born, he had studied with Silvio Scionti there. Davis then won a Fulbright to Italy, where he studied with Carlo Zecchi at Santa Cecilia.

In 1961 he won the Liszt Competition in New York. It was a onetime affair, sponsored by Columbia Pictures as promotion for a film about Liszt. On the jury were Abram Chasins, Byron Janis, and Ania Dorfmann, all friends of Horowitz's. They told him that Davis was very talented. Horowitz telephoned Davis and invited him to dinner. Dorfmann, a Russian-trained pianist who taught at the Juilliard School and had played with Toscanini, was a guest that evening and urged Horowitz to listen to Davis. After dinner Davis played some Scarlatti.

Horowitz said, "Ha, ha. Good fingers. I understand you play Sixth Rhapsody."

"Yes," said Davis.

"I used to play Sixth Rhapsody," said Horowitz.

Davis played it, saying to himself, "Octaves, don't fail me tonight." The last part of the Sixth Rhapsody is all in flashy octaves. It went well. Horowitz said, "You have good octaves. Most pianists do not have good octaves. But you get tired, don't you?" Horowitz said he would give Davis the secret of playing octaves without getting tired. Davis waited, trembling. "Oh, my God. What every pianist has waited for all their lives." Horowitz said: "I practice slow, high from the wrist and in rhythm." Davis hoped that his disappointment did not show. Every teacher says that to his pupils.

Later Horowitz told Davis, "You already are a pianist with personality. You play wonderfully, but sometimes I don't think you hear what you do. I would like to be big ears for you."

Davis said that it was not really a pupil-teacher relationship.

Rather it was more like that of two musical friends. "Horowitz seemed eager for input from somebody else. We did a lot of talking and playing. Then we would wind up the evening listening to recordings: Russian operas, old singers, his own Carnegie Hall performances." Many of Horowitz's Carnegie Hall appearances between 1945 and 1950 had been privately recorded by him (they are now in the Horowitz Archives at Yale). Horowitz would play them and giggle like a little boy showing off his toys. Davis remembered one performance of the Liszt Sixth Rhapsody. Horowitz said about it: "I was so naughty! I decided to do it the fastest I have ever done. Do it wild!" Davis said it was the most extraordinary performance of the piece he had ever heard.

He went with Horowitz to a concert in which Serkin was playing the Mozart Two-Piano Concerto with his son, Peter. In those days Horowitz seldom left his house, but Serkin was a close friend. Horowitz went backstage after the performance. What happened made Davis feel sorry for Serkin. A number of pianists were present, and when Horowitz made his appearance Serkin and his son were forgotten. Everybody gathered around Horowitz. Those who did not know Horowitz sidled up to Davis with desperate whispers. "Introduce me! Introduce me!" Serkin handled it gracefully. He went to Horowitz with his sweet smile and thanked him for coming. "This is a big moment for me," Serkin said, "because my son has always wanted to meet the greatest pianist in the world."

The only time Horowitz and Davis played together was when Horowitz took the second piano to play the accompaniment for the Rachmaninoff Rhapsody. Davis said that he would have "killed" to have had a tape of that performance. "I could barely think of what I was doing because what I heard from the other piano was really so extraordinary, full of orchestral sound."

Horowitz never discussed technique with Davis, "unless you consider pedaling part of technique. He showed me half pedalings and he helped me there a great deal. Horowitz used more pedal and less pedal than other pianists. He thought in extremes. He could play softer than anybody and louder than anybody. Sometimes he used hardly any pedal at all. One of his last recordings, the Schubert-Liszt *Serenade,* is one of the great piano records of all time. There he uses long pedaling, so there are little blurs and things which add to the coloring and the sense of the huge line."

Horowitz hated it when a pupil imitated his records. Davis played the Chopin Andante Spianato and Polonaise for him. Horowitz got angry. "I don't like it. You have copied my record!" Davis said, "Well, I was influenced by it." Horowitz said, "But that's not the way I would play it now. That's the bad thing with records. They are a thing of the moment."

In 1962, Davis received a phone call from Horowitz, who said that he felt like going out. He wanted to sit quietly, relax, see people. "Where will you take me?" Davis got on the phone to friends. Where could one take a legend? He and Horowitz wound up at O'Henry's Steak House in Greenwich Village, sitting outside so that Horowitz could people-watch. Davis put some of his friends on alert, telling them that Horowitz would be there at 9:45 or so. "But don't talk to him." Horowitz, said Davis, was paranoid about being introduced to strangers in public. On the way to O'Henry's, Horowitz said, "If anybody comes, just introduce me as Mr. Howard." Davis thought to himself, *Who's he kidding?*

The friends Davis had tipped off arrived, looked, and ambled on. Horowitz sat quietly, sipping his Poland water. Presently a group of young people carrying Schirmer scores started looking and pointing, and one of them approached the seated couple. Horowitz urgently said to Davis, "Mr. Howard! Remember! Mr. Howard!" The young man came to the table carrying a copy of the Liszt Sonata and said, "Excuse me, but aren't you Ivan Davis?" Horowitz, said Davis,

> made a funny kind of strangulated sound. I said yes, and he said, "Would you please sign this?" I took the music and wrote: "You fool. You have no idea who is sitting next to me." And he thanked me and giggled and went away, and Horowitz sat there and he said, unbelievingly, "But they did not know who I was." I said, "Of course they don't. They're too young. They haven't ever seen you." And Horowitz said, his voice going up an octave, "They didn't know who I was." And I said, "Exactly. The young don't know you. You need to play again." Horowitz thought a little and then said, "Maybe." I think that really did trigger his mind. It really got to him.

Davis was right. Horowitz had the itch. But he was still torn two ways. On the one hand he was not too anxious to return to the rigors of concert life—the traveling, the discomfort, the fear of memory lapses, the critics, and all the other pressures. There was also his colitis, seemingly cured, but could he be sure? On the other hand he missed his public. He knew he could play as well as ever, and could give the new heroes who had come up since his retirement something to think about.

Julius Bloom, the executive director of Carnegie Hall, helped him come to a decision.

At Wanda's suggestion, Horowitz approached Bloom toward the end of 1964. He wanted to play on the stage of Carnegie Hall to see if he felt comfortable enough for a return to concert life, and he asked if such a thing would be possible. Bloom immediately made all the arrangements.

Horowitz and Bloom soon became friends. Bloom was a thoughtful man, trained in sociology and philosophy, a visionary, knowledgeable about music, experienced in all of the ins and outs of the music business. Bloom felt—or, as he later said to a journalist, he *knew*—that Horowitz wanted to return. The more Horowitz insisted that he did *not* want to return, the more Bloom knew that he did. But never once did he try to push Horowitz into playing. "That would have stopped everything then and there. He needed to be persuaded, to be oozed in."

After some serious talks, during which Bloom offered to manage Horowitz's musical affairs and take care of all his business, an understanding was reached. Horowitz, pledging everybody to secrecy, sneaked into the Steinway basement to select a piano and fell in love with the concert grand numbered CD 186, which was thereafter to be his recital instrument, reserved for him alone. He immediately responded to its crashing bass, its even regulation, and the way it sang in the treble. Franz Mohr, the newly appointed Steinway chief technician, took care of it. The instrument had to be tuned to an exact 440-A. It had an unusually light action, with a key pressure of 45 grams as against the usual 48 to 52 of most Steinway concert grands.

The "oozing" process took place on selected afternoons on the stage of Carnegie Hall. Starting on January 7, 1965, Horowitz played a number of secret rehearsals until April for a tiny, hand-picked audience. Meanwhile Bloom reserved Carnegie Hall for a May 9 concert.

All of this was a well-kept secret. "I knew that the last thing Horowitz wanted was publicity," said Bloom. At the first Carnegie Hall tryout Bloom was of course present. "We all sat there stunned while he played. It was absolutely fantastic." The most thrilled person in the tiny audiences was Wanda. She, like Bloom, knew better than to try to nail Horowitz to a definite return. All she did was encourage him and tell him how well he was playing.

Pledged to secrecy, the New York *Times* was in on some of the practice sessions. The *Times* kept its pledge not to break the story until Horowitz was ready. In return the *Times* demanded an exclusive. But such things cannot be kept secret, and it was the *Herald Tribune* that broke the story on March 14, 1965. In a short item, the paper announced that Horowitz was planning a comeback and rehearsing in Carnegie Hall. An angry *Times* music editor called Horowitz. "See what we get for going along with you?" Horowitz said, in all truth, that he did not know how the *Herald Tribune* got the story. A few hours later, Bloom called the *Times,* and told the music department to send somebody to Carnegie Hall the next day, with a photographer. Horowitz would be rehearsing there and the *Times* would get an exclusive.

Howard Klein was there the next afternoon. Klein was a young pianist who had been plucked from the Juilliard School to become a junior critic on the *Times*. This was his first exposure to Vladimir Horowitz; and Klein, who had heard Horowitz only on records, was overwhelmed. To him Horowitz was a legendary figure. He even had a photograph of Horowitz in his living room. He was terribly nervous when, after listening to the rehearsal, he went backstage to ask Horowitz the questions he had written down. Horowitz, still blowing hot and cold about returning to the concert stage, asked Klein what he thought. Twenty-five years later Klein could not forget the flutters he felt when he approached the pianist who had been an idol to him and all of his Juilliard friends:

> Horowitz was the ideal toward which we all aimed. I went to Carnegie Hall not knowing what to expect. The minute he started to play I felt as though my ears had been pinned to the rear wall. I was absolutely in shock. I continued to listen, and I took notes, and I tried to be a good reporter and be very objective. When he finished he went back to the green room. I went back with my pad. He was lying on a chaise longue, smiling at me. Instead of going into the questions, I was so moved that what I said was, "Mr. Horowitz, there's a whole generation that has no idea what you sound like. Your recordings do not do you justice." And he looked at me. I asked him

the questions, went back to the *Times* and wrote a piece that was put on the front page.

Klein's remark about the younger generation's having no idea about what Horowitz represented hit home even harder than Ivan Davis's similar comment at the Greenwich Village episode. Horowitz told Bloom that he would give the concert on the agreed May 9 date, and that the press should be notified.

There was hysteria on the announcement in the *Times* of the Horowitz return. It was the start of a media blitz that astonished even veterans who thought they had experienced everything. Papers from all over the world picked up the *Times* story. Impresarios from Europe and Japan immediately requested Horowitz's services. There was even an official request from Moscow. Horowitz gave a press interview on March 19 in Carnegie Hall. This too received international coverage. Horowitz said in effect that he was a new man. He said he would no longer play flashy transcriptions (though in 1967 he did revive the *Carmen* Variations). His programs, he said, would concentrate more on important pieces and he would program music that had not previously been in his repertoire.

When his program was announced, there was indeed some new (to Horowitz audiences) music on it—the Scriabin Ninth Sonata and *Poème* in F sharp. The opening piece would be the Bach-Busoni Toccata, Adagio, and Fugue in C, followed by the Schumann Fantasy. After intermission would come the Scriabin pieces. Chopin of course was included on the program: the F major Etude (Op. 10, No. 8), the C sharp minor Mazurka (Op. 30, No. 4), and the G minor Ballade. The encores Horowitz prepared were Debussy's *Serenade to the Doll*, Scriabin's Etude in C sharp minor (Op. 2, No. 1), the Moszkowski A flat Etude, and Schumann's *Träumerei*. About the Moszkowski encore Horowitz remarked, "I had to show them some of the old Horowitz." It is a fleet, dazzling little salon piece.

When it was announced that tickets for the May 9 concert would go on sale at the Carnegie Hall box office on April 26, more than 1,500 Horowitzphiles were standing three or four abreast in a line that extended east from Carnegie Hall down to the Avenue of the Americas on that day. Some had arrived two days early. Most had camped out overnight. The first in line got his fifteen minutes of fame; he was Michael Lintzman, a music teacher from Brooklyn, and he was in all the papers. The weather was terrible—rainy and cold. Wanda came down the evening before the box-office opening and looked at the sodden group of Horowitz fans. She immediately went into the Nedick's coffee shop on the corner and ordered coffee for all. The lineup outside Carnegie Hall would be a permanent feature of nearly all future Horowitz concerts. People would start lining up two days before, and they would expect to be given coffee by Wanda Horowitz some time during their camping-out period. Wanda never failed them. And the press never failed her.

Ticket sales were limited to four per person. Top price was $12.50 ("one of the highest in the history of the 2,760-seat house," said the *Times*), scaled down to balcony seats for $4 and $3. When the box office closed, only 300 purchasers had been taken care of. Assuming that each of the 300 had purchased four tickets, that still left about 1,500 seats unaccounted for. There was a public outcry and the newspapers started asking questions. Wanda indignantly said that she had purchased a block of 296 seats, all but eight of which she had paid for. The Steinway people said they had purchased only 20. What had happened to more than 1,000 seats? The New York State Attorney General's office said there would be an investigation.

In any case, no ticket went to waste. The hall was sold out, and scalpers were charging outrageous prices for the few tickets they had managed to locate. Critics from the wire services and newspapers all over America, and many from overseas, put in their request for tickets. First in line for the standing-room tickets, in case posterity is interested, was Lois Attisami, a twenty-two-year-old music student.

The media blitz continued. On the day of the concert there appeared in the *Times* an interview with Mrs. Horowitz, written by Murray Schumach. Mrs. Horowitz told him that she was her husband's librarian, and had made a card file of all of the music in the house. But Horowitz ignored it. "He cannot use the file. Even on his piano he piles up the music till it's up like *this*," Wanda said, raising her arm as high as it could go.

Now all that remained was for Horowitz actually to give his concert. The progress of an artist from stage door to the center of the stage has been described as the longest, loneliest walk in the world. This entrance would be by far the longest, loneliest walk that Vladimir Horowitz had ever taken.

16

Still the Master

When you are on stage you are the king and you should try to
look like one. In Mozart's time every gesture was reverence. Lace,
a little snuff, a little black spot on the face. . . . Look at Chopin!
He was a dandy—he picked out every silk! Liszt too. The public
pays money and they want to see something esthetic.
   —*Vladimir Horowitz, in a* Times *interview with Helen Epstein*

May 9, 1965, was a sunny, humid day in New York.
Horowitz went through his usual preconcert routine as though this
were just another performance. But of course it wasn't. What was
going through his mind? He never said. And nobody asked him.
On the day he gave a concert Horowitz was not to be approached
by anybody during his preparations.

For Horowitz, getting ready for a concert was always more
than a normal toilette. It was a ceremony, a purification rite, even
a sort of baptism. On this Sunday, Horowitz got up around noon,
as usual, and had breakfast. Nobody was permitted to speak to
him. After breakfast he washed, shaved, and dressed. For his afternoon concerts—this one was scheduled for 3:30—he always wore
the once-traditional gray trousers and a swallowtail coat. He was

the last pianist alive to do so. "I think about the small details," he told Helen Epstein in a New York *Times* interview:

> To put on the socks that they don't press me. To see that the shoes are closed. The fly is closed. If they are open, they are terrible. Not to be nervous. Not to rush. All the movements quiet. I don't think about music at all because, you know, the tragedy of an artist is like Pagliacci. At a certain time you have to be inspired, wanting to play and being in good form. It could be at four—just at four—that I could have a stomach-ache. So I am trying to be very quiet. Nobody should interfere with me and if anyone interferes he gets such a scandal that he never heard.

As soon as Horowitz put on his bow tie and cutaway he felt he was in uniform. "It's like a horse before the race. You start to perspire. You feel already in you some electricity to do something. At that moment I am absolutely an artist. I feel a pressure to be on time. I like to be ten, fifteen minutes early to warm up the fingers. I am a general. My soldiers are the keys and I have to command them."

The one unusual thing Wanda noted on the day of the May 9 concert was that Horowitz moved like a snail. She said that she had never seen him dress so slowly. Was he tense? Of course he was tense, she said. He was never nervous before a concert but he always was tense, keyed up to give his very best.

Shortly before 3 P.M. Horowitz, Wanda, and Jack Pfeiffer got into a limousine and headed for Carnegie Hall.

Schuyler Chapin and Carnegie Hall officials were at the stage entrance on West Fifty-sixth Street waiting for Horowitz to appear. Chapin was fulfilling his promise to take care of Horowitz during their association. Today he would act as his valet. Also waiting was a gaggle of reporters, photographers, and television crews. After a while everybody had palpitations. The hall was full—it had been since 3 P.M.—and everybody was there except the pianist. Chapin started thinking of what he would say to the audience if Horowitz had panicked and decided not to show up. He looked desperately at Goddard Lieberson. Lieberson looked desperately at Chapin. They stood and waited. There was nothing else they could do.

Horowitz arrived at the Carnegie Hall stage entrance at 3:25 P.M. for his 3:30 concert. His limousine, he explained getting out of the car, had got caught in traffic. (Pfeiffer later said this was true. The area around Central Park, two blocks north of Carnegie Hall, is always crowded on a pleasant Sunday afternoon.)

Horowitz was immediately surrounded by media people. He did not seem to be disturbed. Everybody else was still shaking. Chapin rushed Horowitz to his dressing room, let him warm up for five minutes on the practice piano there, and escorted him to the wings. Horowitz stood there, looking bemused. Chapin put his hand on Horowitz's back and gently pushed him on to the stage.

The audience stood and roared as the pianist appeared. Horowitz bowed to the balcony, the boxes, the parquet. Everybody in the audience was rooting for him and waves of love were radiating through the hall, as well as waves of anxiety and fear. "I was more nervous," said Gary Graffman, "than at any concert I ever gave. Would he come out, look at the audience, scream and run off?"

Horowitz launched into the Toccata. With so many professionals in the audience, it was possible to look in any direction and see moving fingers, pianists playing along with the soloist. Horowitz hit a particularly exposed wrong note shortly after the opening, and there was an audible gasp. Later on there were also a few wrong notes. But Horowitz did not seem bothered, and he calmly went along, singing out the Adagio and clarifying the part writing of the Fugue as only he could. There was a shout of approval at the end.

Then came the Schumann C major Fantasy. Horowitz played the first movement in a rather reflective, introspective manner. In the second movement he articulated the bold chords with his old authority. But during the coda there was a moment where he teetered on the edge of disaster. Schumann was cruel here; the writing calls for wide, fast jumps in both hands, and few pianists get through it unscathed. Suddenly Horowitz lost control. It was only for a fraction of a second, but everybody who knew the piece *knew* that Horowitz was going to break down. He didn't. He recovered, finished the coda, kept his foot on the pedal, reached for a handkerchief, and mopped his face. Then he started the slow, lovely last movement and played it simply and beautifully.

The Scriabin Ninth Sonata, spooky and complicated, was Horowitz at his best. No living pianist could have matched the color he brought to it, the clarity of the voicings, the identification with the composer's diabolical mysticism. It is not for nothing that it is called the *Black Mass* Sonata. The shorter pieces also went beautifully. In Chopin's F major Etude he ended with a diminuendo on the four last chords where Chopin's marking is forte. That drives purists and many critics crazy. They consider it a cheap, cutesy effect. (As a matter of fact, it was common practice with pianists of the preceding century. Rosina Lhevinne, the widow of the great pianist Josef and one of America's best piano teachers, used to refer to that practice as a "reverse accent.") The concert ended with Chopin's G minor Ballade. This time Horowitz had new ideas about it. But he always had new ideas whenever he played the piece. He never did figure out exactly how he wanted it to go, but he chased after it as relentlessly as Lancelot ever sought the Grail.

Then came the encores, mostly quiet pieces. The only technical excitement was provided by the Moszkowski A flat Etude. Horowitz played the scale passages prestissimo, every note clear, relishing the effect he was making, and at the end there were yips of approval. This was the old Horowitz. He sang his way through the Debussy *Serenade to the Doll* and Scriabin C sharp minor Etude, and at the end there was Schumann's *Träumerei*. The audience gave Horowitz a standing ovation. He was recalled again and again. Finally the house lights were turned on and a stagehand came out and lowered the keyboard lid.

During the concert Wanda was in the wings, crying, her face streaked with mascara. "I never thought I would live to see this day," she said. Sonia was at the concert, seated alone in the rear of the auditorium. She did not go backstage. Hundreds of admirers did. More hundreds thronged the Carnegie Hall stage door. A path was cleared when Wanda and Horowitz were ready to enter their car. At home, he stretched out on a sofa and sipped champagne. Later he went to his room to watch the eleven-o'clock news. The concert was featured on all telecasts. Horowitz went to bed an exhausted, happy man.

The *Times* sent a reporter to the Horowitz household the next day. He found a house full of flowers sent by admirers. There were also many telegrams, including ones from Sviatoslav Richter, Arthur Rubinstein, and Isaac Stern. Was Horowitz satisfied with his playing? "Pianistically speaking, yes," he said. He added, "I am sure I can play better under different circumstances. It was too emotional for me."

All the New York critics raved. Alan Rich of the *Herald Tribune* described his feelings when Horowitz started the Bach-Busoni. "A few seconds thereafter he reaffirmed beyond any possible doubt his place among the supreme musicians of all time." The *Times* critic did not, unlike most of the other reviewers, see a new maturity. The old Horowitz was good enough for him, and here was the old Horowitz in all his glory.

Columbia rushed to get out the recording of the concert. Horowitz kept insisting that this concert was a historic document, and that he wouldn't change a note. But he did. Some of the slips in the Bach-Busoni are on the record, but not the terrifying moment in the Schumann Fantasy.

Columbia sent a test pressing to the senior music critic of the *Times,* who noticed that the Schumann had been cleaned up. He called Columbia and asked what had happened. An hour later his phone rang:

"Mr. Schonberg?"

"Yes."

"This is Vladimir Horowitz. I understand you have question about my record?"

"The coda of the Schumann . . . ?"

"Yes. Let me explain?"

"Of course."

"You remember how hot it was in the hall? And you know how nervous pianists get when they come to the coda? So while I was playing it, even before I got to the coda, the perspiration ran into my eyes and I could not see the keyboard. So I played blind. So you know how important records are for posterity. I did not want to be represented by something that was not my fault. It was an act of God, the heat and the perspiration. So I corrected the passage after the concert."

"All very well, Mr. Horowitz. But Columbia is advertising it as the return of Vladimir Horowitz to Carnegie Hall, and it isn't."

"But it was an act of God!"

"What about truth in advertising?"

Horowitz kept repeating "act of God." His respondent kept repeating "truth in advertising." They got nowhere.

Howard Klein, who had been at the concert, reviewed the record for the *Times*. He noticed that the Schumann performance on the disc was cleaner than he had remembered. He phoned Horowitz, who said, "Well, they tell me that that's the way it was." Then Klein called the Columbia recording people and asked, "Is this in fact what happened?" They told him yes, that the disc indeed was the actual concert. Klein rushed a review into print. Not long after, Klein discovered that he had been had.

Two years later, when Klein had another Horowitz disc to review, he brought up the issue of splicing together a finished product from various tapes and then advertising the result as a live concert.

The honesty of records had been an ethical issue ever since magnetic tape recording started to be used after 1948, the year the LP disc was introduced. Experienced listeners soon learned never to trust any LP record. The old 78-rpm discs were entirely honest; if an artist did not like what came out in the playback, there was nothing that could be done about it. He or she had to record the entire thing over again. Now, with magnetic tape, a measure or even a single note could be corrected.

In studio recordings, it was expected that the artist would correct inexact passages. But many innocents continued to believe that a recording advertised as an actual performance really was recorded "live" and sold in an unaltered state. Klein mentioned that after his review of the Horowitz comeback he had learned that the ending of the second movement of the Schumann Fantasy was not the actual concert performance. "The question here is one of ethics." In the case of the comeback disc, why not be honest and tell what was actually done? For in pretending to be the recording of a live concert, the disc offered most but not all of the truth.

Klein was not going to be bitten again. He queried Thomas Frost, the producer of the disc, which was released in 1967. Called *Horowitz in Concert,* it was advertised as containing selections from actual concerts. It turned out, wrote Klein, that these "practically note-perfect performances" had been patched together from the sources listed on the record and also from some Horowitz rehearsals in Carnegie Hall. "One of the recordings—the Scriabin Tenth Sonata—was recorded at a preview for 200 Rutgers students who had come to hear Horowitz practice at Carnegie Hall the afternoon of the Big Blackout, November 9, 1965!" Klein continued:

> One admires the candor on the part of the pianist and his producer, and only laments the fact that it is after the fact. The

album with its misleading assertions is out. Horowitz cannot be blamed for being a perfectionist—that is what makes him Horowitz, and there is only one like him. But one wonders if the volatile pianist is in fact the best judge of what constitutes his best performances on records.

For, remarkable as the playing in this album is, the kind of direct communication Horowitz electrified his audiences with is only heard sporadically. Maybe the conglomerate performances lack the natural give and take of performance—the spontaneous control of momentum and thrust, the minute accelerations and corrections which give the live performance its human vitality. Do the perfect parts make a perfect whole?

Thinking back over the imbroglio, Klein said in 1990 that he had been very disturbed by Horowitz's lie, "by the fact that he couldn't admit that he had fudged the first time. It was like a weight on my heart. He was an idol, and I thought: Oh, why? An artist of his stature. What difference did it make?"

Klein's mention of the Big Blackout was a reference to the day when there was a massive power failure on the East Coast. When the blackout occurred on November 9, 1965, Horowitz had just started the Chopin Polonaise-Fantaisie. Suddenly Carnegie Hall went black, and it is hard to convey a sense of how black Carnegie Hall is when not a single light is on in the big auditorium. Those listening to the rehearsal were startled, and probably Horowitz also was. But without faltering once, he continued playing into the blackness. About two minutes later, a stagehand came out with a flashlight and focussed it on the keys. When Horowitz finished the Polonaise-Fantasy, he was notified that the lights of the entire area were out. All rushed to the stage door to peer outside into a New York lit only by the headlights of automobiles. Everybody thought it was a local power failure and did not realize that the entire eastern seaboard had been hit. A *Times* reporter at the rehearsal walked down to the newspaper's offices on West Forty-third Street and added his little anecdote to the big story, by candlelight.

17

The New Horowitz?

Almost four thousand seats! The house will be only half full! It will be a fiasco! A disaster! A disgrace!
—*Vladimir Horowitz to a journalist about his forthcoming Metropolitan Opera recital*

*I*t was a happy and relaxed Horowitz who faced the world after his 1965 return. He told the press that his long sabbatical had solved his problems: "Before, I was always aware there was a public in the hall, and I played to please the public. Times are different now. Today I play the music I want and I just try to do my best." He said that now he was at a point where he had become a free agent. He had no managers. Julius Bloom took care of his business affairs, and he did exactly what Horowitz told him to do. "If I want to play in New York, I play in New York. If I want to play five times, I play five times. I make the decisions."

He said that he had also simplified business arrangements by making all the concerts he played single admission. "They are not part of a series. I also continue to insist on afternoon concerts because that's when I'm freshest and I believe it is also the best time for the audience." Here Horowitz was working along the lines of the Charlie Wilson theory. "Engine Charlie" of General Motors had, many years previously, achieved a kind of immortality with his statement: "What's good for General Motors is good for the country."

The first New York concerts after Horowitz's 1965 return were held in Carnegie Hall on April 17 and November 27, 1966. On the programs were pieces either new to his repertoire or that he had not played for years. The Scriabin Tenth Sonata, Mozart's Sonata in A (the one with the "Turkish March"), Beethoven's C minor Variations (which he had not played since the early 1950s), and Chopin's Polonaise-Fantaisie, which he had not played in concert since 1951, were on the April 17 program. On November 27 there were Liszt's *Vallée d'Obermann*, Haydn's F major Sonata (No. 23), Debussy's *L'isle joyeuse* and three preludes (*Bruyères, Les fées sont d'exquises danseuses,* and *La terrasse des audiences au clair de lune*), and Schumann's *Blumenstück.*

Horowitz was taking seriously his promise to expand his repertoire. From 1965 to his death his audiences could count on something new at almost every concert. In the next two decades he programmed for the first time in the United States Scriabin's Fifth and Tenth sonatas, several Mozart and Haydn sonatas, Liszt's B minor Ballade, Schumann's *Kreisleriana* and F minor Sonata, several Clementi sonatas, Liszt's Scherzo and March, the Mendelssohn *Scherzo a Capriccio,* and Schubert's B flat Impromptu. He also revived Rachmaninoff's Second Sonata, which he had not played since 1948.

Then in 1968 television entered his life. Horowitz and Luciano Pavarotti were the two most popular, highly paid classical musicians of their time, and it was inevitable that Horowitz, like the great Italian tenor, would turn to television.

Howard Taubman, critic at large of the *Times* and an old friend of the pianist's, had been appointed by CBS to approach Horowitz with the idea of a televised recital, and he had long talks with him about the project. Horowitz, who had watched classical-music telecasts, at first resisted the idea. He felt that the classical music on television he had looked at was either hyped up or, if presented "straight," simply dull. With a singer on television, he told *Time* in an amusing interview, "you see nothing but tonsils."

But after his specifications were met, he agreed. He wanted no glitz, no ceremony, no advertising on his show, just Horowitz playing the piano.

Taubman was the executive producer, Thomas Frost the sound engineer and Roger Englander the director. Englander was an old hand at classical music on television. A trained musician, he had produced shows for all three networks and had won Emmy and Peabody awards. But Frost withdrew after he and Taubman got into a dispute over the medium of recording. Frost wanted to use film, which he thought provided greater fidelity, whereas Taubman and Englander favored videotape. Frost was replaced by Paul Myers, another CBS record producer.

During the taping Wanda created her own kind of tension. She kept ordering cameramen around, she even objected to close-ups of Horowitz's hands, and she complained bitterly that Horowitz's face was not being properly photographed. If she had been allowed to have her own way, said a technician in the project, the show would have been as stiff as photographs of California redwoods. Goddard Lieberson had to be summoned from his office in the CBS Building. He ordered Wanda to let the television professionals do their job.

At CBS the projected show was called Project X and had a top-secret tag attached to it because Horowitz would have been furious had there been a publicity leak. Rehearsals were held in Carnegie Hall. Special pains were taken to ensure that the highest technical standards obtained. The floor of the stage was sprinkled with talcum powder to avoid squeaking. The television crew wore velvet slippers. Programs were printed on silk so that there would be no rustling. In all, the project cost CBS about $275,000.

Horowitz watched some of the playbacks. He was somewhat startled at what he saw. In his interview with *Time* he said that he had never before seen a close-up of his hands on the keyboard. "It's fantastic, but sometimes the technique is awful. Things I tell my students not to do, I'm doing!" And of the close-ups of his face: "To me it's almost an invasion of my privacy."

The videotape was made by CBS at Carnegie Hall on January 2 and February 1, 1968. For both tapings the hall was full, and reviewers were present. The program contained two Scarlatti sonatas; Chopin's G minor Ballade (Horowitz's old friend and adversary), F sharp minor Polonaise, and F minor Nocturne; the

Schumann *Arabesque;* Scriabin's Etude in D sharp minor; and, as always, Schumann's *Träumerei* as an encore, followed by the *Carmen* Variations. The TV special was sponsored by General Telephone and Electronics. Called *Vladimir Horowitz: A Television Concert at Carnegie Hall,* it went out over the CBS network on September 22, 1968, and later in the year on Christmas Day.

On this show many music lovers and piano students were seeing and hearing Horowitz for the first time; and even those who had watched his playing through the years could see things not visible in the concert hall—the close-ups of the Horowitz hands, for instance. There must have been reverberations between teachers and students all over the country as they watched the fabulous Horowitz hands doing all the "wrong" things. In his review, Robert Finn of the Cleveland *Plain Dealer* was amused at this aspect of the film. "I think," he wrote the following day, "this concert should have borne an 'adults only' label, for if many piano-looking youngsters get the idea that they should hold their hands like Horowitz, American piano playing will be set back 50 years."

By and large the telecast was respectfully greeted by television and music critics around the country, who were grateful that there was little hype, no tricks or gimmicks. Paul Hume of the Washington *Post* wrote that with this show "television took a great step forward." Martin Bernheimer of the Los Angeles *Times* called the telecast "a valuable memento of a formidable artist at work. . . . His heroic individuality and romantic temperament emerged vividly, even on a tiny screen."

The show had a low Nielsen rating. It was up against the popular *Bonanza* on one network and the film *Zorba the Greek* on the other. Yet, as the *Times* pointed out, on this telecast Horowitz played to more listeners in one evening than he could reach in several years on the concert stage.

Then, suddenly, only four years after proudly proclaiming himself a new Horowitz, he disappeared from the stage. This time nobody seemed to be prepared for it. Could it have been an adolescent Horowitz response to a bad criticism? Some thought so.

In 1969 Horowitz gave a recital in Boston and was mauled by the Boston *Globe* critic. Michael Steinberg, never hospitable to Horowitz, praised his technique. But his music making? Steinberg repeated what Virgil Thomson said in the 1940s, citing what he considered the broken lines, the fussy approach, the "incoherencies." Steinberg was a literalist very much of the new school, and his ideal of piano playing centered on such sober, architecture-minded artists as Alfred Brendel.

Was it cause and effect? Wanda said no. She said that in Boston he had "an overdose of sunshine" and became very ill. But that does not sound like a convincing excuse for a long absence. And, as was quickly pointed out, it was after the bad reviews of his Schubert B flat Sonata in 1953 that Horowitz disappeared for twelve years.

This time it was not twelve years. But Horowitz did not play another concert for almost five years. When he stopped in 1969 after the Steinberg review he was, all agreed, "a bundle of nerves," as Jack Pfeiffer described it. Horowitz made it clear that he was not going to play in public for the time being. The only thing he seemed to relish were his Social Security checks (he had turned sixty-five on October 1, 1968). When they came in on the first of the month he cashed them with great satisfaction.

During his absence from the concert life, however, he made records for Columbia—five discs over the next four years. He re-recorded old repertoire, such as the Beethoven *Moonlight* and *Appassionata,* and standard Chopin works. He learned four Schubert impromptus. He recorded Beethoven's *Waldstein* Sonata and Schumann's *Kreisleriana.* He became interested in a relatively obscure Chopin work, the Introduction and Rondo (Op. 16). He restudied a few Scriabin pieces.

He also watched the sales of his records go down. So did the Columbia bottom-line men. With Horowitz no longer before the public, the public began to forget him. Horowitz's association with CBS Masterworks was coming to an end. It was the same pattern that had occurred at RCA more than a decade earlier.

In 1969 and 1970 he had psychiatric help and shock therapy, and by 1971 he was nearly back to normal. He even started an association with Harold Shaw, an experienced New York concert manager, which meant that although he was not yet ready to resume his career, he was at least thinking about it. He realized that he needed more active help than Julius Bloom, his former business manager who was still running Carnegie Hall, could give him.

David Rubin, the artists' representative of Steinway & Sons, had brought up Shaw's name to Horowitz. When Horowitz said that he would not mind talking to Shaw, Rubin brought the two men together. Shaw and Horowitz soon began seeing each other on a regular basis.

For over a year they indulged in a ritual dance. Shaw would come to dinner twice a week, sometimes three times, arriving promptly at 7:45 P.M. He and the Horowitzes had an aperitif. Dinner was served at 8 P.M. Horowitz, who watched his diet very carefully, always ate the same thing, and so did everybody else. The menu consisted only of fish or chicken, with peas or rice. Shaw, a gourmet, heroically ate the unpalatable mess. After dinner Horowitz would disappear for a short rest, while Shaw and Wanda gossiped. When Horowitz returned at 9:45, he and Shaw would talk until midnight.

What they talked about was what Shaw called "living-room tours," discussing various cities and working out an itinerary. Shaw was amazed at the intimate knowledge Horowitz and Wanda had about American concert halls and the concert business, and he said that he learned a lot. "I also learned how to listen to what an artist says and thinks."

Shaw thus found out at first hand what everybody in music management knew. When it came to business, Horowitz and Wanda were a redoubtable team. Between them they knew more about the business of music than any manager. "They had the most uncanny sense of timing, of promotion, of ticket prices," said Shaw. "They knew how to build up excitement. They knew the seating capacity of any concert hall in America," said an agent who used to work for them. "They knew exactly what the ticket-price scale should be, and they insisted on a broad range so that no matter how outrageously high the top prices were, there were always seats for the Horowitz fans and groupies."

At that time Horowitz was a Fellow of Yale University and would occasionally talk to students there. As Shaw remembered it, Horowitz went to New Haven in the early seventies and was shocked when one of the students told Horowitz that not one person in the class had heard him play. Horowitz felt as he had that evening in the sixties when Ivan Davis took him to O'Henry's. He mentioned this to the dean of the university, who suggested that Horowitz play for his students. Horowitz thought about it and agreed. But the university would have to send the students to his Manhattan town house.

Horowitz then talked it over with Shaw, suggesting a program lasting less than half an hour. Shaw said that was not enough, that he should play a full program. Wanda, knowing that Shaw was trying to get him back before the public, enthusiastically lent her support. On the designated Sunday about twenty-five students arrived, and Horowitz played a full program for them, building it around Clementi's Sonata in F sharp minor and the Schumann *Kinderscenen.* "Now they know who I am," he said.

That was the moment Harold Shaw struck. Would Horowitz feel like playing the following Sunday, May 12, 1974? Yes. "Then why not give the same program in Cleveland?" Horowitz was taken aback, thought a bit, and then agreed to go ahead. Shaw got busy. He secured Severance Hall and took out one advertisement. Immediately the house was sold out. He had to arrange for a room that resembled the bedroom in Horowitz's own house: black curtains over the windows and so on. Fresh fish had to be flown in. Wanda oversaw everything. There was only one oversight. Horowitz's suspenders were not packed and nobody noticed that they were missing until the morning of the concert. Shaw borrowed suspenders from Lorin Maazel, then the conductor of the Cleveland Orchestra.

Horowitz came out and played with verve and confidence, kicking off a round of tours for the next few years. But he kept his number of appearances to a minimum. "He really didn't like to be away from home," Shaw said.

This tendency toward last-minute decisions on whether or not to give a concert may have had its roots in the old Russian tradition. "When Horowitz was starting out in the Soviet Union," one manager pointed out, "that's the way people played concerts. Nobody planned ahead of time. Opportunities would arise and off the artist would go, on one day's notice. But in his last decades only Horowitz, with his box-office appeal, was in a position to do that. The mere announcement of a concert was enough to sell out a hall immediately. And because of Horowitz's performing times—only at 4 P.M. on Sundays—it was relatively easy to get halls. Even if a hall was booked for a matinee and an evening performance, Horowitz could be squeezed in."

The return of Horowitz after five years was news, and Donal Henahan of the New York *Times* was sent to Cleveland. He called the concert "a typically Horowitzian show, in which there were many moments that perhaps no living pianist could equal." He noted one characteristic of a Horowitz appearance. "The recital began almost fifteen minutes late, and the intermission dragged on as well, which made some members of the audience jumpy, even if Mr. Horowitz may have been entirely calm."

When Harold Shaw started managing the Horowitz concerts in 1974, the pianist's fee was $11,000. Shaw soon boosted that to 80 percent of the gross receipts. All of a sudden Horowitz was making $50,000 and up per concert. It was no great secret, even outside the business. It was also no secret that whoever presented him would almost always be making money. Pavarotti bragged that nobody ever lost money at one of his concerts despite his outlandish fee. The same could be said of Horowitz. These Horowitz concerts were generally billed as special events, with ticket prices hiked accordingly. The 20 percent that came to the presenter easily covered all expenses, with a good sum left over. And the Horowitz price went ever upwards. Toward the end of Horowitz's career, reports from Europe indicated that he was clearing as much as $300,000 a concert; and he peaked with his first appearances in Tokyo, where he got $1 million for his two concerts and the television rights. When the Japanese public learned about that, they were enraged: not so much because of the enormous fee but because Horowitz was off form in 1983 and the Japanese felt that they had been cheated.

Horowitz was once asked where all the money he made went to. "To Internal Revenue," he immediately answered. Horowitz had the reputation of being money-mad. As a matter of fact he turned down many lucrative offers, refusing for years to play on the radio, to make sound tracks for films, to appear on television (eventually he did turn to television, but on his own terms).

As one of his managers insisted, "It is important to realize that for Horowitz a concert had to be the right combination of what was interesting artistically to him as well as rewarding financially. When the balance was right he would do it. He would never do anything for money alone."

Or, as Horowitz once said, "I want to be paid, but I will not be bought."

The biggest moment in the year of the Horowitz return came on November 17, 1974, when he gave a concert at the Metropolitan Opera House. It was the first concert ever given in the eight-year-old, 3,900-seat auditorium, and also the first New York appearance by Horowitz in six years. The concert was a benefit for the Met, now being run by Horowitz's old friend Schuyler Chapin.

The event also coincided with the entrance of Peter Gelb into Horowitz's life. Gelb was with the New York public relations firm of Gurtman and Murtha. He was a bright, energetic young man, full of ideas. In 1974 he read about Horowitz making a return in Cleveland after a five-year absence from the concert stage. Gelb knew Harold Shaw, and approached him as a representative of Gurtman and Murtha, offering to get publicity for Horowitz. Shaw was intrigued by the young man's imaginative ideas and said that he would engage him through Gurtman and Murtha—if Horowitz liked him. Horowitz had never had a press agent before and certainly would not pay for one. Why should he? Everything he did was news. But he was getting older and, Shaw thought, perhaps would welcome the help of a smart public relations man who was tactful enough not to get in his way. Certainly Horowitz had nothing to lose, and if things did not work out Gelb could be dismissed.

Of course it did not escape Horowitz's calculating mind that Gelb was the son of Arthur Gelb, assistant to the executive editor of the New York *Times;* and one of Arthur Gelb's domains was the newspaper's cultural coverage. When it became known that Peter Gelb was now a public relations man for Horowitz, the news created a great deal of buzzing in the New York musical beehive. Would Horowitz now own the great *Times?*

Arthur Gelb immediately let Seymour Peck, the cultural editor of the *Times,* know that Peter was on his own. He also notified the music department to that effect. Any Horowitz story, he wrote in his memo, and in conversation with department heads, would be run at the discretion of the music editor. If it was real news, run it. If not, spike it. Of course that did not stop the knowing wagging of heads when any Horowitz story appeared in the *Times,* but the fact was that the music department leaned over backward *not* to print Horowitz stories. Raymond Ericson, the music editor, and, later, Donal Henahan, when he became the senior critic in 1980, were determined that the *Times* would never be accused of shilling for Horowitz.

Peter Gelb and Horowitz got along famously. The first thing Gelb did was organize a press conference in Horowitz's living room after his return from Cleveland. The subject was Horowitz's projected concert on November 17 at the Metropolitan Opera, and

Gelb whipped up a great deal of press interest in the event. Journalists were invited by Gelb to the second rehearsal at the Met, and
one result was a front-page story in the *Times*. Horowitz was delighted with the publicity, and Gelb officially became his personal
representative at Gurtman and Murtha. That continued for four
years. In 1978 Gelb left New York to work for the Boston Symphony as publicity director and eventually an assistant manager of
the orchestra. Later he would return to New York and form an
even closer association with Horowitz.

The rehearsals at the Metropolitan Opera were necessary because Horowitz had to make sure that the acoustics satisfied him.
Chapin, after discussions with Cyril Harris (the hall's acoustician),
provided a screen at the rear of the stage to throw the piano's sound
into the auditorium. Horowitz was given two rehearsals.

At the first, Horowitz tried out many locations, conferring
with Wanda from the stage. She and a few of the invited guests
prowled the parquet while Horowitz was playing, and they contributed their acoustic assessments. Horowitz was happy with the
sound from a particular location, and the spot was duly marked on
the stage floor. He was worried—or pretended to be—about the
size of the big house and said to a critic at the second rehearsal that
he would never be able to fill it. The critic told Horowitz that he
was being childish, and that he was willing to bet every seat would
be taken.

"Bet?" asked Horowitz. "How much?"

"Fifty dollars?"

They shook hands on the bet. Of course the house was filled,
and of course Horowitz paid his debt in due time, and of course
the critic never cashed the check, keeping it as a souvenir.

The program consisted of the Clementi Sonata in F sharp
minor; Schumann's *Kinderscenen;* the Scriabin Sonata No. 5 (new
to his repertoire); Chopin's Introduction and Rondo in E flat, two
mazurkas, and (still once again the challenge) the Ballade in G
minor. For encores, Horowitz played Scarlatti, Mendelssohn, Chopin, and Scriabin. The Metropolitan Opera cleared over $100,000
from the recital, of which Horowitz got half.

Once again a Horowitz concert was accompanied by a ticket
scandal. The Metropolitan Opera House has about 3,900 seats.
The Shaw office said that 1,300 tickets had been sent to the Metropolitan Opera, of which 1,200 went to the Metropolitan Opera

Guild and 100 for the Metropolitan Opera staff. Which meant that at least 2,500 seats should have been available for the public but, somehow, many of them did not get to the box office. Another investigation was promised by Louis J. Lefkowitz, the New York State Attorney General, who must have been getting pretty tired of this thing. If a report was ever issued, nobody knows anything about it.

Everywhere Horowitz played in 1974 he was interviewed. He invariably sounded relaxed, charming, witty. Donal Henahan of the New York *Times* spent an hour or so with him. The sixty-nine-year-old Horowitz said that he felt fifty. "My blood pressure is that of a twenty-five-year-old. I walk thirty to forty blocks a day. I eat only fruit and fish, no meat, and have not had a drink in twenty years." He limited himself to two cigarettes a day. Henahan watched Horowitz charm a photographer. "Not from the bottom, please. Look, I have no belly, I am everywhere symmetrical, nice green bow tie, matching handkerchief, everything. Only the nose is a little too long. So take from above, please."

Horowitz seemed happy and pleased with himself. But those happy days were shattered by the news he and Wanda received on January 10, 1975. Their daughter, Sonia, was found dead in her Geneva apartment.

18

Sonia

She was a strange child and I did not understand her. Perhaps I was not so good a father.
—*Vladimir Horowitz to Harold C. Schonberg about Sonia*

Sonia's life had not been happy; and Wanda, who had a terrible attack of guilt feelings, brooded about her daughter's death for a long time. Horowitz too went through a bad period, though many did not realize this because he never talked about it. In any case, his mind-set was such that his own routine had to take precedence over everything else, even the death of his daughter.

Still, it nevertheless was a searing experience. Twelve years after Sonia's death, Horowitz and Wanda still found it painful to talk about it.

"Between Sonia and us," Wanda said, "was a tremendous love and hate. She grew up hearing her grandfather screaming about Mussolini and Hitler. There was an air of hate in the house. And she was brought up with no nationality, really. She had a Jewish

father and a Catholic mother, but was baptized because her grandfather wanted it." Wanda didn't want to baptize her, but Toscanini
had his way, as always. Sonia grew up in the shadow of two religions, though neither parent was a believer.

In Milan Sonia had a nannie, Sister Annie, who was with her
much more than her parents were. They were always on tour. Sister
Annie, said Wanda, gave her a sense of security. But "when we
moved to the States there was no more Sister Annie, and that was
a personal and psychological rupture."

When the family settled in America just after the outbreak of
World War II, Sonia was about five. The Horowitzes lived at first
in the Hotel Astor, then moved to the Hotel Madison and other
hotels. "Sonia had no ground under her feet," said Wanda. "She
was not brought up as an Italian, as a Russian, as an American.
What happened was a complete confusion." Wanda would not send
her to boarding school because, as she explained, Italians sent only
"bad" children there. Looking back, Wanda realized that a boarding school might have given Sonia some security:

> For her education we sent her first to the Lycée Français
> and then to the Convent of the Sacred Heart, where she lived
> five days a week and came home for weekends. She was around
> seven at that time. We thought that this way she would not feel
> rejected by the family. But that was the worst thing that could
> have happened, because we were always on tour, we still did
> not have a house, so she went to Riverdale on weekends to live
> with her grandparents, or she stayed with friends. That's about
> the worst thing that could have happened. She felt that she
> never had a home. The child had no continuity in her life. She
> had no security whatsoever. Every time we left, she felt aban-
> doned. She felt that we would never come back. Had we
> brought Sister Annie to America with us, things would have
> been different.

By all accounts, Sonia was a precocious child, the most intelligent of all the Toscanini grandchildren. Wanda had a letter from
Maestro in which he said he never had a special liking for any of
his children, but among the three grandchildren, he said, "Sonia is
my favorite."

She might have developed into a good pianist had she put her
mind to it. Rachmaninoff said that Sonia had hands like Anton
Rubinstein's—a thick palm, spatulate fingers, a wide stretch. In

short, an ideal piano hand. She had a fine musical memory and a superior ear, with a Toscanini-like ability to hear a single wrong note among a welter of violins. Horowitz's cousin Natasha Saitzoff, staying with the family in Switzerland before the move to America, came down one morning to hear the four-year-old Sonia singing themes from the Brahms B flat Concerto. She had been listening to her father practice it the day before.

At the age of six she already was at the piano, studying with Siegfried M. Lichstein, a teacher at the Chatham Square Music School. Lichstein had been recommended by Samuel Chotzinoff. In 1940 Lichstein told the New York *Times* what his first visit to Villa Pauline, where the Toscaninis lived, felt like.

He was nervous as he approached the door, and more nervous when Toscanini himself opened it. "Come in, come in." Then Toscanini yelled, "Sonia! Quick! Your professor is here!" Toscanini retired to a corner of the room, but his presence was palpable. Lichstein said that he could hardly think straight during that first lesson. But Toscanini seemed pleased, complimented Lichstein on his teaching method, and told Sonia to practice hard for her professor.

Two years later Isabelle Vengerova, who divided her teaching between the Curtis Institute and New York, gave the eight-year-old girl lessons when she came to Manhattan. For these lessons Sonia had to go to Vengerova's studio. Vengerova had no intention of teaching the child with Toscanini and Horowitz hovering about.

During Sonia's adolescence one of her confidantes was Natasha Saitzoff, then living in New York. She and her husband had managed to get out of Europe during World War II, thanks largely to cousin Volodya, who had stood sponsor for them. He had promised to take financial care of them in America, and on the strength of the Horowitz sponsorship they got a visa and were able to take out first papers. Natasha often stayed with Sonia while Horowitz and Wanda, then living in the Madison Hotel, were on tour.

Natasha remembered one illuminating experience with Sonia when the child was eleven or twelve. Her parents were away on tour, and she and Sonia were walking in Central Park. Sonia asked Natasha, "What would you do if one day you woke up and found a big box full of money? What would you do?"

"First," said Natasha, "we buy a ranch and get a group of people who are going to collect all the stray dogs that are miserable, that people don't like, and we take care of them, and we make a paradise for dogs."

Sonia loved animals, as Natasha well knew, and so she loved the idea of a paradise for dogs.

"And then we will give something to your friends."

Sonia beamed. "Oh, sure!" she said.

Then Sonia said, "To Merovitch, what are you going to give him?" Merovitch, though he had little relationship with Horowitz at that time, was still part of Sonia's memory, and she understood how much Horowitz had meant to him. Natasha agreed that it was a good idea to take care of Merovitch.

"We'll find him a beautiful office," said Sonia.

"All right," said Natasha. "What else?"

At that point Sonia turned to Natasha and said, "And then we will buy a hotel."

Natasha was astonished. "What for?" she asked.

"Oh," said Sonia. "Hotels make a lot of money."

"But we have some money," said Natasha.

"No," said Sonia. "We have spent so much we need to make more money."

Natasha suddenly realized that Sonia, who had been living with her parents in hotels, had been hearing them complain about the high rent and cost of living. She would buy a hotel, which made a lot of money, and would put her parents in there free of charge so that they wouldn't complain anymore.

What Sonia did not have, with all of her obvious intelligence, was application. She never pursued anything all the way through. She gave up her piano studies as a young teenager. She dabbled in painting and tried to write poetry, but became bored and dropped those pursuits. In school she never was a good student. As she grew up the subject that interested her most was religion, especially comparative religions, about which she read a great deal.

In her early teens she started to act up, defiantly smoking, constantly arguing with her parents, and using foul language. Anybody with experience would have known that all this was a desperate scream for attention, for help, but her parents did not have experience.

Sonia's bid for attention having failed, the trouble really

began. She refused to go to school anymore. Her parents found her unmanageable. So they sent her to a psychiatrist who suggested she be put into the George Junior Republic School near Ithaca, New York. It was a school that worked on the lines of the American republic. It had a president, a vice president, and the equivalent of a Congress. Everybody in the school had a vote. Wanda said that the move was "a catastrophe. The school had the most horrible, disturbed children, and that was not the place for Sonia."

But she finished high school there before going home to live with her parents.

Sonia was a loner. She did make friends easily and was enthusiastic about them for a while, but she dropped them just as quickly. Wanda wondered if she ever had any real friends. Perhaps she sublimated that need in religion. Exposed to Catholicism, Sonia made a thorough study of the Gospels. Then she broke away from the church, became absorbed in Judaism, studied with a rabbi and became a Jew. By that time, at the age of seventeen, she was able to speak French and Italian, which she got from the family, and she then started to study Russian.

When Sonia became a young woman, friends tried to fit her into jobs. She never could hold one. She was a liberal and an idealist, said Naomi Graffman, who knew the young woman while her husband, Gary, was studying with Horowitz. "She was passionately interested in people and humanity. She threw herself into the civil rights movement and talked about going to Mississippi and joining the marches there. She identified with the plight of the Israelis. But she never really did anything concrete about anything, and her passions seemed to be short-lived."

At around the age of twenty Sonia decided she did not want to live in America. "She really didn't like any place," said Wanda. "She couldn't find any place on this earth."

Sonia started her *Wanderjahre* by going to Paris, and then to Israel, where she lived on a kibbutz. Finally Judaism did not satisfy her. Wanda got a letter from Sonia: "Give Israel back to the Arabs." Wanda considered Sonia "a Wandering Jew herself." She lived for a while in Italy, then Switzerland. Occasionally she would return to America and stay with her parents.

As far as Wanda knew, Sonia never took drugs, "but she almost lived on sleeping pills and toward the end she started drinking. Then she stopped drinking. Then she started again." Wanda realized she was an unhappy, disturbed young woman but did not know what to do about it:

> She remained in contact with us, and was always angry. She was angry with the French, with the Italians, with the Americans, with everybody. She couldn't find peace. She was extreme in everything. Love and hate—there was no half way. She could weigh 180 pounds and then go down to 130. On January 10, 1975, she was found dead in her rooms in Geneva. She had taken too many sleeping pills. By accident or design— nobody will ever know. She couldn't find peace. She was forty when she died.

Sonia had wanted to write a biography of her father, and she discussed the project with Natasha. Of course nothing came of it. Finally her mental problems were beyond her control. Toward the end she had trouble articulating her thoughts. She would talk to friends, but incoherently. Horowitz told Natasha that he believed her motorbike accident in 1957 had caused severe brain damage.

When Sonia died in Geneva, history repeated itself. Wanda immediately got on a plane, while Horowitz stayed home. His way of coping with a crisis was to flee from it.

Wanda had brought Sonia to Geneva in 1974, asking the pianist Nikita Magaloff, who lived near there, to look after her, which he did. Sonia said she wanted to take piano lessons again, and also wanted to continue her Russian studies. Magaloff put her in touch with a Russian pianist, Alexis Golovin. She never got around to taking lessons, but she and Golovin became friends and she would spend much time on the phone with him, discussing her problems. The main problem seemed to be her father. She told Golovin that she loved her father but that he had rejected her. She kept waiting for him to show any desire to see her, any suggestion of love from him.

It never happened.

In Geneva and elsewhere it was generally believed that Sonia had taken her own life. But there was no evidence one way or the other. Natasha believed that it was an accidental death from an overdose of drugs. "If she had wanted to commit suicide she would have done it long before."

Wanda returned from Sonia's funeral in Milan distraught. One night some friends came to East Ninety-fourth Street to pay their respects. Horowitz came downstairs and, said Vera Michaelson, a public relations woman who was a neighbor in Connecticut, where Horowitz and Wanda had a summer home, it was the first time she had ever seen him haggard, untidy, looking as though he had not slept for weeks.

Mrs. Michaelson and her husband soon said they had to leave.

"No," said Horowitz. "I want to play." He went to the piano.

Mrs. Michaelson said that she did not remember what he played, except that "it was not sad, not funeral music." Mrs. Michaelson was looking at Wanda while Horowitz played. "She looked at him with such tremendous love. She was terribly in love with him at that moment." Horowitz played for about two hours. It was a tribute that Sonia would have appreciated and perhaps even understood.

19

Traveling à la Paderewski

What's important is contrast. Always contrast. And if the audience is not with me, then for ten, fifteen minutes there is a little hole. But in the end—unless I am not playing well—they will be with me.
—*Vladimir Horowitz, in a* Times *interview with Helen Epstein*

About two months after Sonia's death, Horowitz was once again on the road with Wanda, meeting the rest of his commitments for the 1974–75 season, during which Horowitz played about twenty concerts in the United States and Canada. It was the biggest tour he had undertaken since the 1950s.

If Horowitz had any deep feelings about Sonia's death, he managed to hide them very well. And Wanda refused to talk to the press about Sonia in any detail. Her only comment was that she thought she would never get over it, but that life must go on. Horowitz made no statement at all. But he was willing, even eager, to talk about everything else.

Something new in his relations with the media was entering Horowitz's life. Ever since his American debut in 1928 he had been in the public eye, always an object of intense curiosity to the musical public. But he never gave much of himself in his interviews, constantly repeating the same old stories—his relationship with Rachmaninoff, his childhood meeting with Scriabin, and so on. Generally he ended up saying the same things over and over again, and his observations were never particularly original or stimulating. In all fairness, this is true of most artists. They are forced back to the same stories, year after year. After all, they can't *invent* new things to say.

But now, all of a sudden, Horowitz seemed to relish public attention and he actively courted the media. He liked to hear himself talk, and he began to fancy himself a wit, a raconteur. Since he was not as witty as he seemed to think he was, this activity bothered many of his admirers. By exposing himself too much, by sometimes coming close to making a fool of himself, Horowitz lost some of the mystery and awe he had previously commanded. He began to be known as a character, an eccentric. He not only relished being a celebrity, he began to try to live up to it, even to the extent of appearing on television talk shows.

On some of those shows and in press conferences during the last decade of his life Horowitz often tried to be both wit and *grand seigneur*. It was a pose that did not ring true. Horowitz, unlike Rubinstein, was not cut out to be a *grand seigneur*. His wisdom—and he could be very wise—was sometimes clouded by an adolescent quality and a vanity that could lead him into silly verbal extravagances. His repartee in press conferences could usually best be described as embarrassing.

And then, in those last decades, there was his mode of travel, gleefully described by the American press.

He traveled in grand style. In the old days, that was traditional among superstars. Idols like Adelina Patti, Paderewski, or Nellie Melba, with their private railway cars, their forty pieces of luggage, their chefs and servants, delighted the public with their lavish mode of life. It was part of their mystique, and it became part of Horowitz's.

Typical was a 1977 concert in Miami, which hit all the newspapers. The Horowitz entourage included his wife, his valet, his secretary, his tuner, his recording engineers, and his cook. His own piano went along with him. In Miami, Judith Drucker, the local impresario, let it be known that Horowitz said he would not play unless a supply of fresh gray sole was on hand. She had it flown in from New Bedford, Massachusetts, and it was delivered to the Horowitz cook so that the fish could be prepared à la Horowitz. (Naturally any suite in which Horowitz stayed had to have a kitchen.)

Drucker also told the press of other Horowitz requirements. He demanded blacked-out bedroom windows. There were to be no calls until noon. He needed a room large enough for two concert grands. A limousine had to be standing by at all times. Drucker reaped a million dollars' worth of publicity from the episode. So did Horowitz.

As Horowitz's manager, Harold Shaw was the one who had to instruct Drucker—and other impresarios around the country—on the way to keep his pianist happy. If Horowitz was not happy, Wanda was unhappy; and if Wanda was unhappy, the entire community would know about it. Woe betide any local manager who did not meet the Horowitz requirements for physical well-being, or who failed to sell every seat in the hall. Not that the latter happened very often.

Shaw remembered that Miami concert for another reason. Horowitz had a series of mishaps in the Chopin B flat minor Sonata and played a great many wrong notes. At intermission he wryly said to Shaw, "Oh, what I wrote for Chopin today." He finished the recital and went back to his dressing room in a vile mood. At best, Horowitz did not like to see many people after a recital. This time he refused to see anybody.

Shaw noticed two ten-year-old children hanging around backstage, twins, waiting for Horowitz to come out. Shaw spoke to them. "They were piano students and lovely kids," he said. "They hoped to get Horowitz's autograph on their program. I knew they didn't have a chance, so I took them into Horowitz's dressing room. He couldn't have been nicer, and he signed their programs. One of the boys then looked at him and said, 'What happened in the Chopin?' Horowitz stared at him and then broke up. He simply howled with laughter."

The American public read the reports about Horowitz's requirements with amusement and even delight. This, by golly, was the way superstars were *supposed* to act.

Was Horowitz spoiled rotten? By normal standards, yes. But a neurotic genius like Horowitz could not be judged by normal standards. Two of his business associates had a ready explanation for Horowitz's behavior. Peter Gelb, his manager after 1981, explained that Horowitz "was operating by his own necessities."

The behavior may have been eccentric, Gelb said in a long, analytic justification, but it was born out of "practical reasoning." For instance, Gelb said, Horowitz had a habit of not signing a contract until a month or so before a concert because he did not want to cancel. "He knew that the only way he could live up to his commitments was by not making commitments until the last possible moment. He knew enough about himself to know that he would never know how well he would feel a few months ahead of time. By limiting his commitments until the last moment he could fulfill them." As for the living requirements he expected:

> When he demanded special food and special treatment from his hotel it was in his mind that it was the only way he could survive. He really thought that. If he didn't have his water, if he didn't have his Dover sole in the period he was having Dover sole, he was not going to live to the next day. In that sense he was a hypochondriac, but he really wasn't being some kind of prima donna. He was being very practical. He wouldn't—he *couldn't*—play anywhere unless he had all the things he was accustomed to. It wasn't a question of being spoiled. It was something much more basic. Believe me, I have dealt with spoiled people, and I know. Having the things he needed was essential to him. He couldn't live without them. And if he couldn't live he couldn't play the piano.

Harold Shaw thought much the same way. He said that he never found Horowitz personally difficult. Demanding, yes. Difficult, no. Most great artists who are considered demanding, he believed, are really not. They need certain things to produce their best work. "His doctor told him that because of his high blood pressure he had to stretch out at intermissions, relax, maybe even take a catnap. Horowitz tried it and it helped him a lot. He *needed* the sofa that had to be put in the artist's room for his concerts. He was not being difficult, he was being practical. He needed it to do his job."

Shaw had another observation to make, one that would be backed by all managers: "It is the middle rank of artists who are difficult. They know that they are never going to make it to the top, and they can drive you crazy with their incessant complaining and the way they change their minds from day to day. They blame everybody but themselves that they are not Vladimir Horowitz, Jessye Norman, or Kathleen Battle."

Horowitz put it more simply. "I have my habits and cannot change."

Shaw noticed that Horowitz was always keyed up before a performance. "But I also noticed that once he acknowledged the applause and sat down, he was at home. He forgot the audience, forgot everything, concentrated only on the piano. Everything else was erased." Robert Marsh, the Chicago critic, once asked Horowitz about his relation with the audience while he was playing. "I don't mind if they're there," Horowitz said. But in a New York *Times* magazine interview with Helen Epstein, he said that he never lost contact; that he monitored the audience while playing:

> I want when I cry on the piano or when I laugh, that the public also cries and laughs. That is my goal. It takes time to achieve. So with me, the longer the recital progresses, the more people are with me. I can measure by the length of the silence. To applaud loud is very easy, but it is when they are silent that you are doing something. Sometimes I feel they are not with me and I am unhappy. So I gradually try to seduce them. If I don't succeed with one piece, I try another, with another sound, from another century, with a more spectacular playing.

Another new feature of his life was that he started to travel in airplanes. Up to 1976 he had been terrified of them. But once he was inveigled into a flight he acted as though he had invented air travel, and he began to look forward to his sorties above the earth. Always first class, of course. Stewardesses pampered and flattered him, and he loved every bit of it.

In 1975 Horowitz left Columbia and went back to RCA. One reason was Kenneth Glancy, with whom he had worked at Columbia. They got along well together. When Glancy went over to RCA as president and general manager of the record division, he was very anxious to get Horowitz back and offered him a handsome contract. Glancy thought it important not only to have Horowitz recording again for RCA, and he also, correctly as it turned out, was conscious of the publicity that Horowitz would bring to RCA.

Glancy also knew exactly what the status of Horowitz as a recording artist was at that time. Horowitz was a free agent, no longer with Columbia. In 1962 and 1963 Columbia had issued his first two records with extraordinary publicity that involved almost everything except a twenty-one-gun salute and the Marine Band playing *The Stars and Stripes Forever*. After that, Horowitz records were normally issued, without any special publicity. And Horowitz also went into a repertoire that not even he could popularize—his Scriabin record, for instance. Sales dropped. Toward the end of the association, Columbia did little promotion. Horowitz's advance of $50,000 for each disc did not cover the sales, and the accountants wanted to reduce it. Horowitz's attorneys said that was not possible. His contract was not renewed.

When Horowitz resumed recording for RCA, the great majority of his discs came from concerts, all of which were taped. Jack Pfeiffer, his producer, followed him all over the country on his tours. Pfeiffer would take the performances, or parts of them, from several concerts and put them together to form a disc. He worked out a system where he could splice from the various halls without much acoustic change. For the most part, these concerts consisted of standard repertoire, and both RCA and Horowitz were pleased with the commercial results.

But one concert that would have galvanized pianophiles the world over did not come off.

Horowitz had agreed to play some four-hand pieces with Rudolf Serkin at the Marlboro Festival during the summer of 1975. The program was to contain, among other things, the Schubert F minor Fantasy and the Mendelssohn *Allegro brillante*. The two old friends got together in New York and worked on the music. Sampson Field, a New York businessman who was a good pianist and active in Marlboro and New York Philharmonic affairs, alerted the press about the event.

But as the Marlboro date approached, Horowitz had second thoughts. Field all but had a stroke. He was constantly on the phone to Horowitz, begging him to keep his promise, telling him how much the concert would mean to Marlboro and to Serkin. It was to no avail. Horowitz finally canceled. His excuse was that he was too busy learning Schumann's F minor Sonata. Field later told a reporter that Serkin, "that saint," took the news with a philosophical shrug of his shoulders. Field was not so saintly, and he never forgave Horowitz.

A highlight of Horowitz's 1975–76 season was a reunion with an important figure from his past.

Early in 1976, Horowitz was playing in California and gave a concert on February 22 at the new hall of Ambassador College in Pasadena. At that time Sergei Tarnowsky, Horowitz's second professor at the Kiev Conservatory, was teaching in Los Angeles. He and Horowitz had never lost touch, but neither were they close friends. Tarnowsky, now ninety-four years old, had always been a dogmatic and unyielding man who made enemies easily. He always said exactly what he thought and did not hesitate to criticize his former pupil. Tarnowsky once angrily lectured Horowitz in the 1930s about his approach to the Chopin G minor Ballade, after a concert in Chicago, and Horowitz brooded about it for a long time.

Among Tarnowsky's pupils was the thirteen-year-old Horacio Gutierrez, whose parents had fled Cuba after Castro took control. Tarnowsky thought that Gutierrez, who studied with him in Los Angeles from 1962 to 1967, was the most phenomenal pianistic talent he had encountered since the young Horowitz, and said exactly that in a testimonial letter to the young pianist. He never charged the Gutierrez family, which was in financial straits, anything for the lessons.

Tarnowsky decided to go to Pasadena for the Horowitz concert. He discussed the oncoming event with Gutierrez a month or so previously. Horowitz was going to play the Schumann F minor Sonata, known as the *Concerto without Orchestra*. Tarnowsky said that he had heard the Horowitz recording of the third movement and did not like it. Gutierrez had the feeling that Tarnowsky, who still regarded Horowitz as his pupil, would have no hesitation about criticizing him when he went to the concert. "Maestro," asked Gutierrez as delicately as he could, "if you don't like it do you have to tell him?" Tarnowsky, who was famous for blurting out what was on his mind, pondered a bit. "No, I suppose not," he finally said.

Orrin Howard and his wife, both of them Tarnowsky pupils, drove the old man to the concert. Howard at that time wrote the program notes for the Los Angeles Philharmonic. At the concert Mrs. Howard sat next to Tarnowsky. Their seats were close to the stage. After Horowitz played the Schumann *Arabesque*, Tarnowsky slapped his knee, looked at Mrs. Howard, and said in a stage whisper that carried several rows but fortunately did not reach Horowitz's ears, "He still doesn't play it right!"

When the concert was over, the Howards ushered their venerable mentor backstage. The reunion, said Howard, was "very warm and emotional." Horowitz and Tarnowsky embraced each other. "This is the only man alive," Horowitz told everybody in sight, "who knew my family." Then he embraced Tarnowsky again. Everybody present was relieved; they had been warned that Horowitz could be unpredictable. What if he snubbed his old teacher or was curt to him? But no. "It was genuine emotion on Horowitz's part," said Howard. "At first they spoke in English. Then they automatically lapsed into Russian. Soon everybody left the room, letting them talk to each other alone."

Tarnowsky went home from the Pasadena concert in a daze of happiness. Horowitz called him the next day to make an appointment, but Tarnowsky, who was not in good health, was unable to see him. One month later, on March 22, 1976, Tarnowsky, the last link with the Horowitz of the Kiev conservatory, was dead.

20
Anniversaries

Am I not well preserved? Come. Feel my muscles.
—*Vladimir Horowitz, age seventy-five, to his photographer,*
Christian Steiner

*I*n May of 1976 it was going to be the eighty-fifth anniversary of the opening of Carnegie Hall. The Music-Hall, as it was originally called, had opened on the corner of Seventh Avenue and West Fifty-seventh Street on May 5, 1891, thanks to the philanthropy of the steel magnate Andrew Carnegie, and it had brought Peter Ilyich Tchaikovsky from Russia for the opening night and the ensuing week of concerts. So Julius Bloom, running the venerable auditorium eighty-five years later, decided to try for a heroic splash on the order of the 1891 opening. The program he worked out was advertised as The Concert of the Century.

Perhaps it was. It is hard to think of another event that brought together such luminaries as Leonard Bernstein (conducting members of the New York Philharmonic), Isaac Stern, Yehudi

Menuhin, Dietrich Fischer-Dieskau, Mstislav Rostropovich—and Vladimir Horowitz. Also gracing the scene was the Oratorio Society (which had sung at opening night and later that week in 1891).

Horowitz was a prominent participant in the program. He accompanied Fischer-Dieskau in Schumann's complete *Dichterliebe* cycle, played the first movement of Tchaikovsky's A minor Trio with Stern and Rostropovich, and the slow movement of the Rachmaninoff Cello Sonata with Rostropovich. The Horowitz-Rostropovich collaboration in the Rachmaninoff came about because the soprano Martina Arroyo canceled at the last minute, whereupon pianist and cellist volunteered to fill in. Menuhin and Stern played the Bach Two-Violin Concerto with Bernstein and the orchestra. Bernstein also conducted Beethoven's *Leonore* No. 3. The Oratorio Society under Lyndon Woodside sang Tchaikovsky's *Pater Noster* and Handel's "Hallelujah" Chorus. All of the musicians donated their services; and the concert, given on May 18, 1976, brought in $1.2 million in cash and pledges for the hall's endowment fund.

As it turned out, Horowitz had a marvelous time collaborating with his colleagues. But he had to be cajoled into appearing. He was not happy to be working with Stern; he told friends that Stern was no longer the violinist he used to be, that he did not practice enough, that he was too interested in being a public figure. Bloom all but got down on his knees begging Horowitz to honor Carnegie Hall even if he had to put up with Stern. Finally Horowitz, who after all owed a great deal to Bloom, agreed.

Bernstein, Stern, Menuhin, Fischer-Dieskau, Rostropovich, Horowitz—a goodly, even godly, group of musicians, these. But it was Horowitz who received the most adulation, as indicated in the *Times* the next day:

> Of all the musicians on stage, Vladimir Horowitz raised the most excitement. It was because he was the most mysterious, most unpredictable, most electrifying. . . . In all of this music Horowitz sat quietly (as he always does) and played as a musician rather than virtuoso. He was determined to work with the ensemble. But that did not stop his electricity from giving everybody in the audience a sizable jolt.
>
> It is curious, this electricity. He never seems to work at it. The first piece on the program, Beethoven's Third *Leonore* Overture, saw Bernstein jumping all over the place, wiggling and waggling and levitating and having a wonderful time bath-

ing his ego in the music. That is his way. Music seems to act on him like an aphrodisiac. But Bernstein made nowhere near the effect that Horowitz did. Horowitz *scares* listeners. There is the feeling of unleashed force in that taut body; a feeling that he, and the stage, and the piano are somewhere along the line going to explode, taking the audience with them.

The concert ended with the "Hallelujah" Chorus. All of the celebrities and also Julius Bloom advanced to the front of the stage and sang along, holding their vocal parts before them and lustily bellowing. They looked amused, Fischer-Dieskau most of all. He was probably listening to the peculiar sounds made by the great instrumentalists.

Later in the year, on October 12, 1976, Horowitz made a personal appearance to sign his discs at the record department of Korvette's department store in New York. He had a tremendous turnout; a few thousand music lovers lined up to meet their hero. A Korvette's spokesman said, "We have never had a response like this for anyone, not even Nureyev or Shirley Bassey." The very fact that Horowitz turned up was indicative of the new attitude he had about public appearances. He bantered with his fans, he gleefully signed records, and appeared to be enjoying himself immensely. Horowitz the recluse had become Horowitz the populist.

In 1977 Horowitz said he would give master classes at the Mannes College of Music. Nothing much came of it. When the director, Risë Stevens, quit, about eight months after he had said yes, so did Horowitz. During that brief time, however, he worked with a young pianist named Dean Kramer, who seems to have disappeared from the concert scene.

Toward the end of 1977, on December 26, Horowitz was interviewed at home by Mike Wallace on *60 Minutes*. Wallace and Horowitz were casual friends. Wanda was an active participant on the show. There were those who found it embarrassing. Horowitz did not show up as an intellectual giant. He looked ill at ease, as evidenced by his nervous, gargled giggle, and he tried too hard to be a regular guy. Wanda was constantly prompting or correcting him. This was not the kind of publicity Horowitz needed.

Two years after the anniversary year of Carnegie Hall came another anniversary, this one more personal. January 12, 1978, marked fifty years since Horowitz had made his American debut with the Tchaikovsky under Beecham in Carnegie Hall. Horowitz celebrated it, almost to the day, with his first orchestral appearance in twenty-five years. On January 8, 1978, in Carnegie Hall, he played the Rachmaninoff Piano Concerto No. 3 with the New York Philharmonic conducted by Eugene Ormandy.

Horowitz had said that he would never again play a concerto, but a golden anniversary is, after all, something special, and he relented. But what conductor could he work with? He would have nothing to do with Leonard Bernstein, who, Horowitz thought, would try to steal the show. He would want to be the stud, Horowitz said. But in a concerto he, Vladimir Horowitz, had to be the stud. Who else among the big names was available? Horowitz went through the roster, criticizing nearly everybody before settling on Ormandy. With him he would feel comfortable.

Avery Fisher Hall in Lincoln Center was the home of the New York Philharmonic, but Horowitz would not play there. He did not like the acoustics. So the Philharmonic packed up and moved south for this one concert. It was fascinating for the audience to hear the Philharmonic in Carnegie Hall for the first time in more than fifteen years.

When Lincoln Center's Philharmonic Hall went up in 1962, the New York Philharmonic left Carnegie Hall to make its home in the glamorous new cultural center. But Philharmonic Hall turned out to be an acoustic disaster. After years of tinkering around at an expense of millions of dollars, Lincoln Center bit the bullet and literally gutted the auditorium, using about half of an $8 million gift previously donated by Avery Fisher. Cyril Harris was the acoustician for the new auditorium. The rebuilt Philharmonic Hall, now named after its benefactor, opened its doors on October 19, 1976. Everybody agreed that there was a tremendous improvement, but Carnegie Hall still remained the premier concert hall of New York. Avery Fisher Hall, it was felt, was somewhat dry, lacking the bass and golden sonority of its distinguished elderly neighbor eight blocks south.

The Philharmonic's appearance in Carnegie Hall for the Horowitz jubilee reinforced that impression. Under Ormandy the orchestra sounded rich and glowing, much more so than in its own home, and there were those at the concert who shed a quiet tear.

The concerto was preceded by Beethoven's *Egmont* Overture and Symphony No. 7. When Horowitz came out after intermission and played the concerto, there was pandemonium at its conclusion.

Naturally the Horowitz-Ormandy Rachmaninoff recording was immediately released, in a touched up version (as the 1965 return concert had been). But the reviews were mixed.

Something was creeping into Horowitz's playing that alarmed some of his admirers. The *Times* reviewer was unhappy about the self-indulgence of the performance. It ended up a collection of details, he said. For a few years the *Times* man had been grumbling about Horowitz's increasingly noticeable mannerisms and his concentration on detail to the detriment of the melodic line. In 1974 he had greeted a Horowitz performance of Chopin's G minor Ballade as "mannered and even inexplicable." There were further complaints about disjointed playing in 1976: "It seems to be getting more pronounced as he grows older. A large-scale work ends up episodic."

Horowitz was entering a bad period, one in which mannerism took precedence over style. His playing still generated the old electricity. But it sometimes had something unsettling about it, something exaggerated, calculated, artificial. The overpronounced rubatos and tempo fluctuations approached bad taste. Sometimes the rhythm was slack, and that almost never was characteristic of his previous work. Sometimes the playing even approached parody, lending support to those who had been claiming all along that Horowitz distorted a melodic line. There could be no defense against these charges with the Rachmaninoff performance, for instance. It was an exhibition of affected sentimentality that had nowhere near the dignity and integrity of the Coates or Reiner recordings.

Also, for some reason, Horowitz started having his piano regulated in a peculiar manner. It sounded hard and bleak, much to the dismay of his technician, Franz Mohr. "In my estimation," Mohr said, "it was overbrilliant, but I was not going to argue with Vladimir Horowitz. Specifically, the piano he used for his performance with Ormandy of the Rachmaninoff Third. Horowitz got it into his head that he needed more volume, that he would not be heard over the orchestra, that the instrument [the famous CD 186 in the Steinway basement, reserved for Horowitz alone] had to be more brilliant. How do you make a piano more brilliant? You file the hammers down so there is little felt, and the hammer is more compact." Then Mohr lacquered the hammers. He worried about the forthcoming Ormandy performance. He thought that the piano sounded ugly, and he told David Rubin of Steinway that he would not take responsibility for the instrument Horowitz was playing. (Sometime later Mohr put a new set of hammers into CD 186, making the piano "only as brilliant as I thought it should be." Horowitz loved it and used it thereafter for his recordings. His favorite instrument, CD 279 503, which had been the Steinway & Sons wedding present and which had been in his house ever since, was sent to the Steinway basement for concert use four years before his death. It was replaced by CD 443, on which he made his at-home recordings.)

It was around this time that Christian Steiner became Horowitz's regular photographer. Steiner, Berlin-born, had been trained as a concert pianist and had grown up on the Horowitz records. After settling in New York he turned to photography and became well known for his portraits of musicians. The first time he heard a Horowitz concert was at the 1965 return. "It was like making a pilgrimage," he said.

In 1978 Steiner got an assignment from the advertising firm of N. W. Ayer to go to Los Angeles and photograph Horowitz. Jack Pfeiffer had suggested his name. When Steiner arrived, it took Horowitz only a short time to realize that the handsome young photographer had a comprehensive knowledge of the piano and its literature. "He couldn't have been more charming," Steiner said. Steiner also had the feeling that Horowitz was trying to impress him. He kept on saying he was seventy-five years old and in wonderful shape. He took off his shirt and displayed his biceps, and Steiner played along. "Oh, yes. Fantastic!" he said.

Horowitz wanted Steiner to play for him. But Steiner said he was out of practice. "There was no way I was going to sit down and play for Horowitz." Steiner concentrated on his photography and got what he considered some fine shots. But when Wanda saw them she was unhappy. Horowitz had combed his hair in a different way, and she did not like the way he looked. Later sessions were more successful. Most of the Horowitz publicity photographs of his last years were Steiner's.

On February 26, 1978, Horowitz played at the White House. It was the first time he had been there since 1931. Harold Shaw engineered the invitation. He had invited Gretchen Poston, the social secretary for President and Mrs. Carter, and several White

House officials to one of Horowitz's Carnegie Hall concerts. There Shaw spoke to Poston about the possibility of a Horowitz appearance at the White House. An hour-long concert was proposed. Poston relayed the message to the president, a music lover who was constantly playing Horowitz records. Carter thought it a fine idea.

When Horowitz arrived, he went to the East Room and tried out his piano, which had preceded him to Washington. He was unhappy with the acoustics and suggested some rugs on the floor. The president and his wife scurried around, found some carpets, and got on their hands and knees to push them around, assisted by White House aides. Shaw looked on all this with amazement. "Where is the press corps? Where are the cameras? What a story!" he kept saying to himself.

Horowitz played the Chopin B flat minor Sonata, two Chopin waltzes (C sharp minor and A minor), and the A flat Polonaise. For encores there were *Träumerei,* Rachmaninoff's *Polka de W. R.,* and his own *Carmen* Fantasy with a new coda. Political figures were present, and also a sizable group of musicians including Eugene Ormandy, Samuel Barber, and Mstislav Rostropovich. President Carter was thrilled to have Horowitz in the East Room, and his introductory comments were from the heart. Horowitz played magnificently. One of his encores, the Rachmaninoff *Polka,* charmed everybody. Horowitz opened the recital with *The Star-Spangled Banner.* That was his idea, and he was very emotional about it.

The concert was televised live by WETA-TV, the Washington Public Broadcasting Service station, and it was picked up by more than a hundred other stations around the country. Not much later it was revealed that Horowitz made money from the foreign television rights of the concert. An article by Linda Charlton in the New York *Times* on May 12, 1978, disclosed that the White House concert had been picked up by Fernseh-Produktionsgesellschaft in Munich, which offered at least $180,000 for foreign distribution rights of the videotape. Horowitz was guaranteed $150,000 immediately, against 67.5 percent of the overseas receipts. WETA-TV was to receive 10 percent of the receipts.

The White House, it was reported, was not happy to be used as part of a commercial enterprise. But Harold Shaw said that he had discussed the financial arrangements with Gretchen Poston and the president. "President Carter," said Shaw, "felt that Horowitz was entitled to everything he could get. He said he deserved it, or words to that effect."

The anniversary concerts continued, around the country and in New York. There were two Carnegie Hall golden jubilee concerts: March 12 and 19, 1978. There was the usual lineup outside the hall. There was the usual ticket scandal; about a thousand tickets were unaccounted for. There was the usual investigation. It turned out that a scalper had managed to get a large number of tickets. It also was reported in the press that Vera Stern had provided some three hundred Carnegie Hall benefactors with tickets so that they would not have to stand in line. Horowitz and Wanda were furious. The scandal was such that the Carnegie Hall box-office head resigned.

For his golden jubilee concerts Horowitz brought back the Liszt Sonata in B minor. He also played the Schumann *Arabesque,* Mozart's C major Sonata (K. 330), which he had never played, and some Fauré—the Impromptu No. 5 and the Nocturne No. 13— also new to his repertoire. There was some Rachmaninoff (the *Moments Musicaux* in B minor and E flat minor [Op. 16, Nos. 3 and 2]) and two Chopin polonaises, the C sharp minor (which he would drop almost immediately) and the inevitable A flat.

Bringing back the long, demanding Liszt B minor Sonata took some daring on Horowitz's part. Some years previously he had told a critic that he was too old to play it anymore. It was for young men, he said. He no longer had the technique and stamina for it. But nobody could have guessed that from his blazing jubilee performance. The Horowitz octaves were functioning as well as ever, the variety of color was all but blinding, and the piece was held together in a masterly manner.

The way he prepared the Fauré pieces was typical. When he looked at music by a composer with whom he was not too familiar, he did a great deal of preliminary reading. "First of all," as reported in the New York *Times* magazine by Helen Epstein,

> I study the whole composer. I play everything he wrote. Ensemble music, everything. I play myself—not listen to recordings. Records are not the truth. They are like post cards of a beautiful landscape. You bring the post cards home so when you look at them, you will remember how beautiful is the truth. So I play. I'm a very good sight reader. The texture of the music

talks to me, the style. I feel the music, the spiritual content of
his compositions.

I also know everything about the composer. I always believe the composer and not what the others write about him. I
read the letters of Fauré, what he was thinking. They gave me
the characteristics of the composer. What he liked in music,
what he didn't like. The first time I play a new piece of music,
I listen. I think there is something here, something is hidden. I
read it again the next day. Then two days I leave it alone. Then
I repeat the third day. Five days. Six days. And then I am in
that music just like I play "Tea for Two."

While he was working on Fauré, Horowitz had talks about
the composer and his style with the well-known French pianist
Jean-Philippe Collard. He had been introduced to Collard in 1977,
and the young man played for Horowitz several times in New
York. Horowitz had a high opinion of him and considered him too
finished an artist to be taken on as a pupil.

Horowitz played in Carnegie Hall again on May 7, 1978, in
what Shaw called an "international concert." During the years since
his 1965 return Horowitz had played only in the United States and
Canada, vowing that he would never again go overseas. Shaw, who
had been besieged by managements in Russia, England, France,
and Germany, all of which wanted to pay fabulous fees for Horowitz, took it philosophically. Then he dreamed up an idea. If Horowitz would not play in foreign cities, perhaps the inhabitants of
foreign cities could hear him in New York.

Shaw got in touch with international travel agents who
worked out package deals. Visitors would get the concert, a stay in
a first-class hotel, a boat ride around Manhattan, visits to New York
museums, time out for shopping, sight-seeing tours, and even a
trip to Niagara Falls if they opted for it. When Horowitz gave this
"international concert," in Carnegie Hall on May 7, more than a
thousand foreigners from fourteen countries were in the Carnegie
Hall audience to hear him play Chopin. As far as Peter G. Davis of
the *Times* was concerned, "The people who had traveled so far for
one concert got what they came for: brilliantly conceived and executed musical statements by one of today's most remarkable pianists."

Capping the golden jubilee concerts was a live television special with Zubin Mehta and the New York Philharmonic on Sep-

tember 24, 1978. It came from Avery Fisher Hall, but only the second half of the program, in which Horowitz played the Rachmaninoff Piano Concerto No. 3, was shown. The *Times* review cited the excitement that Horowitz and Mehta brought to the concerto, but also mentioned self-indulgence from the pianist that approached vulgarity. There was a report from *Variety* on September 27. The broadcast, said *Variety,*

> became an explosion of virtuosity around the world thanks to the Bell System, NBS and satellite transmission. Came an answering wave of astonished delight from all over Europe, a telephone call from the President of the United States. For 20 minutes an audience in Avery Fisher Hall had been standing, applauding, shouting in a way almost never witnessed. Later the doorman at an East Side co-op after the Horowitz fireball was described commented, "You mean he was better than Liberace?"

To celebrate his seventy-fifth birthday on October 1, 1978, Horowitz went with Wanda to a Manhattan discotheque. Horowitz wore plugs to protect his expensive ears, made a few passes on the dance floor with Wanda, and quoted Toscanini as saying, "You can't be serious twenty-four hours a day. You have to take half an hour or an hour a day to be childish." Of course that got him in all the papers, including even the B'nai B'rith *Messenger* of October 13. Most of the stories had pictures of a gleefully stomping Horowitz. More populism. What would he do next to get his picture into the papers?

Horowitz had been in general good health through the years. He was always complaining about this or that, but structurally he was sound. In December, however, he had an operation for the removal of his prostate gland. Concerts for several months were canceled. On March 18, 1979, Horowitz resumed work, with a concert in Atlanta.

Finally Horowitz made up his mind to give a recital in Avery Fisher Hall, and he played there on May 6, 1979. His program contained Clementi's *Sonata quasi concerto* in C (Op. 33, No. 3); the Schumann *Humoresque,* Rachmaninoff's *Etude-Tableau* in E flat minor, Barcarolle in G minor, and *Humoresque* (Op. 10, No. 5); and, to display his still unique technical wonders, Liszt's *Mephisto Waltz* touched up by Busoni with additions by Vladimir Horowitz.

Some of these pieces were new to his repertoire, others he had not played for a long time.

He gave two more Avery Fisher Hall concerts the following season, on May 4 and 11, 1980. Both were in commemoration of Lincoln Center's twentieth anniversary season. Even those who had reservations about Horowitz's artistry could not fail to respond to the high voltage and command over an audience that marked those two recitals. Nicholas Kenyon, a young critic from London who had never heard Horowitz in the flesh, wrote about the experience in the *New Yorker* issue of May 19, 1980. Kenyon was struck by the Horowitz aura: "I have not experienced a more electric sense of anticipation in an audience here all season, or such rapt concentration when the music began." Kenyon found some things in the interpretations that bothered him: effects that to him sounded capricious or fussy. However, "I do not think that this quirky genius could ever be my favorite pianist, but in the space of one concert he taught me more about a virtuoso's command of the keyboard than I could have heard from a dozen weightier recitals."

21
Collapse

PRINCE CHARLES: You and Mrs. Horowitz must come over next
week and have a drink.
HOROWITZ: I don't drink.
PRINCE CHARLES: All right, then, we'll make you some borscht.
HOROWITZ: Ugh!
—*Dialogue between Vladimir Horowitz and Prince Charles,
backstage at Festival Hall, London, 1982*

*I*n 1981 Horowitz left the Shaw management for Columbia
Artists Management, Inc. (CAMI), where he came under the wing
of Ronald Wilford, the CAMI head. Horowitz and Wanda called
him "the barracuda." It was at this time that Peter Gelb renewed
his association with Horowitz. It came about through Wanda, after
some delicate negotiations.

While with the Boston Symphony, Gelb had kept in touch
with the Horowitzes and, when in New York, visited them occasionally. Gelb finally decided to leave Boston. He had worked out
an arrangement with CAMI where he would have his own division
as an idea man for Wilford, with emphasis on television production.

When Wanda heard the rumors in 1981, she called Gelb in

Boston and asked if they were true. Yes, said Gelb. Wanda then asked Gelb if he would like to be Horowitz's personal manager. Gelb was getting ready to leave for New York and CAMI. He promptly got in touch with Wilford.

Gelb had not been thinking along these lines. Working with Horowitz had been the last thing on his mind. But "the idea of handling the greatest artist in the world—at least, I thought he was the greatest artist—was something I certainly wasn't going to turn down," said Gelb. The Horowitz association also would give Gelb an opportunity to become a film and television producer, which interested him enormously. He had dreamed of producing television shows with great musicians.

Wilford thought it a fine idea and suggested that Gelb for the time being should concentrate only on handling the Horowitz affairs. When Gelb spoke to Horowitz he told him that he needed a producer more than a manager. Horowitz and Wanda agreed.

The New York *Times* had a story about CAMI's new division, written by Edward Rothstein, that appeared on August 13, 1981. Horowitz told Rothstein that after seven years with Shaw it was time for a change. He said he admired Shaw, but that at this stage he needed somebody like Gelb, who was starting a new department at CAMI and would be put on special duty to take care of his needs. Shaw of course also was interviewed, and his comment had a measure of bite in it: "As you know, caring for Mr. Horowitz has requirements that exceed those of other artists."

Shaw later said that losing Horowitz was his own fault. As a member of the Horowitz circle who had dinner with him and Wanda at least once a week, Shaw had been watching with consternation the decline of Horowitz's health. It was the beginning of his medicated period, where his psychiatrist was giving him drugs that seemed to be detaching him from reality. Horowitz was gulping down sleeping pills and antidepressants of enormous potency, and for the first time in his life he was drinking. His tipple was a large glass of Campari and Cinzano. Wanda called his doctor to find out what to do about the drinking problem, which was something new in her experience. "Try to have him drink less," was his only advice. Wanda said that she felt like killing him.

Like many others, Shaw honestly believed that Horowitz could no longer function and would never play again. So, horrified, he backed away from the situation. Looking back, some years later, he said that he had no regrets. Indeed, he thought that Peter Gelb was one of the best things that had ever happened to Horowitz. Gelb was the right man at the right time, and he got Horowitz into film and television, an area that Shaw knew little about. "I wouldn't have done as good a job as Gelb," he said, "and I even had a feeling of relief when it was all over between me and Horowitz. Handling him was a full-time job for several people at once." The Shaw office suddenly became a quieter place.

Gelb settled in. There was the Metropolitan Opera concert of November 1, 1981, to take care of. For this, Horowitz was preparing two big pieces, Chopin's F minor Ballade and his first performance in New York of the Liszt B minor Ballade. (He had just learned the Liszt piece and had tried it out at one concert during his 1981 tour.) The concert also was scheduled to be recorded (it was).

There were other things to discuss with Horowitz that Gelb felt were more important than the concert. He strongly advised Horowitz to return to Europe, where he had not played for decades. Horowitz vacillated and went through his usual routine: he was too old, the trip would take too much out of him, they had forgotten him in Europe, it would be a disaster.

Gelb persisted, suggesting London as the beginning of the tour. He dangled an invitation from the Royal Family as bait; Horowitz would go at the personal invitation of Prince Charles. The Royal Festival Hall concert would be broadcast on an international television hookup. Horowitz suddenly became very interested. Gelb flew to London, and things were quickly arranged. Horowitz would give a benefit concert for the Royal Opera (which was trying to raise funds for a major renovation), with Prince Charles the patron of the event.

Horowitz then had (or pretended to have) a change of heart. He put up his usual objections. He was too old to travel. He was nervous. "I don't know what will happen, what to expect. Will they have my food, my water?" It was Wanda who insisted that he go. She was frightened of what was happening to Horowitz, who seemed to be losing his will to play. She believed that the massive drug treatments his psychiatrist was prescribing were beginning to make "a vegetable" out of her husband. Concerts in Europe might stimulate him and bring him back to life.

Things were arranged to satisfy Horowitz. The Connaught,

one of London's leading hotels, took care of the creature comforts. The piano was shipped, and his tuner and regular entourage accompanied him. He flew over on the Concorde on May 6, to give himself enough time to practice and overcome jet lag.

The London public was agog. The Royal Festival Hall concert on May 22, 1982, was Horowitz's first London appearance since October 19, 1951. One of the major pieces on his program was the Schumann *Kinderscenen*. Horowitz was very pleased with himself about that choice. He told everybody he had selected it in honor of Prince Charles and Lady Diana, who were expecting their first child. He also prepared a surprise: he would play the British national anthem before his first number.

Also on the program were six Scarlatti sonatas, Chopin's Polonaise-Fantaisie and G minor Ballade, and the Rachmaninoff B flat minor Sonata. His encores were a Chopin waltz, the Rachmaninoff *Polka de W. R.*, and Scriabin's D sharp minor Etude. The live broadcast, produced by Gelb and directed by Kirk Browning, would be simultaneously relayed via satellite to the United States, Japan, West Germany, and France. (A Sony videocassette of the concert was shortly made available. It was titled *Horowitz in London: A Royal Concert*.)

The benefit brought in over £65,000 for the Royal Opera. A week later, on May 29, also in Festival Hall, Horowitz gave another recital, with a somewhat different program. The major changes were the Fourth Ballade by Chopin and Liszt's B minor Ballade. But this time there was no royal hoopla.

The London concert was a critical success. Many of the reviewers were hearing Horowitz in the flesh for the first time and reacted in wonderment. Dominic Gill in the *Financial Times* of May 24, 1982, called Horowitz "the Grand-Romantic Master of them all." Gill noted "some finger fluffs and a few uncharacteristically cautious ritardandi." But, in summation, "Horowitz' extraordinary alchemical gifts, fundamentally and profoundly musical, go far beyond considerations of mere mechanical expertise." Joan Chisell in the London *Times* wrote of the Horowitz performance of the national anthem *(God Save the Queen)* that it immediately demonstrated "the divine right of keyboard kings." The program "emerged wholly his own, sometimes provocatively so in this Urtext-conscious age, but shot through with enough scorching bursts of flame, enough tonal ravishments, to explain how legends are made." Her only reservation came in the *Kinderscenen,* where the idiosyncratic playing "sometimes worked against true simplicity, despite the beauty and wonder of Mr. Horowitz' confidences." (She was correct; the recording of the concert contains some of Horowitz's most mannered, labored playing.)

Edward Greenfield in the *Guardian* was equally carried away. "It was not so much his virtuosity that left one gasping (astonishing as that is in a man of 77) as his sound." Indeed, in the Chopin, "one had the suspicion that the lovely keyboard sounds were at least as important as the emotions." The Rachmaninoff was a triumph. "Here more than anywhere else the years fell away, leaving one to marvel at a living legend who unlike some of his kind remains a legend even on renewed inspection." Then there was Peter Stadlen in the *Telegraph:* "The charm of his pianism and the excitement it aroused in the keyboard-minded simply defies rational analysis."

But to those familiar with his playing there was a noticeable deterioration. Horowitz was still under toxic medication, and one of the by-products of the drugs seemed to be a loss of self-criticism and judgment. In London it was not as evident as it soon would be, but it was there. Some pianists noticed it without knowing the reason. The London-based American pianist Craig Sheppard, in an obituary notice in the London *Independent* of November 28, 1989, wrote that the 1982 Horowitz performance of the Rachmaninoff B flat minor Sonata in the Festival Hall "was a mere shadow of what he had done with the same work in Carnegie Hall, New York in 1968. . . . One missed the lion, the prowess, the unbelievable tonal control that were *the* Horowitzian trademarks of the past." (This Rachmaninoff performance, incidentally, was not on the Victor disc of the London concert.) Sheppard, of course, had no way of knowing about Horowitz's sad physical condition. What he did know was that "there will never again be another phenomenon like him."

When Horowitz returned to America after London, he prepared to go on tour. By then he was losing physical control. Horowitz thought he was playing well even when he was having memory lapses and lack of finger coordination. He seemed not to realize what was happening, and insisted on going on a tour that extended from Philadelphia to Chicago and Pasadena, ending with his first appearances in Japan.

Wanda knew the tour would be a disaster and she was strongly against it. Indeed, she was frantic. But she couldn't talk him out of it. He was adamant that he play and wouldn't listen to anybody. Once he made up his mind he was stubbornly immovable. When Wanda suggested that he stop his medication and psychiatric sessions, Horowitz blew up. He told her that it was she who needed mental help. Off on his tour he went.

"He knew he was not in top shape—that much he realized," said a member of his entourage. "But he thought he could get away with it. He needed to play, to get some kind of contact with reality. I honestly believe that if he hadn't played he would have totally gone to pieces. It was because he played that he was able to keep that tenuous grip on reality."

The deterioration in his physical appearance and pianistic skills frightened those who came in contact with him. In 1983, before his upcoming tour, he went to Steinway's to try out pianos, and was greeted by Richard Probst, Steinway's director of the Concert and Artists Department. Probst, new on the job, had revered Horowitz all his life and was trembling as he arrived.

"I actually had tears in my eyes at the end of the session," Probst recollected, "because I was so crushed to see this idol, this legend, in such physical disrepair. Yet even in this condition he was still able to make that gossamer pianissimo." Probst, who was standing at Horowitz's shoulders, was amazed that he could play in so unorthodox a manner and still get such amazing results. "All of a sudden, from a pianissimo, he drew a triple forte, sforzando, and I could not see a single movement in his arms or shoulders. It was like a steel bear trap going *plop*. Later, after he had gone, I went to the piano and tried to duplicate that sound. No way!"

Horowitz led off the tour with a concert on May 15, 1983, at the Metropolitan Opera, playing Beethoven's Sonata in A (Op. 101), Schumann's *Carnaval*, Chopin's Polonaise-Fantasy, three etudes, and the Polonaise in A flat. It was the wrong program for him. He had not played the Beethoven in a long time, and late Beethoven never was one of his stronger points. He had never played the *Carnaval* in the West and did not even particularly like the piece. He walked on stage in a semistupor because of the medications he was taking. Those medications were a well-kept secret, but anybody who listened to his playing knew that *something* was wrong. Donal Henahan wrote the next day in the *Times* that the

Beethoven began disconcertingly, "with lots of wrong notes, clotted chords and rhythmic distortions. The famous Horowitz precision was only intermittently in evidence." In each subsequent concert on the tour Horowitz had memory lapses and his playing was incoherent. The concerts degenerated into a shambles, but the critics let him off as lightly as possible. After the Chicago concert his dear friend Gitta Gradova went home and cried.

Wanda did not attend any of these concerts. She was in London, washing her hands of the whole affair. There were those who thought ill of her desertion. Not Probst. "She wanted everybody to know that these concerts were not sanctioned by her. It was a difficult and wonderful thing for her to do. It took such courage. It was a mark of her character that she would have the strength to do that."

But there was even more to it than that. Whatever her differences with Volodya, Wanda idolized him as a pianist, and she fled the country because it would have killed her to watch him making a fool of himself at the keyboard.

The tour ended with Horowitz's first appearance in Japan. He entered Tokyo like a monarch on one of his royal progresses. Wanda flew to Japan to be with him. They were put up in a hotel suite that cost $1,200 a day. A kitchen had to be built into the suite, and the job was so complicated that the wiring ran afoul of the Tokyo fire laws. New wallpaper and a special floor had to be installed. A Mercedes and chauffeur were put at his disposal. Horowitz never used it. He left his rooms only for a short afternoon walk. Otherwise he watched television and his videocassettes.

Tickets for his June 11 and June 16, 1983, concerts at the NKH Hall were selling in the range of $300 (the yen was then very strong). Horowitz was getting an extraordinary fee, later revealed to be in seven figures (television included). For his concert on June 11, 1983, he played the same program he had carried through America: Beethoven's Sonata in A (Op. 101), Schumann's *Carnaval*, Chopin's Polonaise-Fantaisie, several etudes, and the A flat Polonaise. He did not play any encores.

During the concert the public was receptive enough, and Horowitz was called forth many times at the end. But when the reviews appeared, Horowitz was taken apart. "A cracked antique," wrote Hidekazu Yoshida in the *Asahi Shimbun,* Japan's largest newspaper. "I could find only a fragment of the legendary Horowitz." Clyde Haberman, Tokyo bureau chief of the New York *Times,* reported that Tokyo felt it was getting an inferior Horowitz. There also were tart comments about his life-style and the size of his fee.

This time even Horowitz knew that the concert was a fiasco. At its end, Franz Mohr later reported, Horowitz sat exhausted in his dressing room mumbling "I know . . . lots of wrong notes— lots of wrong notes. . . . I don't know what is happening to me." Wanda started to cry. "This was a funeral," she sobbed to Mohr. "We will never hear Horowitz again. He was terrible. Absolutely terrible."

When Horowitz was read a translation of the reviews after he had returned to New York, he said it was worse than the bombing of Pearl Harbor. He said he would never play again, and for a while it seemed that he might keep his promise. He didn't appear in public for a year after that. Critics everywhere wondered if the great career had come to an end. A newspaperman visited Horowitz at home and was shaken by what he saw. Horowitz was in deplorable shape. He had put on much weight, his belly hung over his belt, he was unable to talk coherently. No interview was possible under the circumstances. "He moved like a zombie," said a friend, aghast. Another friend drew Wanda aside, asked if Horowitz had Alzheimer's disease. On October 1, 1983, Ronald Wilford gave him a birthday party for a close circle of friends. The eighty-year-old Horowitz sat on a couch, saying very little, looking like a shriveled old man. People would go up to him to pay homage and walk away puzzled. Horowitz did not seem in contact with the world. Anybody who came near him in that distressing period knew that he would never play again.

22
Resurrection

It has to be note perfect, because that's the world we live in. It has to be musical and it has to make sense.
—*Vladimir Horowitz to Tom Frost on what he wanted in his records*

*F*or a while nothing was heard of Vladimir Horowitz. There was a total blackout on East Ninety-fourth Street. Not even Horowitz's closest associates—neither Peter Gelb, nor Jack Pfeiffer, nor Ronald Wilford, nobody—had the faintest idea of what was going on behind those closed doors. Vladimir Horowitz became the forgotten man.

But suddenly, unexpectedly, around March 1985, Gelb got a phone call from Horowitz and went to see him. He was impressed with what he saw. Horowitz looked almost like his own self. He was off all medications, felt much better, and—surprise of surprises—had decided to play again.

Not much is known about his recovery. Those involved with

it have refused to talk, especially Giuliana Lopes, the person who by all accounts did the most to pull him through. Mrs. Lopes had been engaged in 1959 to be Sonia's companion. After Sonia's death she found herself back in the Horowitz household as the maestro's companion.

Mrs. Lopes, married to an engineer at RCA Records, became Horowitz's confidante. She knew more about him than anybody except Wanda. Perhaps more. He leaned on her and confided to her all of his problems. She cooked for him, traveled with him, became his prop. Mrs. Lopes always refused to be interviewed. She felt that the relationship between herself and Horowitz should forever remain private.

But members of the Horowitz circle claimed that it was Mrs. Lopes who saw him through the terrible period after 1983. While Wanda was away, which was often, Mrs. Lopes kept in touch with his physicians and psychiatrists, mothering him, administering to him, trying to keep his spirits up, comforting him in his withdrawal symptoms. It took time and infinite patience. She admired and respected Horowitz, and she acted in effect as nurse and loving daughter. Finally she brought him back to himself.

When Horowitz summoned Gelb, it was to discuss the future. Horowitz said he was old, had just recovered from severe emotional and physical problems, and did not yet have the strength for concerts. How could he get started again?

Gelb proposed the idea of a film to be shot in the Horowitz living room. It would be a documentary made over the course of a month. Thus Horowitz would have the chance to ease himself back.

Horowitz was very nervous about it. "Even frantic," an associate said. But he started working very hard, and his fingers came back. Pfeiffer and Wanda looked at each other. He sounded like the old Horowitz. Probst from Steinway was stunned. "He was remarkably different. Very strong, very vigorous, everything under control. He was like his old pianistic self."

After a while Horowitz loved making the show. He started kidding around and enjoying himself. When the filming was over —it took six shooting days, starting on April 24, 1985, but spread out over a longer time—he was confident he could return to concert life. In the film Horowitz did some talking and Wanda was very much in evidence. When the film was completed, it was enti-tled *Vladimir Horowitz: The Last Romantic* and was released by MGM.

At the beginning of the filming Gelb alerted RCA and Colum-bia to the fact that Horowitz was back in form. No one in those two companies believed him and would not even send anybody to Ninety-fourth Street to listen. So Gelb picked up the phone and called Gunther Breest, at that time the artists and repertoire direc-tor for Deutsche Grammophon records in Germany. "Here's your chance. You always wanted Horowitz," he said. Breest got on the next plane and immediately signed Horowitz to a contract for the sound track recording of the film.

Horowitz played the Bach-Busoni *Nun komm' der Heiden Hei-land;* Mozart's Sonata in C (K. 330); Schubert's A flat Impromptu (Op. 90, No. 4); Chopin's Mazurka in A minor (Op. 17, No. 4) and Scherzo in B minor; Liszt's *Consolation* in D flat and *Au bord d'une source;* Rachmaninoff's Prelude in G sharp minor; Schu-mann's *Novellette* in F (his first performance of the piece); Scriabin's Etude in C sharp minor (Op. 2, No. 1); Chopin's A flat Polonaise; and Moszkowski's Etude in F.

It is a fascinating film, as much for the portrait of the Horo-witz personality as for his playing. He was dressed in a dark busi-ness suit with a red polka-dot bow tie and a matching handkerchief coyly peeping from his breast pocket. He was relaxed, happy, and charming. For the most part his comments were natural-sounding as he rambled on in a stream-of-consciousness manner about his early life and whatever else came to mind. "I can play still! I can play still!" he kept on exultantly repeating. At the keyboard he can be heard noodling a bit, and among his noodles are a few measures of *Stars and Stripes Forever* and *Tea for Two*. He loftily dismissed the occasional wrong note that could be heard. "I don't want perfec-tion. I'm not Heifetz. I'm Horowitz."

Occasionally he prattled a bit too much and his cutesy side was rather adolescent (though in a peculiar sort of way that was part of his charm because it was so innocently transparent). He said he could give a Carnegie Hall concert the following week if he had to. Then he went into his innocence act. Would anybody come? Would people have forgotten him? He and Wanda, who was very much a part of the film, engaged in a bit of badinage, she as sharp and contentious as always. By now the two of them had made peace with each other. Franz Mohr, Jack Pfeiffer, and some members of the filming team are also on camera. Everybody walks on eggs, catering to Horowitz, assuring him that he is wonderful, wonderful.

And often the playing in this film *is* wonderful. The old color is back, the fingers are still the commander of the keys, and above all there is none of the mannered, neurotic playing of a few years back. Some of the shorter pieces—the Rachmaninoff, the Scriabin etude—are pristine Horowitz. The A flat Polonaise has drive and power, the Mozart simplicity and grace. Only in the B minor Scherzo is there a feeling of struggle. It is a peculiar conception, rather small scaled with very little pedal, and it sounds like an incomplete statement.

There is one great overhead shot of the camera beaming directly down on the Horowitz hands during the famous E major left-hand octave passages of the A flat Polonaise. It would be fascinating to watch this in slow motion. Horowitz uses a rotating technique. The thumb slides from the D sharp to the C sharp to provide a legato. The last three bottom bass notes seem to be played by the third, fourth, and fifth fingers. The way he devours those octaves, one feels that he could go on for hours, so effortless does it appear.

Considering what Horowitz had been the previous year and what he now was doing, it can be considered something of a miracle. It marks the beginning of the glorious playing of his last five years. There was no evidence of the nervous tension that had been one of the marked characteristics of his style. This last period was much simpler and purer. Horowitz gave the impression of enjoying his playing, of being utterly relaxed. It was ripe music making of infinite nuance: relaxed, simple and natural, sweet and singing.

After the film was completed, Horowitz got in touch with Frost and said he was going to make studio recordings again. Would Frost be the producer? Of course. Which meant that Breest and Deutsche Grammophon Gesellschaft also got the next three records Horowitz made, which were among the best-selling records in the history of classical music. Several million copies were purchased. Breest eventually left Deutsche Grammophon for Sony/CBS Records, and Horowitz went with him. That is why the very last disc Horowitz ever made was issued on the Sony Classical label in April 1990, about five months after his death.

When Frost started working again with Horowitz after *The Last Romantic* film, he noticed some changes in the pianist's routine. Horowitz would record only twice a week instead of thrice. He was eighty-two years old and needed more warm-up time to get into the mood. At the recording studio he might spend a half hour improvising, or playing pieces that had no relation to the recording session. Wanda in the control booth was amazed. "My God, I haven't heard him play this piece for thirty years!"

Christian Steiner, the official Horowitz photographer, was in on some of the recording sessions. One session that he especially remembered took place in 1985 at a Deutsche Grammophon recording session in an RCA studio. Horowitz arrived in wonderful spirits and, said Steiner, played Schubert's B flat Impromptu "ravishingly. He knew he was in good form, and every time he did something special he would raise one of his fists in a gesture of triumph when he had a free hand. It was very endearing." Horowitz listened to the playback, liked what he heard, and said that was enough for the day.

As one who had been dealing with superstars for years, Steiner knew their foibles and their vanities. He did not consider Horowitz very temperamental. He was rather surprised, as a photographer, that Horowitz was more interested in his clothes than his face, and he put together an ensemble with great care. Everything was color coordinated. Otherwise, Horowitz "clowned around an awful lot during the photo sessions," Steiner said. "He never took them very seriously. The childlike nature of his personality came out."

Nor did he usually indulge in serious musical talk. But at his last photo session with Steiner, not long before he died, Horowitz started talking with him about the German conductor Carlos Kleiber. While fooling around with his television set, Horowitz had come across a Kleiber broadcast from Vienna and been terribly impressed. Steiner, who was well acquainted with Kleiber's work, was amazed by Horowitz's perceptive, sensitive analysis of the conductor's technique and approach to music. (A few months before his death, Horowitz met Kleiber and discussed with him the possibility of a recording of the Beethoven Third Concerto. Had he lived long enough he would have done it.)

In 1985 the German critic Joachim Kaiser, who had written an important book on twentieth-century pianists, came to New York to interview Horowitz during several of the Deutsche Grammophon studio sessions, and also to provide the program notes for the ensuing compact disc, which contained Schumann's *Kreisleriana*, the Schubert-Tausig *Marche militaire*, and short pieces by Liszt, Scriabin, and Schubert.

Kaiser was in awe and not a little frightened. "After all, he's said to be as withdrawn as Garbo, deified like Liszt." No such thing. Kaiser found "a delightful old gentleman" eager to engage in conversation. He watched Horowitz warm up, indulging "his sense of fantasy," playing some Scriabin and Liszt, "insouciantly combining three Schubert impromptus with the *Wanderer* Fantasy." Horowitz then settled down to Schumann's *Kreisleriana:*

> As he says himself—and demonstrates—he used to play *Kreisleriana* too fast. Now the passages of twilit lyricism seem to have become his favorites. And now he conceives the middle section of the first piece much more beautifully and poetically. There may be a hint of a Schumann-Eichendorff Lied buried there. I allowed myself to point it out to the maestro: the first line of *Auf einer Burg* is "Eingeschlafen auf der Lauer." Suddenly Horowitz switches to German to give me the second line, "oben ist der alte Ritter." (I wonder if any young German Schumann players know their Eichendorff so well.)

After the end of the film and the resumption of recording, Horowitz felt stimulated. He took the summer off and it was agreed that he would perform in Europe in the fall. Two recitals in Paris and another two in Milan were arranged. Horowitz would be playing in Paris for the first time in thirty-four years, and in Milan for the first time in a half century.

Horowitz arrived in Paris on October 18, 1985, about a week before his October 26 concert. He attended a concerto performance by the pianist Jean-Philippe Collard, dined in elegant restaurants, and was interviewed many times. One journalist asked him about his film, *The Last Romantic*. Horowitz said that it was not the title he would have chosen. He would have called it *Le dernier des Mohicans—The Last of the Mohicans.*

Tickets went on sale two weeks before the concert, and the pattern of the New York concerts was repeated (with the exception of a box-office scandal). People started to line up at the Théâtre des Champs-Elysées the day before the box office opened. Max Massei was in the line and reported:

I arrived at six in the morning and was the seventy-fifth person. At eleven, the line was formed and many admirers began to talk together of the pianist until 2 P.M., when the sale began. There were many Frenchmen, of course, but also East Europeans and others (I spoke with a Mexican). On the afternoon of October 26, 1985, there was in the hall an electric atmosphere. Suddenly the director of the hall opened a door in the wings and Horowitz appeared on the scene. He walked slowly toward his keyboard and sat down quickly during the applause. And when he started to play the sonata of Scarlatti we felt that an old friend had come back, after thirty-four years of absence. . . . All of the works were played with a touch of poetry, but some wrong notes in the beginning of *Kreisleriana* showed that Horowitz was a little nervous. The main point was that his pianistic gifts were totally used for the expression of feelings, and the virtuosity completely mastered. The second recital, on November 2, was more peaceful. In the audience were many musicians: Martha Argerich, Krystian Zimerman, Michel Beroff, Jean-Philippe Collard, Nelson Freire, Jean-Pierre Rampal, and all the young French pianists.

Besides *Kreisleriana,* Horowitz played Scarlatti sonatas, Scriabin etudes, Schubert's B flat Impromptu, three short Liszt pieces, Chopin mazurkas and the A flat Polonaise. On November 2 Horowitz played Mozart's Sonata in C (K. 330) and his usual assortment of shorter pieces, though the Schubert-Liszt *Soirée de Vienne* No. 6 was new. Between the recitals, Horowitz was honored in a reception at the Palais de l'Elysée given by President François Mitterrand, who awarded him the title of Commandeur de la Légion d'honneur.

The concerts had the critics searching for adjectives. From Jacques Longchampt in *Le monde* down, all the French critics raved. They saw something new in the playing, something autumnal, something like (in Longchampt's words) "a deep and black lake." The review by Brigitte Massin in *Le matin* was headed: ON HEARING A LIVING MYTH. She went on to say that there was no point going into detail; this was the playing of a man in his "secret garden," with a sound that was sheer alchemy, bathed in "a halo of light."

Dominique Jameux, writing in *Diapason-Harmonie,* started his long piece with a most arresting two paragraphs:

He is the greatest . . . pianist of all time. The greatest what? He does not lack faults. Abusively personal playing, arbitrary, with lapses of taste. Wrong notes. Lack of equilibrium in the undue emphasis on inner voice, impetuous accents, unsteady rhythms. Rubato from another era. His own kind of saturated virtuosity. Repertoire highly limited. Always the same pieces. Four concertos in sixty years of his career. Not curious about music of his own time. Generally uncultured. Vanity that has its own place in piano history: *I am the legend.* Not a very sympathetic personality. He does not serve music; it serves him. Circus artist. Out-of-date diva.

The greatest pianist in history.

And Jameux went on at great length to explain why Horowitz was the greatest pianist in history. Basically, according to his analysis, it was a combination of astounding virtuosity, variety of sound, and an ability to see the long line in big pieces and the charm in small ones. Forget whatever defects Horowitz has as a man, Jameux wrote. "A poet speaks: we listen to him. Emotion first, mastery second. A pianist of the nineteenth century? Most assuredly: that century knew how to say 'I.' " Most modern pianists, Jameux concluded, are anonymous, lacking in individual expression. But Horowitz, "that old, sad and cunning elephant, is definitely more alive than ever."

When Horowitz gave his two Milan concerts on November 17 and 24, the Italian critics were equally stunned. The headline in the *Corriere della sera* told the world that Horowitz was greater than his legend. The reviewer, Duilio Courir, wrote that Horowitz gives the impression of being "an absolute pianist, totally, the interpreter *par excellence.*"

Horowitz resumed concert life on his return to America; and he and Wanda still continued to plan the programs and itinerary, establish the fees, and study the small print of the contract stipulations. In that, their skill had nowhere diminished. Probst was in on some of the sessions:

> I was always impressed about how savvy Horowitz was about the music business, about the production of concerts, about how to build a program so as to lead to a climactic moment. He was very skilled at that and the whole business of

how to manipulate or how to get the presenter to get exactly the results he wanted. And nobody better knew the psychology of the audience. Wanda worked with him on all this, and she also knew exactly when to stop him and when to let somebody else take over.

Probst admired Wanda's decisive way of doing things and considered her scrupulously fair. The one time she bawled him out, she discovered the next day that Probst had not been at fault, and she phoned him from Paris to apologize. Horowitz was more easygoing than she except when it came to his art. "The only strong feeling he had," Probst said, "was about his public career—the halls, his programs, the instrument, the ambience. When that was tampered with, he could lash out."

On November 15, 1985, *The Last Romantic* was shown in Carnegie Hall. Horowitz did not attend. Had he done so, it would have been the first time in history that a pianist attended his own recital as a member of the audience.

It was around this time that Horowitz began thinking of writing his memoirs. Could the conclusion of the two-volume Rubinstein memoirs have been a factor? He also knew that Milstein was preparing his autobiography. Horowitz had been approached many times by publishers hungry for such a book, but he had turned down all requests. Now perhaps he was ready.

Ileene Smith, senior editor of Summit Books, an imprint of Simon & Schuster, very much wanted to sign Horowitz up, and her friend Marion Wiesel was aware of this. When Mrs. Wiesel happened to meet Peter Gelb at a dinner party, she told him about Smith's wish to acquire the Horowitz memoirs. Smith and Gelb met and agreed that the time was right.

But Gelb had a bit of persuading to do. For instance, Horowitz insisted on having a Russian-speaking coauthor. This immediately created problems because there were few Russian-speaking writers who knew music and the piano inside out and had a style that could attract American readers. There was a series of delicate meetings among Horowitz, Wanda, Gelb, and Smith. At the first one Horowitz suggested that Wanda's autobiography would be more interesting than his own. Wanda, who was present, looked vaguely amused, said Smith. Then Horowitz, looking at Smith, asked, "What is book editor?" Wanda was the one who answered: "Volodya, book editor is KGB for words."

The project never came to fruition. But other things did: the 1986 trip to Russia, appearances in Germany and Austria after half a century, Horowitz's love affair with Mozart, and some of the best records he ever made. Horowitz had a great deal to do before the norns of his beloved *Götterdämmerung* suddenly cut the string in 1989.

23
Globetrotter

I want to show the Japanese that I am rehabilitated.
—*Vladimir Horowitz to Peter Gelb in 1986*

Horowitz's Russian concerts of 1986 were by all odds the emotional highlight of his life. After sixty-one years he had returned as a legend, and he had lived up to his reputation. Russians are an outgoing people, and at the end of his visit Horowitz felt bathed in their warmth, love, and admiration. He was pumped full of adrenalin, he talked and acted like an eager youngster, and he looked years younger. There was no trace of the physical and mental crisis of only two years before.

Now he had another part of the world to conquer. He was returning to Germany to concertize for the first time in about half a century.

It was an absolutely exhilarated Horowitz who left Leningrad to begin a short tour of the country he had put on his enemies list when Hitler started his ascent to power. Horowitz had not played there since 1932. His schedule called for a concert in Hamburg's Music Hall on May 11, 1986, to be followed by one in Berlin at the Philharmonie a week later, on May 18.

On his arrival in Germany he underwent a media blitz not unlike the one in New York during his return to action in 1965. The televised Moscow concert had received enormous coverage and discussion all over Europe, and had made everybody aware of Horowitz. The German press and television were not going to let their clienteles down.

When Horowitz's flight from Leningrad touched down in Frankfurt for the connecting forty-five-minute flight to Hamburg, a small army of reporters, television crews, and photographers was waiting for him. An article by Kläre Warnecke in the May 5, 1986, issue of *Die Welt* described the reception accorded the eighty-two-year-old "God of the Piano."

Horowitz came off the plane wearing a black hat and an overcoat. He was dressed for chilly Leningrad, not Hamburg in the spring. Besieged with questions, Horowitz laughed and parried the reporters, loving every bit of it. Wanda attracted almost as much attention as Horowitz. Reporters thickly grouped around her. Entering the first-class cabin on the Hamburg plane, Horowitz was "very carefully guarded by Wanda." He joked about her, calling her his Cerberus.

During the flight he refused to answer questions. He sat in his cabin drinking apple juice. "The diet freak," reported Warnecke, "does not drink a drop of alcohol." The flight ran into an electrical storm, and the pilot ordered all passengers to fasten their seat belts. "I am afraid," Horowitz was overheard saying.

The following day there was a press conference in Hamburg that the *Abendzeitung* headlined as THE BIG VLADIMIR AND WANDA SHOW. Horowitz spoke in English; he had forgotten most of his German. A large and distinguished audience turned out for "the greatest pianist of the century." As usual, said the *Abendzeitung*, "Mrs. Horowitz led the way to the stage." She marched straight to the podium, "parting the crowd as God did for Moses and the Red Sea." The cameramen and reporters were cowed by "her arrogant look." *Der Spiegel* called her "The voice of the Lord." Horowitz lingered behind her, joking with the journalists and shaking hands everywhere. Any plans for the press conference that the organizers might have prepared went out the window. Wanda and Horowitz said whatever was on their mind, with Wanda generally taking the lead. She was "the caring mother," whispering things into his ear. Thus:

Q: What do you think of young pianists?

A: *(Wanda to Horowitz):* They're all the same.

A: *(Horowitz to press):* They're all the same.

Elsewhere Horowitz was equally coy:

Q: Are you the last Romantic?

A: No.

Wanda: Why not?

A: Because I don't know what is a Romantic.

There were the usual questions. One journalist, Rolf Hosfeld, asked Horowitz, "What does Germany mean to you?"

"I love it," Horowitz quickly said.

"Nobody believes him," wrote Hosfeld, "but they accept the answer as given."

Wanda was keeping her eye on the clock. After about half an hour she took out the most recent Horowitz compact disc, slammed it on the table "so forcefully that the microphones whistled," and announced, "Enough is enough!" She "stormed out of the hall," leading Horowitz by the hand, "towing away the most famous pianist in the world."

The papers made much of Horowitz's enormous fee, which forced ticket prices to an unprecedented high. Tickets for the Hamburg Music Hall, which seats about two thousand, were priced from 400 marks down to 100. At that time the mark was worth about 35 cents in American money.

Press and public were fascinated with Horowitz and he was the subject of incessant interviews and feature stories. The *Süddeutsche Zeitung* of May 10 looked upon Horowitz as a cross between a film star and a stand-up comic. The story called Horowitz "a wise Jewish clown who demonstrates that he probably is the very last of the big pianists, who looks as though he is constantly making fun of himself and the phalanx of fans who follow him on their knees." The paper was charmed when Horowitz went to the best fish restaurant in Hamburg harbor and calmly asked for chicken and camomile tea. The *Süddeutsche* also reported that Horowitz practiced in his hotel room until his neighbors complained. When they were told who was playing, they stopped complaining and ran around telling everybody that they had heard Vladimir Horowitz.

For his programs in Germany, Horowitz repeated what he had played in Leningrad. Schumann's *Kreisleriana* was the major work, along with Scarlatti, Mozart, Chopin, and Liszt. Stories about the May 11 concert started appearing the next day.

All the critics agreed that they had been faced with a legend. The gist of the *Hamburger Morgenpost* review was that Horowitz was "a genius who stands above all things and is fighting for the ultimate musical truths." *Der Spiegel* pointed out that there were some rocky moments in the recital, and that Horowitz could "no longer shake technical tricks out of his sleeve. . . . Still there was a fullness of sound like an organ, which no youngster of the present can manage." *Die Zeit* of May 16 said that Horowitz brought to life a vanished era.

In the *Süddeutsche Zeitung* of May 12, Karl Schumann wrote a very long, detailed review, and it was not exactly a rave. But he, like all the other critics, was carried away by The Presence, by a style that had just about vanished from the earth. He called Horowitz "the last embodiment of the nineteenth century, and he proves it measure by measure. He knows about charm as an artistic ingredient, which makes him different from all other pianists since Kempff." He had some reservations about Horowitz's scholarship in the Scarlatti sonatas. Horowitz played them "like Debussy with a wig," applying delicate tints of color that "must have raised goosebumps" among the purists.

In *Die Zeit* of May 16, Heinz Josef Herbort, following much the same line, wrote that Horowitz tried to present Scarlatti as "the Chopin of the eighteenth century." Herbort thought that the *Kreisleriana* performance was somewhat reserved and held back: meditative, soft, lyrical. In Liszt and Chopin, Herbort had no reservations. Here the Horowitz left hand, "the most expressive in the history of piano playing," was given full rein, even if the *Petrarca* was "overloaded" with inner voices. In the Chopin A flat Polonaise "the demon of the steppes, the world champion of octaves and a full fortissimo," unleashed his full powers. Herbort concluded that other pianists might be as good as Horowitz in some of the pieces on the program, "but nobody in the A flat Polonaise."

Gerhard Koch, in the May 13 *Frankfurter Allgemeine Zeitung,* wrote that there was something new in Horowitz. The formerly shy person was now "a clownlike character" with platform manner- isms and coy gestures to the public. Koch found some of this rather engaging. Horowitz, he said, "shows his happiness at still being able to do amazing technical feats." To be sure, there was no longer the infallibility of yore. To compensate, there was an intensity of interpretation, more so than in more exact younger pianists. If *Kreisleriana* had some bad moments, there nevertheless were "cer- tain other insights, more color, greater sensitivity." The Liszt was great. Horowitz, said Koch, can still sing like nobody else; his tone and touch were still astounding. What he could not do technically he made up for with an intensity of expression peculiarly his own. Horowitz in this concert, Koch wrote, opened new worlds of "de- pressive fragility" and proved himself the master of "painful intro- version."

Horowitz played at his usual hour, 4 P.M. on Sunday. That very evening in the same concert hall Placido Domingo sang, at tickets priced at 450 marks, 50 marks over the Horowitz top. But, as was pointed out, Domingo was not singing for himself. He was singing for Mexico; the proceeds went to the aid of the victims of the earthquake there.

From Hamburg Horowitz went on to Berlin and almost did not play his scheduled concert. He was to perform in the Philhar- monie, the 2,400-seat avant-garde concert hall, home of the Berlin Philharmonic, designed by Hans Scharoun. It opened in 1963 and was promptly dubbed "Karajan's Circus." A concert hall in the round, meaning that the stage is surrounded on all sides by the audience, it does look something like a circus tent. When Horowitz and Wanda entered the premises, their first thought was to get out of Berlin as fast as they could. Horowitz hated it, and a great deal of pressure had to be put on him before he agreed to go on with the concert.

As things turned out, he was happy there and later said he loved the acoustics. Not everybody does. The Philharmonie has some very bad spots. But Horowitz was so elated after his Berlin concert on May 18 that, at dinner with the Berlin cultural senator, he impulsively said that he would stay in Berlin an extra week to give a recital on May 24 at half price for those who could not get into the first one. To prove his sincerity, Horowitz then and there wrote out his promise on the dinner menu. Klaus Geitel in *Die*

Welt exclaimed that "the music world is dumbfounded" by this action of "the czar of the piano." When the announcement was made, the Philharmonie was sold out in three hours.

In Berlin, Horowitz played the same program he had given in Hamburg. The first review appeared on May 20 in the *Bild,* not one of the world's supreme newspapers. Its headline ran: DIVINE HOROWITZ: BERLIN WEEPS AT THE PHILHARMONIE. It was more a news story than a review. "The atmosphere," wrote the reporter, "was a cross between an upper-league football match and a prayer in church." Words like "divine playing" and "piano genius" were thrown at the reader. There was a half-hour standing ovation when it was all over, after which, the article reported, Horowitz and Wanda repaired to a casino for blackjack and roulette.

On May 21 a long review by Albrecht Dümling came out in *Der Tagesspiegel.* After a look at Horowitz's career in Germany in 1926, and his subsequent career, Dümling got down to business. The concert, he said, was, except for the Scarlatti, an homage to Romantic music and the Romantic piano. Horowitz was above all comparisons and standards, and could be compared only with his own recordings. In his 1969 recording of *Kreisleriana* he was stronger and very free. Now he is more subdued and suffused with feeling. As for his sound, "Once you have heard a pianissimo by Horowitz you will never forget it." And Horowitz still had a very big technique, with stunning octaves in the A flat Polonaise. The immaculate, effortless, and virtuosic playing in the Liszt *Soirée* was a sheer wonderment.

Hans-Jörg von Jena's review in the *Volksblatt* took much the same approach. At this concert a musician triumphed, "not a technocrat of the keys." Arthur Rubinstein's charge that Horowitz was not a good musician was wrong—in 1986, at least. The *Kreisleriana* was "a portrait of a soul divided into eight sections."

The May 21 *Morgenpost* had a review by Klaus Geitel with the headline: OLD MAGIC OF THE LEGENDARY PIANIST REMAINS UNBROKEN. Geitel pointed out that Berliners had been waiting years and years for this concert. "The old magic of his playing does not die away" even at such an advanced age. It has an unequaled combination of charm, brilliance, and elegance. Horowitz is "a dreamer at the piano and he knows how to dream more splendidly than the others." Today "his dreams are different": he is more introverted, more melancholy. He is the "belcantist" of the piano and knows how to make it sing.

Geitel reviewed the second concert for *Die Welt*. Horowitz played Mozart's Sonata in C (K. 330), the Schumann *Arabesque*, Chopin's B minor Scherzo, and repeated some pieces from the previous week's concert. To Geitel, the concert was "a fantasy of sound" in which the listener was all but drugged. The Mozart was a world unto itself, with its opera buffa elements, the intensity of the slow movement and the elegance of the last. Horowitz, wrote Geitel, gave the listener a "brilliant insight into the simplicity of the complicated." In all the music, and especially the Schumann, Chopin, and Liszt pieces, the playing reflected the bel canto tradition. "The time of thundering and special effects is over. Now Horowitz reasons at the piano, with all sounds in absolute balance."

Hellmut Kotschenreuther was the critic in the *Tagesspiegel* for the second concert. His was a sad story. Such were the crowds around the Philharmonie, he said, that there was no parking space. He finally ended up behind the National Gallery, missing a good part of the concert. Only after the intermission could he get to his seat and hear the Schumann *Arabesque*. What he heard was a *Wunder,* a miracle. He heard eighteen different sounds, "not played by human hands," coming out of the silence. After the B minor Scherzo the audience rose and gave him an ovation "of more splendor than even Herbert von Karajan had ever achieved."

Not only were the critics ravished. Musicians also were. The members of the Berlin Philharmonic petitioned for admittance to Horowitz's second Berlin concert. Because the house was sold out, stage seats were supplied for them. After the concert they begged the Horowitz management to make arrangements for Horowitz to record a concerto with them—any concerto, any time, any place. They said they would drop whatever they had, rearrange their schedule, give anything to play with Vladimir Horowitz.

There was one untoward event just before the recital, though Horowitz did not know about it until later. While Franz Mohr was tuning the piano he discovered that the entire bass was sharp, and he had to lower the whole section. This took time, and he was busy at his work while the audience started to enter. When Mohr came to the last B flat the string broke. What to do? If he put a new string on the piano, it would go out of tune during the concert. So

Mohr rushed backstage and found a Steinway that belonged to the hall. He removed its bass B flat string and put it on the Horowitz piano, finishing just before the concert was to start. He begged the hall's manager, and also the Berlin Philharmonic musicians who were already on the stage, not to tell Horowitz.

After leaving Germany for a successful appearance in London, Horowitz spontaneously decided to play in Tokyo. He felt that he was on a roll, playing well, and he very much wanted to redeem his reputation after the 1983 disaster.

This time the Japanese public was wary. The concerts nevertheless sold out. In Tokyo Horowitz went so far as to apologize for 1983, saying that he had drunk too much, eaten too much, and taken too many sleeping pills.

In Japan, Horowitz played the same program he had recently presented in Leningrad and Germany. The concert, on June 22, 1986, was given in a hall on the campus of the Showa Women's University in western Tokyo. Horowitz had made up his mind so quickly to play in Tokyo that it was impossible to get a hall in any central site. "So rushed were recital preparations," reported Clyde Haberman for the New York *Times,* "that programs also were not available until the intermission."

As soon as he started playing, everybody realized that this was not the Horowitz of 1983. His old electricity galvanized the audience. He was repeatedly called back after his final piece, and played three encores, after which there were eight curtain calls. Backstage, wrote Haberman, Horowitz was tired but happy. He felt that he had played well.

When the reviews appeared, they were ecstatic. Hidekazu Yoshida of the *Asahi Shimbun,* who in 1983 had called Horowitz "a cracked antique," now called him "a magician." All the critics expressed amazement over the Horowitz "revival." Horowitz was content; he had indeed rehabilitated himself. His general behavior this time was different, too. Instead of sulking in his hotel room he went shopping and even went out for dinner although, Haberman reported, "he has stayed safely to his preferred diet of sole and chicken. The only Japanese fare he is known to have sampled is tea."

On his return to America in the fall of 1986 Horowitz gave a few concerts, including an appearance at the White House on October 5, 1986. This event made front-page news when Horowitz was upstaged by Mrs. Reagan. While the president was describing the pianist's harsh life in Russia during the Revolution, Mrs. Reagan inadvertently moved the legs of her chair over the edge of the small platform that serves as a stage in the East Room, and she toppled into the audience, landing at the feet of former ambassador to Great Britain Walter H. Annenberg. There was a gasp and everybody rushed to the rescue. She was not injured and laughingly walked back on the platform, to be embraced by Horowitz. "That's the reason I did this," she told the audience. The president quipped, "Honey, I told you to do it only if I didn't get any applause."

The East Room of the White House was crowded with musicians, diplomats, and politicians. Horowitz was being honored not only as a musician but also as a cultural ambassador who was helping to improve relations between the United States and the Soviet Union.

Ambassador Hartman was there. So were Yuri Dubinin, the Soviet ambassador to the United States; George P. Shultz, the American secretary of state; Zubin Mehta, Isaac Stern, Yo-Yo Ma, assorted pianists great and small, heads of great libraries and museums, philanthropists, administrators—in short, the cream of the American cultural establishment.

The audience heard music that Horowitz had played in Moscow: Mozart's Sonata in C (K. 330); Liszt's *Sonetto 104 del Petrarca* and the Schubert-Liszt *Soirée de Vienne* No. 6; two Chopin mazurkas and two etudes by Scriabin; Schumann's *Träumerei*; and Moszkowski's *Etincelles*. He was in good form, exhibiting his sensitively spun and unabashedly Romantic Mozart, and having fun with the other works on the program. As always, it was the virtuoso pieces that brought down the house. There were smiles and nudges after his elegant performance of the delicious Schubert-Liszt *Soirée,* which Horowitz ended with a stylish cadenza of his own; and the fleetness and accuracy of the prestissimo scales in *Etincelles* had everybody cheering.

Back in New York, Horowitz worked hard on a record that was to contain Schubert's big B flat Sonata, the Mozart Rondo in D and B minor Adagio, Schubert's *Moment musical* in F minor, and the Schubert-Liszt *Ständchen* and *Soirée de Vienne* No. 6. Frost edited the tape and brought it to Horowitz, who turned it down. He told Frost that his concept of the Mozart pieces and the Schubert B flat Sonata had changed while he was making the record. Especially the Mozart; he suddenly got new ideas about Mozart embellishments, he said, and would have to revise his thinking. The Schubert sonata he found too fussy, and the only things he liked were the *Ständchen, Soirée,* and *Moment musical.* Those three pieces ended up in a disc, *Horowitz at Home,* released about three years later. Late in 1991 the rejected Schubert B flat Sonata shared a compact disc (named *Horowitz the Poet*) with the 1987 Vienna performance of Schumann's *Kinderscenen.* (The Schubert should not have been released; Horowitz was right in calling it too fussy, and its appearance was a disservice to his memory.)

During the summer of 1986 Horowitz started sending material to Yale University for a Horowitz Archives there. Most of the arrangements were handled by Wanda. Horowitz came to Yale through Tom Frost, a Yale alumnus, who thought that his alma mater would be the ideal repository for the Horowitz artifacts after his death—his music, the many acetates he had made of actual concerts, his library, letters, iconography, clippings, everything. Even his piano. Negotiations with Harold E. Samuel, the music librarian of Yale, had started around 1985, but not until the following year were the papers signed and some material shipped.

Horowitz had a special affinity for Yale because of Woolsey Hall. He liked the acoustics of the big (about 2,700 seats) auditorium and often would play there to try out new programs. His audience would consist of Yalies, and his association with the university was honored when he was made a Fellow of Silliman College there.

In the fall of 1986 Horowitz returned to Europe where, on November 16, he played in Frankfurt at the opera house, the Alte Oper. There was general hysteria in the quest for tickets and the house was of course sold out.

"The Horowitz fever," wrote the critic Klaus Bennert on November 18, "not exactly dampened by the media, finds many victims, and those who fall sick, incurable with ecstasy, follow their idol all over Europe." Bennert pointed out that Horowitz was no longer the thunderer of yore and that his repertoire had been cut down. No matter. "Horowitz repeats pieces but never repeats himself," and thus his recitals were always "artistic adventure trips." Where Hamburg critics had likened Horowitz's Scarlatti to Chopin or Debussy, Bennert said it was something like "a Baroque Scriabin." The Schumann *Arabesque* spun "a soft, impressionistic web." Horowitz was dealing with "the art of the sublime." Mozart's B minor Adagio had "a painful beauty" and the D major Rondo was played in a stylized manner with "breathtaking colors." As for Mozart's C major Sonata (K. 330), what attracted Bennert were the anticipations of Romanticism that Horowitz brought to it.

Gerhard Koch in the November 18 *Frankfurter Allgemeine Zeitung* found in Horowitz's playing a new introverted quality, relaxed and often witty. He raised the question of style, particularly in Mozart, and ended with "Style? Whatever it is, Horowitz changes the conception of what style is. He redefines it his own way." Koch raved about the concert, with one reservation. Chopin's B minor Scherzo, he thought, was too taxing for the octogenarian, even if it did have remarkable energy. Elsewhere the playing was enchanting, miraculous, melancholy at times, with a narcotic quality.

Wanda had one reason not to remember Frankfurt with love. The afternoon that she was at the Alte Oper listening to Horowitz check out the acoustics, their hotel room was rifled and her jewelry stolen. She did not stay in Amsterdam, the next stop on the tour, but went directly to London.

Horowitz had not appeared in Amsterdam since February 20, 1936, when he played the Brahms D minor with the Concertgebouw under Bruno Walter. The Dutch critics at that time raved. "Beautiful." "Remarkable presence." "Flawless grip." "The public gasped." "Hardly any words can do justice to . . ." "Phenomenal." The only reservation was about Brahms. The D minor Concerto was a weak, uninteresting work, many critics said. Today we can laugh. But in 1936 the Brahms was still pretty much a novelty.

A half century later, in 1986, Amsterdam went wild at the Horowitz return. Before the November 22 concert, there were full-page features about "The Tornado from the Steppes." Dutch television reran *The Last Romantic* and the Moscow film a few days before the concert. There was constant reference to the ticket prices —$135 throughout the house, with only a few low-priced seats set aside for students. All tickets promptly disappeared. At the Concertgebouw a dressing room had to be built for Horowitz; the old building was undergoing renovation, and the backstage areas were a mess.

At the opening concert Queen Beatrix and her husband,

Prince Klaus (a serious music lover on the board of the Concert-gebouw), and Ruud Lubbers, the prime minister (it was said in Amsterdam that this was the first concert he had ever attended), were in the audience. Some listeners were observed weeping. Critics from all Dutch newspapers were there. They had to pay for their seats. As often as not, the papers on November 24 carried not only a review but also accompanying news stories and background features.

Horowitz's program was the same as in Germany—Scarlatti, Mozart, Scriabin, the Liszt *Petrarch* 104 and *Soirée,* three Chopin mazurkas and the B minor Scherzo. For encores there were *Träumerei* and *Etincelles.*

In his review, Eddie Vetter in *Het Parool* expressed the consensus: A phenomenon like Horowitz could not be criticized. Vetter pointed out, as others did, that Horowitz in his old age was still the best even though he had refined his repertoire to a point where three-quarters of it could be played by a gifted amateur. But now, wrote Vetter, there was a maturity, a ripeness, that made his interpretations even more spellbinding. Vetter came up with a very nice sentence describing the way Horowitz played Scarlatti: "It seems as though he tells Scarlatti what happened to his music after all those centuries." Vetter concluded that "in old age, poet and virtuoso are brought together in a complete musician."

About Horowitz's Mozart there were two dissenting voices. Hans Heg in the *Volkskrant* wrote that the C major Sonata was "ruined" by Horowitz "in a soft and gentle way." And Van der Ven in the *Haagische Courant* advised Horowitz never to touch Mozart again. K. 330 to him was "a caricature . . . a nonsensical overinterpretation." But most responded to Horowitz's ideas about Mozart. Gérard Verlinden in the *Telegraaf* noticed some wrong notes, but the kind of color Horowitz brought to K. 330 was "the important thing." This Mozart had "a musical heart." Some critics had a little fun with Horowitz's stage mannerisms and eccentricities. To Oene W. Nijdam of the *Leewarder Courant,* the pianist was "a mixture of child, clown and genius." Horowitz loved the Concertgebouw and the Dutch audience so much that he announced he would return the following year, which he did.

On December 14, 1986, not long after his return to New York, Horowitz gave a concert at the Metropolitan Opera. It got a long review from Bernard Holland in the *Times.* Holland pointed out a rebirth in the playing of the eighty-three-year-old pianist. In the past he had listened to Horowitz with a certain reservation. Like many critics of his generation, Holland had been disturbed by what he considered rhythmic liberties, outsized fortissimos and distortion of phrase in Horowitz's musical approach. But now he no longer found the Horowitz of yore. Roughly half of the music —the Mozart C major Sonata (K. 330), Rondo in D and Adagio in B minor, some Chopin mazurkas—was small scale and modest in technical demands. To Holland this kind of repertoire "represented less a weakening technique than a new conduit for an old talent. . . . Power does not necessarily diminish with age but simply changes its shape." And then Holland wrote something extremely perceptive:

> Thus, the opening Scarlatti and Mozart pieces spoke almost in whispers—just as the Schumann *Arabesque* and Liszt's *Valse oubliée* were eerily subdued. Their power, however, was considerable, but transformed, drained of any old brutalities or arrogance and couched in terms of great calmness. It is odd how a whole generation of young pianists has based its collective style on Horowitzian principles, while probably misunderstanding the nature of his playing. . . . It is this amazing gift for using the quality of sound as a metaphor for human speech that sets Mr. Horowitz apart from his admirers and imitators.

The evening after the Metropolitan Opera recital, Horowitz made a brief appearance in Carnegie Hall.

It was on December 15, 1986, and the occasion marked the opening of the newly refurbished Carnegie Hall. The hall had been closed since May in an effort to restore it to the estate it had been in when opened in 1891.

During the period when the Carnegie Hall festivities were being planned, Horowitz had agreed to be the first pianist to give a recital there. Arrangements had been all but finalized when Horowitz picked up the paper before the opening of the hall and read that Daniel Barenboim would be giving a recital before him. The Barenboim engagement may have been Carnegie Hall's booking error, but whatever it was, Horowitz hit the ceiling and canceled his concert. He had nothing against Barenboim but was furious that Carnegie Hall had gone back on its word. Some felt that the December 14 concert at the Metropolitan Opera was Horowitz's implied rebuke to Carnegie Hall.

He did, however, agree to participate in the opening program on December 15. It turned out to be his last appearance on an American stage. He played Chopin's A flat Polonaise and C sharp minor Waltz. Then he went backstage and loudly announced that the Carnegie Hall acoustics had been ruined during the hall's alterations and that he would never play in it again. How much was truth, how much pique, one does not know. But many agreed with his assessment.

Horowitz had superb ears, a lifetime of experience, and strong, often unorthodox, ideas about concert halls. He was, for instance, about the only musician ever to denigrate the sound from the stage of the Musikvereinsaal in Vienna, a concert hall considered one of the acoustic marvels of the world. Horowitz said that he could not hear himself while playing, and the colors he was trying to achieve came out "a mishmash." He loved the Concertgebouw in Amsterdam and Symphony Hall in Boston, both acknowledged to be among the greatest halls in the world, and he was happy in Chicago's Orchestra Hall. He thought the concert hall in Leningrad's Winter Palace one of the finest anywhere. He liked playing in the Philharmonie in Berlin, which is not generally regarded as an acoustic monument. In the Berlin hall, despite its dry acoustics— or because of the dry acoustics?—he could hear everything and thought it was wonderful.

The Horowitz conquest of Europe continued in 1987. He traveled with a program mostly of short pieces—Mozart's D major Rondo and Sonata in B flat (K. 333), Schumann's *Kinderscenen,* Chopin's A flat Polonaise and the B minor Mazurka, Schubert's G flat Impromptu, and the Liszt *Soirée de Vienne* No. 6. His encores were Liszt's D flat *Consolation,* Schubert's F minor *Moment musical,* and Moszkowski's *Etincelles.* He played it in Amsterdam on May 24. A week later, on May 31, he repeated it for his first appearance in a Vienna concert hall in fifty-one years, and then in Berlin on June 7 and Hamburg on June 21.

Two days before the Vienna concert at the Musikvereinsaal, Horowitz was invited by the Musikverein, which had sponsored the concert, to a round table at the Hotel Imperial, and he showed up with Wanda. Horowitz, said Karlheinz Roschitz in the *Abendzeitung,* seemed to be in good humor. His first question was: "Are there any musicians here?" Nobody had the nerve to raise a hand. Horowitz grimaced. He said he liked playing in Europe but not in

London, which did not have a hall with good acoustics. When had he last played in Vienna? Horowitz said that he had forgotten. "December, 1935," Wanda prompted him. "You played with Bruno Walter and the Vienna Philharmonic." Suddenly Horowitz remembered. He was asked if he was eccentric. "I am not," he answered, sticking out his tongue.

The Viennese critics echoed the party line, repeating what their European colleagues had been writing since 1985. His playing was "incomparable," said *Die Presse*. "His age gives him the right and the freedom to shape the music however he feels is right. The listener does not even think to question whether his Mozart, for example, conforms to our current notions of style. The subjective truth of his playing is stronger." In the *Österreichische Musik Zeitschrift* one could read that "the rich Horowitz palette rendered the complete variety of moods, yet without becoming sentimental. . . . The Poet speaks." (These last three words are a reference to the last piece in the *Kinderscenen*, the title of which is *Der Dichter spricht*.)

The concert was televised live. Horowitz was paid about $250,000 for the television rights, and a videocassette was issued by Deutsche Grammophon in 1991. It is strictly a concert; there is no intermission talk or commentator. Horowitz merely comes forth and plays his short program. The playing has all of the traits associated with post-1985 Horowitz except that it is perceptibly weaker in pieces like the polonaise, which is carefully played and even has a few bobbles. Elsewhere the octogenarian was resorting to finesse rather than brilliance, and using extremely slow tempos. For instance, he takes over seven minutes for the Schubert G flat Impromptu. Gieseking in concert used to take it at around four minutes. But Horowitz's running technique remains unimpaired, and the scales in the *Soirée* and *Etincelles* are dazzling examples of the old *jeu perlé*.

After Vienna, Horowitz returned to Berlin for a Philharmonie concert on June 7. Wolfgang Schreiber's review welcomed Horowitz's return a year after his "sensationellen Comeback in Deutschland." Horowitz, Schreiber wrote, can still sing like nobody else. He no longer has the power he once had, but he remains irresistible. Mozart's B flat Sonata (K. 333) was played with élan, charm, and "perhaps too much attention to detail." The Romantic pieces demonstrated Horowitz's ability to create harmonic richness, and the Schubert-Liszt *Soirée* was irresistible. Schreiber, like critics else-where, found a pronounced strain of melancholy in the elderly Horowitz. But what he represents is "an incarnate presence . . . the epoch of the legendary virtuosos."

After he repeated the same program in Hamburg on June 21, 1987, Horowitz returned home. He was to live almost two and a half more years, and he had plans for returning to Europe, but it was not to be. The Hamburg concert was his last appearance any-where as a recitalist.

In New York, Horowitz resumed work on his Deutsche Grammophon series. These last recordings were in many respects probably the best he ever made. They are singing, beautiful, and relaxed. Here virtuoso and musician come into perfect balance. There no longer are the neuroticism, athleticism, and demonism that had long characterized his playing. Everything is simple and natural. Mozart suddenly occupies an honored place in his reper-toire. Horowitz also had always loved Haydn, and his very last disc took a look at a lovely, witty Haydn sonata that he had never previously played.

Horowitz was wise enough to realize that he could no longer be the thundering virtuoso, and he avoided large-scale pieces in the last years of his life, choosing his recorded repertoire very carefully. Aside from Schumann's *Kreisleriana,* he kept away from anything that would tax him physically. The celebrated electricity was still present, but not with the voltage of previous years. Instead there was gentleness, an infinite variety of sound and flexibility of rhythm, a singing color world in which conception, ear, feet, and finger worked together in perfect, artistic harmony. It was a new Horowitz, and if he was not as stunning as before, the rewards—as critics all over the world were quick to point out—were perhaps greater.

24
Last Pupil

You do not have to be afraid of playing for me. You know, I'm a pretty good pianist myself. I understand every pianist, what they want to do with the music, and I understand how difficult it is to be a pianist. So I am very forgiving.
—*Vladimir Horowitz to his pupil Eduardus Halim at their first meeting*

*E*ver since he taught Byron Janis in 1944, Horowitz had been listening to talented young pianists as much as his schedule would permit. Many were called, few were chosen. And of those few who could be considered real pupils—those who had worked steadily with him for a year or more—only Janis and Gary Graffman had gone on to major careers. Still, Horowitz welcomed promising talents and relished the role of Godfather.

Yet for two decades after his return to the stage in 1967 he found nobody who interested him very much.

In 1988, however, Horowitz met Eduardus Halim, and he became really excited. He considered Halim to be of an extraordinary potential, an artist who could well carry on the Horowitz kind of Romanticism, and Horowitz made no secret of his admiration.

He discussed him with such managers as Harold Shaw, and trumpeted his praises to Peter Gelb and also to Franz Mohr and other Steinway executives. He even lent Halim his piano when the young man gave a concert at the Ninety-second Street Y.

But after some forty lessons, the affair came to an end. The Horowitz-Halim relationship illustrated some of the wonders—and perils—of working with Vladimir Horowitz.

In 1988 Halim was a twenty-seven-year-old, Indonesian-born pianist, tall, thin, and exotically handsome. That did him no harm with Horowitz, who was always responsive to male beauty. And Halim had a blazing talent plus an unusual empathy with nineteenth-century Romanticism. That meant rhythmic freedom, beautiful sound, and a world-class technique.

He was brought to Horowitz by David Dubal, a pianist who wrote about the piano world, taught at Juilliard, and knew all of the piano students. Dubal was seeing Horowitz regularly. When Horowitz told him that he wanted to hear some of the younger Juilliard pianists, Halim was one of the first to be introduced. Horowitz listened to Halim and was immediately fascinated. Of all the young pianists he had heard since Byron Janis in the 1940s, Halim had the most instinctive response to Romanticism and the grand manner.

Halim was born in 1961 in Bandung, which is about a hundred miles south of Jakarta. At the age of six he was studying with a local teacher, a Hungarian pianist named Alfons Becalel. The boy was born with nimble fingers, and technique came naturally. He also had perfect pitch. Playing the piano, he said, was easy. He made his debut at eleven with the Beethoven Third Concerto. Then came his solo recital, in which he played the Liszt Sonata, Chopin B flat minor, and other difficult things. He heard the few touring pianists, none of them very important, who passed through Indonesia. Then, he said, he "drifted" for a few years.

At seventeen he started work under Stephan Sulungan, an Indonesian who had studied in Belgium. Sulungan put him to work on finger independence: slow exercises, one finger at a time, striving for evenness and control.

In 1980, not yet twenty, Halim made his way to New York and the Juilliard School, where he asked for Sascha Gorodnitzki, a Russian-trained virtuoso who had turned out a large number of competition winners. Gorodnitzki accepted him. Halim said that he needed the discipline that Gorodnitzki would give him. He won a few competitions, came out high in several international ones, but never took first in any of the majors. Halim's style bothered many jurors, especially the more academic ones; it ran counter to the approved literal school, and Halim's critics considered him too free if not actually anarchic.

After Gorodnitzki's death in 1986 Halim was accepted by Rudolf Firkusny, who worked on polishing his jewel. Halim supplemented his work at the piano by constantly studying recordings of nineteenth-century pianists and was inspired especially by Ignaz Friedman, whose recording of the Chopin E flat Nocturne (Op. 55, No. 2) opened a new world to the young pianist. The freedom, the coloring—all was different from anything he had been taught. Listening to records made by nineteenth-century pianists was, Halim said, "a big jump in my thinking."

Halim's first meeting with Horowitz was set for September 18, 1988. He and Dubal arrived at 9:15 P.M., which was Horowitz's invariable hour for receiving evening visitors. Horowitz was waiting on top of the stairs, greeted them and did his best to put Halim at ease. An easy conversation followed. Horowitz asked Halim the usual questions. How did he develop pianistic skills in Indonesia? What was his background? Then he asked Halim if he wanted to play.

Halim was in a state of near paralysis. Vladimir *Horowitz*! He stumbled to the piano and played one of Horowitz's war horses, the Bach-Busoni Toccata, Adagio, and Fugue in C. Horowitz's piano, Halim said, took some getting used to. It was a beautiful instrument with a very light action, a lot of ping, and responsive to any kind of touch. Its crashing bass had to be approached with care.

Halim followed the Bach-Busoni with Chopin's E major Nocturne and then the Etude in Thirds. About the etude, Horowitz commented, "Very good, but it does not have to be so fast. With correct pedaling you could play it slower and it would sound faster." He also had a few comments about the Bach and briefly demonstrated at the piano. At this first encounter there was nothing much specific otherwise, Halim said. Horowitz just wanted to hear him play and size him up.

"Would you like to hear me?" Horowitz asked. Halim thought that was a silly question. Horowitz, he later noted in his diary, played some strange things. One was his own transcription of the "Dance of the Seven Veils" from Strauss's *Salome* and the waltz from Tchaikovsky's *Eugene Onegin*. "You know, that's my favorite," said Horowitz. Then he played a Schumann novellette. Horowitz said he was thinking of recording it.

"Horowitz apparently never practiced at that time," Halim said. "He just worked on pieces when he had to play them." The brilliance of his playing was breathtaking, but what struck Halim more was the emotional content and the color of the performances. "The man could play three or four melodies separately or independently. It was multidimensional," said an awed Halim.

Around 1 A.M. the first session came to an end. Horowitz took Halim downstairs to the kitchen and said that he had personally gone out and bought some pastries. "Take these home for your wife," he said. Halim's wife, Judy, a petite Chinese woman from Taiwan, was a pianist and also a Juilliard student. Then Horowitz said to Dubal, "I want to hear him again." An appointment was made for three days later.

Halim says he walked out of the house "on cloud nine." The first thing he did when he got home was to grab a notebook and start a diary, which he kept up during the entire course of the relationship. The two were in constant touch through most of the next year except for the time, when Horowitz was occupied with the recording of *Horowitz at Home*. In all, Halim had some forty lessons with Horowitz. He was determined never to forget a single thing Horowitz told him.

At the second session Halim played the Schumann *Kinderscenen* and the Bach-Busoni again. Horowitz congratulated him on the Schumann. "It is very difficult," he said. "Much more so than a virtuoso piece." He discussed the piece's tempos and changes of mood. He told Halim that he played too much with his right hand. "It's fine, the right hand should be beautiful. But you have completely forgotten your left hand." He went to the piano. "It should be like a string quartet," he said. "Or the opening of [Beethoven's A flat Sonata] Op. 110. All subsidiary fingers should be of equal strength." Horowitz discussed the rubato in the slow movement of the Bach-Busoni. The bass, he said, should not deviate at all. Everything else should be free and colored.

Horowitz played for him Mozart's B minor Adagio, and Halim, who had studied it himself and played it in concert, was amazed. "It sounded like a different piece, so free and full of color." Horowitz told Halim, "Mozart should be free. As free as Chopin." He said that the colorings of the left hand were of the greatest importance. With coloration and differentiation of finger strokes a pianist could make the Steinway sound like a period instrument or a modern one. "You should train your fingers as though they were vocal cords. Singing, always singing." When Halim played the Mozart Sonata in C (K. 330), Horowitz demanded color. "You must practice for color. Each color you must be able to get on each finger," he said. "When you are able to do that, when you have the real color in your playing, the interpretation cannot be artificial. You don't have to force your interpretation any more by slowing down or trying different tricks. With the color, the register in your fingers, you can create an atmosphere without slowing down or speeding up." He insisted that the little finger be the strongest of all.

Halim's hand position at the piano—fingers often flat, wrist below the keys—strongly resembled that of Horowitz. Horowitz wanted to know if this was accidental or if he had copied from him. Halim explained that he had developed it long before ever seeing Horowitz in concert. He said he always used a low wrist in Indonesia. He got it from Sulungan, who worked intensively with him on finger independence.

When the wrist is low, Sulungan insisted, the fingers already are raised, and the downstroke can be easily controlled. That way of playing also has much more power. Halim had a large hand with skinny fingers. It was much bigger than Horowitz's beautifully proportioned but not very large hand, which could at best stretch a tenth. Halim could take an easy eleventh (C to F).

The hands of most great pianists, incidentally, have been thick and spatulate, with a wide space between thumb and first finger; the expression "the beautiful hands of a pianist" comes primarily from sentimental fiction. Halim considered his thin fingers a decided handicap and had to work very hard to get a rich, sonorous sound from them. A low wrist and flat fingers helped solve his problem. The low wrist that Horowitz used, Halim believes, was responsible for the sparkle of the Horowitz passage-work. Each note was distinct and seemed to be weighted exactly the same way. "You get a better sound that way," Horowitz said. "The entire ball of the finger, not merely the tip, is on the key."

Wanda listened to many of the sessions and never hesitated to offer suggestions. Generally, Halim said, her suggestions were right, too. In the Bach-Busoni she told him to hold back; he was too brilliant; he pushed too hard. She told all this to Horowitz, in the French they always spoke together. Horowitz then translated it into English for Halim and added, "You know, she's right." After some fifty years of listening to Horowitz play, Wanda had a very good knowledge of the repertoire and of piano playing.

Halim played the Godowsky arrangement of the Strauss *Künstlerleben*, and Wanda and Horowitz listened to it with fascination. They had never heard this long, glitzy, supertechnical piece before. Wanda's comment was, "The music is overly transcribed. There is too much going on. There are too many opening pages. I was waiting for the waltz. It is coming! It is coming! But it never came. I got so tired waiting for it." Halim said that was very true. He had already contemplated making a cut in the introduction, and Wanda's comment cemented his decision.

Soon Horowitz began to take a great interest in his protégé, and the relationship, Halim felt, was almost that of father and son. Horowitz would think about something Halim had done after he left, and a day or two later would telephone him to discuss various points. "You must do this, you must do that." He said, "You know, Eduardus, I want to make for you a special sound, a sound that belongs to you alone. It will be the Halim sound. That's my job. It's my duty to do that. I will help you all the way to develop your kind of sound."

Horowitz never neglected musical structure. Halim said that when he played the Chopin B minor Sonata, Horowitz showed him how to put it together. He cut out a lot of Halim's rubatos and tempo changes, and wanted it played much more strictly than Halim had been doing. One thing he especially insisted on: the opening of any piece of music should be very direct, no fooling around. Later there would be places for tempo changes or inner voices. Never at the beginning, Horowitz said. If there is too much rubato at the beginning, it is not effective when it is used later.

Any technique, he told Halim, can be developed if you have the right attitude and the right way of practicing. "He taught me how to practice. That was one of the most important things he did for me," said Halim. "We were working on the runs in the last movement of the Chopin B minor Sonata. Horowitz told me that the tendency of most pianists was to accelerate here. That made it too fast. So Mr. Horowitz told me to practice it fortissimo, slow, each note very even. 'When you overcome your urge to play it too fast,' Horowitz told me, 'then you do it forte, mezzo-forte, piano, pianissimo, pianississimo. That is what we call discipline.' Which I did. It was fantastic, the finger control that I got, and the agility. Mr. Horowitz, I think, had figured out everything about piano playing."

Horowitz hated playing by rote and wanted pieces never to be played the same way twice. When a performer's interpretation becomes predictable, he told Halim, "that is the end." The sense of improvisation always had to be there. His attitude was, "Sometimes it works, and it's so wonderful. Sometimes it doesn't work but at least you tried. It's better to have risky playing than have everything safely planned."

A great deal of time was spent on rhythm. Playing rhythmically, Horowitz explained, has nothing to do with playing metronomically. "It's the other way around." What Horowitz meant is that when a basic, unfaltering pulse is maintained, almost anything can be done in the way of metrical displacement.

Horowitz also spent much time on pedaling with Halim. His ideas, thought Halim, were highly unorthodox. "Most teachers try to get their pupils to pedal clearly, never going through changes of harmony. But," said Halim,

> Horowitz had no hesitation blending several harmonies at the same time. It was a beautiful effect. When he played a singing line he felt that the pedal should be used sparingly, letting the fingers take care of the legato. He considered the left pedal very important. Before I came to Horowitz I had experimented with the left pedal and thought it was too soft-edged. But Horowitz used the left pedal almost all the time, even when he played forte. It was part of his distinctive sound, the soft textures of the left pedal always mixing with the right. He got different overtones that way.

Harmonies seemed to be suspended in the air, helped by the slight harmonic clash when the harmonies were pedaled through. Horowitz showed Halim various kinds of pedalings: half pedal, full pedal, flutter pedaling. It takes considerable work and experience, and a very good ear, to master the effects that result. Halim slaved over it.

Then there was the matter of repertoire. Horowitz showed Halim a great deal of music to open his mind to new composers. He would go to his library and emerge with, say, an armload of pieces by Poulenc. He would play these for Halim to see if he was interested.

Preparing for a concert at the Ninety-second Street Y, Halim played his program for Horowitz. It was very much a Horowitz kind of program: the Bach-Busoni Toccata, Adagio, and Fugue in C; Schubert's G flat Impromptu; the Chopin B minor Sonata; Schumann's *Humoresque*; and the Liszt Twelfth Rhapsody. They spent some time on it and Horowitz was pleased. "When you give your recital," he said, "I will tell Steinway to see that you have a good piano. Try my piano in the Steinway basement too. It's a good piano. But you don't have to like it. If you don't like it, don't choose it." Horowitz immediately phoned Franz Mohr, and when Halim went to the Steinway basement, Mohr took him in hand.

Halim tried several instruments and then the Horowitz CD 186, and loved it. "I never felt in the slightest way uncomfortable playing it. The dynamics from pianissimo to fortissimo I was able to do with ease. It was bright with a lot of timbre. Naturally I picked that piano. I thought it would be fantastic for the program." Horowitz was pleased but warned Halim, "Remember, you play at the Y and it is a small hall. The piano may be too big for it." Halim took note, but felt that as long as he was comfortable with the instrument, he could control it regardless of the hall.

As things turned out, Halim was wrong. The Horowitz piano was a mistake. Halim was not yet experienced enough to hear what the people in the audience were hearing. The piano simply sounded too loud and overbrilliant when Halim came down on it. At the intermission Tom Frost told Peter G. Davis of *New York* magazine that the piano was Horowitz's. Davis made something of that fact in his review, and Halim learned an important thing. He had to take great care if he did not want to be regarded as a Horowitz clone.

Wanda had already indicated as much to him. In a private conversation, when Horowitz was out of the room, she said to Halim, "You know, Horowitz's name might not be very good for you. You should be very careful." Halim did not realize it at the time, but it was her way of telling him that he ran the risk of being called a Horowitz imitator when the reviews of his playing would start to come in. In a way Halim was a junior Horowitz before he started working with him, and some of his playing was so Horowitz-like that there was a real danger he would be labeled an epigone.

From the beginning, Halim tried to establish the ground rules of the relationship. Were his sessions with Horowitz to be a secret? Yes, said Horowitz. Nobody should know. Halim then said that at least he had to tell his teacher, Rudolf Firkusny, an artist for whom he had the greatest respect. He would not want Firkusny to hear it from somebody else. "Oh, yes!" said Horowitz. "Firkusny is a very good friend of mine." Finally Halim worked up the nerve to tell Firkusny, who thought it was wonderful and congratulated Halim. He thought Halim was going to Horowitz at just the right time. Halim was twenty-seven. A few years earlier, and Halim could have ended up being swamped by Horowitz, becoming a mere copy. A few years later, and Halim's own style would have been solidified.

Horowitz, of course, was naïve to think that his work with Halim could be kept a secret. If nothing else, Dubal was bringing other Juilliard pianists to Horowitz, and they knew what was going on. Halim was walking on eggs all the time. He was terrified that Mr. and Mrs. Horowitz would think he was using them. Halim once asked Mrs. Horowitz what he should do when asked if he were studying with Maestro. She thought a bit and said, "You can say yes, you play for Mr. Horowitz and you know Mr. Horowitz. But do not elaborate."

But Horowitz and his wife surely must have realized that there is no way of keeping a secret in musical New York, especially when Horowitz himself was telling powerful figures in the musical establishment about Halim. Word got out very fast. Juilliard piano students would come up to Halim and ask, "Is it true that you are studying with . . . Him?" He told them only what Mrs. Horowitz had told him to say.

Of course everybody at Steinway knew about Horowitz's great interest in Halim, and when Halim went there to try pianos he was given the red-carpet treatment. Then the *Times* called Halim and wanted a picture of him with Horowitz. Halim ran the other way.

But the relationship was not to last. Halim does not know what caused the rupture. It may have been the suspicious quality imbedded in the natures of Wanda and Horowitz. Was Halim using them? It may have been because Halim did not get very far in the 1989 Cliburn Competition, which Horowitz did not at first want Halim to attend. (Halim's free style was always anathema to strict-constructionist jury members.) It may have been that Wanda thought Horowitz was spending too much of his time with Halim, was perhaps becoming too interested in him personally.

Halim had no regrets. He had the privilege of friendship with a legendary figure who played an important part in his musical and pianistic development. He considered Horowitz one of the most generous and considerate persons he had ever met. He also thought that Horowitz was "a sad man, happy only at the piano."

25

Mozart and Liebestod

From looking at the music of a composer-pianist, say Godowsky or Friedman, I can tell how they played. That's why the transcriptions of Busoni are the closest to me.
　　—*Vladimir Horowitz, talking about Busoni and Mozart in 1987*

*H*orowitz had been thinking about a concerto recording for well over a year, and early in 1987 he discussed repertoire with his friends. He talked about the Liszt E flat. He said he might pair it with the Chopin F minor. Or maybe Liszt's A major Concerto, which he adored. He even spoke about the Saint-Saëns C minor Concerto. But he ended up with the A major Mozart (K. 488). Horowitz had never played K. 488 in public but was not unfamiliar with it. In 1939 he learned the work when he was going to play it at the Lucerne Festival with Toscanini, but at the last minute it was replaced by the Brahms Second.

Recording sessions for the Mozart were arranged. The locale would be La Scala, Milan, in March, 1987.

Since 1985, Horowitz had been having a great love affair with

Mozart. In his old-age look at Mozart, Horowitz, knowingly or unknowingly, was experiencing what the great Italian-German pianist Ferruccio Busoni had experienced in the final years of *his* life. Busoni, famous for his Bach, Beethoven, and Liszt, suddenly turned to Mozart, giving series of the concertos in a day when most of them were unknown.

Horowitz never heard Busoni, who died in Berlin in 1924, the year before Horowitz left Russia. But he had looked through all the Busoni oeuvre and felt a peculiar affinity with the great Italian-German composer-pianist:

> All my life I have been playing his Bach transcriptions. I often use his editions of Liszt. All those colors. Such colors! He must have been a fantastic colorist. I never heard him. But with all his eccentricities there is a timbre and color that makes him, I think, very much in my style.

Busoni made a few records and many piano rolls. None were of Mozart. But he did write cadenzas for some of the concertos; and in 1987, when Horowitz was getting ready for his recording of K. 488, it was the Busoni cadenza that he used.

He did not like Mozart's own cadenza, which had been written for a pupil. Horowitz found it "uninteresting and too naïve." He looked at cadenzas by Landowska, and whatever else he could find, and did not like any of them. His friend David Dubal dug out the Busoni and showed it to Horowitz, who loved it. "It was as though Mozart himself composed it," Horowitz said.

Wanda unbelievingly watched Horowitz get the concerto ready for Milan. He did very little work on it. No more than an hour a day once or twice a week, she said, and that was in February for a session coming up in less than a month. She did not know how he could get it into his fingers in so short a time with so little practice, but on this occasion she underestimated the old pro. Horowitz knew how to pace himself. And besides, this was a recording session, not a concert. He could have the sheet music in front of him.

When Horowitz felt that he had the concerto more or less in his fingers, he went to the Steinway basement to play it with the orchestral accompaniment on a second piano. Mordecai Shehori was the other pianist.

The Israeli-born Shehori had studied with the well-known

teacher Mindru Katz. At Juilliard he worked with Ilona Kabos, Beveridge Webster, and Claude Frank. Those were impressive credentials. Like so many young pianists, Shehori had a Horowitz fixation and had always wanted to meet him. He went to various recitals within striking distance of New York—Boston, Philadelphia, Rutgers University in New Jersey. "To me," Shehori said, "he was the most intriguing pianist. When I hear the old master recordings I know where he came from. In my time he was the only one."

One day Shehori got a call from Thomas Frost, who had heard one of his concerts and was impressed. "Would you like to play a Mozart concerto with Mr. Horowitz?" Frost asked. "K. 488?" It so happened that Shehori had played the second piano part of the Mozart for other pianists and knew it inside out. Of course he jumped at the chance. Knowing Horowitz's approach to the piano, he spent a few days changing the dynamics of the orchestral reduction to what he thought would be along the lines of Horowitz's conception of the solo part.

They met in the Steinway basement at the appointed day. Horowitz sat down and played some of his usual warm-up improvisations. "What was amazing to me," Shehori said, "was that he was nervous. Finally he started playing one difficult passage in the Mozart over and over, many times." Obviously Horowitz had not yet mastered the piece; he was still practicing. But, said Shehori, "it got better and better and better. By that time he had no nerves anymore. I was the one who had nerves."

Finally Horowitz was ready. Shehori said, "Maestro, would you like me to skip the introduction?" Almost always pianists working on a Classic concerto, with its opening orchestral introduction, will ask the accompanist to begin just a few measures before the solo entrance. "No!" said Horowitz. "Every note I have to hear. Every note!" So Shehori started off and they went through the entire concerto. "We didn't look at each other. When the musical lines are clear there is no need to. I anticipated what he was going to do. We did the slow movement twice. What I found very interesting was that he didn't like to make crescendos. His greatest color was when he started strong and went into a diminuendo. He also didn't like scholarly things that don't translate into practice."

Horowitz was so pleased with the accompaniment that Shehori began to be invited to East Ninety-fourth Street and had many evenings with the Horowitzes. He discovered what many musicians exposed to Horowitz at home came to realize: "He was very serious. That was what a lot of people did not understand." Horowitz, as always, spent a great deal of time at the keyboard late at night, and what struck Shehori was his economy of means. "He knew exactly the minimum movement needed for any kind of phrase. His body was immobile. If you looked at his face you did not see one muscle move, eyebrow, nothing. He was listening totally."

In March, Horowitz went to Milan to make his record, which contained the last of the few concertos he ever recorded. Instead of another concerto to go with the Mozart, Horowitz finally decided to play Mozart's Sonata in B flat (K. 333). Conductor and orchestra were Carlo Maria Giulini and the Scala Orchestra of Milan.

Not many orchestras or major conductors had been available on such short notice. Milan was selected because the Scala was available. Giulini came into the picture because he was a major conductor and he too was available because he spent most of his time at home with his ailing wife. He would no longer travel, and he lived close to Milan, so he would have no problem going home after the recording sessions. Normally a concerto session with any pianist other than Horowitz would take two days at most. With Horowitz and his frequent rest breaks, it might take ten days, and the world's top busy conductors would not give up that much time. Giulini could. Horowitz and Giulini were on good terms, and Horowitz felt that Giulini would not fight him and his free way of playing Mozart.

Nevertheless there were problems. Onlookers at the sessions said that Giulini, who considered himself a great authority on Mozart, was steamrolled by Horowitz. This was not his kind of Mozart, but he went along nevertheless, with a peculiar look on his face. There were a few tense moments. At one point Horowitz wanted an appoggiatura played short and Giulini said, "No, it's an acciaccatura." (An acciaccatura is a short accessory note to the main note, sounded the same time as the main note and promptly released. An appoggiatura is a melodic ornament a half step above or below the main note, played against the bass to supply a momentary dissonance.) Horowitz felt it as an appoggiatura, and neither Giulini nor any documentation would persuade him otherwise. It ended up with Horowitz saying something like, "You play it your way and I'll play it mine." Giulini gave in.

After the sessions were over, Horowitz was not too happy with Giulini, and it had nothing to do with appoggiaturas or acciaccaturas. He felt that Giulini was a little stodgy and did not breathe life into the music. Also there were fundamental differences about tempo. Giulini would try to take a slow opening tutti, even though he knew that Horowitz, at his entry, would establish a faster tempo. Finally Giulini was persuaded, very much against his will, to use the Horowitz tempo. But the finished product did not reflect a meeting of minds.

The performance was filmed as well as recorded, and the film cassette was a best-seller. It had its premiere at Lincoln Center's New York Film Festival on October 8, 1987. Like *The Last Romantic,* it was a Peter Gelb Production directed by the Maysles documentary team—Albert Maysles, Susan Froemke, and Charlotte Zwerin. The music was punctuated by some on-screen talk by Mr. and Mrs. Horowitz. Wanda was in good form. There was one shot of her listening to European music critics quizzing Horowitz. "Always the same questions," she mutters, with a disgusted look. At the end of the film she was asked what she thought of the performance. She looked at the questioner unbelievingly. "Do you want me to say that I don't like how he played?"

Horowitz made his last public appearance some months after he returned from Milan. It was not in a concert hall but at a record-signing promotion on October 11, 1989, at the Sam Goody record store on West Fiftieth Street in Manhattan. Horowitz had done such things in the past and seemed to enjoy them. He had made a previous Goody appearance in 1978, and an appearance at Tower Records in 1986, and in both cases had been gratified to learn that the lines started hours before his scheduled appearance, just as it had formed for his concerts. At Goody's he happily signed his records for the adoring throng that surrounded him. The old man appeared indestructible.

At the East Ninety-fourth Street town house, Eduardus Halim was not the only pianist regularly playing for Horowitz in the last year of his life. A steady visitor was Murray Perahia.

Perahia, who had concentrated on Mozart and the Austro-German classics, had decided to expand his repertoire, and he worked with Horowitz on some large-scale Liszt pieces and the Franck Prelude, Chorale, and Fugue. It was not a pupil-teacher relationship. Perahia, after all, had a great international career and was even something of a cult figure. In a 1991 *Gramophone* interview he said that Horowitz merely gave him tips, "as one artist to another." What could Horowitz give so finished an artist? "A lot. The potential of the piano to express itself in coloristic terms." It was a myth, Perahia said, "that all Horowitz thought about was technique. That was always connected with musical sounds, with phrasing, a larger picture. Horowitz hated mechanical playing. . . . I had previously found Liszt unattractive—the showmanship was foreign to me—but he showed me that Liszt could be musical too." The major impression Perahia received from these sessions was the realization that Horowitz "never liked exaggeration or heart-on-sleeve Romanticism. Of course he believed in rubato, but he didn't like it if you couldn't discern the pulse. Everything had to be natural, not artificial."

Otherwise few faces were seen at Ninety-fourth Street. Friends had died, or he had broken off relationships with such admirers as Jack Pfeiffer. Rudolf Serkin was ill and seldom left his Vermont retreat. Perhaps Horowitz did not wish to see anybody anymore. Toward the end of his life he asked Franz Mohr about Serkin. "Why don't you call him?" asked Mohr. "Rudi would love it so much." Horowitz said, "No. He has to call me. He is younger than I am." Horowitz was wrong. Serkin, born on March 28, 1903, was six months older. He died in 1991 after a long illness.

Perhaps Horowitz was too busy making recordings at his home to see people. His living room was cluttered with recording equipment and there were electrical lines all over the floor. Horowitz had come to the conclusion that his best records were made at East Ninety-fourth Street. He did not want to go back to the RCA studios, where the acoustics were not to his liking. He tried the Grace Rainey Rogers Auditorium at the Metropolitan Museum and was not happy there either. So home it was.

Early in 1989 Thomas Frost recorded what was released as the *Horowitz at Home* album. It contained some Mozart, including the B flat Sonata (K. 281), which was new to the Horowitz repertoire, and also the three Schubert-Liszt pieces from the discarded 1986 recording—*Ständchen* and the *Soirées* Nos. 6 and 7. The Mozart sings and dances, and the Liszt arrangements are among the greatest of their kind in recorded history. This combination of relaxed control, linear independence (in the *Ständchen*), pure song, long-arched phrases, and blinding colors makes the playing unique, even for Horowitz.

For a few months after the completion of the disc Horowitz took it easy. He hardly touched the piano at all, at least during the day. Virginia Bach, who worked there at that time as a sort of assistant—keeping his music in shape, seeing that he signed his autograph pictures, sorting his mail, doing some light bookkeeping—was herself a pianist and was dying to hear him play. But, she said, he never touched the piano during the first few months she was there.

It was only when he started thinking about a new recording that he worked a little bit. Around the end of August 1989, he was going through the repertoire for what turned out to be his last recording. Mrs. Bach never heard him play scales or any kind of exercise. He would just play through the music, occasionally stopping and repeating a phrase. He never played any single piece more than five times. Usually it was only three.

One afternoon, she remembered, Wanda was out, the house was empty, and she crept from upstairs and sat on the settee outside the living room listening to Horowitz play.

It was the *Liebestod,* and, she said, "it was so wonderful I started to cry. I went into the living room and said to him, 'Maestro, you have made me cry.' " Horowitz was touched and engaged her in conversation. "He was so sweet, trying to share something with me for what I had said to him."

Once again Mrs. Bach was struck by how childlike he could be at times, "and a total genius at other times." She had been watching him for some months and thought that he was very well organized. He always would have a little notebook on him, and if he heard or read something that interested him he would jot it down. He also impressed her as a very unhappy man. But he functioned well. "He was an eighty-six-year-old man who was with it. Oh, yes!"

Recording sessions started on October 20. Frost thought it was going to be another CD for Deutsche Grammophon. Horowitz thought so too. He was perfectly happy there. But CBS/Sony wanted the next Horowitz record, and Gunther Breest, who had brought Horowitz to Deutsche Grammophon, was now with CBS/Sony. Horowitz finally went with Breest. Insiders say that CBS/

Sony offered a much more lucrative contract than did Deutsche Grammophon.

The disc consisted of music Horowitz had never publicly played in America. His original idea was to play only Haydn and Chopin. But he changed his mind. He did start out, as planned, with Haydn and Chopin, recording the Haydn Sonata No. 49 in E flat and Chopin's Etudes in A flat and E minor (Op. 25, Nos. 1 and 5), Mazurka in C minor (Op. 56, No. 3), Nocturnes in E flat (Op. 55, No. 2) and B (Op. 62, No. 1), and the Fantaisie-Impromptu.

But after the second session he told Frost: "You are going to be very surprised. I found something better to end the record with than the Fantasy-Impromptu." He had been looking through volumes of Liszt because he was unhappy with the Chopin. He felt that he needed a bigger ending, and he looked again at the Liszt arrangement of the *Liebestod,* on which he had worked with Halim. "That's the perfect ending!" In a few days he had the piece entirely in his fingers, and it was made the ending of his record. It turned out to be symbolic. He also found a little-played Liszt work, the Praeludium to Bach's cantata *Weinen, Klagen, Sorgen, Zagen.* Liszt later composed a large-scale set of variations on the cantata theme that sometimes is heard, but the short, highly chromatic, dark-colored, intense Praeludium was a complete novelty to most.

Usually Horowitz asked for two sessions a week, two hours each session. Frost, the producer of the record for CBS/Sony, figured that the sessions would last about three weeks before Horowitz was satisfied. But, as he wrote in a *Times* piece on April 11, 1990, on the occasion of the disc's release, "this time, however, he was driven by some mysterious source of energy that made him eager to complete the recording in a couple of weeks. He was back on his old three sessions a week, having a wonderful time, enjoying himself." He was more energetic than Frost had seen him for a long time. And he was looking forward to attending the *Traviata* performance that his new friend Carlos Kleiber would conduct at La Scala on December 5. Then there were the two recitals he planned to give in Berlin and Hamburg in mid-December.

The recording took six sessions in a period of twelve days. The last session took place on November 1. Four days later Horowitz was dead.

26

Artist-As-Hero

Le grand piano ne sonnera plus . . .
—*Start of a poem by Jean-Philippe Collard on learning of the death of Vladimir Horowitz*

*V*ladimir Horowitz died instantly at his home on Sunday, November 5, 1989, at about 1 P.M. The medical report said that his eighty-six-year-old heart had just stopped beating.

There had been no indication that anything was basically wrong with Horowitz's health. He had always taken care of himself. His diet was Spartan, he did not smoke or drink, he walked his mile or two each day, and shortly before his death he had a medical checkup at which he was assured that he was in fine shape.

But his death had been preceded by what he and everybody else thought was a temporary stomach upset. On Friday, November 3, Horowitz woke up and did not feel well. He was nauseated and dizzy, and he called Tom Frost to cancel that day's recording session, telling him that he had thrown up the night before. He thought he had a digestive problem. His doctor came the next day and could find nothing wrong. Horowitz told him that he now was feeling fine.

At the canceled recording session he was going to work on several Chopin etudes from Op. 25—Nos. 2, 3, and 4. He had previously played the C minor Etude (Op. 25, No. 12) and the *Winter Wind* (Op. 25, No. 11) but abandoned them. Frost could not understand why he dropped the *Winter Wind* because he played it "very well."

On the morning of his death, Horowitz had followed his normal routine. He had risen late and had breakfast. He then went to Wanda's bedroom and sat down to discuss the menu for the evening dinner. Celine Knight, the housekeeper, entered the room. Wanda turned her head for a moment to talk to her. Mrs. Knight suddenly gasped. When Wanda turned around, Horowitz was slumped in the chair. He then slid to the floor. Wanda took one look at him and said, "He's dead."

She dialed 911 for an ambulance and then called Giuliana Lopes, who rushed over. Mrs. Lopes called Peter Gelb, who had just returned to his office in the CAMI Building on West Fifty-seventh Street from a tennis game. He was still in his tennis clothes. She told him to come right over, right away, immediately. From the tone of her voice, Gelb knew that something had happened to Horowitz. When he arrived, an ambulance was parked outside the house. Gelb raced upstairs. Paramedics were working on Horowitz, but he was already dead. They tried for an hour to resuscitate him. A doctor with the team signed the death certificate.

Frost called in early Sunday afternoon to find out how Horowitz was and got the news. He rushed down from his summer home in Massachusetts and joined the shocked group. Wanda tried to be composed, though every once in a while she broke into tears. Gelb and Frost tidied up the living room, which was still full of recording equipment. Later Murray Perahia arrived.

Gelb notified the Associated Press, and word immediately flashed around the world. All the media people got busy. Obituary writers got to work. Advance obits were updated. Critics were hastily summoned to newsrooms to write appraisals of the Horowitz career and what it represented. Television specialists rooted out stills and film clips. Magazines immediately commissioned experts to write long articles. Horowitz's death was in the news on every radio and television station that evening, and was on Page 1 of virtually every American paper the following morning.

Letters and telegrams of condolence overwhelmed the Horowitz home. Wanda received messages from the White House and from musicians and admirers the world over. One she especially cherished was a sweet, understanding letter that came a few days later from Leonard Bernstein.

Eduardus Halim learned of Horowitz's death at the intermission of a concert he was playing that Sunday afternoon in New Jersey. When he returned to the stage he told the audience the news (he saw some people break into tears) and dedicated the last half of his concert to the memory of Vladimir Horowitz.

The body was taken to the Frank E. Campbell Funeral Home on Madison Avenue. Gelb handled the details of the funeral arrangements. Amid all the confusion—hysteria, even—he kept an eye on Wanda. She was "stoic, holding up very well," he said.

Burial was to be in the Toscanini family plot in the cemetery in Milan.

The body was on view at Campbell's on November 6 and 7, and thousands came to pay their respects. In the background was a tape of music played by Horowitz, put together by Frost. He went through the Columbia and Deutsche Grammophon discs and picked out slow, lyric pieces—Schumann's *Arabesque* and *Träumerei*, Scarlatti sonatas, the slow movement of Mozart's Sonata in C, and the like.

The body lay in state at Campbell's for two days instead of one because of an error by the *Times* reporter who helped write the obituary. He forgot that when a reporter writes about an event that will take place the following day he writes "today" because he is writing for tomorrow's paper. The reporter unthinkingly wrote "tomorrow" instead of "today," and when the Monday paper came out, everybody of course read "tomorrow" as Tuesday.

The body was flown to Milan on Wednesday, accompanied by Wanda, Mrs. Lopes, and Peter Gelb. On their arrival in Milan, they were greeted at the airport by the mayor of Milan and other dignitaries. Photographers were everywhere. There was a motorcade from the airport to La Scala, where the coffin was carried by ushers into the opera house and placed in the lobby. Frost had supplied another, shorter, tape for background music. On the stage of the great auditorium, where Horowitz had played, was a piano with the lid symbolically closed. The hall was lit as though for a concert. Nobody was admitted into the auditorium. A large crowd had gathered in the piazza, and thousands entered the lobby to view the coffin.

After a few hours the body was brought to the cemetery. It was a very large, walled burial site, with huge monuments, lavish sculptures and graveled walks. A short Catholic religious service was held in the chapel of the Cimitero Monumentale. Horowitz was Jewish and, strictly speaking, he should not have been buried there. Nor should he have had a service. Catholic doctrine would normally forbid such a thing. It was rumored that Wanda got around the problem by assuring the priest that Horowitz had been thinking of converting to Catholicism. But Wanda's official statement was that nobody asked any questions, that it was taken for granted that Horowitz would be interred in the Toscanini family crypt, and that he was buried without question in a Catholic cemetery simply because he was Vladimir Horowitz. The whole affair would have amused Horowitz, who never practiced any form of religion. Sometimes he would say to Wanda, "I'm Catholic. I'm Catholic." It made no difference to him. At the end of the service, a Horowitz recording of *Träumerei* was played. He was interred in the Toscanini family crypt, near Sonia. During these final rites Wanda was, said Gelb, "very strong."

Musicians around the world were asked to talk or write about Horowitz, and for several months magazines were full of articles and interviews. All, inevitably, made the point that an era had come to an end. One of the more sensitive and thoughtful assessments came from Vladimir Feltsman:

> When I learned from that day's television broadcasts that he died, it hit me, but somehow I was asking myself why I did not feel any real sadness. Of course I felt very sorry for Wanda and for all of us, but why wasn't I sorry for Horowitz? I realized that his life as a musician, despite all the complications, was an extremely lucky one. He was born to play the piano, he got all possible fame in the world he lived in, he lived a long life, he rediscovered Mozart, he went back to his motherland, and the circle of his life was complete. He had fulfilled himself. It was the happy life of an artist, and I can only wish all of us to have this sort of life. He left a legacy. His sound is here and it is still floating, somewhere above us.

In *Le monde de la musique,* the pianist Jean-Philippe Collard, who had played for Horowitz and had discussed the music of Fauré with him, wrote an article, prefacing it with a four-line poem:

Le grand piano ne sonnera plus . . .
Finis les pirouettes, les clins d'oeil, les cascades . . .
Envolées les harmonies mêlées comme les couleurs de ses
      tableaux qu'il affectionnait tant . . .
Figé à jamais, le sourire de ce grand enfant.

The concert grand will sound no more . . .
Ended are the pirouettes, the winks, the cascades . . .
Flown away are the harmonies mixed like the colors of the
    paintings he loved so much . . .
Imprinted forever is the smile of this great child.

Humble music lovers expressed their sorrow by taking out little squibs in newspapers during the next few months. Typical was one that was published in Amsterdam's *Het Parool* on December 12, 1989: HOROWITZ; I WILL NEVER FORGET YOU. It was signed "Marcel Tristesse."

When the contents of Horowitz's will were revealed, it was learned that Wanda and Gelb were named the coexecutors of the estate, which was valued at $6 to $8 million. Horowitz gave $300,000 to Juilliard for scholarships. His memorabilia, recordings, and library were to go to Yale. To Giuliana B. Lopes, "my friend and companion," he left $200,000. The remainder went to his wife.

Wanda, shortly after her husband's death, started packing all of his memorabilia and sending it to the archives at Yale. She decided not to sell the town house on Ninety-fourth Street, but felt she needed a quiet retreat, so she purchased a house in Ashley Falls, Massachusetts. There she busied herself with a renovation job. The house was stocked with American antiques, about which she was an expert. Several cats had the run of the house, and they could gaze upon the walls and admire picture after picture of cats, from American primitives to moderns. There also were other things: a set of original Boz etchings for the illustrations in the Dickens books, some trompe l'oeil paintings, cabinets of rare china, and informal photographs of Horowitz scattered through the house. In the driveway was a sign with the name of the little estate: Pinci's Acres.

On May 8, 1991, Wanda flew to Rome. She had received news of her sister Wally's death that day. Wally had been in poor health for almost ten years, had become senile, and Wanda considered her death a blessing. She returned depressed, feeling all alone in the world. All of her immediate family were now gone. She felt useless and depleted, an eighty-three-year-old woman without a mission.

In the meantime, it was clear that Horowitz had not been forgotten. Reissues of his records continued to be released on CDs. Two years after his death his last disc—*Horowitz: The Last Recording*—continued to be a best-seller.

Horowitz remained the archetype of the Romantic pianist, his name still a legend to all pianists and the public, the most potent and electrifying virtuoso of the twentieth century, the musician with the strongest, most individual personality, a reincarnation of the nineteenth-century artist-as-hero.

He was unique, the last of his kind; and when he died there was nobody to replace him. In his day, in his way, he was, as the Countess d'Agoult had said of Liszt almost 150 years before, the only one.

The Horowitz Recordings

Appendix I
1926–53

The most extraordinary thing. I listened to the radio and there
was some pianist. Wanda was there. It was the Liszt B minor
Ballade. I listened and said to Wanda, it is horrible. I have to
know who that is. Tempi too slow and tempi too fast, all like
that. I said it's probably somebody good and I don't like it. It
turned out to be Vladimir Horowitz. I hated this performance. It
was horrible. I would not play one note like that today. So that
means the taste changes.
—*Vladimir Horowitz on his recordings*

Vladimir Horowitz took recording very seriously. It is true that he fretted
about certain built-in factors. Recordings, he said, were like photographs,
resemblances of things past. A photograph of a thirty year old man dif
fered from a photograph of the same man thirty years later. "Sometimes
you recognize the person and sometimes you don't." A Horowitz recording of a specific piece made in 1935, he said, would differ from his
recording of the same piece made in 1975.

Nor did he think that recordings were necessarily a force for good.
Ever since the introduction of magnetic tape and the LP disc in 1948,
editing had become so easy that recordings no longer represented what
an artist really could do. Through splicing, even a second-rate technician
could now sound like a Hofmann or Horowitz. Tape editing created a
race of (apparently) perfect technicians of a kind who did not exist in the
concert hall and opera house, where fingers and vocal cords could, alas,

sometimes show their human imperfections. In addition, the public started to grow up on technically perfect performances that bore no relation to what actually happened in the concert hall.

Horowitz told Elyse Mach, in her *Great Pianists Speak for Themselves,* that too many pianists were influenced by recordings. "They are so used to hearing note-perfect performances on record that they want to duplicate the same note-perfect performance in the concert hall. The result is that instead of projecting the spirit of the music they concern themselves only with the notes. . . . With recordings today, it is mechanically [Horowitz should have said electronically] possible to do what it took me so many years to develop."

At the same time Horowitz realized that a musician could live forever only through recordings, and he took full advantage of whatever new techniques were available.

For some sixty years Vladimir Horowitz made records. By the time he had made his last one, only four days before his death, a good part of his repertoire was forever available to posterity. Max Massei, the French expert on Horowitz who made a study of the recordings, estimated that Horowitz recorded about 85 percent of the Schumann works he played in public, 80 percent of his Chopin and Scriabin, 70 percent of his Scarlatti, 65 percent of his Rachmaninoff, and—surprisingly—only 55 percent of his Liszt.

In the process he consistently won Grammy Awards, far more than any other pianist. The Grammy Awards were initiated in 1959 for records issued the previous year. Horowitz got his first one in 1963 for his *Columbia Presents Vladimir Horowitz.* In all he got twenty-three Grammy Awards, a Merit Award and, after his death, the Lifetime Achievement Award. This does not take in the many awards he received in Europe, and he continued to receive them after his death. In 1991 his last record won a posthumous Grammy for the best classical-music instrumental recording.

He had prefaced his first series of recordings with a few Welte-Mignon piano rolls (made in Germany) and Duo Art (made in America). He was one of the last of the great piano-roll artists to record; in 1926 and 1928, when he made the rolls, the player-piano industry was almost dead. Electrical recordings and a new thing called radio captured the public's imagination. Before long, piano rolls, which had been popular since 1904, disappeared.

The Horowitz rolls reflect the faults of the medium. For instance, accurate pedaling was next to impossible to capture. Nor was there much metrical flexibility. And the rolls could be heavily edited, with wrong notes repaired. Piano rolls tended to lack nuance. Hence the expression "He sounds like a player piano," referring to a pianist who plays metronomically with no color or inflection. The story goes that Schnabel was once approached by a piano-roll company to sign a contract. "We have seven degrees of nuance in our rolls," the manufacturer bragged. "Sorry," Schnabel wired back. "I have eight."

With all that, and keeping in mind the fact that Horowitz himself disavowed the rolls, his playing on them is still recognizably Horowitzian. And there is on the rolls one major work he never played in America, the Mozart-Liszt *Figaro,* ardent yet controlled, brilliantly unfolded. Another typical example of the young Horowitz is the Schubert-Liszt *Liebesbotschaft,* which demonstrates a lovely long line. He never played this after his first few seasons in America. There are also the Adagio from the Bach-Busoni Toccata in C, some Chopin mazurkas and etudes with which he later became identified, his own *Moment exotique,* and some Rachmaninoff.

When Horowitz started to make flat-disc recordings in 1928, the process was new. Only a few years before, the Bell Telephone Laboratories had tested a means of electrical recording in which the frequency response was greatly expanded. Up to then—from 1877, the year Edison invented the phonograph, to 1925—musicians had to record into a horn that had a limited frequency response. Now, with the new electronic process, musicians could play and sing into microphones instead of the acoustic horn, and the advantages were immediately apparent. In 1925 the first commercial electrical recordings were made, and the technique was able to capture sounds, especially of such large groups as symphony orchestras, with then unheard-of fidelity. A complete rethinking of the phonograph as a medium for music resulted.

The first recordings made by Horowitz were, of course, 78-rpm discs. Several things can be said about 78s. There was more in those old grooves than even the manufacturers realized, and a mint or even decent copy of the best of them, played on today's top-quality audio equipment, could easily be mistaken for a CD. There is startling presence and surprisingly little background noise. The best that a CD transfer of a 78-rpm disc can do is aspire to be as good as the original. Another thing about the 78-rpm discs: they were honest. In those days before tape, there was no way of correcting a mistake. If an artist was not happy with what he did in the recording studio, there was only one option: to record the entire piece over again. What is heard on a 78-rpm disc is what the artist really did, and that cannot be said of LPs or CDs.

Of the many recordings Horowitz made between 1928 and 1953 (the year of his second retirement), by which time the LP record had triumphed and 78s were beginning to disappear, two stand out—the Rachmaninoff Piano Concerto No. 3, with Albert Coates and the London Symphony Orchestra (1930), and the Liszt B minor Sonata (1932).

Both were Horowitz specialties, and neither was much of a repertoire piece before he espoused them. Such a thing is hard to believe, because the Rachmaninoff Third Concerto has become perhaps the most-played piece for piano and orchestra in the international repertoire, and the Liszt B minor Sonata has been undergoing a major reassessment.

But in the 1930s both composers were derided as not worthy of attention by serious musicians. Liszt was equated with flashy, meretricious virtuosity. Rachmaninoff, in the fifth edition of *Grove's Dictionary,* was dismissed in only five contemptuous paragraphs, with such statements as: "His music is well constructed and effective, but monotonous in texture, which consists in essence mainly of artificial and gushing tunes accompanied by a variety of figures derived from arpeggios. The enormous popular success some few of Rachmaninoff's works had in his lifetime is not likely to last, and musicians never regarded it with much favor." So much for Rachmaninoff in 1935.

Of course he no longer needs defending, and it was Horowitz with his blazing performance of the Third Concerto who did much to establish its real value. Horowitz was to record the Rachmaninoff three times, and many consider his 1930 performance the best. It is propulsive, even savage, and he simply eats up the notes. There are none of the mannerisms of which he was later accused, and the slow movement emerges in a singing, natural kind of poetry. In the last movement he is one of the few pianists (Rachmaninoff himself *not* included) who, in the two Più mosso sections of the last movement, maintains a steady metric without allowing the patterns to fall into triplets. The prevailing tempos, like those of the composer, are faster than today's.

Horowitz took some of the cuts sanctioned by Rachmaninoff. So did everybody else in those days. In the last movement there is a tiny ensemble mishap that the participants did not bother to remake; it passes almost unnoticed. This is a massive, thrilling performance that, along with the composer's own, set the standard for all to follow.

Because of today's slowdown in tempo, the 1932 Horowitz performance of the Liszt Sonata may sound fast. But it wasn't in its day. Horowitz's timing is 26 minutes, 30 seconds. Timings from the 1950s and 1960s show Rubinstein at 25'28", Alexander Brailowsky at 26'02", Clifford Curzon at 25'35", Van Cliburn at 26'50", and Emil Gilels at 25'38". Today the average is around 30 minutes and getting longer.

The Horowitz performance is typical: raw excitement coupled with moments of delicate lyricism and washes of color. As expected, there are the flashing octaves and awesome technical command. He holds the sprawling piece together beautifully. Even in the last measures he suggests a feeling of motion, and this is hard to do. Old pianists used to say of the Liszt B minor Sonata that he composed it and then he decomposed it.

Pianists who are too funereal at the end decompose the piece. Horowitz maintains the tension.

It was in 1932, also, that Horowitz took a foray into Classicism with his recording of the last Haydn sonata, No. 52 in E flat (which in those days was the only Haydn sonata in the repertoire, and seldom played at that). Horowitz may have been especially attracted to it by the slow movement, which has a proto-Chopin kind of melisma. He plays the sonata with a minimum of pedal, unflagging rhythm, precise fingerwork, sharp contours—and no repeats, the omission of which is today considered a sin.

But few musicians of his time, or indeed of the nineteenth century, took repeats, and there is every indication that they were not taken even in the composers' own time. At best they were optional and, as recent research has indicated, not many took the option. In the slow movement Horowitz manfully sings the melodic line without ever getting sloppy; and the grace of his phrasing and precise articulation in the finale, the relationships of the dynamics (never above a forte), the lack of musical trickery or cheap effect, all give the listener a Haydn to treasure. The sheer technical mastery plus the unfaltering rhythm and expressiveness combine in a performance that makes most others sound anemic.

Horowitz was never accepted as a pianist with an affinity for the Classic repertoire, and he certainly could have his problems with some of the Beethoven works he played, but his Haydn and Mozart performances generally have a purity that few associate with his name. In 1947 he recorded his first Mozart sonata—in F (K. 332). It has much the same musical approach as the Haydn. Horowitz was not afraid to use the piano as a piano, which means delicate pedal colorations, a highly expressive slow movement, and glittering passage-work in the finale.

The other concerto recordings, after the Rachmaninoff, that Horowitz made in the period before his 1953 retirement were of the Tchaikovsky B flat minor, the Brahms B flat, and the Beethoven *Emperor*.

The Brahms came first, in 1940. In 1987 Horowitz said that he did not like this performance with Toscanini and the NBC Symphony. He said it was too fast and too metronomic, and he was right about the speed if he was thinking of the concerto in terms of 1980s performance practice. Horowitz—or, one should say, Toscanini, for the concerto goes according to *his* idea of the correct tempo—takes 43'21". In the 1950s and 1960s, Rubinstein took 48 minutes, Serkin 47, Richter 46, Cliburn 46, and Wilhelm Backhaus 47. In the late 1970s and in the 1980s, such pianists as Vladimir Ashkenazy, Daniel Barenboim, and Vladimir Feltsman were clocked between 48 and 49 minutes in concert performances. Of his collaboration with Toscanini, Horowitz said:

Not long ago I heard a broadcast of the Brahms B flat
Concerto that I recorded with Toscanini and I asked myself why
I ever did it. Whatever its status as music, it is not a concerto for
me. I never liked it very much, and I played it so badly, and my
ideas about the music were so different from Toscanini's. Metrically he was so much stricter than I was. I didn't enjoy rehearing
this performance at all.

The Horowitz/Toscanini performance gives the feeling of power
rather than poetry. And the slow movement is (uncharacteristically, for
Toscanini) dragged, with Horowitz uneasily imitating a metronome. He
is happiest in the last movement, the most pianistic of the four, and he
hurtles through the tricky double thirds with a nonchalant flourish. Grace
and style are here, but this cannot be described as one of the great Horowitz performances.

There were two performances of the Tchaikovsky with Toscanini: the
first, a studio recording, in 1941, and the second live from Carnegie Hall
at a war bond concert on April 25, 1943. Both performances take about
half an hour, roughly four minutes faster than today's average.

The 1941 performance is not as good as the 1943. In the earlier
version Toscanini is absolutely unyielding. Horowitz goes precisely along
with him. The performance has its brilliant and even majestic moments,
but one can feel Horowitz dying to let loose. Restrained by Toscanini, he
did not dare. But the 1943 performance is more relaxed. In the second
movement there is a serious disagreement between oboe and piano, and
one shudders to think of the Toscanini explosion that must have devas-
tated the backstage area after the performance.

But the recorded performance of the Tchaikovsky that is the most
exciting of all never was officially released, and is available only on a
pirated recording. It was the Horowitz Silver Jubilee Concert on January
12, 1953, and he played the Tchaikovsky with George Szell and the New
York Philharmonic in Carnegie Hall.

Wherever the pirated tape came from, it was of top quality, and when
Jack Pfeiffer heard it, he thought of bringing it out under the RCA label.
But too many technical difficulties interfered. Among other things, Szell
was under contract to Columbia.

Copies of course inevitably made their way to collectors, first on reel-
to-reel tapes. Then, in the middle 1960s, microminiaturization was
coming along, and recording machines not much larger than a pack of
cigarettes were on the market. Music lovers were, joyously and illegally,
taking them into the concert halls and going home with tapes of concerts
given by their favorite artists. Now collectors could easily copy something

precious and send it to friends. Pirated tapes started making the rounds, and were even sold under the counter in specialty record stores. Thus it was with the Horowitz/Szell Tchaikovsky. Pianophiles had to have a copy, and there was little trouble locating one.

It is a staggering performance, very different from the Toscanini pair. It is taken at about the same speed—30 minutes, 40 seconds—but does not sound particularly fast except for the two big octave heroics and the last-movement coda, where Horowitz races to the finish line in record speed, skidding off the last note. He employs a rubato and a kind of freedom that he did not attempt with Toscanini. Listening to the performance, it is hard to see what Olin Downes in his review meant by his comment about not everything going as had been planned in rehearsal. The liaison is perfect—no trouble with the oboe in the second movement here!—and Szell anticipates every move.

The story goes—at least, that is how a Philharmonic musician told it to a critic—that before the first rehearsal Szell faced the orchestra and said that the Tchaikovsky B flat minor was a piece of junk. (Only he did not exactly say "junk.") "So let's let Horowitz do what he wants. We'll follow him anywhere." And Szell and the orchestra did.

Still another off-the-air recording of the Tchaikovsky made the rounds, and in 1990 it was transferred to a commercial compact disc by AS Disc, an Italian company registered in Monaco. The performance, with Bruno Walter and the New York Philharmonic from the broadcast of April 11, 1948, is magnificent, even if the last-movement octaves are little more than a glorious blur. Horowitz was still running the octaves race so decried by Rachmaninoff. The octaves apart, it has a feeling of relaxation and poetry that the other two performances lack. The Horowitz/Szell may have the most animal excitement, but the Horowitz/Walter could well be the single greatest performance ever made available to the public.

Some of the pre-1953 Horowitz recordings present a repertoire that disappeared from his concerts after a few years. In 1946 Victor issued his Mendelssohn album, dominated by a lovely performance of the *Variations sérieuses*. Here we have simple, flowing, elegant playing very much in the sparkling Mendelssohn style. Using very little pedal, employing a reduced scale of dynamics, Horowitz manages to suggest Mendelssohn's own kind of Neoclassic playing. (Mendelssohn was considered one of the great pianists, but not a Romantic one; he had been taught in the Mozart-Clementi style by the classicist Ignaz Moscheles.)

1946 also saw Beethoven's *Moonlight* Sonata, a low-level recording with noisy surfaces. The first movement is painfully regular except for some artificial, overcalculated dynamic effects that interfere with the natural flow of the music. For most of the movement Horowitz was trying too hard to be "Classic," and it did not work. The second movement is better, and the finale is an explosion. He was to make a much better recording of the *Moonlight* ten years later.

The best Beethoven Horowitz ever recorded is probably the 32 Variations in C minor (1934). Rhythmically precise, magnificently fingered, supple in phrase, logical in contour, coherent and natural all the way through, it is a stunning performance. So was his performance of the Schumann *Arabesque* that same year.

What was Horowitz's all-time favorite recording? He was asked that, two years before he died, and immediately replied that it was the Czerny *Ricordanza* Variations of 1944. One can see why. This unknown piece resurrected by Horowitz is triumphant in every respect: it is beautifully written for the piano, it has a good deal of period charm, it is played with purling passage-work and exquisite tonal adjustments, and it gives a better idea of the Horowitz tone and color than do most of his records.

Of the large-scale Chopin works that he recorded in those days, one of the most interesting is the Chopin album of 1945 because it contains the Andante Spianato and Polonaise, which he seldom if ever played after that year. A pity. The piece is one of the most effective of Chopin's early works, and the performance is Horowitz at his best: poetic, flowing, brilliant, sprightly.

The Chopin-Liszt album of 1947 also is a prize, mostly because of the Liszt. It contains Chopin's G minor Ballade in a performance so thought-out that it lacks spontaneity and ends up a collection of details. Horowitz fought this ballade all his life, constantly playing and recording it, never really making up his mind about how it should go. But the album also contains a ravishing performance of Liszt's *Au bord d'une source* and a pulverizing one of the Sixth Hungarian Rhapsody.

Of the three Prokofiev sonatas that Horowitz introduced to America, he recorded only No. 7, in 1945. Horowitz plays it with very little pedal, which accounts for the unusually clear textures. He maintains steady rhythm, takes the toccatalike finale slower than one would have expected, and builds to an enormous climax. No wonder his old friend from Paris, Serge Prokofiev, was carried away when the first copy off the assembly line was sent to him in Moscow.

Then—talking about Russian music—there was Horowitz with the Mussorgsky *Pictures at an Exhibition*. He made two arrangements, the first of which he recorded in 1947. The second, more elaborate, was recorded from a 1951 Carnegie Hall recital. To read some of the outraged reviews about the Mussorgsky-Horowitz *Pictures* one gets the impression that mayhem was committed. Not really. In his reconstruction of the familiar piece Horowitz touched up here and there, always with taste and respect for the original. The only significant changes were in the last section, where he added a very effective bell-like counterpoint to the massive chords.

Horowitz gave the piece a pair of transcendent performances, "orchestrating" it on the keyboard and getting a coloristic quality that no pianist, not even the great Sviatoslav Richter, has achieved. The contingent that finds the Mussorgsky *Pictures* unpianistic and something of a bore think that the Horowitz version is an improvement. Horowitz played the *Pictures* for only three seasons, the last in 1951, and his version remains unpublished. Thus the chances are that it will never be heard again on the concert stage.

In the pre-LP era of the single 78-rpm disc, Horowitz recorded many short pieces—Chopin mazurkas and etudes, Mendelssohn *Songs without Words,* works by Debussy, Poulenc, Rachmaninoff, Schumann, and others. Many are very beautiful, and one of the colossal Liszt recorded performances of all time is on one of the early ten-inch singles—Horowitz in 1930 playing the Paganini-Liszt-Busoni Etude in E flat. The articulation in the scale passages is not of this world, nor are those fast, controlled left-hand octaves. This was the etude that Rubinstein heard Horowitz play in Paris in 1926, and Rubinstein was carried away by its "easy elegance." Horowitz never played it after his first years in America.

Nor did he often play Stravinsky's *Petrushka,* but he did record the "Danse russe" in London. Too bad he never recorded the complete three-movement transcription. The recorded performance of the "Danse russe" is terribly exciting, a thrilling example of virtuosity (which one must have for this work) coupled with all kinds of coloristic effects and a special feeling for the Russian element.

Another piece that Horowitz dropped in the 1930s (though he briefly brought it back some three decades later) was the Schumann Toccata, which he recorded in London in 1934. It so happens that his Kiev classmate Simon Barere also recorded the Schumann Toccata, that murderous study in double notes and octaves. The 1937 Barere recording followed the 1934 Horowitz. Barere is not only faster than Horowitz; he plays the fastest version ever recorded. His timing was 4 minutes, 17 seconds. Horowitz took 4 minutes, 37 seconds. Of course in both recordings the repeat was omitted.

The story goes that when Barere was ready to record the Schumann piece, he was asked by Victor what he would use as a filler on the second side. After all, that fabulous technician Josef Lhevinne had made a Victor recording of the Toccata in 1928, and did not get it on one side of the 78-rpm disc. Barere laughed. He said that he could easily get it on one side, and he did. Easily. Both Barere and Horowitz play the notes as written, but Horowitz, with his coiled-spring intensity, is much more convincing musically. Barere just shows how fast he could play.

When Horowitz returned to the stage after his retirement in 1953, he no longer ended his programs with the sensational virtuoso tricks he and his public enjoyed so much. But at least he had put nearly all of them on records. His first disc recording of the *Carmen* Fantasy was made in 1928, followed by another in 1947 and still another in 1968. The Saint-Saëns–Liszt–Horowitz *Danse macabre* came out in 1942. The Mendelssohn-Liszt-Horowitz *Wedding March* was issued in 1946; the LisztHorowitz *Rákoczy March* and the Sousa-Horowitz *Stars and Stripes Forever* in 1950; and the Liszt-Horowitz Hungarian Rhapsody No. 2 in 1953.

All of these are examples of inimitable virtuosity, with the kind of technique—so effortless, so thrown off, so exultant in its easy execution of the impossible—that carries its own esthetic probity. "Is there not a time for cakes and ale?" asked Sir Toby Belch. There is indeed, and as served up by Horowitz in concert it provided a kind of *frisson* that created hysteria. But Horowitz grew to dislike this kind of exhibitionism; he worried about it and finally discarded it. In an interview with Jacob Siskind of the Montreal *Gazette* (April 24, 1976) he explained:

> When you play these pieces, like I have my variations on *Carmen,* I find out very funny things, that the people when they hear those pieces for encores, they forget the whole program. It kills the whole effect. They say, Oh my God, did you hear him in *Carmen*—look what is he doing there, in the *Stars and Stripes* he is like a band, a band for himself—and you know that is not so good for a program.

But a lot of fun from concerts disappeared when Horowitz dropped his death-defying tightrope act. Incidentally, he considered his arrangement of the Hungarian Rhapsody No. 2 the most difficult he ever created, much more so than *Stars and Stripes*.

After 1948 all of the future Horowitz records would be LP discs, then stereo discs, then cassettes and finally the compact disc. With the CD, the long, proud reign of the flat, grooved, Berliner disc, from 1895 to the middle 1980s, came to an end. But what a glorious spin it had!

Appendix II
LP and Stereo

> Clementi was a great composer. He was admired by Beethoven, he anticipated some of the Romantics, he was a great pianist who created the modern school of playing. Yes, even more than Mozart and Beethoven!
> —*Vladimir Horowitz on why he recorded Clementi*

With the advent of the long-playing record, Horowitz began to put some of the major pieces of his repertoire on disc for RCA Victor. But even there he thought of the LP disc as a mini-recital, which meant that one major piece was generally accompanied by short items.

(In the following discussion of the Horowitz LPs, the actual names of the discs as they were issued, such as *Horowitz Plays Chopin* or *Horowitz in Concert,* are for the most part not given. All of those discs have long been out of print. In the discography at the end of this book, information about CD reissues of any Horowitz performance—which means almost everything—can be found.)

Was the LP kinder to him than 78-rpm discs? Yes and no. Yes, because now works of up to almost a half hour in length could fit on each side of the disc (previously the record had to be turned every four and a half minutes), and because more of the Horowitz dynamics could be captured on LP. No, because the engineer exercised a great deal of control, and not all engineers had in their ears music as actually heard in the concert hall. Too much early LP recording favored close-up microphoning. Some Horowitz records, especially the early Victor LPs, sounded as though the listener's ear was right over the strings of the piano. In the concert hall the Horowitz sound was much more subtle. Critics who were familiar with it only on records often heard a misrepresentation, and many of their complaints about a kind of hard clangor were legitimate.

But occasionally an early Victor LP captured the Horowitz essence. Two of the best were issued in 1950 and 1951. The first contained Schumann's *Kinderscenen* and seven Chopin mazurkas, and the second was a Liszt disc containing the *Funérailles,* the *Sonetto 104 del Petrarca,* the *Valse oubliée* No. 1, and the Horowitz arrangement of Liszt's *Rákoczy March.*

The *Kinderscenen* represents Horowitz at his most eloquent and elegant. Horowitz was always more comfortable in Schumann than in Chopin. In Chopin he had a tendency to want to "do" something, and the listener sometimes can become more conscious of Horowitz than of the musical architecture. In Schumann he was content to let the music flow in a natural manner, with a fine feeling for tempo fluctuation and telling dabs of color achieved through imaginative pedaling and the exploitation of inner voices. As for the mazurkas that accompany the *Kinderscenen,* they go with charm, rhythmic snap, and a delicate rubato, as they always did with Horowitz.

In the *Funérailles* his amazing octaves come into play, and also his ability to voice full chords. This powerful performance is followed by the unabashed virtuosity of the *Rákoczy March.* The arrangement has little to do with Liszt's original, which Horowitz largely ignored. Instead, he takes the theme as a point of departure for some giddy acrobatics. Of all the Horowitz transcriptions, this is the most conspicuously showy. He soon dropped it.

His first recording of the Chopin B flat minor Sonata came out in 1950, coupled with the Piano Sonata in E flat minor by Samuel Barber. Barber wrote it for Horowitz, and after the premiere it entered the international repertoire, where it has stayed.

This performance is definitive. Barber and Horowitz worked on it together, and what emerges is propulsive, sharply etched, massive playing. No pianist who has since taken it on has been able to command the Horowitz articulation in which every strand has X-ray definition as the architecture is laid bare.

The performance of Chopin's *Funeral March* Sonata is perplexing. It is slow, mannered, and contrived. For some reason Horowitz takes the first-movement repeat; never a good idea. The modulation at the end of the exposition is one of the ugliest that Chopin, the master of modulation, ever conceived. (But Charles Rosen, the pianist-scholar, argued in 1990 that all twentieth-century editions of the sonata are incorrect, and that according to the manuscript the repeat, if taken, should start at the very opening and not the fourth measure.) Naturally there are wonderful moments, especially in the orchestration of the march, but this is not a convincing performance, and Horowitz was to record a much better version a few years later for Columbia.

The first disc of Horowitz "live" performances came in 1951, and it contains some of his most cherishable playing. Especially notable is his performance of Schumann's *Variations on a Theme by Clara Wieck* (the third movement of the F minor Sonata). Horowitz captures the songlike quality of the music, its sadness close to tears. It is a radiant, intimate, emotionally controlled performance.

On the disc is Chopin's Polonaise-Fantaisie, a work seldom played fifty years ago (since then, largely thanks to Horowitz, it has been "discovered" and today is very much with us). Horowitz draws together its sprawling organization, makes magic out of the mazurkalike section, and builds to a tremendous climax. He also put Haydn's E flat Sonata on this disc—the sonata he had recorded in 1932. This time the performance is more Romantic and very fine in its way, but without the Classic logic and elegance displayed in the great 1932 recording. For dessert there is the *Stars and Stripes,* even more coruscating than in the 1950 studio recording. Audiences always stimulated Horowitz to supreme efforts.

A vintage Horowitz year, 1951 also saw the Horowitz/Fritz Reiner recording of the Rachmaninoff Piano Concerto No. 3 with the RCA Victor Symphony Orchestra. Impulsive, daring, full of raw energy, Horowitz duplicates the feats he had accomplished with Coates in the landmark 1930 recording. He shapes the melodies with more color than before (or does one imagine this because of the more modern sound?) and adopts a looser rhythmic scheme. In the finale he takes the cut sanctioned by the composer. The only time he loses the rhythm is in the Più mosso section, the second time it comes around (Section 65 of the Boosey and Hawkes score). Here he gets excited and lapses into jerky triplets. On the whole this is a monumental performance, a true Horowitz experience. But there are those who insist that of the three Horowitz versions of the Rachmaninoff Third, it is the 1930 version with Coates that has most grandeur and steadiness, the one that most closely matches the splendor of Rachmaninoff himself.

There are, incidentally, early off-the-air recordings of Horowitz in the Rachmaninoff Third held by private collectors. One of them, with Barbirolli and the New York Philharmonic in May 1942, is wild. Horowitz storms through it faster than any player before or since. His timing is 32 minutes, 53 seconds. (Add another two minutes or so for the cuts.

The performance even then is about ten minutes faster than the 1990s norm.) One's first impulse is to say, "Too fast! Ridiculous!" Then one listens again, notices that every note is perfectly articulated, gets caught up in the visceral excitement, responds to the loving shape of the lyrical elements, is floored by a technique of supreme mastery, and surrenders— gladly.

The following year, 1952, Horowitz recorded the Beethoven *Emperor* Concerto, also with Reiner and the RCA Victor Symphony Orchestra. Horowitz was on his best behavior. This is—one can feel it going through his mind—*Beethoven!* One could take dictation from the piano part, so accurate is it. Every note is precisely struck, every indication carefully followed. The piano part is logically unfurled, and never is there the thickness one has heard from certain Beethoven specialists. This is an objective, supple, non-Romantic performance that turns out to be a much more Classic *Emperor* than many of the weightier, thicker, self-indulgent performances that are so often encountered today. It also, at 37'44", runs four or five minutes faster than prevailing 1990 tempos. In many respects, the Horowitz/Reiner *Emperor* is a revelation, even if it has been bad-mouthed by purists.

Horowitz's first big Chopin disc on LP, for Victor in 1952, contains the A flat and F minor Ballades and the B minor Scherzo. There are also the F minor Nocturne, E major Etude, and A flat Impromptu.

For some reason Horowitz seldom played the A flat Ballade. This is his only recording. He is warm and relaxed in this interpretation, and sounds as though he is enjoying himself. On the other hand the B minor Scherzo remained with him almost to the end, and he recorded it five times. The playing here is slashing, nervous, almost febrile. Horowitz swallows it whole, ending with a burst of interlocked octaves (which he always used). Chopin wrote unison scales instead of octaves, and the Horowitz addition bothered some musicians. Yet there was precedent for it. Carl Tausig, Liszt's phenomenal pupil, used to play the ending of the Chopin E minor Concerto with interlocked octaves, and it produced such a grand effect that audiences swooned and the players in the orchestra stood up and cheered. Yes, the Horowitz double octaves ending the B minor Scherzo are an "effect." But no notes or harmonies are changed; it is only a reinforcement, and if an artist can do it with panache it does not falsify the music.

The Ballade No. 4 in F minor was a Horowitz staple, and it stayed with him until he felt he was too old to handle its technical demands. He played it differently every time. In this recording he used a highly inflected line with all kinds of agogics. (Agogics involve the temporal variation of notes within a metrical framework; it is a first cousin of rubato.) Horowitz never loses the pulse of the music, no matter how many rhythmic changes he adopts. At the impossibly difficult coda he uses very little pedal in an astonishing display of sheer finger independence. Power and poetry are united in one of the all-time great recorded performances of the piece.

Horowitz gave his twenty-fifth anniversary concerts all over America in 1953, and Victor put most of the Carnegie Hall recital of February 23 on disc. The big piece was Schubert's B flat Sonata. He had never played it before—he had played almost no Schubert up to then—and his ideas about the work did not get universal approval; his approach ran counter to the received opinion of how Schubert should go. Of course he was accused of Romanticizing the work. Even had he played it à la Serkin or Brendel he automatically would have been accused of Romanticism.

Yet, listening to the record without preconceived opinions, and keeping in mind performances of this work by a dozen or so of the most acclaimed pianists of our day, one wonders about the alleged Romanticisms. Horowitz certainly plays the music in a cleaner manner than any of the others. He maintains a perpetual singing line; the playing at all times moves with a fluent lyricism and transparency of texture. It is also full of striking ideas. The accentuations are different from, say, those of Pollini or Brendel, and are infinitely more exciting. The menacing pianissimo trills in the bass of the first movement, so perfectly calibrated, sound like distant mutters of thunder and are even scary.

As for the "Romanticisms," Horowitz is, as in the *Emperor,* again on his best behavior, paying full respect to Schubert's big form and intensity of utterance. But his rhetoric and inflections are so different from those of the Schubert specialists that one can understand the frightened reaction of many musicians. Perhaps the time has come for a reassessment of Horowitz in such icons as the Beethoven *Emperor,* the Haydn and Mozart sonatas, and this Schubert B flat. (The Horowitz performance of Schubert's B flat Sonata that Deutsche Grammophon released in 1991 is nowhere near as good. He recorded it in 1986 and never approved it. His instincts were correct; this is labored and artificial playing, full of overdone rubatos that make the music sound like kitsch, and its release did no service to Horowitz's reputation.)

The other big pieces in the anniversary album are the Chopin B minor Scherzo, Scriabin's Sonata No. 9, and the Liszt-Horowitz Hungarian Rhapsody No. 2. The Chopin is probably Horowitz's most successful of the versions he recorded. There is no lingering in the middle section, which can sound interminable at a slow tempo, and the final octaves are a burst of glory. In the Scriabin some details are obscured, but the performance remains one of fire and ice. Horowitz always had a remarkable insight into the dotty but wonderful world of late Scriabin. He was to play the work even more convincingly at his return concert in 1965. In the familiar Liszt Rhapsody No. 2, Horowitz does not tear up the form of the work as he had done in the *Rákóczy March*. What he did was add countermelodies, insert some new and difficult cadenzas, and change a few harmonies. At the end, two themes come together à la Godowsky. Horowitz was proud of this arrangement. He said it was one of the most difficult pieces he had ever played.

Horowitz never played this rhapsody again after 1953, the year he retired. But although he was not before the public for the next twelve years, he continued to record. His first record after the retirement, released in 1954, was devoted to sonatas by Muzio Clementi. That alone was a story. A supervirtuoso playing *Clementi!* Clementi, who wrote those *Gradus ad Parnassum* exercises on which every pianist is weaned!

The three sonatas that Horowitz carefully selected—he had read through every sonata Clementi had written—backed up all of Horowitz's claims about the importance of Clementi as a creative figure. He played them simply, tenderly, lovingly. And with extraordinary virtuosity, too. In complicated passage-work every finger is equally weighted, and only a phenomenal technician could have achieved such clarity, such transparency of texture.

After the Clementi binge, Horowitz turned to Scriabin, and the recording of the Sonata No. 3 and sixteen preludes was issued by Victor in 1956. The sonata is not one of Scriabin's more arresting works, and not even Horowitz could popularize it. Normally, pianists everywhere rushed to play a work that Horowitz featured. Not this time. Horowitz helped Scriabin along by introducing a short, unwritten repeat in the last section of the second movement. It improves the structure of the music. The preludes are idiomatic, colorful pieces that were seldom played at the time —and are seldom played today, for that matter. Scriabin's etudes are much more popular with pianists than are the preludes. Horowitz lavished all he could upon the music, and if he could not evoke much interest in it, nobody could.

In 1956, Horowitz also got around to his second Beethoven *Moonlight,* coupling it with the *Waldstein*. The *Moonlight* performance is much better than the 1946: looser, more personal, with much more freedom in the first movement. He burns up the keyboard in the finale and considered it one of the best things he had ever done. The *Waldstein* is along the lines of the *Emperor*—objective, clearly contoured, Classic in approach even with the resounding chords and fantastic articulation. He plays the notorious octave passage in the finale presto and staccato. No glissando, as written in the score. A glissando, Horowitz said, could be played on the light-actioned Viennese instrument that Beethoven owned but is not feasible on a modern piano.

The only other Beethoven sonata that Horowitz recorded during his long sabbatical was the D major (Op. 10, No. 3). It was made in 1959 and was the first time Horowitz had been recorded in stereo. The first movement prepares the listener for an elegant example of early-Beethoven playing. It is beautiful: a concert-grand approach with strong basses and impeccable taste. The rhythms are bracing throughout, the fingerwork sparkling, and one gets the feeling that Horowitz is having a wonderful time. But from there on all is downhill. He makes too much of the second movement, and the explosive dynamics are out of proportion. They would work in the big sonatas, such as the *Waldstein* and *Appassionata*. Here they make the playing sound overstressed, and what we get is rhetoric rather than poetry. The finale also suffers from undue emphases.

The main interest of Horowitz's Chopin recital in 1957 is the inclusion of two Chopin scherzos—No. 2 in B flat minor and No. 3 in C sharp minor. Those were not part of his normal repertoire. With them he now had all four of the scherzos on record. In 1936 he had made a brilliant recording of No. 4 in E. No. 1 in B minor dated from 1951. Incidentally, Horowitz once said that all four Chopin scherzos should have the same tempo, adding that in No. 3 most pianists were so anxious to show off their octaves that they played too fast. Horowitz followed his own precepts by playing the octaves strictly in time, making them sound powerful and ominous rather than flurried. In the coda he is absolutely demonic.

The B flat minor Scherzo has some incredible articulation in it, along with charm and ravishing color. Horowitz, as always, got a good deal of that color by a deft emphasis of inner voices, and by his canny way of handling the bass. There was always a firm harmonic underpinning to Horowitz's playing that anchored and reinforced what was going on in the treble.

This Chopin record also includes four nocturnes that Horowitz never again played: in B (Op. 9, No. 3), F (Op. 15, No. 1), C sharp minor (Op. 27, No. 1), and the popular E flat (Op. 9, No. 2). He plays them with appropriate sensuousness and grace. In addition there is the first Horowitz recording of the Barcarolle in a performance that suggests crystals flashing light. Here we experience Horowitz at his best: rhythm is always embedded in rock; fioritura perfectly adjusted; melodies projected in a manner reminiscent of great vocal stylists. The interpretation has poetry, power, and drama and is one of Horowitz's greatest performances.

Closing Horowitz's association with Victor was the 1959 recording of the Beethoven *Appassionata* Sonata. Again, as in most of Horowitz's Beethoven performances, he holds back, avoiding pronounced Romanticisms. His aim was to deliver a strong, clear *Appassionata*. His tempos are deliberate (slower than those of Richter, Kempff, and Rubinstein in that period), the outlines are sinewy and well proportioned. It is an impressive achievement that was not universally well received, because everybody of course *knew* that Horowitz was not really an exponent of Beethoven. But, to repeat, when musicological revisionists get busy on early nineteenth-century performance practice, the Horowitz *Appassionata* will be high on their list as an example of monumental Beethoven playing.

For the next three years Horowitz made no more recordings; and Victor, unhappy with his record sales—Clementi and Scriabin, indeed!—showed no desire to lure him back to work. Perhaps Victor was relieved when he went to Columbia in 1962. Of course it was a terrible mistake for the company to have let Horowitz go. The first three Columbia records that ensued were best-sellers. Horowitz looked at his new association as a challenge; and he probably had the all-too-human determination to show the Victor executives what idiots they had been.

Columbia also gave Horowitz a richer, more mellow quality of recorded sound than Victor had offered, much closer to what Horowitz actually sounded like in the concert hall. And with a different company Horowitz could start rerecording his repertoire. He also recorded some new music that he had been looking at during his retirement. The first disc contained Chopin's B flat minor Sonata, the Schumann *Arabesque,* Rachmaninoff's *Etudes-tableaux* in C (Op. 33, No. 2) and E flat minor (Op. 35, No. 5), and his own version of Liszt's virtually unknown Hungarian Rhapsody No. 19.

In his old age Liszt composed four rhapsodies after No. 15. Nos. 16, 17, and 18 are of no particular interest, but No. 19 as Horowitz arranged it is a dazzler, a throwback to the plangent *zigeuner* music of such rhapsodies as Nos. 6, 11, and 12. It has no great technical problems, and Horowitz touched it up to make it much more virtuosic. As much of Horowitz as of Liszt is in it, and Horowitz threw himself into the performance with abandon. It is one of the most brilliant, exciting transcriptions he ever created, and he plays it like an angel or a devil—take your choice.

The Chopin Sonata is more relaxed and better thought out than the 1950 Victor. Tempos are faster and the line more secure. Horowitz this time avoided the first-movement repeat, and the sonata unfolds with a feeling of logic and inevitability, from the bold initial statement to the sotto-voce mutterings of the finale. Horowitz never played it better.

For his second Columbia record, also in 1962, Horowitz played Schumann's *Kinderscenen* and Toccata, some Scarlatti, Schubert's G flat Impromptu, and several Scriabin pieces—two etudes and the lovely *Poème* (Op. 32, No. 1). In the Toccata he sets the piano on fire with the velocity and clarity of the double notes and the grace of the octave section.

The *Kinderscenen* has all the characteristics of Horowitz's mature style: careful, even sharp-edged phrasing, freedom of tempo, and an unusual feeling for the polyphonic lines embedded into the fabric. Few pianists today know what to do with Schumann's polyphony, and therefore they ignore it. But in Schumann it is ever-present. Alban Berg once analyzed the apparently simple *Träumerei* from the *Kinderscenen* to show how it is, throughout, a piece in the strictest four-part harmony. Horowitz knew exactly how to balance the lines in Schumann, bringing out inner details that not only provide harmonic interest but also an amazing variety of color.

The Schubert Impromptu in G is an anomaly. Schubert wrote it in G flat. For some reason Horowitz, in his 1953 recording of the piece, had used the Bülow arrangement, which transposes it to G major. In this 1962 recording he goes to the original G flat.

For his 1963 Columbia disc, Horowitz made his first recording of Beethoven's *Pathétique* Sonata, took another look at his old friend the Chopin B minor Scherzo, added Chopin's *Revolutionary* Etude and the C sharp minor (Op. 25, No. 7), and then turned to Debussy for his only recordings of three preludes from Book II—*Les fées sont d'exquises danseuses, Bruyères,* and *General Lavine—eccentric.*

In the intimate world of the preludes Horowitz is very much his own man. This is not "authentic" Debussy, as the term is generally understood. For some it may be too hard edged. Yet the color is there, the wit of *Lavine* and the charm of *Les fées* are fully captured, and *Bruyères* has a steady, atmospheric flow. It is a most interesting look at Debussy.

The *Pathétique* has all the characteristics of the previous *Moonlight, Waldstein,* and *Appassionata.* It is carefully organized, it is warm, powerful, lyric in the slow movement, and dramatic elsewhere. And the fingerwork has a clarity that supersedes all previous and subsequent recorded performances. Only some pulled-out ritards are questionable. The B minor Scherzo has some great moments and some spasmodic ones. As with Chopin's G minor Ballade, Horowitz never fully came to terms with this piece.

His next Columbia record was issued in 1964, the year before his return to the stage. It contained twelve Scarlatti sonatas, carefully selected for variety and contrast among the 550 or so that Scarlatti composed. It is safe to say that Horowitz had played through every one of the 550. When he developed a passion for a composer, as he had done with Clementi, he went through the entire oeuvre. Horowitz had played Scarlatti sonatas from the beginning. Now that he had retired, he could make a close study of that remarkable composer, one of the most original in music history.

What came out was a labor of love. Horowitz did not attempt to recreate harpsichord sounds. Instead he adapted Scarlatti to the concert grand with amazing success. After all, Scarlatti sonatas were composed for the harpsichord; hence, played on the piano, they amount to a transcription. He played the notes accurately as written, and with his ability to vary touch he was able to suggest the Scarlatti period, though in modern terms, playing always with taste and refinement. One of the most delightful of all the Horowitz recordings resulted.

The next Horowitz record commemorated his grand return to the stage. It is as thrilling on records as it was for the listeners in Carnegie Hall on that memorable day of May 9, 1965.

Appendix III
1965–82

It is not enough to emphasize the upper voice to make the melodic line sing; it must pulsate like the voice of a great singer. The wrist must *feel* the movement. Rubato can never be a substitute for insufficient dynamic shadings. The moment you know how to color a phrase, the excessive rubato disappears by itself. A rubato in tone has replaced it.
—*Vladimir Horowitz to Jan Holcman*

When Horowitz returned to the stage on May 9, 1965, the Columbia engineers were in Carnegie Hall to immortalize the event. The album, issued shortly afterward, was advertised as *The Return of Horowitz to Carnegie Hall*. But, as we know, it was not exactly that. Horowitz, working under extreme pressure, was not his usual infallible technical self, and he went back to the hall to touch up some sections that were not in accord with his legend. This included the one really scary spot in the recital, where he momentarily threatened to lose control—the coda of the second movement of the Schumann Fantasy.

Nevertheless the disc remains a compelling document. And some of the technical mishaps were retained. The famous slip at the beginning of the Bach-Busoni Toccata in C can be heard, for example. It is of no importance except to let listeners know that Vladimir Horowitz could be nervous and hence human. The slow movement is a miracle of color, with chords seemingly suspended in air. With the left-hand octaves of the Fugue, the old Horowitz is talking, and the audience knew that he was really back.

The Schumann Fantasy is interesting. Horowitz takes the first movement at a somewhat slow tempo, playing it powerfully, with moments of deep introspection. Throughout this work he sounds different from all other pianists. He phrases differently, he moves the basses differently, he finds nuances nobody had ever imagined. Some critics greeted this as the "new" Horowitz. It is true that there were dimensions in this performance he had not previously shown. But, then again, Horowitz never played a work twice the same way, and this performance reflected a rethinking rather than a new philosophy.

He had played the weird, wonderful Scriabin Ninth Sonata at his twenty-fifth anniversary concert in Carnegie Hall in 1953, and that performance had been recorded. It was fast, taking 6'17". Now, twelve years later, he plays it more slowly, at 9'06". The result is a better performance. The 1953, exciting as it was, had some scrambled moments. Here everything can be heard, with no loss in power or drive. It is stupendous playing.

The other big piece on the recital was the Chopin G minor Ballade, which was always one of Horowitz's problem pieces. This time he plays it with certain left-hand accentuations never heard before or since. But Horowitz plays what is written, and if he wanted to bring out things in the music not normally heard, he was being characteristically Horowitzian. If the effects do not always convince, they bring the listener up short and make him rethink the piece.

Two years later, in 1967, Columbia released an album that contained major pieces from two 1966 Carnegie Hall recitals, those of April 17 and November 27. There was Haydn's Sonata in F, flowing and glittering, full of joy and wit. There was the first Horowitz recorded performance of Mozart's Sonata in A, the one with the "Turkish March." He plays it simply, the first two movements with somewhat faster tempos than are today's norm, shepherding the notes alertly along. The "Turkish March" is, however, played rather slowly, with a steady pulse and a lovely suggestion of cymbals and percussion in the *turquerie* sections.

Also on the disc was Schumann's seldom-heard *Blumenstück*, enchantingly played. Schumann always brought out the best in Horowitz. And there was a simply staggering performance of Liszt's *Vallée d'Obermann*, an extraordinary piece. It opens with a plangent melody that could have come right out of Tchaikovsky's *Eugene Onegin*, except that the Liszt was composed before 1854, the Tchaikovsky in 1878. In this interpretation Horowitz maintains incredible tension and drama, yet never neglecting the poetry. Or the virtuosity: the controlled left-hand octaves are hair-raising. The result is a sound-world that Horowitz alone could re-create, and a sound-world that also shows how big, innovative, and daring a composer Liszt was. There also is Scriabin's Tenth Sonata, new to the Horowitz repertoire, with incredible detail and shading despite the exceptionally difficult writing. Again this is Horowitz at his greatest.

The September 22, 1968, Horowitz television broadcast from Carnegie Hall was immediately put on disc by Columbia. The big pieces were Chopin's F sharp minor Polonaise, G minor Ballade (yet again), the Schumann *Arabesque,* and the *Carmen* Fantasy. The F sharp minor Polonaise is played with high drama; the two savage-sounding arpeggiated passages that lead to the reprise are actually terrifying. Here Horowitz, as in the *Carmen* (which he never again recorded), is at the height of his powers. The G minor Ballade goes spasmodically and unconvincingly.

The series of live Horowitz performances on Columbia records continued with pieces taken from recitals in 1967 and 1968. Some unusual things were present. One was the only Horowitz recording of Beethoven's Sonata in A (Op. 101) in a problematic performance. Every note is crisp and clear, but the interpretation sounds labored, overaccented (some of the explosive attacks are disturbing), and hard. It is not Horowitz at his best, even if the last movement is articulated with superb *maîtrise*. Claude Frank, the Beethoven specialist, once said that he would much rather play the entire *Hammerklavier* than the last movement of Op. 101. The double-note passages, he said, were the most treacherous in the Beethoven canon.

Another oddity in this album is Liszt's Scherzo and March, a virtually unknown piece. Horowitz played it in public, in his own touched-up version, only once in his life, at a Queens College recital on October 22, 1967. It is a wild work, and Horowitz is at his most awesome technical heights. But there really is not much substance to the music, which is Liszt at his most bombastic, and that may be one reason Horowitz immediately dropped it. The effort involved was not worth the musical reward.

To counteract the high-wire act of the Liszt, there is on this record a lovely performance of Haydn's two-movement Sonata in C (Hob. XVI:48). It is a work with an introspective first movement, and Horowitz plays it as such, giving a demonstration of how the dynamics of the Haydn fortepiano can be successfully transferred to the modern concert grand. The joyous quality of the last movement is fully captured, with the bouncing rhythm and the finger independence that Horowitz alone had. Playing like this makes the early-music specialists of the 1990s sound like amateurs.

In 1969 Horowitz brought into his repertoire Schumann's *Kreisleriana,* and of course it was promptly recorded. Most agree that this is one of his greatest records. It encompasses all aspects of Schumann's wild imagination, from simple lyricism to dramatic outburst. The biggest contribution that the performance makes to the understanding of the piece is Horowitz's knowledge of its polyphony. He cannily brings out the inner lines of the music, balancing them against bass and melody in a lovely, natural-sounding flow.

Also on the record is Schumann's *Variations on a Theme by Clara Wieck,* which he had previously recorded so lovingly for Victor in 1951. Now he has new ideas about the piece, and plays it in a stronger, more assertive manner. It is beautiful, but the earlier recording was even more beautiful in its quieter way.

In his search for repertoire, Horowitz in 1971 came up with Chopin's Introduction and Rondo in E flat (Op. 16). It is rarely heard. While it has some of Chopin's most imaginative and brilliant figurations, it is musically lightweight—one of the few Chopin pieces that can be categorized as salon music. Basically it is nothing more than an effective showpiece, and Horowitz cheerfully plays it as such, with supervirtuosity. But he dropped it almost immediately.

A peculiar performance of Chopin's A major Polonaise (the *Military*) was made in 1972. For some reason Horowitz seldom played this popular work. Could it be that he did not like it very much? Nothing in this performance suggests love. He plays it doggedly and metronomically, taking all repeats, hitting all the notes, but sounding bored. He takes no ritards, not even at the end. On the disc also are, among other things, mind-blowing performances of Chopin's Etude in C sharp minor (Op. 10, No. 4) and the *Revolutionary* Etude.

On another 1972 Columbia disc, Horowitz recorded Beethoven's *Appassionata* for the second time and also a peculiar *Moonlight* Sonata, his third recorded try at that work. The *Appassionata* is respectful, strong, beautifully organized. The *Moonlight* is another, sad, story. Its first movement is painfully rigid, and the finale is positively perverse. The forte–subito-piano chords are both played staccato without the loud–soft shift, and the meaning of the passage is lost. Mannerism was beginning to creep into Horowitz's playing.

But no mannerism can be heard in his 1972 Scriabin disc for Columbia, which contains seven etudes from Opp. 8 and 42, the Tenth Sonata (previously released), two *poèmes, Vers la flamme,* and other pieces. The etudes, which contain some of Scriabin's best music, come off brilliantly, especially the great C sharp minor (Op. 42, No. 5). Those left-hand smashes in the climax may seem out of proportion, but they fit the bigness of the piece. Today's right-hand pianists are much more polite, but they lack the surge and passion that Horowitz achieved. There are other delights on the disc—the unabashed, thrilling virtuosity of the double-note

D flat Etude, the precision of the tiny, spooky F sharp major Etude (all fifty seconds of it), and the wild, menacing trills of *Vers la flamme*.

The May 18, 1976, "Concert of the Century" at Carnegie Hall presented Horowitz in an unfamiliar role. He played the first movement of the Tchaikovsky A minor Trio with Isaac Stern and Mstislav Rostropovich, partnered the cellist in the slow movement of Rachmaninoff's Cello Sonata and accompanied Dietrich Fischer-Dieskau in Schumann's *Dichterliebe*. The Tchaikovsky went splendidly, with Horowitz listening carefully, playing accompaniment passages in a properly subdued manner, taking command without unduly asserting himself in his solos. The Rachmaninoff saw two brilliant Russian musicians happily playing Russian music, Rostropovich singing away with his endless bow, Horowitz making near-equivalent sounds on the piano.

In the *Dichterliebe* Horowitz maintained expert liaison with the singer, but there could never be any doubt as to who was at the piano. Horowitz was generally reserved but could not resist some of his usual practices—the sudden agogic changes, the little hesitations and expressive devices that his public adored and that infuriated the anti-affettuoso crowd.

On his return to RCA Victor in 1975, Horowitz was represented by excerpts from actual concerts in his first series of discs. His tours were accompanied by a retinue from the recording company, who took down virtually everything he played. Then a composite of a piece could be made. One movement might have come from New York, another from Chicago, and so on. Or perhaps Horowitz may have liked a single performance well enough to let it go through. His performance of the Scriabin Fifth Sonata certainly has the feeling of a single performance; it moves with coherence and grand sweep. Sometimes the playing is actually brutal—deliberately so. It far eclipses all other recorded performances of the work.

Less can be said of his performance of Schumann's Sonata No. 3, the *Concerto without Orchestra*. The least-played of Schumann's three piano sonatas, it is a sprawling, thick-textured, terribly difficult piece with only one point of relaxation—the lovely third movement, which is a set of variations on a theme supplied by the composer's beloved wife Clara and which Horowitz had recorded twice before. Throughout most of the sonata there is a lack of rhythmic steadiness in Horowitz's playing, which imparts an unsettled feeling. Even technically Horowitz seems ill at ease, and he sounds as though he is working very, very hard. One wonders if he really liked the piece. He dropped it after one season.

In 1978 he returned to the Liszt B minor Sonata, which he had last recorded in 1932 and had not played for many years. His basic ideas had not changed very much. The only major difference is a quality of relaxation from a seventy-five-year-old veteran, as opposed to the more impulsive playing of a twenty-nine-year-old. Now Horowitz is more careful, and some of the difficult sections are tough going for him. Yet the playing has all the power needed for the big moments, and all the musical parameters are perfectly commanded. The Liszt B minor was still "his" piece.

But not the Rachmaninoff Third, which he once had owned. His Golden Anniversary concerts of 1978 included a Carnegie Hall performance of the concerto on January 8 with the New York Philharmonic under Eugene Ormandy, and of course it was recorded. This time none of the Rachmaninoff-sanctioned cuts were observed. Horowitz's fingers were still up to the notes, but otherwise the performance was a near travesty, with Horowitz constantly changing tempo, introducing interminable ritards, and with many accentuations rhythmically incorrect. His timing was 43′18″, about ten minutes slower than he had been in 1930. He was entering a period where the psychopharmaceutical drugs he was taking were clouding his judgment.

Yet he still could be capable of consummate playing. In an album of pieces from his 1978–79 recitals, he plays the Schumann *Humoresque* gorgeously. It is a beautiful work that he had not played for many years, and he clearly relished it much more than the previous season's Schumann F minor Sonata. He also takes on the Liszt-Busoni *Mephisto* Waltz, with some large-scale rewriting of his own. The Horowitz fingers could still create thunder and lightning, and Liszt would have applauded this kind of *diablerie*. In one of the trickier spots—the fast, big jumps toward the end—Horowitz substitutes a series of convoluted maneuvers that are actually more difficult, if less hazardous.

From Horowitz's 1979–80 recitals Victor put together an album containing a lovely performance of Clementi's *Sonata quasi concerto*—poised, elegant, with a witty last movement. There is also a warm and loving Chopin Barcarolle, unfortunately a little mannered toward the end, where Horowitz holds on to certain key notes far too long. On the disc he turned to a Rachmaninoff piece he had never recorded—the coruscating E flat minor *Moment Musical* in a performance that matches in its finish the composer's own 1940 recording, though it is completely different in approach. Horowitz is more virtuosic and uses greater dynamic extremes. He also plays Rachmaninoff's *Polka de W. R.*, that tasty bonbon, in a much freer way than Rachmaninoff did. Rachmaninoff is ever the reserved musical aristocrat; Horowitz is simply having fun camping it up.

More Schumann is on another disc of selections from 1979–80 concerts. Horowitz came up with the seldom-played *Fantasiestücke* (Op. 111). He also plays the third and fourth pieces from the *Nachtstücke* (Op. 23), and here we have Horowitz the poet, with simple, tender lines and delicate dynamics. In Mendelssohn's *Scherzo a Capriccio* he gives a demonstration of how fingers can do virtuoso work almost unaided by the pedal. His big piece was Rachmaninoff's Piano Sonata No. 2 in his own version. Rachmaninoff wrote it in 1913 and revised it in 1931. Horowitz created a montage of both editions. He plays it so brilliantly, with such controlled abandon, that he almost succeeds in convincing the listener that it is an important piece of music.

At his Metropolitan Opera House concert of November 1, 1981, the novelty was Liszt's B minor Ballade. Severe critics tend to look on this piece as Lisztian-fustian. But granted its abundance of Romantic rhetoric, it also has some of the more startling harmonies of its period and some unusually penetrating melodies. Horowitz loved the piece, and the performance is in a class by itself, even with some stretched-out sections that are more self-indulgent than musical. Some of that indulgence can also be heard in the Chopin F minor Ballade on this disc, which is otherwise a flexible and tonally sumptuous account of one of the greatest piano pieces ever written.

In the live recording of Horowitz's May 22, 1982, concert in London's Festival Hall, he plays the British national anthem. Otherwise the program contained no surprises: Chopin's Polonaise-Fantasy and G minor Ballade, Schumann's *Kinderscenen,* and the Rachmaninoff Piano Sonata No. 2. The album came packaged with a floppy disc on which Horowitz reminisced about his life and career. Pianistically the concert went pretty well. Musically it was mannered and, in some spots, actually awkward. Horowitz was not in good shape. He collapsed physically and mentally soon after his tour, and this was to be his last record for several years.

Which did not mean that Horowitz recordings were not released during this time. Almost every piece he ever recorded did double, triple, quadruple duty. Horowitz was a one-man recording trust. Say he recorded a Chopin mazurka. Two years later it might turn up on an LP named *My Favorite Chopin.* Another year or two after that it might reappear in *Horowitz Encores.* Then it would appear once more on a digitally remastered disc. When CD became the prime recording medium, nearly all of the Horowitz recordings were promptly transferred to the new format. Not even the beloved Arthur Rubinstein was ever accorded this kind of treatment.

Appendix IV
1985–89
with a Digression
on Horowitz and Mozart

> Pablo Casals once told me that Mozart must be played like Chopin, and Chopin should be played like Mozart. He was correct.
> —*Vladimir Horowitz, talking about Mozart*

In the last five years of his life Horowitz concentrated on Mozart as he had never done before. He previously had recorded a few sonatas, but after 1985 he went on an intoxicating Mozartean jag: the Sonatas in C (K. 330), B flat (K. 333) and B flat (K. 281), and the Adagio in B minor and Rondo in D, as well as the A major Concerto (K. 488).

Where does Horowitz the Mozartean stand?

Although a great deal of musicological work has been done on it, Classic performance practice remains a mystery. After all, when a composer named Wolfgang Amadeus Mozart is on record as saying that he never played the same piece twice the same way; that he improvised the solo parts of his concertos and, of course, the cadenzas; that he played adagios as andantes; that he used a good deal of rubato (which is mistakenly supposed to belong only to the Romantics); that the concept of a beautiful sound was integral to his thinking—with all this, we are on ground that nobody today can tread with any great confidence. In a way Mozart was the Rachmaninoff of his day, composing difficult concertos hand tailored to his own abilities, exulting in his virtuosity. "This will make them sweat," he wrote to his father about a concerto he had just composed.

Every age makes music its own way, and the new style that came in after World War II featured fidelity to the printed note rather than what Bach would have called the *Affekt*—the emotional meaning of the music. Modern practice meant the use of the Urtext—the authoritative published version of a work, pure and honest, based on the manuscript, purged of editorial insertions and other excrescences of Romanticism. Musicians felt that any artist who did not play from an Urtext edition was an uncultured barbarian.

But the trouble was, as Horowitz well knew, there really can be no such thing as an Urtext, and in recent years performers have started to realize the paradoxical fact that in an attempt to be "authentic" by slavish adherence to approved Urtexts, they get further away from the essential Bach, Mozart, Haydn, Beethoven, whomever. What also resulted, thanks to the urge for "authenticity," was the negation of personality to a point where everybody began to sound like everybody else.

That was all wrong, artistically and historically. Nearly all composers historically have expected their interpreters to take their notes and make a living organism of them, in a process where the interpreter almost achieves parity with the creator. Music, after all, means nothing on the printed page. Somebody—the performer—has to bring it to life.

In bringing Mozart to life, many exponents of the early-instrument movement have failed completely. They seem to be more interested in translation than interpretation. The fact is that whereas the early-instrument players may give an idea of what classic forces *sounded* like, they convey little idea of how it actually was *played*. It is hard to believe that their consistently dull, metronomic Mozart performances served up on the platter of "authenticity" were actually played that way by the brilliant, mercurial, impulsive, ebullient, musically aristocratic Mozart.

Horowitz was familiar with the early-instrument movement and read some of the pronouncements with interest and also disdain. He would have none of it. Horowitz insisted that Mozart himself, in his letters, told pianists how to play Mozart. And what did Mozart say? Horowitz could quote chapter and verse from memory. He would recite Mozart on rubato, Mozart on a singing line, Mozart on empty, meaningless virtuosity, Mozart on tempo and fluctuation of tempo, Mozart on key structure, Mozart on improvisation, Mozart on pianos, Mozart on piano sound, Mozart on singers and singing, Mozart on taste, Mozart on expression.

Mozart, Horowitz believed, must be played so that every note sounds. His music must be played with a singing line, with taste, and, above all, with expressiveness. Because Mozart's textures are so spare and transparent, he needs more color, not less. Horowitz believed that the modern piano could achieve a Mozartean sound by a canny use of the pedal, though the pedals of course should not be used in Mozart as lavishly as in Romantic music. It could well be that Horowitz was closer to the essential Mozart than the modern, early-instrument specialists, who —as such revisionists as Richard Taruskin and Robert Levin have recently been pointing out—play Mozart not in Mozart's style but in a modern, literal, objective style.

Now we are beginning to know better about "the Mozart style." Sandra P. Rosenblum in her *Performance Practices in Classic Music* has done major research, and her findings indicate that in Mozart's day music was allied to rhetoric. Music was, in the words of the violinist-composer-theorist Heinrich Christoph Koch (1749–1815), "the expression of passionate feelings." Rosenblum quotes many contemporary treatises to that effect. Quantz: "The orator and the musician have, at the bottom, the same aim . . . , namely to make themselves masters of the heart of their listeners, to arouse or still their passions, and to transport them now to this sentiment, now to that," and she backs Quantz up with an impressive list of contemporary authorities. Pre-Romanticism already is in the air.

Tempos, Rosenblum says—and many scholars are beginning to agree —were faster in the Mozart-Haydn period and the first half of the nineteenth century than they are today. Mendelssohn and Berlioz, by all accounts, took fast tempos. It was Wagner who started slowing down. Writes Rosenblum: "Wagner turned in the direction that led eventually to his exaggeratedly slow tempos based in part on what he considered the expression of the melodic line." Wagner's disciples, such as von Bülow and Seidl, showed their profundity through slow tempos.

Rosenblum, quite correctly, points out that the tradition of Wagnerian tempos, especially in regard to slow movements and "moderate" minuets, is very much alive today; that "it has been an important element in the strong resistance of many contemporary musicians to adopting, or at least experimenting with and trying to understand, Beethoven's own metronomizations and the next best that we have, those of Czerny and Moscheles." Czerny studied with Beethoven, and his metronome markings to the Beethoven sonatas are considerably faster than today's, just as Beethoven's own metronome marks are considerably faster than today's.

It thus seems clear that tempo has been slowing since Mozart's day. In the late 1980s some of the early-instrument protagonists, notably Roger Norrington, started conducting the Beethoven symphonies using the composer's own metronome marks, which are considerably faster than what was customary up to then. In Norrington's recording of the Beethoven Ninth, for instance, his timing is about one hour, two minutes. Some slow-tempo conductors in the 1980s—Leonard Bernstein, for instance—could take fifteen or twenty minutes over the hour to deliver their message. But in the 1950s, Charles Munch and Pierre Monteux were taking *less* than one hour for the Ninth, with all repeats, and the average timing of such conductors as Toscanini, Walter, Bernstein (yes, Bernstein), Reiner, and Koussevitzky was one hour, four minutes.

Then there is the problem of rubato, which Mozart wrote about in great detail. Rubato is the delicate displacement of rhythm for expressive purposes. Mozart's and Chopin's rubato were alike: the left hand remained steady, the right hand could wander. As early as 1723 Pier Francesco Tosi wrote that good taste in playing included "going from one note to another with singular and unexpected surprises, and stealing the time exactly on the true motion of the bass." (*Rubato* in Italian means "stolen.") All sensitive artists use fluctuation of tempo, otherwise their performances would be metronomic. It is believed that Mozart wrote out some measures of how he played tempo rubato. They can be found in the Adagio of his F major Sonata (K. 332). In this notation, he syncopates the right hand against the left-hand bass.

Horowitz set forth his ideas about Mozart on the piano in his program notes for the Deutsche Grammophon *Horowitz at Home* recording in 1989. He took the position that "all music is the expression of feelings, and feelings do not change over the centuries." Therefore he discarded such labels as Classic, Romantic, Modern, Neo-Classic. *All* music is Romantic. Style and form may change, but not the basic human emotions. "Purists would have us believe that music from the so-called Classical period should be played with emotional restraint, while so-called Romantic music must be played with emotional freedom." The sad result, according to Horowitz, is exaggeration on both sides: overindulgent, uncontrolled performances of Romantic music, and dry, sterile, dull performances of Classical music.

To play Mozart properly, Horowitz wrote, the requirement is not interpretation but a process of subjective re-creation. He pointed out what every experienced musician knows: "The notation of a composer is a mere skeleton that the performer must endow with flesh and blood." Expression is more important than an Urtext. "Shouldn't the performer listen to his heart rather than to intellectual concepts of how to play Classical, Romantic, or any other style of music?" True, mastery implies control. "But control that is creative does not limit or restrain feelings or spontaneity. It is rather a setting of standards and boundaries in regard to taste, style, and what is appropriate to each composer."

Horowitz spoke about Mozart playing for his projected autobiography:

> In five days I could memorize and play the *Funérailles* of Liszt but I could not play a sonata by Mozart. If you give me a Mozart sonata, I promise you that I can learn the notes by heart in one day. That is not hard. No problem. But if I am going to play it the way I think it should be played, with the colors I hear in the music, emotionally, with a singing line, I have to spend a long time working like crazy. In any movement of a Mozart sonata are forty colors, fifty colors, sixty colors. But pianists are no longer receptive to color. Mozart demands a unique kind of color. I try to give him that color. He had the same blood, the same veins as we have. Now in the last years of my life I go to Mozart because he is the most difficult composer. I am familiar with the authentic instrument craze but am not impressed. Mozart is much better on the modern piano. You can do much more. It's the same with Bach and Scarlatti. You lose more with Chopin on the modern piano than you do with Mozart. Chopin could play his etudes on his light-action Pleyel, but some of the etudes are impossible to play on the modern piano.

Horowitz's performances of the Classic repertoire adhered to his strictures. In his early Mozart and Haydn performances on records, Horowitz played with a wonderfully bouncing rhythm, very little pedal, some delicate tempo fluctuations, and a perpetually singing line. In the Classic performances of his last years, the rhythm and articulation remained much the same, but the tempos were a shade slower and more delicate color washes were applied.

In the Mozart C major Sonata (K. 330), which he first played in his 1985 *Last Romantic* film (Deutsche Grammophon immediately put it on CD) and then in Moscow, the musical approach is simple and direct, even with the infusions of color. The dynamics are carefully calculated, all between piano and forte (no pianissimos or fortissimos). The clarity of the playing contradicts some assertions of early-piano specialists who insist that the modern grand piano is not capable of a fortepiano's subtleties. In the slow movement Horowitz practices what others preach: he actually makes the music sound like an extended operatic aria, and the last four measures are simply melting: Susanna and the Countess in a hitherto unknown *Figaro* aria. The finale is sweet and graceful.

Mozart's B flat Sonata (K. 333) as recorded by Horowitz in 1987 has some unusual ornaments. He substitutes turns and other devices for more conventional appoggiaturas and uses them in the best of taste. It is hard to believe that the playing is that of an eighty-four-year-old man.

There is life in it, relish and joy, even rapture. Horowitz takes all of the repeats, including the long one in the first movement.

Whether he believed in repeats as important to structure or used them to fill out a not very long compact disc is a moot question. There is every reason to believe that in Mozart's own day (and Beethoven's, too) repeats were generally ignored. At best they were optional. The conductor George Smart, who introduced many Haydn, Mozart, and Beethoven symphonies to London in the early 1830s and 1840s, seldom took repeats. Once in a while he entered in his score, "Took repeat." That did not happen very often.

On this Deutsche Grammophon disc is also the A major Piano Concerto (K. 488), with Giulini and the Scala Orchestra. The performance can also be seen on a videodisc (without the sonata). As in all of the Horowitz videodiscs, the cameras concentrate on his hands, and one marvels at his flat-fingered approach to the technical problems. Not that there are any problems for him in this work. The first movement has, if one can use an oxymoron, a calm tension. The melodic elements are of course emphasized in this most melodic of concertos, but there is an inexorable buildup to the ingenious Busoni cadenza (which flashes and disappears after seventy-two seconds). Horowitz conceived the second movement as a siciliana (a slow dance in six-eight time) rather than an adagio as marked. This means a faster than normal tempo for the movement, though Horowitz never races. He is intent on keeping the music in constant, elegant flow, and what comes out is an elegy rather than a dirge. The finale is all fun and games. Giulini accompanies faithfully, but one feels that his ideas about the music are much more sober and post–World War II traditional than those of Horowitz.

The last Mozart that Horowitz played appeared in the Deutsche Grammophon *Horowitz at Home* album. It contained the Sonata in B flat (K. 281), the Adagio in B minor, and the Rondo in D. In the sonata Horowitz again takes all repeats. The first movement is brisk, beautifully articulated, with the controlled flow that Horowitz always brought to his scale passages. In the second movement he starts with a rhythmic error, the right hand coming in with accented upbeats that throw the rhythm off for two measures. He gets it right when he takes the repeat. At measures 53–56 he makes a slight textual change, and in the last movement he inserts a tiny cadenza at measure 70. If one were to be *really* authentic, it would be mandatory to add many more cadenzas, and to embroider the slow movement much more than anybody today (Horowitz included) would dare to do.

Horowitz responds fully to the piercing sadness of the B minor Adagio's chromatic harmonies. This is a demonstration not only of expressive playing but also of the way the two hands of a pianist can be in perfect balance. Horowitz uses the left hand to apply just the right combination of harmonic solidity and color without being obvious about it. Yes, it is a "Romantic" performance. But this piece could well be, with the Rondo in A minor, Mozart's most Romantic writing. The harmonies are far in advance of their day.

Of course Horowitz in his last years recorded other things than Mozart. For Deutsche Grammophon in 1985 he recorded the Schumann *Kreisleriana.* Could he have had anything further to say about this piece after his great 1969 recording for Columbia? Yes. The tempos are now a bit slower (31'04" as against 28'04"), there is a more relaxed feeling, and a simpler, more reflective approach to the music. The 1969 performance swept the listener away with its ardent Romanticism. The new one, less physically exciting, has more warmth and even more color. The technique remains solid; everything is in splendid order. This was the most ambitious work Horowitz recorded in his last five years.

Also on the disc was a rarity: a nocturnelike Liszt Impromptu in F sharp, unknown even to most Liszt specialists. Liszt had Chopin in mind here, as the Horowitz performance makes very clear. The disc contains, in addition, a curiously subdued performance of the oft-recorded (by Horowitz) Scriabin D sharp minor Etude. Schubert's B flat Impromptu (Op. 142, No. 3) and the Schubert-Tausig *Marche militaire* fill out the disc. Grace and suppleness, with purling, precisely weighted scale passages in the last variation, mark the B flat Impromptu. It is interesting to compare Horowitz with the recording made by Schnabel around 1950. Schnabel's is equally great, with overpowering authority and a masculine sense of poetry (and he too does those scale runs with extraordinary finesse). The Horowitz is more feminine, more interesting harmonically (thanks to the inner voices he brings out), more colorful.

As for the Schubert-Tausig, it is great fun. At the turn of the century it was very much in the repertoire, and was recorded by such giants as Hofmann and Godowsky as well as a host of lesser pianists. Horowitz touches up the music a bit, adds a flourish here and there and almost reminds one of the Horowitz of *Stars and Stripes* or *Carmen.*

About two years later, in 1988, Deutsche Grammophon brought out a disc containing three of Horowitz's most enchanting performances. All are Liszt transcriptions of Schubert: the *Soirées de Vienne* Nos. 6 and 7, and the *Ständchen,* better known as the celebrated Schubert Serenade. They make the listener wiggle with pleasure, especially the Serenade, with its amazing separation of voices—such control!—and its subtle colorations, together with a melodic line that extends into infinity.

The last Horowitz disc, completed just before his death, is remarkable. It contains music he had never before recorded: Haydn's Sonata in E flat (No. 49), a Chopin group consisting of the Fantaisie-Impromptu,

Mazurka in C minor (Op. 56, No. 3), the Nocturnes in E flat (Op. 55, No. 2) and B (Op. 62, No. 1), and the Etudes in A flat (Op. 25, No. 1) and E minor (Op. 25, No. 5). Then there were the Praeludium to the Liszt *Weinen, Klagen, Sorgen, Zagen* Variations, and the Wagner-Liszt *Liebestod.*

Every piece on the disc is a spectacular example of great piano playing. The Haydn sonata, a witty and unconventional work full of charm and unexpected darts, receives a performance that extracts everything in the music. Horowitz uses more dynamics here than he generally did for Classic pieces, but everything he does comes out beautifully without erasing the Haydnesque character. If Haydn is to be played on the modern grand, this is the way to play it. If Haydn is to be played on a period instrument, the player would do well to listen and learn from Horowitz's expressiveness.

One wonders if Horowitz selected the E flat Nocturne because of the Ignaz Friedman recording of the mid-1930s. Horowitz said many times (and he was so right) that nobody had ever played it better. Perhaps he wanted to show that he, Vladimir Horowitz, was no slouch either. There are a few Friedmanesque ideas in the Horowitz performance, and also a great deal of prime Horowitz in the registrations and the way he moves the bass line to get such rich textures. Is he more convincing than Friedman? Let's call it a standoff.

The B major Nocturne is one of the sexiest things that Horowitz ever did: positively orgiastic, yet never in bad taste. It is a prime example of what the British critic Bryce Morrison called Horowitz's "Romantic polyphonic style, one which could 'voice,' scatter or realign any harmony or texture at will." The Fantasy-Impromptu is cooler playing. Determined to avoid sentimentality in the middle section, Horowitz alertly moves it along and suddenly it no longer seems interminable. The fingerwork of the fast sections is a *Wunder*. Of the two etudes, the A flat is supple and singing, but one wonders why at the end of an otherwise deliciously played E minor Etude he holds on to the fortissimo trills so long and so loud. It rather overbalances the piece.

Nobody had ever heard of the *Weinen, Klagen* Praeludium until this disc came out. There is a big Liszt set of *Weinen, Klagen* Variations on a theme from a Bach cantata, recorded by Alfred Brendel and others, but that is not what Horowitz plays here. He found among his sheet music a short, separately published work on the Bach theme that Liszt appears to have composed before his big variations. It is a dense, harmonically fascinating example of Liszt's later period, moody and gripping, and Horowitz plays it with extraordinary richness and intensity. Here again he is in a sound-world that only an old magician like him could bring to life. It was the last piece of music he recorded for this disc, though the *Liebestod* was, inevitably, placed last. Toward the end of the *Liebestod,* Horowitz makes a change in the bass to provide a thrilling effect.

It was billed as *The Last Recording,* and indeed it was. But that does not mean no Horowitz records will be issued in the future. A disc of his last Vienna concert was released early in 1991. So was a CD of the Vienna *Kinderscenen* and the rejected 1986 Schubert B flat Sonata. More inevitably will be forthcoming. There still is unreleased material in the "icebox" of the various companies that made his records. The Horowitz Archives at Yale contain full concerts he gave in the 1940s and 1950s, and it may be that these will eventually go public. Collectors have pirated cassettes of Horowitz recitals, and those too may be made commercially available. The public will most certainly be deluged with "new" Horowitz recordings for many years to come. And who knows but that in some attic, or hoarded by some reclusive collector, are off-the-air copies of Horowitz in the two Liszt concertos that he was playing in the early 1930s.

It was a huge discography that Horowitz left, and it exemplified what he once said to the German critic Joachim Kaiser: "Piano playing consists of intellect, heart, and technique. All should be equally developed. Without intellect you will be a fiasco, without technique an amateur, and without heart a machine. The profession has its perils."

Perils, yes. But also joy, wonderment, and, sometimes, fulfillment. All artists pursue a Grail, that all-but-impossible quest for those rare moments when the light of the music transfigures them to the point where performer, composer, and audience are as one. Vladimir Horowitz consistently achieved that goal, and that is why he was the dominant force in piano playing for the last half of the twentieth century.

Discography of Horowitz

Compiled by Jon M. Samuels

This is a working discography aimed at the general reader. Only basic information is given. Thus such minutiae as matrix and take numbers, or complete issue information, are deemed irrelevant here. Eventually a scholarly Horowitz discography based on the following material will be published independently or in a trade journal. As it stands, this discography provides a chronological inventory of all the commercially released Horowitz recordings, followed by a detailed index.

It is divided into two parts. The first is the Chronological Section. It contains every Horowitz recording date, each of which is assigned a session number in chronological order. When a recording or group of recordings was made over a series of dates, those dates are assigned a single "sessions number." The name of the company that made the recordings is listed above the first session in which it participated. Every session that follows the initial mention of a record company was recorded by that same company until the name of another company is listed. To save space, the titles of compositions are in abbreviated form in this section.

The second part, the Index and Release Section, serves several functions. First, it acts as an index to the Chronological Section. The number in parenthesis at the end of every listing in the second section is a cross-reference to the session number in the first. Secondly, the Index and Release Section provides detailed composition titles. It also contains a complete inventory of all the Horowitz compact discs, videodiscs, and videotapes at the point of writing.

When a Horowitz recording has not yet been published in one of those formats (CD, videodisc, or videotape), the last previously available form of recording is given (LP, 45 rpm, 78 rpm, or piano roll). When more than one version was made of a particular piece, a date is provided to distinguish among them.

In 1986 Horowitz donated his private collection to Yale University. It contained recordings of numerous live concerts between 1941 and 1950. There is a strong possibility that in the near future some of them will be issued on compact disc.

This discography would not have been possible without the help of many people. These include Caine Alder, Morgan Cundiff, formerly of the International Piano Archives at Maryland, Ruth Edge of EMI Records, Thomas Frost, Tina McCarthy of CBS Records, Donald Manildi, Joseph Patrych, John Pfeiffer and Bernadette Moore of BMG/RCA records, and Steven Reveyoso. My thanks and appreciation to all.

The completion date of this discography is July 17, 1992.

Chronological Section

Welte & Soehne Piano Roll Session
Session No. 1, January or February 1926?: M. Welte & Soehne Studios, Hamburg

Rachmaninoff: Prelude in G minor (Op. 23/5)
Horowitz: *Danse excentrique*
Horowitz: *Carmen* Variations
Schubert-Liszt: *Liebesbotschaft*
Liszt: *Valse oubliée* No. 1
Rachmaninoff: Prelude in G (Op. 32/5)
Rachmaninoff: Prelude in G sharp minor (Op. 32/12)
Bach-Busoni: Adagio and Fugue from Toccata in D minor
Chopin: Mazurka in C sharp minor (Op. 30/4)
Chopin: Mazurka in F minor (Op. 63/2)
Chopin: Mazurka in C sharp minor (Op. 63/3)
Bach-Busoni: Organ Prelude and Fugue in D
Mozart-Liszt-Busoni: *Figaro* Fantasia
Chopin: Etude in F (Op. 10/8)
Chopin: *Black Key* Etude

RCA Victor Recording Sessions

Session No. 2, March 26, 1928: Victor Studio No. 1, Camden, N.J.
  Chopin: Mazurka in C sharp minor (Op. 30/4)
  Debussy: *Serenade for the Doll*

Session No. 3, April 2, 1928: Victor Studio No. 1, Camden, N.J.
  Horowitz: *Carmen* Variations
  Scarlatti-Tausig: *Capriccio* (Sonata in E, K. 20, L. 375)

Aeolian Company Piano Roll Session

Session No. 4, between June and September 1928: Duo-Art Studios, New York
  Horowitz: *Carmen* Variations
  Saint-Saëns–Liszt: *Danse macabre* (Op. 40)
  Tchaikovsky: *Dumka*
  Chopin: Etude in E flat minor (Op. 10/6)
  Chopin: Etude in C minor (Op. 25/12)
  Schubert-Liszt: *Liebesbotschaft*
  Rachmaninoff: Prelude in A minor (Op. 32/8)
  Rachmaninoff: Prelude in B minor (Op. 32/10)
  Horowitz: Waltz in F minor

RCA Victor Recording Sessions

Session No. 5, December 4, 1928: Victor Studio No. 1, Camden, N.J.
  Dohnányi: *Capriccio*—Concert Etude in F minor (Op. 28/6)

Session No. 6, February 25, 1930: Liederkranz Hall, New York
  Liszt: *Valse oubliée* No. 1

Session No. 7, March 4, 1930: Liederkranz Hall, New York
  Horowitz: *Danse excentrique*
  Liszt-Busoni: *Paganini* Etude in E flat

Gramophone Company Recording Sessions

Session No. 8, December 30, 1930: Kingsway Hall, London
  Rachmaninoff: Concerto No. 3. London Symphony Orchestra/
    Coates
  Prokofiev: Toccata

Session No. 9, June 12, 1931: Beethovensaal, Berlin
Rachmaninoff: Prelude in G minor (Op. 23/5)

Session No. 10, November 11, 1932: Abbey Road Studio No. 3, London
Poulenc: *Pastourelle*
Poulenc: Toccata
Haydn: Sonata in E flat (Hob. XVI:52)
Rimsky-Korsakov—Rachmaninoff: *The Flight of the Bumble-Bee*
Stravinsky: "Russian Dance" from *Petrushka*

Session No. 11, November 12, 1932: Abbey Road Studio No. 3, London
Liszt: Sonata in B minor

Session No. 12, November 15, 1932: Abbey Road Studio No. 3, London
Schumann: *Presto passionato*
Liszt: *Funérailles*
Chopin: Mazurka in F minor (Op. 7/3)
Chopin: Etude in F (Op. 10/8)
Schumann: *Traumeswirren*

Session No. 13, May 29, 1933: Abbey Road Studio No. 3, London
Chopin: Mazurka in E minor (Op. 41/2)

Live Recording
Session No. 14, October 5, 1933: Copenhagen
Debussy: *Serenade for the Doll*

Gramophone Company Recording Sessions
Session No. 15, May 6, 1934: Abbey Road Studio No. 3, London
Bach-Busoni: Chorale Prelude *Nun freut euch, lieben Christen*
Schumann: *Arabesque*
Debussy: *Pour les arpèges composés*
Beethoven: 32 Variations in C minor

Session No. 16, May 12, 1934: Abbey Road Studio No. 3, London
Schumann: Toccata
Chopin: Etude in F (Op. 25/3)
Chopin: *Black Key* Etude

Live Recording
Session No. 17, October 18, 1934: Copenhagen
    Tchaikovsky: Concerto No. 1 (only third movement survives).
    Denmark Radio Symphony Orchestra/Malko

Session No. 18, March 17, 1935: Carnegie Hall, New York
    Brahms: Concerto No. 1. New York Philharmonic/Toscanini

Gramophone Company Recording Session
Session No. 19, June 2, 1935: Abbey Road Studio No. 3, London
    Chopin: Mazurka in C sharp minor (Op. 50/3)
    Chopin: Etude in C sharp minor (Op. 10/4)
    Chopin: *Black Key* Etude
    Scarlatti: Sonata in G (K. 125, L. 487)

Session No. 20, June 4, 1935: Abbey Road Studio No. 3, London
    Scarlatti: Sonata in B minor (K. 87, L. 33)

Live Recording
Session No. 21, February 20, 1936: Concertgebouw, Amsterdam
    Brahms: Concerto No. 1 (part of first movement missing). Concert-
    gebouw Orchestra/Walter

Gramophone Company Recording Session
Session No. 22, March 9, 1936: Abbey Road Studio No. 3, London
    Chopin: Sonata No. 2—first movement
    Chopin: Scherzo No. 4

Live Recording
Session No. 23, May 6, 1940: Carnegie Hall, New York
    Brahms: Concerto No. 2. NBC Symphony Orchestra/Toscanini

RCA Victor Recording Session
Session No. 24, May 9, 1940: Carnegie Hall, New York
    Brahms: Concerto No. 2. NBC Symphony Orchestra/Toscanini

Live Recording
Session No. 25, April 19, 1941: Carnegie Hall, New York
    Tchaikovsky: Concerto No. 1. NBC Symphony Orchestra/Toscanini

RCA Victor Recording Sessions
Sessions No. 26, May 6 and 14, 1941: Carnegie Hall, New York
    Tchaikovsky: Concerto No. 1. NBC Symphony Orchestra/Toscanini

Sessions No. 27, August 27 and September 29, 1942: Hollywood Recording Studio, California
    Tchaikovsky: *Dumka*

Session No. 28, September 10, 1942: Hollywood Recording Studio, California
    Saint-Saëns–Liszt–Horowitz: *Danse macabre*

Session No. 29, April 25, 1943: Carnegie Hall, New York (recorded live)
    Tchaikovsky: Concerto No. 1. NBC Symphony Orchestra/Toscanini

Session No. 30, December 23, 1944: Hunter College Auditorium, New York
    Czerny: Variations on Rode's *La ricordanza*

Sessions No. 31, September 22 and October 6, 1945: Hunter College Auditorium, New York
    Prokofiev: Sonata No. 7
    Chopin: Andante Spianato and Polonaise
    Chopin: Polonaise in A flat (October 6)

Session No. 32, September 23, 1945: Hunter College Auditorium, New York
    Chopin: Waltz in A minor

Session No. 33, October 24, 1946: Town Hall, New York
    Scarlatti: Sonata in E (K. 380, L. 23)
    Scarlatti: Sonata in G (K. 455, L. 209)

Sessions No. 34, October 25 and November 22, 1946: Town Hall, New York
    Mozart: Sonata in A (K. 331)—third movement ("Turkish March") (October 25)

Mendelssohn: *Variations sérieuses*
Mendelssohn-Liszt-Horowitz: *Wedding March* and Variations (November 22)

Session No. 35, October 29, 1946: Town Hall, New York
Mendelssohn: *Shepherd's Complaint*
Mendelssohn: *May Breezes*
Mendelssohn: *Elegy*
Mendelssohn: *Spring Song*

Sessions No. 36, November 21 and 26, 1946: Town Hall, New York
Beethoven: *Moonlight* Sonata

Session No. 37, November 27, 1946: Town Hall, New York
Scarlatti: Sonata in A (K. 322, L. 483)
Scarlatti: Sonata in E (K. 46, L. 25)

Session No. 38, November 29, 1946: Town Hall, New York
Chopin: Waltz in C sharp minor

Sessions No. 39, May 16 and 19, 1947: Town Hall, New York
Debussy: *Serenade for the Doll* (May 16)
Poulenc: Presto in B flat (May 16)
Liszt: Hungarian Rhapsody No. 6 (May 16 and 19)
Chopin: Ballade No. 1 (May 19)
Chopin: Nocturne in F sharp (May 19)
Liszt: *Au bord d'une source* (May 19)

Session No. 40, September 6, 1947: Republic Studios, Hollywood, California
Bach-Busoni: Chorale Prelude *Nun komm' der Heiden Heiland*

Session No. 41, November 6, 1947: Town Hall, New York
Mozart: Sonata in F (K. 332)

Sessions No. 42, November 7 and December 22, 1947: Town Hall, New York
Scarlatti: Sonata in E (K. 531, L. 430) (November 7)
Mussorgsky-Horowitz: *Pictures at an Exhibition*
Kabalevsky: Sonata No. 3 (December 22)
Horowitz: *Carmen* Variations (December 22)
Chopin: Mazurka in F minor (Op. 7/3) (December 22)

Session No. 43, November 21, 1947: Town Hall, New York
Mussorgsky-Horowitz: *By the Water*
Schumann: *Träumerei*
Prokofiev: Toccata
Scarlatti: Sonata in B minor (K. 87, L. 33)

Live Recordings
Session No. 44, April 11, 1948: Carnegie Hall, New York
Tchaikovsky: Concerto No. 1. New York Philharmonic/Walter

Session No. 45, October 23, 1948: Studio 8-H, Radio City, New York
Brahms: Concerto No. 2. NBC Symphony Orchestra/Toscanini

RCA Victor Recording Sessions
Session No. 46, May 9, 1949: Town Hall, New York
Liszt-Horowitz: Hungarian Rhapsody No. 15—first half

Session No. 47, May 11, 1949: Town Hall, New York
Chopin: Ballade No. 3
Chopin: Mazurka in C sharp minor (Op. 41/1)

Live Recording
Session No. 48, August 2, 1949: Hollywood Bowl, Hollywood, California
Tchaikovsky: Concerto No. 1. Hollywood Bowl Orchestra/Steinberg
Scarlatti: Sonata in E (K. 380, L. 23)
Moszkowski: Etude in A flat (Op. 72/11)
Schumann: *Träumerei*
Sousa-Horowitz: *The Stars and Stripes Forever*

RCA Victor Recording Sessions
Session No. 49, December 28, 1949: Town Hall, New York
Chopin: Ballade No. 4
Chopin: Mazurka in D flat (Op. 30/3)
Chopin: Mazurka in C sharp minor (Op. 30/4)

Session No. 50, December 30, 1949: Town Hall, New York
Chopin: Mazurka in F minor (Op. 63/2)
Chopin: Mazurka in C sharp minor (Op. 63/3)
Chopin: Mazurka in C sharp minor (Op. 50/3)

Sessions No. 51, May 10 and 17, 1950: Town Hall, New York
  Schumann: *Kinderscenen*
  Chopin: Mazurka in F sharp minor (Op. 59/3) (May 10)
  Liszt-Horowitz: Hungarian Rhapsody No. 15—second half (May 17)
  Clementi: Sonata in B flat (Op. 24/2)—third movement (May 17)
  Scriabin: Etude in C sharp minor (Op. 2/1) (May 17)

Session No. 52, May 13, 1950: Town Hall, New York
  Chopin: Sonata No. 2

Session No. 53, May 15, 1950: Town Hall, New York
  Barber: Sonata in E flat minor

Sessions No. 54, June 22 and 29, 1950: RCA Studio No. 2, New York
  Brahms: Violin Sonata No. 3. Nathan Milstein/violin

Live Recording
Session No. 55, August 31, 1950: Hollywood Bowl, Hollywood, California
  Rachmaninoff: Concerto No. 3. Hollywood Bowl Orchestra/Koussevitzky

RCA Victor Recording Sessions
Session No. 56, October 10, 1950: Town Hall, New York
  Brahms: Waltz in A flat
  Moszkowski: Etude in A flat (Op. 72/11)
  Moszkowski: Etude in F (Op. 72/6)

Session No. 57, December 27, 1950: Hunter College Auditorium, New York
  Schumann: *Arabesque*

Session No. 58, December 29, 1950: Hunter College Auditorium, New York
  Sousa-Horowitz: *The Stars and Stripes Forever*
  Liszt: *Funérailles*

Session No. 59, March 5, 1951: Carnegie Hall, New York (recorded live)
  Schumann: Sonata No. 3 in F minor (Op. 14)—third movement (Wieck Variations)
  Chopin: Mazurka in B flat minor (Op. 24/4)

Session No. 60, April 23, 1951: Carnegie Hall, New York (recorded live)
  Haydn: Sonata in E flat (Hob. XVI:52)
  Brahms: Intermezzo in B flat minor (Op. 117/2)
  Chopin: Polonaise-Fantaisie
  Mussorgsky-Horowitz: *Pictures at an Exhibition*
  Scarlatti: Sonata in E (K. 380, L. 23)
  Moszkowski: *Etincelles*
  Sousa-Horowitz: *The Stars and Stripes Forever*

Session No. 61, April 28, 1951: Hunter College Auditorium, New York
  Liszt: *Sonetto 104 del Petrarca*
  Liszt: *Valse oubliée* No. 1
  Chopin: Nocturne in F minor (Op. 55/1)

Session No. 62, April 29, 1951: Hunter College Auditorium, New York
  Chopin: Scherzo No. 1
  Chopin: Etude in E (Op. 10/3)

Sessions No. 63, May 8 and 10, 1951: Carnegie Hall, New York
  Rachmaninoff: Concerto No. 3. RCA Victor Symphony Orchestra/
    Reiner

Gramophone Company Recording Session
Session No. 64, October 11, 1951: Abbey Road Studio No. ?, London
  Chopin: Nocturne in E minor
  Chopin: Impromptu No. 1
  Scarlatti: Sonata in A minor (K. 188, L. 239)
  Scarlatti: Sonata in A (K. 322, L. 483)

RCA Victor Recording Sessions
Session No. 65, January 5, 1952: Hunter College Auditorium, New York
  Chopin: Nocturne in E minor
  Chopin: Etude in C sharp minor (Op. 10/4)

Session No. 66, April 26, 1952: Carnegie Hall, New York
  Beethoven: *Emperor* Concerto. RCA Victor Symphony Orchestra/
    Reiner

Session No. 67, May 8, 1952: Manhattan Center, New York
  Chopin: Ballade No. 4

Session No. 68, January 4, 1953: Carnegie Hall, New York
    Schubert-von Bülow: Impromptu in G (Op. 90/3)

Columbia? Recording Session
Session No. 69, January 12, 1953: Carnegie Hall, New York (recorded live)
    Tchaikovsky: Concerto No. 1. New York Philharmonic/Szell

RCA Victor Recording Sessions
Session No. 70, February 25, 1953: Carnegie Hall, New York (recorded live)
    Schubert: Sonata in B flat (D. 960) (also December 29, 1952?, and
        January 4, 1953?—Carnegie Hall)
    Chopin: Nocturne in E minor
    Chopin: Scherzo No. 1
    Scriabin: Etude in B flat minor (Op. 8/11)
    Scriabin: Etude in C sharp minor (Op. 42/5)
    Debussy: *Serenade for the Doll*
    Liszt-Horowitz: Hungarian Rhapsody No. 2
    Chopin: Waltz in A minor
    Prokofiev: Sonata No. 7—third movement

Sessions No. 71, October 16 and 21, 1954: Horowitz's home, New York
    Clementi: Sonata in F sharp minor (Op. 25/5)
    Clementi: Sonata in G minor (Op. 34/2)
    Clementi: Sonata in F minor (Op. 13/6) (October 21)

Session No. 72, May 9, 1956: Horowitz's home, New York
    Scriabin: Sonata No. 3

Sessions No. 73, May 10, 11, and June 5, 1956: Horowitz's home, New York
    Beethoven: *Waldstein* Sonata
    Beethoven: *Moonlight* Sonata (June 5)

Session No. 74, May 14, 1956: Horowitz's home, New York
    Scriabin: Prelude in C (Op. 11/1)
    Scriabin: Prelude in C sharp minor (Op. 11/10)
    Scriabin: Prelude in E (Op. 11/9)
    Scriabin: Prelude in G (Op. 11/3)
    Scriabin: Prelude in B flat minor (Op. 11/16)

Scriabin: Prelude in G flat (Op. 11/13)
Scriabin: Prelude in E flat minor (Op. 11/14)
Scriabin: Prelude in F sharp minor (Op. 15/2)
Scriabin: Prelude in B (Op. 16/1)
Scriabin: Prelude in B minor (Op. 13/6)
Scriabin: Prelude in E flat minor (Op. 16/4)
Scriabin: Prelude in G minor (Op. 27/1)
Scriabin: Prelude in A minor (Op. 51/2)
Scriabin: Prelude in D flat (Op. 48/3)
Scriabin: Prelude (Op. 67/1)
Scriabin: Prelude (Op. 59/2)
Scriabin: Prelude in D (Op. 11/5)
Scriabin: Prelude in G sharp minor (Op. 22/1)

Session No. 75, January 15, 1957: Hunter College Auditorium, New York
    Chopin: Scherzo No. 3

Session No. 76, February 23, 1957: Carnegie Hall, New York
    Chopin: Nocturne in B (Op. 9/3)
    Chopin: Nocturne in F (Op. 15/1)
    Chopin: Nocturne in C sharp minor (Op. 27/1)
    Chopin: Barcarolle
    Chopin: Scherzo No. 2

Session No. 77, May 14, 1957: Carnegie Hall, New York
    Chopin: Nocturne in E flat (Op. 9/2)

Sessions No. 78, May 14, 18, and 25, 1959: Carnegie Hall, New York
    Beethoven: *Appassionata* Sonata

Sessions No. 79, May 29 and June 10, 1959: Carnegie Hall, New York
    Beethoven: Sonata No. 7

Columbia Recording Sessions
Sessions No. 80, April 18, 24, and May 9, 14, 1962: 30th St. Studio, New York
    Chopin: Sonata No. 2
    Rachmaninoff: *Etude-Tableau* in E flat minor (Op. 39/5)
    Rachmaninoff: *Etude-Tableau* in C (Op. 33/2)
    Schumann: *Arabesque*
    Liszt-Horowitz: Hungarian Rhapsody No. 19
    Liszt: *Consolation* No. 2 in E (May 9)

Sessions No. 81, November 6, 13, 29, and December 18, 1962: 30th St. Studio, New York
Schumann: *Kinderscenen*
Schumann: Toccata
Scarlatti: Sonata in E (K. 531, L. 430)
Scarlatti: Sonata in A (K. 322, L. 483)
Scarlatti: Sonata in G (K. 455, L. 209)
Schubert: Impromptu in G flat (Op. 90/3)
Scriabin: *Poème* in F sharp
Scriabin: Etude in C sharp minor (Op. 2/1)
Scriabin: Etude in D sharp minor (Op. 8/12)

Session No. 82, June 4, 1963: 30th St. Studio?, New York
Clementi: Sonata in A minor (Op. 50/1)—Adagio

Sessions No. 83, September 16 and 23, 1963: 30th St. Studio?, New York
Clementi: Sonata in B flat (Op. 25/3)—Rondo

Session No. 84, November 4, 1963: 30th St. Studio, New York
Chopin: Etude in E flat minor (Op. 10/6) (also June 17)
Beethoven: *Pathétique* Sonata
Debussy: *Les fées sont d'exquises danseuses*
Debussy: *Bruyères*
Debussy: *General Lavine—eccentric*
Chopin: *Revolutionary* Etude

Session No. 85, November 14, 1963: 30th St. Studio, New York
Chopin: Etude in C sharp minor (Op. 25/7)
Chopin: Scherzo No. 1

Sessions No. 86, April 23, May 4 and 18, June 4, September 24 and 28, 1964: 30th St. Studio, New York
Scarlatti: Sonata in F (K. 525, L. 188) (April 23)
Scarlatti: Sonata in A (K. 39, L. 391) (April 23)
Scarlatti: Sonata in B minor (K. 197, L. 147) (April 23)
Scarlatti: Sonata in C minor (K. 303, L. 9) (April 23, May 18)
Scarlatti: Sonata in G (K. 194, L. 28) (April 23, May 18)
Scarlatti: Sonata in G (K. 201, L. 129) (April 23, May 4, 18, June 4)
Scarlatti: Sonata in F sharp minor (K. 25, L. 481) (May 4, 18)
Scarlatti: Sonata in D minor (K. 52, L. 267) (May 4, 18, June 4)
Scarlatti: Sonata in D (K. 33, L. 424) (not April 23)
Scarlatti: Sonata in A minor (K. 54, L. 241) (not April 23)

Scarlatti: Sonata in F minor (K. 466, L. 118) (not April 23)
Scarlatti: Sonata in G (K. 146, L. 349) (not April 23)
Scarlatti: Sonata in D (K. 96, L. 465) (not April 23)
Scarlatti: Sonata in E (K. 162, L. 21) (not April 23)
Scarlatti: Sonata in E flat (K. 474, L. 203) (not April 23)
Scarlatti: Sonata in E minor (K. 198, L. 22) (not April 23)
Scarlatti: Sonata in D (K. 491, L. 164) (not April 23)
Scarlatti: Sonata in F minor (K. 481, L. 187) (not April 23)

Session No. 87, April 7, 1965: 30th St. Studio?, New York
Chopin: *Nouvelle Etude* in A flat

Session No. 88, May 9, 1965: Carnegie Hall, New York (recorded live)
Bach-Busoni: Toccata, Adagio, and Fugue in C
Schumann: Fantasy in C
Scriabin: Sonata No. 9
Scriabin: *Poème* in F sharp
Chopin: Mazurka in C sharp minor (Op. 30/4)
Chopin: Etude in F (Op. 10/8)
Chopin: Ballade No. 1
Debussy: *Serenade for the Doll*
Scriabin: Etude in C sharp minor (Op. 2/1)
Moszkowski: Etude in A flat (Op. 72/11)
Schumann: *Träumerei*

Session No. 89, April 17, 1966: Carnegie Hall, New York (recorded live)
Mozart: Sonata in A (K. 331)
Scriabin: Sonata No. 10 (Op. 70)
Chopin: Polonaise-Fantaisie
Chopin: Mazurka in B minor (Op. 33/4)
Chopin: Nocturne in E minor

Session No. 90, November 27, 1966: Carnegie Hall, New York (recorded live)
Haydn: Sonata in F (Hob. XVI:23)
Debussy: *L'isle joyeuse*
Liszt: *Vallée d'Obermann*

Session No. 91, December 10, 1966: Carnegie Hall, New York (recorded live)
Schumann: *Blumenstück*

Session No. 92, October 22, 1967: Queens College, New York (recorded live)
> Beethoven: Sonata in A (Op. 101)—first movement (see Session No. 94)
> Liszt: Scherzo and March

Session No. 93, November 12, 1967: Brooklyn College, New York (recorded live)
> Scarlatti: Sonata in F sharp (K. 319, L. 35)
> Scarlatti: Sonata in G (K. 260, L. 124)

Live Recording and Columbia Recording Session
Session No. 94, November 26, 1967: Carnegie Hall, New York (recorded live)
> Beethoven: Sonata in A (Op. 101)—second and third movements (see Session No. 92)
> Chopin: Barcarolle
> Mendelssohn: Etude in A minor
> Scarlatti: Sonata in A (K. 101, L. 494)
> Scarlatti: Sonata in F sharp (K. 319, L. 35)
> Scarlatti: Sonata in G (K. 260, L. 124)
> Scarlatti: Sonata in F minor (K. 466, L. 118)
> Scarlatti: Sonata in G (K. 55, L. 335)
> Rachmaninoff: *Etude-Tableau* in E flat minor (Op. 33/6)
> Rachmaninoff: *Etude-Tableau* in C (Op. 33/2)
> Rachmaninoff: *Etude-Tableau* in D (Op. 39/9)
> Horowitz: *Carmen* Variations

Columbia Recording Sessions
Session No. 95, December 10, 1967: Constitution Hall?, Washington, D.C. (recorded live)
> Rachmaninoff: *Etude-Tableau* in E flat minor (Op. 33/6)
> Rachmaninoff: *Etude-Tableau* in C (Op. 33/2)
> Rachmaninoff: *Etude-Tableau* in D (Op. 39/9)

Sessions No. 96, January 2 and February 1, 1968: Carnegie Hall, New York (recorded live)
> Chopin: Ballade No. 1
> Chopin: Nocturne in F minor (Op. 55/1)
> Chopin: Polonaise in F sharp minor
> Scarlatti: Sonata in E (K. 380, L. 23)

Scarlatti: Sonata in G (K. 55, L. 335)
Schumann: *Arabesque*
Scriabin: Etude in D sharp minor (Op. 8/12)
Schumann: *Träumerei*
Horowitz: *Carmen* Variations

Session No. 97, April 7, 1968: Symphony Hall, Boston (recorded live)
Chopin: Waltz in C sharp minor (also November 13, 1966, in Woolsey Hall, New Haven?)

Session No. 98, May 12, 1968: Orchestra Hall, Chicago (recorded live)
Chopin: Mazurka in F minor (Op. 7/3) (also February 8, 1973?)

Live Recording
Session No. 99, November 24, 1968: Carnegie Hall, New York (recorded live)
Schumann: *Kreisleriana* (Op. 16)
Rachmaninoff: Prelude in G sharp minor (Op. 32/12)
Rachmaninoff: *Moment Musical* in B minor (Op. 16/3)
Rachmaninoff-Horowitz: Sonata No. 2

Columbia Recording Sessions
Session No. 100, December 1, 1968: Academy of Music, Philadelphia (recorded live)
Haydn: Sonata in C (Hob. XVI:48)

Session No. 101, December 15, 1968: Carnegie Hall, New York (recorded live)
Rachmaninoff: Prelude in G sharp minor (Op. 32/12)
Rachmaninoff: *Moment Musical* in B minor (Op. 16/3)
Rachmaninoff-Horowitz: Sonata No. 2

Session No. 102, February 5 and 14, 1969: 30th St. Studio, New York
Schumann: Sonata No. 3 in F minor (Op. 14)—third movement (Wieck Variations)

Session No. 103, June 12, 1969: 30th St. Studio, New York
Bach-Busoni: *Ich ruf' zu dir, Herr Jesus Christ*
Medtner: *Fairy Tale* in A (Op. 51/3)

Live Recording
Session No. 104, October 26, 1969: Symphony Hall, Boston (recorded live)
    Chopin: Scherzo No. 1

Columbia Recording Sessions
Session No. 105, December 1, 1969: 30th St. Studio, New York
    Schumann: *Kreisleriana*

Sessions No. 106, April 14 and May 4, 1971: 30th St. Studio, New York
    Chopin: Mazurka in A minor (Op. 17/4) (April 14)
    Chopin: Introduction and Rondo in E flat (April 14)
    Chopin: *Black Key* Etude (April 14)
    Chopin: Prelude in D flat (April 14 and May 4)
    Chopin: Waltz in A minor (May 4)
    Chopin: Polonaise in A flat (May 4)

Sessions No. 107, April 20, 27 and May 4, 1972: 30th St. Studio, New York
    Clementi: *Gradus ad Parnassum*, Book I, No. 14—Adagio in F (April 20)
    Clementi: Sonata in E flat (Op. 12/2)—third movement (April 20)
    Beethoven: *Moonlight* Sonata (April 20, 27)
    Scriabin: Etude in F sharp (Op. 42/4) (April 27)
    Scriabin: Etude in F sharp (Op. 42/3) (April 27)
    Scriabin: *Feuillet d'album* (Op. 58) (April 27)
    Scriabin: *Poème* (Op. 69/1) (April 27)
    Scriabin: *Poème* (Op. 69/2) (April 27)
    Scriabin: Etude in D flat (Op. 8/10) (April 27)
    Scriabin: Etude in F sharp minor (Op. 8/2) (April 27, May 4)
    Scriabin: Etude in A flat (Op. 8/8) (April 27, May 4)
    Scriabin: Etude in B flat minor (Op. 8/11) (April 27, May 4)
    Scriabin: Etude (Op. 65, No. 3) (April 27, May 4)

Session No. 108, May 31, 1972: 30th St. Studio, New York
    Scriabin: *Feuillet d'album* in E flat (Op. 45/1)
    Scriabin: *Vers la flamme*
    Scriabin: Etude in C sharp minor (Op. 42/5) (also April 27?)

Session No. 109, July 6, 1972: 30th St. Studio?, New York
    Chopin: Prelude in B minor (Op. 28/6) (also May 4, 1971?)
    Chopin: Etude in E (Op. 10/3)

Chopin: *Revolutionary* Etude
Chopin: Polonaise in A

Sessions No. 110, October 25 and 30, 1972: 30th St. Studio?, New York
Beethoven: *Appassionata* Sonata

Session No. 111, December 20, 1972: 30th St. Studio?, New York
Beethoven: *Waldstein* Sonata

Sessions No. 112, January 10 and 24, 1973: 30th St. Studio?, New York
Schubert: Impromptu in E flat (Op. 90/2)
Schubert: Impromptu in A flat (Op. 90/4)
Schubert: Impromptu in F minor (Op. 142/1)
Schubert: Impromptu in A flat (Op. 142/2)

Sessions No. 113, February 8 and 15, 1973: 30th St. Studio, New York
Chopin: Mazurka in C sharp minor (Op. 50/3)
Chopin: Etude in C sharp minor (Op. 10/4)
Chopin: Mazurka in D flat (Op. 30/3)
Chopin: Mazurka in D (Op. 33/2)
Chopin: Mazurka in E minor (Op. 41/2) (February 15)
Chopin: Mazurka in F sharp minor (Op. 59/3) (February 15)

RCA Victor Recording Sessions

Sessions No. 114, February 14 and 15, 1976: Paramount Theatre, Oakland,
California; February 22, 28, and 29, 1976: Ambassador College, Pasa-
dena, California (recorded live)
Scriabin: Sonata No. 5 (February 28, 29)
Schumann: Sonata No. 3 in F minor (February 14, 15, 22, 29)

Session No. 115, May 9, 1976: Massey Hall, Toronto, Canada (recorded
live)
Schumann: *Arabesque*
Schumann: Sonata No. 3 in F minor
Rachmaninoff: Prelude in G sharp minor (Op. 32/12)
Rachmaninoff: *Etude-Tableau* in E flat minor (Op. 39/5)
Liszt: *Valse oubliée* No. 1
Liszt: *Au bord d'une source*
Chopin: Waltz in A minor
Chopin: Ballade No. 1
Schumann: *Träumerei*
Moszkowski: *Etincelles*

Session No. 116, November 21, 1976: Powell Hall, St. Louis, Missouri (recorded live)
    Liszt: Sonata

Columbia Recording Session

Session No. 117, May 18, 1976: Carnegie Hall, New York (recorded live)
    Tchaikovsky: Trio—first movement. Mstislav Rostropovich/cello and Isaac Stern/violin
    Rachmaninoff: Cello Sonata—third movement. Mstislav Rostropovich/cello
    Schumann: *Dichterliebe.* Dietrich Fischer-Dieskau/baritone

RCA Victor Recording Sessions

Session No. 118, June 24, 1977: RCA Studio A, New York
    Rachmaninoff: *Moment Musical* in E flat minor (Op. 16/2)
    Rachmaninoff: Prelude in G (Op. 32/5)
    Rachmaninoff: *Polka de W. R.*

Session No. 119, September 9, 1977: RCA Studio A, New York
    Fauré: Impromptu No. 5
    Fauré: Nocturne No. 13

Session No. 120, January 8, 1978: Carnegie Hall, New York (recorded live)
    Rachmaninoff: Concerto No. 3. New York Philharmonic/Ormandy

Sessions No. 121, April 7, 8 and 15, 1979: Orchestra Hall, Chicago; April 22, 1979: Constitution Hall, Washington, D.C. (recorded live)
    Clementi: Sonata in C (Op. 33/3) (April 7, 8, 15, 22)
    Schumann: *Humoresque* (April 8, 15, 22)
    Rachmaninoff: Barcarolle in G minor (April 7, 8, 22)
    Rachmaninoff: *Humoresque* in G (April 7)
    Liszt: *Consolation* No. 3 (April 22)
    Liszt-Busoni-Horowitz: *Mephisto* Waltz No. 1 (April 7, 8, 15, 22)

Live Recording

Session No. 122, November 4, 1979: Massey Hall, Toronto (recorded live)
    Clementi: Sonata in C (Op. 33/3)
    Rachmaninoff-Horowitz: Sonata No. 2

RCA Victor Recording Sessions

Sessions No. 123, April 13, 1980: Symphony Hall, Boston; May 2, 4, 11,
1980: Avery Fisher Hall, New York (recorded live)
    Rachmaninoff-Horowitz: Sonata No. 2 (April 13, May 2, 4, 11)
    Schumann: *Nachtstück* in D flat (Op. 23/3) (April 13, May 2)
    Schumann: *Nachtstück* in F (Op. 23/4) (April 13, May 2)
    Chopin: *Black Key* Etude (May 4)
    Chopin: Etude in C sharp minor (Op. 25/7) (April 13)
    Chopin: Barcarolle (April 13, May 4)
    Mendelssohn: *Scherzo a capriccio* in F sharp minor (May 2)
    Schumann: *Fantasiestücke* (Op. 111) (April 13, May 2)

Sessions No. 124, October 25 and November 1, 1981: Metropolitan Opera
House, New York (recorded live)
    Scarlatti: Sonata in A flat (K. 127, L. 186)
    Scarlatti: Sonata in F minor (K. 466, L. 118)
    Scarlatti: Sonata in F minor (K. 184, L. 189)
    Scarlatti: Sonata in A (K. 101, L. 494)
    Scarlatti: Sonata in B minor (K. 87, L. 33)
    Scarlatti: Sonata in E (K. 135, L. 224)
    Chopin: Ballade No. 4
    Liszt: Ballade No. 2
    Chopin: Waltz in A flat (Op. 69/1)
    Rachmaninoff: Prelude in G minor (Op. 23/5)

Sessions No. 125, May 18, 20 and 22, 1982: Royal Festival Hall, London
(recorded live)
    Anonymous: *God Save the Queen* (May 22)
    Chopin: Polonaise-Fantaisie
    Chopin: Ballade No. 1 (May 18, 20, 22)
    Schumann: *Kinderscenen* (May 20)
    Scriabin: Etude in D sharp minor (Op. 8/12)

Deutsche Grammophon Recording Sessions

Sessions No. 126, April 19–30, 1985: Horowitz's home, New York
    Bach-Busoni: Chorale Prelude *Nun komm' der Heiden Heiland* (April
       19, 28)
    Mozart: Sonata in C (K. 330) (April 19, 25, 28)
    Chopin: Mazurka in A minor (Op. 17/4) (April 21, 28)
    Chopin: Scherzo No. 1 (April 21, 28, 30)
    Schubert: Impromptu in A flat (Op. 90/4) (April 19, 21, 28)
    Liszt: *Consolation* No. 3 (April 21)

Schumann: *Novellette* in F (Op. 21/1) (April 28, 30)
Rachmaninoff: Prelude in G sharp minor (Op. 32/12) (April 25, 28)
Scriabin: Etude in C sharp minor (Op. 2/1) (April 23, 28, 30)
Chopin: Polonaise in A flat (April 19, 23, 30)
Moszkowski: Etude in F (Op. 72/6) (April 30)

Sessions No. 127, September and October 1985: RCA Studio A, New York
Scarlatti: Sonata in B minor (K. 87, L. 33) (September 12, 16)
Scarlatti: Sonata in E (K. 135, L. 224) (September 12, 16)
Schumann: *Kreisleriana* (September 12, 16, 18, 23, October 3, 9)
Schubert: Impromptu in B flat (Op. 142/3) (September 16, 18, 20, 25, October 9)
Liszt: Impromptu (Nocturne) in F sharp (September 20, 23, 25, 30, October 3)
Scriabin: Etude in D sharp minor (Op. 8/12) (September 20, 25, 30)
Schubert-Tausig-Horowitz: *Marche militaire* in D flat (Op. 51/1) (September 23, 25, 30, October 3, 9)
Liszt: *Valse oubliée* No. 1 (September 30, October 3)

Sessions No. 128, February and March 1986: RCA Studio A, New York
Schubert: Sonata in B flat (D. 960) (February 10, 12, 14, 18, 28, March 4)
Schubert: *Moment Musical* in F minor (Op. 94/3) (February 18)
Schubert-Liszt: *Ständchen* (February 14, March 6)
Schubert-Liszt: *Soirée de Vienne* No. 6 (February 18, March 4, 6)

Sessions No. 129, April 18 and 20, 1986: Tchaikovsky Hall, Moscow Conservatory (recorded live)
Scarlatti: Sonata in E (K. 380, L. 23) (April 18)
Mozart: Sonata in C (K. 330) (April 18, 20)
Rachmaninoff: Prelude in G (Op. 32/5) (April 18)
Schubert-Liszt: *Soirée de Vienne* No. 6 (April 18)
Rachmaninoff: *Polka de W. R.* (April 18)
Rachmaninoff: Prelude in G sharp minor (Op. 32/12) (April 20)
Scriabin: Etude in C sharp minor (Op. 2/1) (April 20)
Scriabin: Etude in D sharp minor (Op. 8/12) (April 20)
Liszt: *Sonetto 104 del Petrarca* (April 20)
Chopin: Mazurka in C sharp minor (Op. 30/4) (April 20)
Chopin: Mazurka in F minor (Op. 7/3) (April 20)
Schumann: *Träumerei* (April 20)
Moszkowski: *Etincelles* (April 20)

Session No. 130, March 1987: Abanella Studio, Milan
    Mozart: Concerto No. 23. La Scala Theatre Orchestra/Giulini
    Mozart: Sonata in B flat (K. 333)

Session No. 131, May 31, 1987: Musikverein, Vienna (recorded live)
    Mozart: Rondo in D (K. 485)
    Mozart: Sonata in B flat (K. 333)
    Schubert: Impromptu in G flat (Op. 90/3)
    Schubert-Liszt: *Soirée de Vienne* No. 6
    Schumann: *Kinderscenen*
    Chopin: Mazurka in B minor (Op. 33/4)
    Chopin: Polonaise in A flat
    Liszt: *Consolation* No. 3
    Schubert: *Moment Musical* in F minor (Op. 94/3)
    Moszkowski: *Etincelles*

Sessions No. 132, December 1988 through February 1989: Horowitz's home, New York
    Mozart: Rondo in D (K. 485) (December 12, 23, January 16, 23)
    Mozart: Sonata in B flat (K. 281) (December 12, 16, 19, 23)
    Mozart: Adagio in B minor (K. 540) (December 16, 19, January 6)
    Schubert-Liszt: *Soirée de Vienne* No. 7 (February 13, 21)

Sony Classical Recording Session

Sessions No. 133, October and November 1989: Horowitz's home, New York
    Haydn: Sonata in E flat (Hob. XVI:49) (October 20, 24, 25, 31)
    Chopin: Fantaisie-Impromptu (October 20, 24, 27, 31, November 1)
    Chopin: Nocturne in E flat (Op. 55/2) (October 20, 24, 27, November 1)
    Liszt: Praeludium to *Weinen, Klagen, Sorgen, Zagen* (October 20, 25, 27, November 1)
    Chopin: Mazurka in C minor (Op. 56/3) (October 24, 27, November 1)
    Chopin: Etude in A flat (Op. 25/1) (October 25, 27, 31, November 1)
    Chopin: Etude in E minor (Op. 25/5) (October 25, 27, 31, November 1)
    Wagner-Liszt: *Liebestod* (October 25, 27, November 1)
    Chopin: Nocturne in B (Op. 62/1) (October 25, 27, November 1)

Index and Release Section

KEY TO ABBREVIATIONS:
CD—compact disc
CDV—digitally recorded, videodisc format
45rpm—45-rpm microgroove record
NTSC—American video standard
PAL—European video standard
LP—33⅓-rpm microgroove record
78—78-rpm record
VHS—VHS HiFi videotape format

Composer Index

Anonymous: *God Save the Queen*
  CD: RCA Victor RCD1-4572 (125)

Bach-Busoni: *Ich ruf' zu dir, Herr Jesus Christ* (BWV 639)
  CD: Sony Classical SK 48093 (103)

Bach-Busoni: Chorale Prelude *Nun komm' der Heiden Heiland* (BWV 599)
  (1947) CD: RCA Victor 60461-2-RG (40)
  (1985) CD: Deutsche Grammophon 419 045-2GH, 427 269-2GH3; VHS: MGM/VA 01085 (126)

Bach-Busoni: Chorale Prelude *Nun freut euch, lieben Christen* (BWV 734)
  CD: EMI References CDHC 63538; EMI References CHS 7 63538 2 (15)

Bach-Busoni: Organ Prelude and Fugue in D (BWV 532)
  LP: Sony Superscope KBI 4-A068 (1)

Bach-Busoni: Toccata, Adagio, and Fugue in C (BWV 564)
(1926) Adagio and Fugue—piano roll: Welte 4124; Adagio only;
CD: Intercord 860.864 (1)
(1965) CD: CBS M3K 44681 (88)

Barber: Sonata in E flat minor (Op. 26)
CD: RCA Victor 60377-2-RG (53)

Beethoven: Concerto No. 5 in E flat, *Emperor* (Op. 73)
CD: RCA Victor 7992-2-RG (66)

Beethoven: Sonata No. 7 in D (Op. 10/3)
CD: RCA Victor 09026-60986-2 (79)

Beethoven: Sonata No. 8 in C minor, *Pathétique* (Op. 13)
CD: CBS MK 34509 (84)

Beethoven: Sonata No. 14 in C sharp minor, *Moonlight* (Op. 27/2)
(1946) CD: RCA Victor 60461-2-RG (36)
(1956) CD: RCA Victor 60375-2-RG (73)
(1972) CD: CBS MK 34509, MK 44797 (107)

Beethoven: Sonata No. 21 in C, *Waldstein* (Op. 53)
(1956) CD: RCA Victor 60375-2-RG (73)
(1972) LP: Columbia M 31371 (111)

Beethoven: Sonata No. 23 in F minor, *Appassionata* (Op. 57)
(1959) CD: RCA Victor 60375-2-RG (78)
(1972) CD: CBS MK 34509 (110)

Beethoven: Sonata No. 28 in A (Op. 101)
CD: CBS MK 45572 (92, 94)

Beethoven: 32 Variations in C minor (WoO 80)
CD: EMI References CDHC 63538; EMI References CHS 7 63538
2 (15)

Brahms: Concerto No. 1 in D minor (Op. 15)
New York Philharmonic/Toscanini. CD: Stradivarius STR 10037
(excerpt of first movement only) (18)
Concertgebouw Orchestra of Amsterdam/Walter. CD: AS Disc AS
400 (21)

Brahms: Concerto No. 2 in B flat (Op. 83)
  (May 6, 1940) LP: Melodram MEL 229 (2 discs) (23)
  (May 9, 1940) CD: RCA Victor 60523-2-RG, 60319-2-RG (24)
  (1948) CD: Classical Society CSCD 103; Hunt Arkadia CDMP
      454; Stradivarius STR 13595; Viola Bellaphon 689-24-002
      (45)

Brahms: Intermezzo in B flat minor (Op. 117/2)
  CD: RCA Victor 60523-2-RG (60)

Brahms: Violin Sonata No. 3 in D minor (Op. 108)
  CD: RCA Victor 60461-2-RG (54)

Brahms: Waltz No. 15 in A flat (Op. 39/15)
  CD: RCA Victor 09026-60463-2 (56)

Chopin: Andante Spianato and Polonaise in E flat (Op. 22)
  CD: RCA Victor 7752-2-RG (31)

Chopin: Ballade No. 1 in G minor (Op. 23)
  (1947) CD: RCA Victor 60376-2-RG (39)
  (1965) CD: CBS M3K 44681 (88)
  (1968) CD: CBS MK 42306, M3K 44681, MK 45829 (96)
  (1976) CD: Music and Arts CD-666 (115)
  (1982) CD: RCA Victor RCD1-4572 (125)

Chopin: Ballade No. 3 in A flat (Op. 47)
  CD: RCA Victor 09026-60986-2 (47)

Chopin: Ballade No. 4 in F minor (Op. 52)
  (1949) 78: HMV DB-21503 (49)
  (1952) CD: RCA Victor 09026-60987-2 (67)
  (1981) CD: RCA Victor RCD1-4585, 7752-2-RG (124)

Chopin: Barcarolle in F sharp (Op. 60)
  (1957) CD: RCA Victor 09026-60463-2 (76)
  (1967) CD: Stradivarius STR 10038 (94)
  (1980) CD: RCA Victor 7752-2-RG (123)

Chopin: Etude No. 3 in E (Op. 10/3)
  (1951) CD: RCA Victor 60376-2-RG (62)
  (1972) CD: CBS MK 42305, MK 42306 (109)

Chopin: Etude No. 4 in C sharp minor (Op. 10/4)
    (1935) CD: EMI References CDHC 63538; EMI References CHS
       7 63538 2 (19)
    (1952) CD: RCA Victor 60376-2-RG (65)
    (1973) CD: CBS MK 42306 (113)

Chopin: Etude No. 5 in G flat, *Black Key* (Op. 10/5)
    (1926) CD: Intercord 860.864 (1)
    (1934) 78: HMV DB-2238 (16)
    (1935) CD: EMI References CDHC 63538; EMI References CHS
       7 63538 2 (19)
    (1971) CD: CBS MK 42305, MK 42306 (106)
    (1980) CD: RCA Victor 7752-2-RG (123)

Chopin: Etude No. 6 in E flat minor (Op. 10/6)
    (1928) Piano roll: Duo-Art 7287-4 (4)
    (1963) CD: Sony Classical SK 48093 (84)

Chopin: Etude No. 8 in F (Op. 10/8)
    (1926) CD: Intercord 860.864 (1)
    (1932) CD: EMI References CDHC 63538; EMI References CHS
       7 63538 2 (12)
    (1965) CD: CBS M3K 44681, MK 45829 (88)

Chopin: Etude No. 12 in C minor, *Revolutionary* (Op. 10/12)
    (1963) CD: CBS MK 42305, MK 42306 (84)
    (1972) LP: Columbia M 32932 (109)

Chopin: Etude No. 13 in A flat (Op. 25/1)
    CD: Sony Classical SK 45818 (133)

Chopin: Etude No. 15 in F (Op. 25/3)
    (1934) CD: EMI References CDHC 63538; EMI References CHS
       7 63538 2 (16)

Chopin: Etude No. 17 in E minor (Op. 25/5)
    CD: Sony Classical SK 45818 (133)

Chopin: Etude No. 19 in C sharp minor (Op. 25/7)
    (1963) CD: CBS MK 42412 (85)
    (1980) CD: RCA Victor 7752-2-RG (123)

Chopin: Etude No. 24 in C minor (Op. 25/12)
   Piano roll: Duo-Art 7287-4 (4)

Chopin: *Nouvelle Étude* No. 2 in A flat
   CD: Sony Classical SK 48093 (87)

Chopin: Impromptu No. 1 in A flat (Op. 29)
   CD: EMI References CDHC 63538; EMI References CHS 7 63538
   2; RCA Victor 60376-2-RG (64)

Chopin: Fantaisie-Impromptu in C sharp minor (Op. 66)
   CD: Sony Classical SK 45818 (133)

Chopin: Introduction and Rondo in E flat (Op. 16)
   LP: Columbia M 30463 (106)

Chopin: Mazurka in F minor (Op. 7/3)
   (1932) CD: EMI References CDHC 63538; EMI References CHS
   7 63538 2 (12)
   (1947) CD: RCA Victor 09026-60987-2 (42)
   (1968) CD: CBS MK 42306 (98)
   (1986) CD: Deutsche Grammophon 419 499-2GH, 427 269-2GH3
   (129)

Chopin: Mazurka in A minor (Op. 17/4)
   (1971) CD: CBS MK 42306 (106)
   (1985) CD: Deutsche Grammophon 419 045-2GH, 427 269-
   2GH3; VHS: MGM/VA 01085 (126)

Chopin: Mazurka in B flat minor (Op. 24/4)
   CD: RCA Victor 09026-60463-2 (59)

Chopin: Mazurka in D flat (Op. 30/3)
   (1949) CD: RCA Victor 09026-60986-2 (49)
   (1973) CD: CBS MK 42306 (113)

Chopin: Mazurka in C sharp minor (Op. 30/4)
   (1926) CD: Intercord 860.864 (1)
   (1928) CD: APR CDAPR 7014; RCA Victor 09026-60463-2 (2)
   (1949) CD: RCA Victor 60376-2-RG (49)
   (1965) CD: CBS M3K 44681, MK 45829 (88)
   (1986) CD: Deutsche Grammophon 419 499-2GH, 427 269-2GH3
   (129)

Chopin: Mazurka in D (Op. 33/2)
    CD: CBS MK 42306 (113)

Chopin: Mazurka in B minor (Op. 33/4)
    (1966) CD: CBS MK 42412, M3K 44681, MK 45829 (89)
    (1987) CDV: Deutsche Grammophon 072 221-1GHG (NTSC),
        072 121-1GH (PAL), VHS: 072 221-3GVG (NTSC), 072
        121-3GH (PAL) (131)

Chopin: Mazurka in C sharp minor (Op. 41/1)
    CD: RCA Victor 09026-60987-2 (47)

Chopin: Mazurka in E minor (Op. 41/2)
    (1933) CD: EMI References CDHC 63538; EMI References CHS
        7 63538 2 (13)
    (1973) CD: CBS MK 42306 (113)

Chopin: Mazurka in C sharp minor (Op. 50/3)
    (1935) CD: EMI References CDHC 63538; EMI References CHS
        7 63538 2 (19)
    (1949) CD: RCA Victor 09026-60987-2 (50)
    (1973) CD: CBS MK 42412 (113)

Chopin: Mazurka in C minor (Op. 56/3)
    CD: Sony Classical SK 45818 (133)

Chopin: Mazurka in F sharp minor (Op. 59/3)
    (1950) CD: RCA Victor 09026-60987-2 (51)
    (1973) CD: CBS MK 42306 (113)

Chopin: Mazurka in F minor (Op. 63/2)
    (1926) Piano roll: Welte 4126 (1)
    (1949) CD: RCA Victor 09026-60987-2 (50)

Chopin: Mazurka in C sharp minor (Op. 63/3)
    (1926) CD: Intercord 860.864 (1)
    (1949) CD: RCA Victor 09026-60987-2 (50)

Chopin: Nocturne No. 2 in E flat (Op. 9/2)
    CD: RCA Victor 60376-2-RG (77)

Chopin: Nocturne No. 3 in B (Op. 9/3)
    CD: RCA Victor 09026-60987-2 (76)

Chopin: Nocturne No. 4 in F (Op. 15/1)
CD: RCA Victor 09026-60987-2 (76)

Chopin: Nocturne No. 5 in F sharp (Op. 15/2)
CD: RCA Victor 09026-60463-2 (39)

Chopin: Nocturne No. 7 in C sharp minor (Op. 27/1)
CD: RCA Victor 09026-60986-2 (76)

Chopin: Nocturne No. 15 in F minor (Op. 55/1)
(1951) CD: RCA Victor 60376-2-RG (61)
(1968) CD: CBS MK 42306, M3K 44681 (96)

Chopin: Nocturne No. 16 in E flat (Op. 55/2)
CD: Sony Classical SK 45818 (133)

Chopin: Nocturne No. 17 in B (Op. 62/1)
CD: Sony Classical SK 45818 (133)

Chopin: Nocturne No. 19 in E minor (Op. 72/1)
(1951) CD: EMI References CDHC 63538; EMI References CHS
7 63538 2 (64)
(1952) CD: RCA Victor 09026-60986-2 (65)
(1953) CD: RCA Victor 09026-60987-2 (70)
(1966) CD: CBS MK 42412, M3K 44681 (89)

Chopin: Polonaise No. 3 in A, *Military* (Op. 40/1)
CD: CBS MK 42306 (109)

Chopin: Polonaise No. 5 in F sharp minor (Op. 44)
CD: CBS MK 42412, M3K 44681 (96)

Chopin: Polonaise No. 6 in A flat, *Heroic* (Op. 53)
(1945) CD: RCA Victor 7755-2-RG (31)
(1971) CD: CBS MK 42305, MK 42306 (106)
(1985) CD: Deutsche Grammophon 419 045-2GH, 427 269-
2GH3; VHS: MGM/VA MV 01085 (126)
(1987) CDV: Deutsche Grammophon 072 221-1GHG (NTSC),
072 121-1GH (PAL), VHS: 072 221-3GVG (NTSC), 072
121-3GH (PAL) (131)

Chopin: Polonaise-Fantaisie in A flat (Op. 61)
(1951) CD: RCA Victor 09026-60987-2 (60)

(1966) CD: CBS MK 42412 (89)
(1982) CD: RCA Victor RCD1-4572 (125)

Chopin: Prelude in B minor (Op. 28/6)
CD: CBS MK 42306 (109)

Chopin: Prelude in D flat, "Raindrop" (Op. 28/15)
CD: Sony Classical SK 48093 (106)

Chopin: Scherzo No. 1 in B minor (Op. 20)
(1951) CD: RCA Victor 60376-2-RG (62)
(1953) CD: RCA Victor 09026-60987-2 (70)
(1963) CD: CBS MK 42306 (85)
(1969) CD: Stradivarius STR 10038 (104)
(1985) CD: Deutsche Grammophon 419 045-2GH, 427 269-
2GH3; VHS: MGM/VA MV 01085 (126)

Chopin: Scherzo No. 2 in B flat minor (Op. 31)
CD: RCA Victor 09026-60987-2 (76)

Chopin: Scherzo No. 3 in C sharp minor (Op. 39)
CD: RCA Victor 09026-60463-2 (75)

Chopin: Scherzo No. 4 in E (Op. 54)
CD: EMI References CDHC 63538; EMI References CHS 7 63538
2 (22)

Chopin: Sonata No. 2 in B flat minor, *Funeral March* (Op. 35)
(1936)—first movement—CD: APR CDAPR 7014 (22)
(1950) CD: RCA Victor 60376-2-RG (52)
(1962) CD: CBS MK 42412, MK 44797 (80)

Chopin: Waltz No. 3 in A minor (Op. 34/2)
(1945) CD: RCA Victor 09026-60987-2 (32)
(1953) CD: RCA Victor 09026-60986-2 (70)
(1971) CD: CBS MK 42306 (106)
(1976) CD: Music and Arts CD-666 (115)

Chopin: Waltz No. 7 in C sharp minor (Op. 64/2)
(1946) CD: RCA Victor 09026-60986-2 (38)
(1968) CD: CBS MK 42306 (97)

Chopin: Waltz No. 9 in A flat (Op. 69/1)
    CD: RCA Victor RCD1-4585, 7752-2-RG (124)

Clementi: *Gradus ad Parnassum,* Book I, No. 14—Adagio in F
    CD: Sony Classical SK 48093 (107)

Clementi: Sonata in E flat (Op. 12/2)—Rondo
    CD: Sony Classical SK 48093 (107)

Clementi: Sonata in F minor (Op. 13/6) (aka Op. 14/3)
    CD: RCA Victor 7753-2-RG (71)

Clementi: Sonata in B flat (Op. 24/2) (aka Op. 47/2)—third movement
    CD: RCA Victor 7753-2-RG (51)

Clementi: Sonata in B flat (Op. 25/3)—Rondo
    CD: Sony Classical SK 48093 (83)

Clementi: Sonata in F sharp minor (Op. 25/5) (aka Op. 26/2)
    CD: RCA Victor 7753-2-RG (71)

Clementi: Sonata in C (Op. 33/3) (aka Op. 36/3)
    (April 1979) CD: RCA Victor 7753-2-RG (121)
    (November 1979) CD: Music and Arts CD-666 (122)

Clementi: Sonata in G minor (Op. 34/2)
    CD: RCA Victor 7753-2-RG (71)

Clementi: Sonata in B flat (Op. 50/1)—Adagio
    CD: Sony Classical SK 48093 (82)

Czerny: Variations on Rode's *La ricordanza* (Op. 33)
    CD: RCA Victor 60451-2-RG (30)

Debussy: *Serenade for the Doll* (No. 3 from *Children's Corner* Suite)
    (1928) CD: APR CDAPR 7014; RCA Victor 09026-60526-2 (1)
    (1933) CD: Danacord DACOCD 303 (14)
    (1947) CD: RCA Victor 7755-2-RG (39)
    (1953) CD: RCA Victor 09026-60463-2 (70)
    (1965) CD: CBS MK 42305, M3K 44681 (88)

Debussy: *Pour les arpèges composés* (No. 11 from Etudes, Book II)
(1934) CD: EMI References CDHC 63538; EMI References CHS
7 63538 2 (15)

Debussy: *L'isle joyeuse*
CD: CBS MK 42305, M3K 44681, MK 45829 (90)

Debussy: *Les fées sont d'exquises danseuses* (No. 4 from Preludes, Book II)
LP: Columbia MS-6541 (84)

Debussy: *Bruyères* (No. 5 from Preludes, Book II)
LP: Columbia MS-6541 (84)

Debussy: *General Lavine—eccentric* (No. 6 from Preludes, Book II)
LP: Columbia MS-6541 (84)

Dohnányi: *Capriccio:* Concert Etude in F minor (Op. 28/6)
CD: APR CDAPR 7014; RCA Victor 09026-60986-2 (5)

Fauré: Impromptu No. 5 in F sharp minor (Op. 102)
CD: RCA Victor 09026-60463-2 (119)

Fauré: Nocturne No. 13 in B minor (Op. 119)
CD: RCA Victor 60377-2-RG (119)

Haydn: Sonata in F (Hob. XVI:23)
CD: CBS M3K 44681 (90)

Haydn: Sonata in C (Hob. XVI:48)
CD: CBS MK 45572 (100)

Haydn: Sonata in E flat (Hob. XVI:49)
CD: Sony Classical SK 45818 (133)

Haydn: Sonata in E flat (Hob. XVI:52)
(1932) CD: EMI References CDHC 63538; EMI References CHS
7 63538 2 (10)
(1951) CD: RCA Victor 60461-2-RG (60)

Horowitz: *Danse excentrique*
(1926) CD: Intercord 860.864 (1)
(1928) CD: APR CDAPR 7014; RCA Victor 09026-60526-2 (7)

Horowitz: *Carmen* Variations
    (1926) Piano roll: Welte 4120 (1)
    (April 1928) CD: APR CDAPR 7014; RCA Victor 09026-60526-
       2 (3)
    (ca. June–September 1928) CD: Fone 90 F 12 CD (4)
    (1947) CD: RCA Victor 7755-2-RG (42)
    (1967) CD: Music and Arts CD-666 (94)
    (1968) CD: CBS MK 42305, MK 44797, M3K 44681, MK 45829
       (96)

Horowitz: Waltz in F minor
    CD: Fone 90 F 12 CD (4)

Kabalevsky: Sonata No. 3 in F (Op. 46)
    CD: RCA Victor 60377-2-RG (42)

Liszt: *Au bord d'une source* (No. 4 from *Années de pèlerinage, Suisse*)
    (1947) CD: RCA Victor 60523-2-RG (39)
    (1976) CD: Music and Arts CD-666 (115)

Liszt: Ballade No. 2 in B minor
    CD: RCA Victor RCD1-4585, 5935-2-RC (124)

Liszt: *Consolation* No. 2 in E
    CD: Sony Classical SK 48093 (80)

Liszt: *Consolation* No. 3 in D flat
    (1979) CD: RCA Victor 5935-2-RC (121)
    (1985) CD: Deutsche Grammophon 419 045-2GH, 427 269-
       2GH3; VHS: MGM/VA MV 01085 (126)
    (1987) CDV: Deutsche Grammophon 072 221-1GHG (NTSC),
       072 121-1GH (PAL), VHS: 072 221-3GVG (NTSC), 072
       121-3GH (PAL) (131)

Liszt-Busoni: Fantasia on Two Motives from Mozart's *Marriage of Figaro*
    CD: Intercord 860.864 (1)

Liszt: *Funérailles* (No. 7 from *Harmonies poétiques et religieuses*)
    (1932) CD: EMI References CDHC 63538; EMI References CHS
       7 63538 2; Fidelio 3465 (12)
    (1950) CD: RCA Victor 5935-2-RC (58)

Liszt-Horowitz: Hungarian Rhapsody No. 2 in C sharp minor
    CD: RCA Victor 60523-2-RG (70)

Liszt: Hungarian Rhapsody No. 6 in D flat
    CD: RCA Victor 09026-60463-2 (39)

Liszt-Horowitz: Hungarian Rhapsody No. 15 in A minor, *Rákoczy March*
    CD: RCA Victor 7755-2-RG (46, 51)

Liszt-Horowitz: Hungarian Rhapsody No. 19 in D minor
    LP: Columbia M 35118 (80)

Liszt: Impromptu (Nocturne) in F sharp
    CD: Deutsche Grammophon 419 217-2GH, 427 269-2GH3 (127)

Liszt-Busoni-Horowitz: *Mephisto* Waltz No. 1
    CD: RCA Victor 5935-2-RC (121)

Liszt-Busoni: *Paganini* Etude No. 2 in E flat
    CD: APR CDAPR 7014; RCA Victor 09026-60463-2 (7)

Liszt: Praeludium to Bach's *Weinen, Klagen, Sorgen, Zagen*
    CD: Sony Classical SK 45818 (133)

Liszt: Scherzo and March
    CD: CBS MK 45572 (92)

Liszt: Sonata in B minor
    (1932) CD: EMI References CDHC 63538; EMI References CHS
        7 63538 2; Fidelio 3465 (11)
    (1976) CD: RCA Victor 5935-2-RC (116)

Liszt: *Sonetto 104 del Petrarca* (No. 4 from *Années de pèlerinage, Italie*)
    (1951) CD: RCA Victor 60523-2-RG (61)
    (1986) CD: Deutsche Grammophon 419 499-2GH, 427 269-2GH3
        (129)

Liszt: *Vallée d'Obermann* (No. 6 from *Années de pèlerinage, Suisse*)
    CD: CBS M3K 44681, MK 45829 (90)

Liszt: *Valse oubliée* No. 1 in F sharp
    (1926) Piano roll: Welte 4122 (1)
    (1930) CD: APR CDAPR 7014; RCA Victor 09026-60463-2 (6)
    (1951) CD: RCA Victor 7755-2-RG (61)

(1976) CD: Music and Arts CD-666 (115)
(1985) CD: Deutsche Grammophon 419 217-2GH, 427 269-2GH3
(127)

Medtner: *Fairy Tale* in A (Op. 51/3)
CD: Sony Classical SK 48093 (103)

Mendelssohn: Etude No. 3 in A minor (Op. 104b/3)
CD: CBS MK 45572 (94)

Mendelssohn-Liszt-Horowitz: *Wedding March* and Variations (from *A Midsummer Night's Dream*)
CD: RCA Victor 7755-2-RG (34)

Mendelssohn: *Scherzo a capriccio* in F sharp minor
CD: RCA Victor 7755-2-RG (123)

Mendelssohn: *May Breezes* (No. 25 of *Songs without Words*, Op. 62/1)
CD: RCA Victor 09026-60463-2 (35)

Mendelssohn: *Spring Song* (No. 30 of *Songs without Words*, Op. 62/6)
CD: RCA Victor 7755-2-RG (35)

Mendelssohn: *Shepherd's Complaint* (No. 35 of *Songs without Words*, Op. 67/5)
CD: RCA Victor 7755-2-RG (35)

Mendelssohn: *Elegy* (No. 40 of *Songs without Words*, Op. 85/4)
CD: RCA Victor 7755-2-RG (35)

Mendelssohn: *Variations sérieuses* in D minor (Op. 54)
CD: RCA Victor 60451-2-RG (34)

Moszkowski: *Etincelles* (Op. 36/6)
(1951) CD: RCA Victor 7755-2-RG (60)
(1976) CD: Music and Arts CD-666 (115)
(1986) CD: Deutsche Grammophon 419 499-2GH, 427 269-2GH3
(129)
(1987) CDV: Deutsche Grammophon 072 221-1GHG (NTSC),
072 121-1GH (PAL), VHS: 072 221-3GVG (NTSC), 072
121-3GH (PAL) (131)

Moszkowski: Etude in F (Op. 72/6)
(1950) CD: RCA Victor 7755-2-RG (56)
(1985) CD: Deutsche Grammophon 419 045-2GH, 427 269-2GH3; VHS: MGM/VA MV 01085 (126)

Moszkowski: Etude in A flat (Op. 72/11)
(1949) CD: Stradivarius STR 10037 (48)
(1950) CD: RCA Victor 7755-2-RG (56)
(1965) CD: CBS MK 42305, M3K 44681, MK 44797, MK 45829 (88)

Mozart: Adagio in B minor (K. 540)
CD: Deutsche Grammophon 427 772-2GH (132)

Mozart: Concerto No. 23 in A (K. 488)
CD: Deutsche Grammophon 423 287-2GH, CDV: 072 215-1GHE (NTSC), 072 115-1GH (PAL), VHS: 072 215-3GVG (NTSC), 072 115-3GH (PAL) (130)

Mozart: Rondo in D (K. 485)
(1987) CDV: Deutsche Grammophon 072 221-1GHG (NTSC), 072 121-1GH (PAL), VHS: 072 221-3GVG (NTSC), 072 121-3GH (PAL) (131)
(1988–89) CD: Deutsche Grammophon 427 772-2GH (132)

Mozart: Sonata No. 3 in B flat (K. 281)
CD: Deutsche Grammophon 427 772-2GH, 431 274-2 (132)

Mozart: Sonata No. 10 in C (K. 330)
(1985) CD: Deutsche Grammophon 419 045-2GH, 431 274-2?; VHS: MGM/VA MV 01085 (126)
(1986) CD: Deutsche Grammophon 419 499-2GH, 427 269-2GH3, 431 274-2? (129)

Mozart: Sonata No. 11 in A (K. 331)
(1946)—third movement ("Turkish March")—CD: RCA Victor 7755-2-RG (34)
(1966) CD: M3K 44681, MK 44797; third movement—CD: CBS MK 42305 (89)

Mozart: Sonata No. 12 in F (K. 332)
CD: RCA Victor 60451-2-RG (41)

Mozart: Sonata No. 13 in B flat (K. 333)
    (March 1987) CD: Deutsche Grammophon 423 287-2GH, 427
       269-2GH3, 431 274-2 (130)
    (May 1987) CDV: Deutsche Grammophon 072 221-1GHG
       (NTSC), 072 121-1GH (PAL), VHS: 072 221-3GVG
       (NTSC), 072 121-3GH (PAL) (131)

Mussorgsky-Horowitz: *By the Water* (from *Without Sun*)
    CD: RCA Victor 60449-2-RG (43)

Mussorgsky-Horowitz: *Pictures at an Exhibition*
    (1947) CD: RCA Victor 09026-60526-2 (42)
    (1951) CD: RCA 60321-2-RG, Victor 60449-2-RG (60)

Poulenc: *Pastourelle* in B flat
    CD: EMI References CDHC 63538; EMI References CHS 7 63538
      2 (10)

Poulenc: Presto in B flat
    CD: RCA Victor 60377-2-RG (39)

Poulenc: Toccata
    CD: EMI References CDHC 63538; EMI References CHS 7 63538
      2 (10)

Prokofiev: Sonata No. 7 in B flat (Op. 83)
    (1945) CD: RCA Victor 60377-2-RG (31)
    (1953)—third movement—CD: RCA Victor 09026-60526-2 (70)

Prokofiev: Toccata in D Minor (Op. 11)
    (1930) CD: EMI References CDHC 63538; EMI References CHS
      7 63538 2 (8)
    (1947) CD: RCA Victor 60377-2-RG (43)

Rachmaninoff: Barcarolle in G minor (Op. 10/3)
    CD: RCA Victor 09026-60526-2 (121)

Rachmaninoff: Concerto No. 3 in D minor (Op. 30)
    London Symphony Orchestra/Coates. CD: EMI References CDHC
      63538; EMI References CHS 7 63538 2; Fidelio EB-3, 3465;
      Viola Bellaphon 689-24-003 (8)
    Hollywood Bowl Orchestra/Koussevitzky. CD: AS Disc 550 (55)

RCA Victor Symphony Orchestra/Reiner. CD: RCA Victor 7754-2-RG (63)

New York Philharmonic/Ormandy. CD: RCA Victor RCD1-2633 (120)

Rachmaninoff: *Etude-Tableau* in C (Op. 33/2)
(1962) LP: Columbia KS-6371 (80)
(November 1967) CD: Music and Arts CD-666; Stradivarius STR 10038 (94)
(December 1967) CD: CBS MK 42305 (95)

Rachmaninoff: *Etude-Tableau* in E flat minor (Op. 33/6)
(November 1967) CD: Music and Arts CD-666; Stradivarius STR 10038 (labeled "Op. 33/5") (94)
(December 1967) LP: Columbia M 30464 (95)

Rachmaninoff: *Etude-Tableau* in E flat minor (Op. 39/5)
(1962) LP: Columbia KS-6371 (80)
(1976) CD: Music and Arts CD-666 (115)

Rachmaninoff: *Etude-Tableau* in D (Op. 39/9)
(November 1967) CD: Music and Arts CD-666; Stradivarius STR 10038 (94)
(December 1967) LP: Columbia M 30464 (95)

Rachmaninoff: *Humoresque* in G (Op. 10/5)
CD: RCA Victor 09026-60526-2 (121)

Rachmaninoff: *Moment Musical* No. 2 in E flat minor (Op. 16/2)
CD: RCA Victor 7754-2-RG (118)

Rachmaninoff: *Moment Musical* No. 3 in B minor (Op. 16/3)
(November 1968) CD: Stradivarius STR 10038 (99)
(December 1968) LP: Columbia M 30464 (101)

Rachmaninoff: *Polka de W. R.* in A flat
(1977) CD: RCA Victor 7754-2-RG (118)
(1986) CD: Deutsche Grammophon 419 499-2GH, 427 269-2GH3 (129)

Rachmaninoff: Prelude No. 6 in G minor (Op. 23/5)
(1926) CD: Intercord 860.864 (1)

(1931) CD: EMI References CDHC 63538; EMI References CHS
7 63538 2 (9)
(1981) CD: RCA Victor RCD1-4585, 7755-2-RG (124)

Rachmaninoff: Prelude No. 16 in G (Op. 32/5)
(1926) LP: Sony Superscope KBI 4-A068 (1)
(1977) CD: RCA Victor 7754-2-RG (118)
(1986) CD: Deutsche Grammophon 419 499-2GH, 427 269-2GH3
(129)

Rachmaninoff: Prelude No. 19 in A minor (Op. 32/8)
CD: Fone 90 F 12 CD (4)

Rachmaninoff: Prelude No. 21 in B minor (Op. 32/10)
CD: Fone 90 F 12 CD (4)

Rachmaninoff: Prelude No. 23 in G sharp minor (Op. 32/12)
(1926) LP: Sony Superscope KBI 4-A068 (1)
(November 1968) CD: Stradivarius STR 10038 (99)
(December 1968) CD: CBS MK 42305 (101)
(1976) CD: Music and Arts CD-666 (115)
(1985) CD: Deutsche Grammophon 419 045-2GH; VHS: MGM/
VA MV 01085 (126)
(1986) CD: Deutsche Grammophon 419 499-2GH, 427 269-2GH3
(129)

Rachmaninoff-Horowitz: Sonata No. 2 in B flat minor (Op. 36)
(November 1968) CD: Stradivarius STR 10038 (99)
(December 1968) LP: Columbia M 30464 (101)
(1979) CD: Music and Arts CD-666 (122)
(1980) CD: RCA Victor 7754-2-RG (123)

Rachmaninoff: Cello Sonata in G minor (Op. 19)—third movement
CD: Sony Classical SM2K 46743 (117)

Rimsky-Korsakov–Rachmaninoff: *The Flight of the Bumble-Bee*
CD: EMI References CDHC 63538; EMI References CHS 7 63538
2 (10)

Saint-Saëns–Liszt: *Danse macabre* (Op. 40)
CD: Fone 90 F 12 CD (4)

Saint-Saëns–Liszt–Horowitz: *Danse macabre* (Op. 40)
CD: RCA Victor 7755-2-RG (28)

Scarlatti-Tausig: *Capriccio* (Sonata in E, K. 20, L. 375)
    CD: APR CDAPR 7014; RCA Victor 09026-60986-2 (3)

Scarlatti: Sonata in F sharp minor (K. 25, L. 481)
    CD: Sony Classical SK 48093 (86)

Scarlatti: Sonata in D (K. 33, L. 424)
    CD: CBS MK 42410 (86)

Scarlatti: Sonata in A (K. 39, L. 391)
    CD: CBS MK 42410 (86)

Scarlatti: Sonata in E (K. 46, L. 25)
    CD: RCA Victor 09026-60986-2 (37)

Scarlatti: Sonata in D minor (K. 52, L. 267)
    CD: Sony Classical SK 48093 (86)

Scarlatti: Sonata in A minor (K. 54, L. 241)
    CD: CBS MK 42410 (86)

Scarlatti: Sonata in G (K. 55, L. 335)
    (1967) CD: Music and Arts CD-666 (94)
    (1968) CD: CBS MK 42410, M3K 44681, MK 45829 (96)

Scarlatti: Sonata in B minor (K. 87, L. 33)
    (1935) CD: EMI References CDHC 63538; EMI References CHS
        7 63538 2 (20)
    (1947) CD: RCA Victor 09026-60986-2 (43)
    (1981) CD: RCA Victor RCD1-4585 (124)
    (1985) CD: Deutsche Grammophon 419 217-2GH, 427 269-2GH3
        (127)

Scarlatti: Sonata in D (K. 96, L. 465)
    CD: CBS MK 42410 (86)

Scarlatti: Sonata in A (K. 101, L. 494)
    (1967) CD: Music and Arts CD-666 (94)
    (1981) CD: RCA Victor RCD1-4585 (124)

Scarlatti: Sonata in G (K. 125, L. 487)
    (1935) CD: EMI References CDHC 63538; EMI References CHS
        7 63538 2; Fidelio 3465 (19)

Scarlatti: Sonata in A flat (K. 127, L. 186)
    CD: RCA Victor RCD1-4585 (124)

Scarlatti: Sonata in E (K. 135, L. 224)
    (1981) CD: RCA Victor RCD1-4585 (124)
    (1985) CD: Deutsche Grammophon 419 217-2GH, 427 269-2GH3
        (127)

Scarlatti: Sonata in G (K. 146, L. 349)
    CD: CBS MK 42410 (86)

Scarlatti: Sonata in E (K. 162, L. 21)
    CD: CBS MK 42410 (86)

Scarlatti: Sonata in F minor (K. 184, L. 189)
    CD: RCA Victor RCD1-4585 (124)

Scarlatti: Sonata in A minor (K. 188, L. 239)
    CD: EMI References CDHC 63538; EMI References CHS 7 63538
        2 (64)

Scarlatti: Sonata in G (K. 194, L. 28)
    CD: Sony Classical SK 48093 (86)

Scarlatti: Sonata in B minor (K. 197, L. 147)
    CD: Sony Classical SK 48093 (86)

Scarlatti: Sonata in E minor (K. 198, L. 22)
    CD: CBS MK 42410 (86)

Scarlatti: Sonata in G (K. 201, L. 129)
    CD: Sony Classical SK 48093 (86)

Scarlatti: Sonata in G (K. 260, L. 124)
    (November 12, 1967) CD: CBS MK 45572 (93)
    (November 26, 1967) CD: Music and Arts CD-666 (94)

Scarlatti: Sonata in C minor (K. 303, L. 9)
    CD: Sony Classical SK 48093 (86)

Scarlatti: Sonata in F sharp (K. 319, L. 35)
    (November 12, 1967) CD: CBS MK 45572 (93)
    (November 26, 1967) CD: Music and Arts CD-666 (94)

Scarlatti: Sonata in A (K. 322, L. 483)
  (1946) CD: RCA Victor 09026-60986-2 (37)
  (1951) CD: EMI References CDHC 63538; EMI References CHS
    7 63538 2 (64)
  (1962) CD: CBS MK 42305, MK 42410, MK 44797; Odyssey
    MBK 42534 (81)

Scarlatti: Sonata in E (K. 380, L. 23)
  (1946) CD: RCA Victor 09026-60986-2 (33)
  (1949) CD: Stradivarius STR 10037 (48)
  (1951) CD: RCA Victor 60461-2-RG (60)
  (1968) CD: CBS MK 42410, M3K 44681, MK 45829 (96)
  (1986) CD: Deutsche Grammophon 419 499-2GH, 427 269-2GH3
    (129)

Scarlatti: Sonata in G (K. 455, L. 209)
  (1946) CD: RCA Victor 09026-60986-2 (33)
  (1962) CD: CBS MK 42410; Odyssey MBK 42534 (81)

Scarlatti: Sonata in F minor (K. 466, L. 118)
  (1964) CD: CBS MK 42410 (86)
  (1967) CD: Music and Arts CD-666 (94)
  (1981) CD: RCA Victor RCD1-4585 (124)

Scarlatti: Sonata in E flat (K. 474, L. 203)
  CD: CBS MK 42410 (86)

Scarlatti: Sonata in F minor (K. 481, L. 187)
  CD: CBS MK 42410 (86)

Scarlatti: Sonata in D (K. 491, L. 164)
  CD: CBS MK 42410 (86)

Scarlatti: Sonata in F (K. 525, L. 188)
  CD: CBS MK 42410 (86)

Scarlatti: Sonata in E (K. 531, L. 430)
  (1947) CD: RCA Victor 09026-60986-2 (42)
  (1962) CD: CBS MK 42305, MK 42410, MK 44797; Odyssey
    MBK 42534 (81)

Schubert: Impromptu in E flat (D. 899/2, Op. 90/2)
  LP: Columbia M 32432 (112)

Schubert-von Bülow: Impromptu in G (D. 899/3, Op. 90/3)
    CD: RCA Victor 60523-2-RG (68)

Schubert: Impromptu in G flat (D. 899/3, Op. 90/3)
    (1962) CD: CBS MK 42305; Odyssey MBK 42534 (81)
    (1987) CDV: Deutsche Grammophon 072 221-1GHG (NTSC),
        072 121-1GH (PAL), VHS: 072 221-3GVG (NTSC), 072
        121-3GH (PAL) (131)

Schubert: Impromptu in A flat (D. 899/4, Op. 90/4)
    (1973) LP: Columbia M 32432 (112)
    (1985) CD: Deutsche Grammophon 419 045-2GH, 427 269-
        2GH3; VHS: MGM/VA MV 01085 (126)

Schubert: Impromptu in F minor (D. 935/1, Op. 142/1)
    LP: Columbia M 32432 (112)

Schubert: Impromptu in A flat (D. 935/2, Op. 142/2)
    LP: Columbia M 32432 (112)

Schubert: Impromptu in B flat (D. 935/3, Op. 142/3)
    CD: Deutsche Grammophon 419 217-2GH, 427 269-2GH3 (127)

Schubert-Tausig-Horowitz: *Marche militaire* in D flat (D. 733/1, Op.
51/1)
    CD: Deutsche Grammophon 419 217-2GH, 427 269-2GH3 (127)

Schubert: *Moment Musical* No. 3 in F minor (D. 780/3, Op. 94/3)
    (1986) CD: Deutsche Grammophon 427 772-2GH (128)
    (1987) CDV: Deutsche Grammophon 072 221-1GHG (NTSC),
        072 121-1GH (PAL), VHS: 072 221-3GVG (NTSC), 072
        121-3GH (PAL) (131)

Schubert-Liszt: *Liebesbotschaft* (No. 1 from *Schwanengesang*, D. 957)
    (1926) CD: Intercord 860.864 (1)
    (1928) CD: Fone 90 F 12 CD (4)

Schubert-Liszt: *Ständchen* (No. 4 from *Schwanengesang*, D. 957)
    CD: Deutsche Grammophon 427 772-2GH (128)

Schubert: Sonata No. 21 in B flat (D. 960)
    (1953) CD: RCA Victor 60451-2-RG (70)
    (1986) CD: Deutsche Grammophon 435 025-2GH (128)

Schubert-Liszt: *Soirées de Vienne: Valse-Caprice* No. 6
(February 1986) CD: Deutsche Grammophon 427 772-2GH (128)
(April 1986) CD: Deutsche Grammophon 419 499-2GH (129)
(1987) CDV: Deutsche Grammophon 072 221-1GHG (NTSC), 072 121-1GH (PAL), VHS: 072 221-3GVG (NTSC), 072 121-3GH (PAL) (131)

Schubert-Liszt: *Soirées de Vienne: Valse-Caprice* No. 7
CD: Deutsche Grammophon 427 772-2GH (132)

Schumann: *Arabesque* in C (Op. 18)
(1934) CD: EMI References CDHC 63538; EMI References CHS 7 63538 2 (15)
(1950) 45rpm: RCA Victor 49-3304 (probably unissued) (57)
(1962) LP: Columbia KS-6371 (80)
(1968) CD: CBS MK 42305, MK 42409, M3K 44681, MK 45829 (96)
(1976) CD: Music and Arts CD-666 (115)

Schumann: *Blumenstück* in D flat (Op. 19)
CD: CBS MK 42409, M3K 44681 (91)

Schumann: *Dichterliebe* (Op. 48)
CD: Sony Classical SM2K 46743 (117)

Schumann: Fantasy in C (Op. 17)
CD: CBS M3K 44681 (88)

Schumann: *Traumeswirren* (No. 7 from *Fantasiestücke*, Op. 12)
CD: EMI References CDHC 63538; EMI References CHS 7 63538 2 (12)

Schumann: *Fantasiestücke* (Op. 111)
CD: RCA Victor 6680-2-RG (123)

Schumann: *Humoresque* in B flat (Op. 20)
CD: RCA Victor 6680-2-RG (121)

Schumann: *Kinderscenen* (Op. 15)
(1950) CD: RCA Victor 09026-60463-2 (51)
(1962) CD: CBS MK 42409; Odyssey MBK 42534 (81)
(1982) CD: RCA Victor RCD1-4572 (125)

(1987) CDV: Deutsche Grammophon 072 221-1GHG (NTSC), 072 121-1GH (PAL), VHS: 072 221-3GVG (NTSC), 072 121-3GH (PAL), CD: Deutsche Grammophon 435 025-2GH (131)

Schumann: *Träumerei* (No. 7 from *Kinderscenen*, Op. 15)
(1947) CD: RCA Victor 60461-2-RG (43)
(1949) CD: Stradivarius STR 10037 (48)
(1950) CD: RCA Victor 7755-2-RG (from complete recording) (51)
(1965) CD: CBS M3K 44681, MK 45829? (88)
(1968) CD: CBS MK 42305, M3K 44681, MK 44797, MK 45829? (96)
(1976) CD: Music and Arts CD-666 (115)
(1986) CD: Deutsche Grammophon 419 499-2GH, 427 269-2GH3 (129)

Schumann: *Kreisleriana* (Op. 16)
(1968) CD: Stradivarius STR 10038 (99)
(1969) CD: CBS MK 42409 (105)
(1985) CD: Deutsche Grammophon 419 217-2GH, 427 269-2GH3 (127)

Schumann: *Nachtstück* in D flat (Op. 23/3)
CD: RCA Victor 6680-2-RG (123)

Schumann: *Nachtstück* in F (Op. 23/4)
CD: RCA Victor 6680-2-RG (123)

Schumann: *Novellette* in F (Op. 21/1)
CD: Deutsche Grammophon 419 045-2GH, 427 269-2GH3; VHS: MGM/VA MV 01085 (126)

Schumann: *Presto passionato* in G minor (Op. 22)
CD: EMI References CDHC 63538; EMI References CHS 7 63538 2 (12)

Schumann: Grand Sonata No. 3 in F minor (*Concerto without Orchestra,* Op. 14)
(1951)—third movement—CD: RCA Victor 09026-60463-2 (59)
(1969)—third movement—LP: Columbia MS-7264 (102)
(February 1976) CD: RCA Victor 6680-2-RG (114)
(May 1976) CD: Music and Arts CD-666 (115)

Schumann: Toccata in C (Op. 7)
  (1934) CD: EMI References CDHC 63538; EMI References CHS
    7 63538 2 (16)
  (1962) CD: CBS MK 42305, MK 42409; Odyssey MBK 42534
    (81)

Scriabin: Etude in C sharp minor (Op. 2/1)
  (1950) CD: RCA Victor 09026-60526-2 (51)
  (1962) CD: CBS MK 42305, MK 42411; Odyssey MBK 42534
    (81)
  (1965) CD: CBS M3K 44681 (88)
  (1985) CD: Deutsche Grammophon 419 045-2GH, 427 269-
    2GH3; VHS: MGM/VA MV 01085 (126)
  (1986) CD: Deutsche Grammophon 419 499-2GH (129)

Scriabin: Etude in F sharp minor (Op. 8/2)
  CD: CBS MK 42411 (107)

Scriabin: Etude in A flat (Op. 8/8)
  CD: CBS MK 42411 (107)

Scriabin: Etude in D flat (Op. 8/10)
  CD: CBS MK 42411 (107)

Scriabin: Etude in B flat minor (Op. 8/11)
  (1953) CD: RCA Victor 6215-2-RG (mislabeled "Op. 8/7") (70)
  (1972) CD: CBS MK 42411 (107)

Scriabin: Etude in D sharp minor (Op. 8/12)
  (1962) CD: CBS MK 42305, MK 42411; Odyssey MBK 42534
    (81)
  (1968) CD: CBS M3K 44681, MK 44797, MK 45829 (96)
  (1982) CD: RCA Victor RCD1-4572, 6215-2-RG (125)
  (1985) CD: Deutsche Grammophon 419 217-2GH, 427 269-2GH3
    (127)
  (1986) CD: Deutsche Grammophon 419 499-2GH (129)

Scriabin: Etude in F sharp (Op. 42/3)
  CD: CBS MK 42411 (107)

Scriabin: Etude in F sharp (Op. 42/4)
  CD: CBS MK 42411 (107)

Scriabin: Etude in C sharp minor (Op. 42/5)
  (1953) CD: RCA Victor 6215-2-RG (70)
  (1972) CD: CBS MK 42411 (108)

Scriabin: Etude (Op. 65/3)
  CD: Sony Classical SK 48093 (107)

Scriabin: *Feuillet d'album* in E flat (Op. 45/1)
  CD: CBS MK 42411 (108)

Scriabin: *Feuillet d'album* (Op. 58)
  CD: Sony Classical SK 48093 (107)

Scriabin: *Poème* in F sharp (Op. 32/1)
  (1962) CD: CBS MK 42411; Odyssey MBK 42534 (81)
  (1965) CD: CBS M3K 44681 (88)

Scriabin: *Poème* (Op. 69/1)
  LP: Columbia M 31620 (108)

Scriabin: *Poème* (Op. 69/2)
  LP: Columbia M 31620 (108)

Scriabin: Prelude in C (Op. 11/1)
  CD: RCA Victor 6215-2-RG (74)

Scriabin: Prelude in G (Op. 11/3)
  CD: RCA Victor 6215-2-RG (74)

Scriabin: Prelude in D (Op. 11/5)
  CD: RCA Victor 09026-60526-2 (74)

Scriabin: Prelude in E (Op. 11/9)
  CD: RCA Victor 6215-2-RG (74)

Scriabin: Prelude in C sharp minor (Op. 11/10)
  CD: RCA Victor 6215-2-RG (74)

Scriabin: Prelude in G flat (Op. 11/13)
  CD: RCA Victor 6215-2-RG (74)

Scriabin: Prelude in E flat minor (Op. 11/14)
  CD: RCA Victor 6215-2-RG (74)

Scriabin: Prelude in B flat minor (Op. 11/16)
CD: RCA Victor 6215-2-RG (74)

Scriabin: Prelude in B minor (Op. 13/6)
CD: RCA Victor 6215-2-RG (74)

Scriabin: Prelude in F sharp minor (Op. 15/2)
CD: RCA Victor 6215-2-RG (74)

Scriabin: Prelude in B (Op. 16/1)
CD: RCA Victor 6215-2-RG (74)

Scriabin: Prelude in E flat minor (Op. 16/4)
CD: RCA Victor 6215-2-RG (74)

Scriabin: Prelude in G sharp minor (Op. 22/1)
CD: RCA Victor 09026-60526-2 (74)

Scriabin: Prelude in G minor (Op. 27/1)
CD: RCA Victor 6215-2-RG (74)

Scriabin: Prelude in D flat (Op. 48/3)
CD: RCA Victor 6215-2-RG (74)

Scriabin: Prelude in A minor (Op. 51/2)
CD: RCA Victor 6215-2-RG (74)

Scriabin: Prelude (Op. 59/2)
CD: RCA Victor 6215-2-RG (74)

Scriabin: Prelude (Op. 67/1)
CD: RCA Victor 6215-2-RG (74)

Scriabin: Sonata No. 3 in F sharp minor (Op. 23)
CD: RCA Victor 6215-2-RG (72)

Scriabin: Sonata No. 5 (Op. 53)
CD: RCA Victor 6215-2-RG (114)

Scriabin: Sonata No. 9, *Black Mass* (Op. 68)
(1953) CD: RCA Victor 09026-60526-2 (70)
(1965) CD: CBS MK 42411, CBS M3K 44681, MK 45829 (88)

Scriabin: Sonata No. 10 (Op. 70)
    CD: CBS MK 42411, CBS M3K 44681 (89)

Scriabin: *Vers la flamme* (Op. 72)
    CD: CBS MK 42411 (108)

Sousa-Horowitz: *The Stars and Stripes Forever*
    (1949) CD: Stradivarius STR 10037 (48)
    (1950) CD: RCA Victor 09026-60526-2 (58)
    (1951) CD: RCA Victor 7755-2-RG (60)

Stravinsky: "Russian Dance" (from *Petrushka*)
    CD: EMI References CDHC 63538; EMI References CHS 7 63538
        2 (10)

Tchaikovsky: Concerto No. 1 in B flat minor (Op. 23)
    Denmark Radio Symphony Orchestra/Malko (only third movement
        survives). CD: Danacord DACOCD 303 (17)
    NBC Symphony Orchestra/Toscanini (April 19, 1941). CD: Bella-
        phon 689 24-001 (25)
    NBC Symphony/Toscanini (May 6 & 14, 1941). CD: RCA Victor
        60319-2-RG, 60449-2-RG (26)
    NBC Symphony/Toscanini (1943). CD: Classical Society CSCD
        103; Melodram MEL 18014; RCA Victor 7992-2-RG, 60321-
        2-RG (29)
    New York Philharmonic/Walter. CD: AS Disc AS 400 (44)
    Hollywood Bowl Orchestra/Steinberg. CD: Stradivarius STR 10037
        (48)
    New York Philharmonic/Szell. CD: Movimento Musica 011.007
        (69)

Tchaikovsky: *Dumka* in C minor (Op. 59)
    (1928) Piano roll: Duo-Art 7281-4 (4)
    (1942) CD: RCA Victor 09026-60526-2 (27)

Tchaikovsky: Trio in A minor (Op. 50)—first movement
    CD: Sony Classical SM2K 46743 (117)

Wagner-Liszt: *Liebestod* from *Tristan und Isolde*
    CD: Sony Classical SK 45818 (133)

Performer Index

Albert Coates, conductor (8)
Concertgebouw Orchestra of Amsterdam (21)
Denmark Radio Symphony Orchestra (17)
Dietrich Fischer-Dieskau, baritone (117)
Carlo Maria Giulini, conductor (130)
Hollywood Bowl Orchestra (48), (55)
Serge Koussevitzky, conductor (55)
London Symphony Orchestra (8)
Nikolai Malko, conductor (17)
Nathan Milstein, violinist (54)
NBC Symphony Orchestra (23), (24), (25), (26), (29), (45)
New York Philharmonic (18), (44), (69)
RCA Victor Symphony Orchestra (63), (66)
Fritz Reiner, conductor (63), (66)
Mstislav Rostropovich, cellist (117)
La Scala Theatre Orchestra (130)
William Steinberg, conductor (48)
Isaac Stern, violinist (117)
George Szell, conductor (69)
Arturo Toscanini, conductor (18), (23), (24), (25), (26), (29), (45)
Bruno Walter, conductor (21), (44)

Index

A

Abendzeitung (Hamburg), 277
"Accelerated" piano action, 126–
     127
Acciaccaturas, 305
Agoult, Marie-Catherine-Sophie
     d', 9, 315
Airplane travel, 243
Aitken, Webster, 167
Alkan, Charles-Valentin
     Morhange, 54
American pianists, 122–23
American Red Cross, 158
American-Soviet cultural
     exchange, 22, 284
Amsterdam Concertgebouw, 125,
     143, 286, 287
Amsterdam critics, 286, 287
Annenberg, Walter H., 284
Annie, Sister, 233
Anti-Semitism, 47, 91, 98, 103,
     104, 145
Appoggiaturas, 305
Arensky, Anton, 54
Arrau, Claudio, 15, 122, 168
Arroyo, Martina, 248
Art collections, 118–19
Asahi Shimbun (newspaper), 264,
     283
AS Disc (firm), 325
Ashkenazy, Vladimir, 14, 112,
     206, 323
Attisami, Lois, 213
Audiences, 243

Auer, Leopold, 56–57
Avery Fisher Hall, 250, 256–57
Ax, Emanuel, 169
Ayer, N. W. (firm), 252

B

Bach, Johann Sebastian, 216, 309,
     339–40, 353
Bach, Virginia, 308
Backhaus, Wilhelm, 73
*Baker's Biographical Dictionary of
     Musicians,* 36–37
Barber, Samuel, 170, 253, 330
Barbirolli, John, 156, 331
Barenboim, Daniel, 288, 323
Barere, Simon, 52–53, 327–
     328
Bassiano, Rofredo, 87
Battistini, Mattia, 59, 185, 193
Beatrix, Queen, 286
Becalel, Alfons, 293
Bechstein pianos, 20, 72, 83
Beecham, Thomas, 102, 105–7,
     108, 125, 150, 173, 249
Beethoven, Ludwig van
   Clementi and, 197, 329
   compositions of
     Concerto No. 3, Op. 37, C
        minor, 54, 141
     Concerto No. 5, Op. 73, E
        flat major (*Emperor*), 92,
        135–36, 138, 139, 140,
        332

Beethoven, Ludwig van, *continued*
   Sonata No. 37, Op. 10, No.
      3, D major, 334–35
   Sonata No. 38, Op. 13, C
      minor (*Pathétique*), 337
   Sonata No. 14, Op. 27, No.
      2, C sharp minor
      (*Moonlight*), 325–26, 334,
      342
   Sonata No. 21, Op. 53, C
      major (*Waldstein*), 121,
      334
   Sonata No. 23, Op. 57, F
      minor (*Appassionata*),
      335–36, 342
   Sonata No. 28, Op. 101, A
      major, 263, 264, 341
   Sonata No. 29, Op. 106, B
      flat major
      (*Hammerklavier*), 152
   Sonatas, 15, 138–39
   Symphony No. 3, Op. 55, E
      flat major (*Eroica*), 132
   Symphony No. 9, Op. 125, D
      minor (*Choral*), 349
   32 Variations, C minor, 326
   metronome markings of, 348,
      349
   pianism of, 167–68
   Rachmaninoff and, 111–12
   Schnabel on, 72
Behrman, Sam, 170
Belgiojoso, Cristina, 9
Bell Telephone Laboratories, 321
Benches, piano, 129–30
Bennert, Klaus, 285–86
Berdichev (Ukraine), 36–38
Berg, Alban, 67, 337
Berlin, 67–68, 100
Berlin Philharmonic, 99, 282,
   283
Berlin Städtische Oper, 67
Berlin Symphony, 74, 77
Berlioz, Hector, 348
Bernheimer, Martin, 224
Bernstein, Leonard, 248, 349
Bertensson, Sergei, 104, 155

Big Blackout (New York, 1965),
   219, 220
Bild (Berlin), 281
Bizet, Georges, 15
Bloom, Julius, 210, 211, 221,
   225, 247, 248, 249
Blumenfeld, Felix, 44, 51, 53, 55,
   64, 65, 197
Blumfield, Coleman, 195–96
Bodick, Alexander, 39
Bodick, Natasha. *See* Saitzoff,
   Natasha
Bodick family, 37–38
Boesen-Courier (Berlin), 97
Le boeuf sur le toit (Milhaud), 87
Bonanza (television program), 224
Bonnard, Pierre, 82
Boris Godunov (Mussorgsky), 51
Boston Symphony, 230
Boulanger, Nadia, 87, 166
Boxing, 30
Box office mismanagement, 169,
   230–31, 254
Bracker, Milton, 189
Brahms, Johannes
   Concerto for Violin, 140
   Concerto No. 1, Op. 15, D
      minor, 142–44, 286
   Concerto No. 2, Op. 83, B flat
      major, 72, 93, 98, 123–
      124, 142, 154
   Paganini Variations, Op. 35, A
      minor, 122
   Trio No. 2, Op. 87, C major,
      99–100
Brailowsky, Alexander, 92, 322
Breest, Gunther, 268, 269, 308
Brendel, Alfred, 225
Broesecke-Schön, Max, 79, 80
Browning, Kirk, 261
Bülow, Hans von, 337, 348
Busch, Adolf, 135, 152
Busch Quartet, 152
Busoni, Ferruccio, 64, 92, 116,
   139, 302, 303, 351
   Etude, E flat major (after
      Paganini-Liszt), 327

Mephisto Waltz (after Liszt), 344
Toccata, Adagio, and Fugue, C
    major (after Bach), 216,
    339–40

C

Cadenzas, 303
Canasta, 185, 186
Cardus, Neville, 124–25
Carnegie, Andrew, 247
Carnegie Hall performances of
    Horowitz
    1928: 109–11
    1931: 115
    1940: 154
    1942–45: 157
    1943: 158, 324
    1945–51: 208
    1945: 158
    1953: 174, 324–25, 333
    1965: 210–20, 339–40
    1966: 222, 340–41
    1968: 223–24, 341
    1976: 247–49, 343
    1978: 249–51, 254–55, 344
    1986: 288–89
Carter, Jimmy, 252–53, 254
Casals, Pablo, 346
Castelbarco, Wally, 133, 137, 145,
    154, 200, 315
CBS, Inc., 26, 30, 223–24. *See
    also* Columbia Broad-
    casting System, Inc.;
    Sony/CBS Records (firm)
Chaliapin, Feodor, 51, 58, 113
Chapin, Schuyler, 202, 205, 215,
    216, 229, 230
Charles, Prince of Wales, 22, 258,
    260, 261
Charlton, Linda, 253
Chasins, Abram, 176, 185, 196,
    207
"Cheating" techniques, 172
Chekhov, Anton Pavlovich, 113
Chernobyl disaster, 34

Chicago Symphony, 98–99, 135
Child prodigies, 40–42
Chisell, Joan, 261–62
Chopin, Frédéric
    compositions of
        Andante Spianato and
            Polonaise, 83, 209, 326
        Ballade, Op. 23, G minor,
            217, 245, 251, 326, 340
        Ballade, Op. 52, F minor, 73,
            345
        Barcarolle, 344
        Concerto No. 2, Op. 21, F
            minor, 65
        Etude, Op. 10, No. 1, C
            major, 73
        Etude, Op. 10, No. 8, F
            major, 217
        Etudes, 57, 57–58
        Introduction and Rondo, Op.
            16, E flat major, 342
        Nocturne, Op. 55, No. 2, E
            flat major, 294, 353
        Polonaise, Op. 40, No. 1, A
            major, 342
        Polonaise, Op. 53, A flat
            major, 269, 279
        Polonaise-Fantaisie, Op. 61,
            A flat major, 220, 331
        Scherzo, Op. 20, B minor,
            269, 286, 337
        Sonata, Op. 35, B flat minor
            (*Funeral March*), 71, 167,
            170, 241, 297–98, 330–
            331, 336
    Cortot edition of, 91–92
    Friedman interpretations of, 94
    Godowsky interpretations of,
        95
    modern pianos and, 350
    recordings of, 326, 332–33,
        335, 352–53
    rubato of, 349
    Slavic interpretations of, 69
Chotzinoff, Samuel, 66, 161, 163,
    234
Civic (concert agency), 120

Classic performance practice, 346–347
Clementi, Muzio, 190, 194, 197–198, 329, 334, 344
Cliburn, Van, 322
Cliburn Competition, 301
Coates, Albert, 124, 251, 321, 331
Cocteau, Jean, 87
Collard, Jean-Philippe, 255, 271, 314
Columbia Artists Management, Inc., 102, 196, 258–60
Columbia Broadcasting System, Inc., 101. *See also* CBS, Inc.
Columbia Concerts (firm), 101, 102, 119, 134
Columbia Pictures (firm), 207
Columbia Presents Vladimir Horowitz (recording), 202, 320
Columbia Records (firm)
  Graffman and, 201–2
  Horowitz and, 202–5, 218–20, 225, 243–44, 268, 284–285, 336
  Judson and, 101
Community Concerts (firm), 101, 120, 121
Concert halls, 289
Concert performances of Horowitz, 92, 120–22, 154–55, 170, 243
  Amsterdam (1936, 1986), 143, 286–87
  Berlin (1926, 1929, 1986, 1987), 74–79, 125, 280–283, 290–91
  Boston (1928), 116
  Cleveland (1974), 227–28
  Dortmund, 123–24
  England (1930, 1932), 124–25
  Frankfurt (1986), 285–86
  Hamburg (1926, 1927, 1986), 79–81, 97, 99, 277–80
  Jacksonville, 121

Kiev (1920), 55, 56
Leningrad (1923, 1986), 32–35, 62–64
London (1951, 1982), 173, 260–62, 345
Los Angeles (1942), 156
Miami (1977), 240–41
Milan (1985), 273
Moscow (1923, 1986), 19–32, 60–61, 181
New York
  1928: 102, 105–11
  1931: 115
  1933: 135–36
  1934: 142–43
  1940: 154
  1942–45: 157
  1943: 158, 166, 324
  1945: 158
  1953 (*Silver Jubilee*): 173–74, 324–25, 333, 340
  1965: 210–20, 339–40
  1966: 222, 340–41
  1968: 222–24, 341
  1974: 228–31
  1976: 247–49, 343
  1978 (*Golden Jubilee*): 249–251, 254–56, 344
  1979: 256–57
  1981: 260, 345
  1983: 263–64
  1986: 287–89
Paris (1926–27, 1933, 1985), 82–95, 100–101, 138, 271–73
Pasadena (1976), 245–46
Philadelphia (1929, 1934), 116, 140
Tokyo (1983, 1986), 228, 264–265, 283
Vienna (1987), 289–90, 354
Washington, D.C. (1931, 1978, 1986), 115, 252–54, 283–84
Zurich (1938), 152
Conductors, 125–26, 132, 139–140

Conversations with Arrau (Joseph Horowitz), 168
Correspondent (Hamburg), 97
Cortot, Alfred-Denis, 69, 90–92, 128, 138
Cottle, Maurice, 155
Courir, Duilio, 273
Critics
  Amsterdam, 286, 287
  Frankfurt, 285–86
  Germany, 97
  Hamburg, 279–80
  New York, 107–9, 165–68, 218
  Paris, 85, 272–73
  Tokyo, 264–65, 283
  Vienna, 290
Croan, Robert, 113
Cultural exchange, Soviet-American, 22, 284
Curzon, Clifford, 322
Cutner, Solomon, 15
Czerny, Carl, 167, 326, 348

D

Darré, Jeanne-Marie, 186
Davis, Ivan, 200, 207–9, 212, 226
Davis, Peter G., 255, 299
Debussy, Claude, 112, 337
Demeny, 90
Deutsche Grammophon Gesellschaft
  CBS/Sony and, 308–9
  Horowitz recordings for, 269–271, 290, 291, 333
  The Last Romantic and, 268, 269
  Moscow concert (1986) and, 26
Devries, Herman, 117, 124
Diaghilev, Sergei, 51
Diana, Princess of Wales, 261
Diesterweg, Adolf, 77
Dobrowen, Issay, 135

Dolberg, Yelena, 23, 31
Dombrowski, Marian, 45
Domingo, Placido, 280
Donizetti, Gaetano, 185
Dorfmann, Ania, 207
Dover sole, 24
Downes, Olin
  Janis and, 163
  Judson and, 102
  on Horowitz
    New York debut, 106, 107–108, 109–10
    Silver Jubilee Concert, 173–174, 325
    with Toscanini (1935), 144
Drucker, Judith, 240–41
Dubal, David, 293, 295, 300, 303
Dubinin, Yuri, 284
Dümling, Albrecht, 281
Duo Art piano rolls, 320
Dynagroove LP discs, 171

E

Early-instrument movement, 347–348
Echo (Hamburg), 79, 81
Edison, Thomas, 126
Electrical recording, 321
Elman, Mischa, 57
Englander, Roger, 223
Epstein, Helen, 214, 215, 243, 254
Ericson, Raymond, 229
Essipov, Annette, 44
Eugene Onegin (Tchaikovsky), 34, 340
Evening World (New York), 107

F

Fauré, Gabriel, 254, 255
La Favorita (Donizetti), 185

Feinstein, Martin, 188, 189
Feltsman, Vladimir, 21, 25, 28–
    29, 31–32, 313, 323
Fernseh-Produktionsgesellschaft,
    253
Field, John, 197
Field, Sampson, 244
Films, 120. See also *Vladimir
    Horowitz: The Last
    Romantic*
Fingering technique, 171–72
Finn, Robert, 224
Fiorillo, Alexander, 200–201
Firkusny, Rudolf, 85–86, 294,
    300
Fischer, Edwin, 73
Fischer-Dieskau, Dietrich, 248,
    249, 343
Fleisher, Leon, 192
Flier, Jacob, 21
Frank, Claude, 304, 341
Frankfurt critics, 285–86
French pianists, 69
Fried, Oskar, 77
Friedberg, Annie, 159
Friedberg, Carl, 117
Friedman, Ignaz, 73, 94, 128,
    153, 294, 353
Froemke, Susan, 306
From Russia to the West (Milstein),
    57
Frost, Thomas, 191, 202–5, 266
    death of Horowitz and, 311,
        312
    final Horowitz recording and,
        308, 309, 310
    Halim and, 299
    Horowitz at Home and, 284–85,
        307–8
    Klein and, 219
    post–*The Last Romantic*
        recordings and, 269, 270
    Project X and, 223
    Shehori and, 304
    Yale University and, 285
Furtwängler, Wilhelm, 72, 98–99,
    106

G

Ganz, Rudolf, 128
Garbousova, Raya, 61
Gaubert, Philippe, 85
Gaveau pianos, 83, 84, 85
Gavoty, Bernard, 92, 173
Geitel, Klaus, 280–81, 282
Gelb, Arthur, 229
Gelb, Peter, 276
    death of Horowitz and, 311,
        312, 313, 314
    Halim and, 293
    The Last Romantic and, 266–68
    Metropolitan Opera House
        recital (1974) and, 229–
        230
    Mozart A major Piano Concerto
        recording and, 306
    on idiosyncracies of Horowitz,
        242
    Royal Festival Hall concert
        (1982) and, 261
    Russian tour (1986) and, 20,
        21, 22, 23–24, 25, 26–27
    Smith and, 274
General Telephone and Electronics
    Corp., 224
George Junior Republic School,
    236
German conductors, 132, 139–
    140
German critics, 97
German pianists, 69, 70, 73, 86
Germany, 100
Gershwin, George, 128, 169
Gieseking, Walter, 73, 93, 290
Gilels, Emil, 15, 52, 206, 322
Gill, Dominic, 261
Gilman, Lawrence, 102, 136,
    142–43, 144
Ginsburg, Gregory, 62
Giulini, Carlo Maria, 13, 305–6,
    351
Glancy, Kenneth, 243–44
Glazunov, Alexander, 58, 60, 62
Glière, Reinhold, 46

Globe (Boston), 116
Godowsky, Leopold, 52, 95, 112,
    297, 352
Goebbels, Joseph, 99
Golden Jubilee Concerts, 249–51,
    254–56
Golovin, Alexis, 237
Golschmann, Vladimir, 118
Gorbachev, Mikhail, 22, 23, 26,
    35
Gorodnitzki, Sascha, 293–94
Gorowitz. *See* Horowitz
Gosconcert, 23, 24
Gostel Radio, 26
Gottschalk, Louis Moreau, 96–97
Gould, Glenn, 14
Grace Rainey Rogers Auditorium,
    307
Gradova, Gitta, 122–23, 155, 195
Graffman, Gary, 189–90, 191–
    195, 201–2, 216, 292
Graffman, Naomi, 192, 236
Grainger, Percy, 128
Grammy Awards, 320
Gramophone (periodical), 307
Gray sole, 241
Great Pianists Speak for Themselves
    (Mach), 320
Greenfield, Edward, 262
Greiner, Alexander ("Sascha")
    Horowitz correspondence with,
        97, 153
    Lhevinne and, 126
    on Merovitch, 119–20
    on piano tuners, 129
    Rachmaninoff and, 103, 104,
        111, 128
    Schnabel and, 72
Grieg, Edvard, 54
Grosz, George, 68
Gruen, John, 142
Gunn, Glenn Dillard, 116–17,
    124
Gurtman and Murtha (firm), 229,
    230
Gutheil (firm), 116
Gutierrez, Horacio, 46, 48, 245

H

Haberman, Clyde, 265, 283
Haggin, B. H., 167
Halim, Eduardus, 292–301, 306,
    312
Halim, Judy, 295
Hambro, Leonid, 160, 171–72
Hamburg critics, 279–80
Hamburger Morgenpost
    (newspaper), 279
Harlem School of the Arts, 184
Harris, Cyril, 230, 250
Harrison, Sidney, 167
Hartman, Arthur A., 23, 24, 26,
    181, 284
Hartman, Donna, 29
Haydn, Joseph, 291, 323, 331,
    340, 341, 353
Heck Brothers (firm), 169
Heg, Hans, 287
Heifetz, Jascha
    Auer and, 57
    Chotzinoff and, 161
    Graffman and, 192
    Horowitz and, 16, 117
    Rabinovich and, 110
    Arthur Rubinstein and, 94
    Thomson on, 166
Henahan, Donal, 227–28, 229,
    231, 263–64
Henderson, W. J., 109, 142
Herald Tribune (New York), 102,
    165, 211
Herbort, Heinz Josef, 279
Herz, Henri, 69
Hess, Myra, 128
Hickenlooper, Lucy. *See* Samaroff,
    Olga
Hitler, Adolf, 81, 100, 103, 124,
    153
Hoërée, Arthur, 84
Hofmann, Josef
    Horowitz and, 14, 48, 126, 127
    in Philadelphia, 116
    Anton Rubinstein and, 34
    in St. Petersburg, 63

Hofmann, Josef, *continued*
  Schubert-Tausig *Marche
    militaire* and, 352
  Steinway & Sons and, 128
  Vengerova and, 191
Holcman, Jan, 339
Holland, Bernard, 287–88
Hollywood Bowl concerts, 142
Hoover, Herbert, 115
Horowitz, Alexander (uncle), 19–
    20, 40, 56, 57, 59
Horowitz, George (brother), 23,
    55
Horowitz, Jacob (brother), 23, 55
Horowitz, Joseph, 168
Horowitz, Regina (*or* Genya,
    sister), 23, 45, 46, 57–58,
    71, 145
Horowitz, Samuel (father)
  Garbousova and, 61
  last years of, 144–45
  marriage of, 37
  Merovitch and, 66
  on Tchaikovsky B flat minor
    concerto, 65
  on Vladimir's future, 42
  residences of, 38, 61
  Russian Revolution and, 54–55
  Saitzoff on, 39
  Zeitlin and, 60
Horowitz, Sonia (daughter), 232–
    238
  birth of, 144
  at Carnegie Hall recital (1965),
    217
  childhood and youth of, 145–
    146, 155, 164–65
  death of, 231, 237–38, 239
  injured, 199–200
  Lopes and, 267
  parents' marital problems and,
    169
  in wartime Europe, 154
Horowitz, Sophie (mother)
  death of, 144, 148, 232
  Dombrowski and, 49
  marriage of, 37

Rachmaninoff and, 49
  residences of, 38, 61
  Saitzoff on, 39–40
  Tarnowsky and, 48
  in Vladimir's development, 43,
    199
Horowitz, Vladimir
  art collections of, 118–19, 207
  awards and honors of, 272, 285,
    320
  compositions and arrangements
    by, 89–90, 121–22
    juvenile, 42–43
    Liszt arrangements, 330,
      333–34, 336
    recordings of, 328
    Sousa *The Stars and Stripes
      Forever,* 158, 198
  death of, 151–52, 310–15
  education of, 41–42, 44–47,
    50–55
  enthusiasms of
    boxing, 30
    canasta, 185
    film, 120
    media attention, 240
    opera, 15, 36, 43, 73–74
  family relationships of, 66, 144–
    145, 165, 200, 237
  finances of, 114, 115, 118–19,
    169, 206–7, 225, 228
  health of
    colitis, 178–79, 210
    crushed finger, 155
    drug/alcohol dependence,
      259, 260, 262–65, 344
    hypochondria, 138
    manic-depressive condition,
      174–75, 198–99
    nausea, 310–11
    nervousness, 225
    normal, 231
    phlebitis, 148–49
    prostate removal, 256
  influence of, 168–69
  marriage of, 131–32, 136–38,
    169, 179, 180–84, 199

memoirs of, 13–14, 274–75
opinions on
  Cortot, 90–91
  Friedman, 94
  Hofmann, 48
  Mozart, 349–50
  Paderewski, 117–18
  pianists, 14–15, 70, 73
  Prokofiev, 89
  recording, 319–20
  Arthur Rubinstein, 188
  Schnabel, 71–72
  technical development, 47
performances. *See* Concert
  performances of Horowitz;
  Recorded performances of
  Horowitz
personal appearance of, 68, 103,
  231, 270
personality of
  childlikeness, 270
  eccentricity, 241–42
  extravagance, 95
  humor, 111
  self-centeredness, 179
  sexuality, 131, 136
  in youth, 47–48
professional relationships with
  Barere, 52–53
  Breest, 268, 269
  conductors, 125–26
  Frost, 202–5, 269
  Peter Gelb, 229–30, 266–
  268
  Giulini, 305–6
  Hofmann, 127
  Merovitch, 64–65, 119
  Milstein, 56–62, 64–65
  Neuhaus, 51–52
  Paderewski, 117
  Perahia, 306–7
  Pfeiffer, 32, 201, 202, 205
  Piatigorsky, 99
  Prokofiev, 88–89
  Rachmaninoff, 103–4, 111–
  113, 149–50, 152, 155–
  157

  Arthur Rubinstein, 93–94,
  186–89
  Rudolf Serkin, 70–71
  Shaw, 225–27
  Shehori, 303–5
  Toscanini, 132, 134–36,
  138–42
pupils of
  Blumfield, 195–96
  Davis, 207–9
  Fiorillo, 200–201
  Graffman, 189–90, 191–95
  Halim, 292–301
  Janis, 159, 160–64
  Kramer, 249
religious affiliation of, 137, 313
retirements of, 147–52, 176–
  213, 224–27
technique of
  Blumenfeld and, 52
  boxing and, 29–30
  Hambro and, 171–73
  hand position, 50, 296
  octave passages, 106–7, 207,
  269
  pedaling, 34, 193–94, 208,
  298
  Probst on, 263
  Anton Rubinstein and, 47
  Tarnowsky and, 46
Horowitz, Wanda (wife)
  art collection of, 119
  in Berlin, 280
  Bloom and, 210
  business acumen of, 159, 202,
  273, 274
  at Carnegie Hall recital (1965),
  215, 217
  Clementi repertoire and, 196–
  197
  as coexecutor, 314
  Columbia Records and, 202,
  204
  death of Vladimir and, 152,
  311, 312, 313
  Deutsche Grammophon and,
  270

Horowitz, Wanda, *continued*
early years of, 133–34
in Frankfurt, 286
friends of, 182, 185
Peter Gelb and, 258–59
Halim and, 297, 299, 300, 301
in Hamburg, 277–78
Ingram and, 198, 199
in *The Last Romantic,* 267–68
as librarian, 213
marriage of, 131–32, 136–38,
169, 179, 180–84, 199
medical views of, 178
memoirs of Vladimir and, 14,
274
Metropolitan Opera House
recital (1974) and, 230
in Moscow, 20, 25, 27
as mother, 145–46, 155, 165,
200, 232–33, 236–37,
237–38
Mozart A major Piano Concerto
and, 303, 306
at New York Plaza, 140
on Samuel Horowitz, 145
on Arthur Rubinstein, 187
on *60 Minutes,* 249
personality of, 180–82, 183–84
at Pinci's Acres, 314–15
Project X and, 223
RCA and, 201
retirements of Vladimir and,
206, 211, 225
Royal Festival Hall concert
(1982) and, 260
Aniela Rubinstein and, 189
self-doubt of Vladimir and, 151
Shaw and, 226
Steiner and, 252
Steinway & Sons and, 129
ticket buyers and, 213
tour of 1974–75 and, 239, 241
tour of 1983 and, 263, 264
in Vienna, 289, 290
in wartime Europe, 153–55
Horowitz-Milstein-Piatigorsky
Trio, 99–100

Horowitz: The Last Recording, 315
Horowitz Archives, 285, 354
Horowitz at Home (recording),
284–85, 307–8, 349, 351
Horowitz in Concert (recording),
219
*Horowitz in London: A Royal
Concert* (video), 261
Horowitz in Moscow (video/CD),
26, 30
Horowitz the Poet (recording), 285
Horwich, Sally, 25, 185
Hosfeld, Rolf, 278
Howard, Orrin, 245–46
Hume, Paul, 224
Huneker, James, 107
Hurok, Sol, 163

I

Imperial Opera (St. Petersburg),
51
Ingram, Lawrence, 198
Irion, Hermann, 128
Istomin, Eugene, 192
Iturbi, José, 93

J

Jameux, Dominique, 272–73
Janis, Byron, 159, 160–64, 192,
194, 207, 292
Jarmel, Dorle, 111
Jazz, 15–16, 169
Jelobinsky, Valérie, 157–58
Jena, Hans-Jörg von, 281
Jeopardy! (television program), 120
Jewish pianists, 69
Joachim, Joseph, 140
Joseph II, Holy Roman Emperor,
197
Judson, Arthur, 101–3, 111, 119–
120, 154, 159
Juilliard School, 314
piano students at, 300

K

Kabalevsky, Dmitri, 34–35
Kabos, Ilona, 304
Kaiser, Joachim, 270–71, 354
Kalb, Bernard, 23
Kapell, William, 56, 123
Katchen, Julius, 168
Katz, Mindru, 304
Keene, Constance, 185–86
Kennan, George F., 86–87
Kenyon, Nicholas, 257
KGB, 27
Kharkov (Ukraine), 40
Kiev, 39–40, 59–60
Kiev Conservatory, 44–47, 50–51, 55
Klaus, Prince, 287
Kleiber, Carlos, 270, 309
Kleiber, Erich, 67, 140
Klein, Howard, 177, 206, 211–212, 218–219
Klemperer, Otto, 67
Knabe pianos, 139
Knight, Celine, 311
Koch, Gerhard, 279–80, 286
Koch, Heinrich Christoph, 348
Kochanski, Paul, 51
Korvette's department store, 249
Koshetz, Nina, 58
Kotschenreuther, Hellmut, 282
Koussevitzky, Serge, 115–16
Kramer, Dean, 249
Krasner, Louis, 135
Kreisler, Fritz, 49
Kroll Opera, 67
Kubie, Lawrence, 178, 198, 199
Kuralt, Charles, 26

L

Lange, Hans, 135
Larrocha, Alicia de, 16
The Last Recording, 352–54
The Last Romantic (film). See *Vladimir Horowitz: The Last Romantic*
Lateiner, Jacob, 192
League of Nations, 153
Lefkowitz, Louis J., 231
Legato playing, 193–94
Lelong, Lucien, 137
Lenin, Vladimir Ilich, 50
Lenin Conservatory, 63
Leschetizky, Theodor, 44, 69, 92, 94
Levant, Oscar, 169–70
Levin, Robert, 348
Levitzki, Mischa, 73, 93, 98, 128
Lewisohn Stadium concerts, 101, 142
Leyda, Jay, 104, 155
Lhevinne, Josef, 126, 327
Lhevinne, Rosina, 217
Liapounov, Sergei, 54
Libidins, David, 159
Lichstein, Siegfried M., 234
Lieberman, Evsei, 58
Lieberson, Goddard, 202, 215, 223
Lincoln Center, 250, 256–57
Lintzman, Michael, 212–13
Lipatti, Dinu, 123, 151
Lipkin, Seymour, 192
Liszt, Franz
  Alkan and, 54
  compositions of
    Ballade, No. 2, B minor, 260, 319, 345
    Concerto No.1, E flat major, 84
    Etudes (after Paganini), 93, 327
    Faust Waltz, 14
    Feux follets, 73
    Hungarian Rhapsody No. 2, C sharp minor, 333–34
    Hungarian Rhapsody No. 6, D flat major, 207, 208
    Hungarian Rhapsody No. 11, A minor, 91

Liszt, Franz, *continued*
Hungarian Rhapsody No. 19,
D minor, 336
Impromptu, F sharp major,
352
Mephisto Waltz, 344
Petrarch Sonnets, 34
Scherzo and March, 341
Schubert transcriptions, 352
Sonata, B minor, 78, 79,
109–10, 254, 321–23,
343–44
Ständchen (after Schubert),
29, 208
Vallée d'Obermann, 340–41
*Weinen, Klagen, Sorgen,
Zagen,* Praeludium (after
Bach), 353
Devries and, 117
ivory carving of, 137
recordings of, 309
Anton Rubinstein and, 44
Schnabel and, 71, 72
Slavic pianism and, 70
Thalberg and, 9
Liszt Competition, 207
Lodaya, Zoya, 58
London Symphony Orchestra, 321
Longchampt, Jacques, 272
Long-play recordings, 329–38
Lopes, Giuliana, 267, 311, 312,
314
Lubbers, Ruud, 287
Lucerne Festival, 302

M

Ma, Yo-Yo, 284
Maazel, Lorin, 161, 227
McCormick, Cyrus, 114
Mach, Elyse, 203, 320
Magaloff, Nikita, 237
Mannerisms, 251
Mannes College of Music, 249
Marcus, Adele, 161–62, 163
Marek, George, 201

Marlboro Festival, 244
Marmontel, Antoine-François, 69
Marsh, Robert, 243
Massei, Max, 271–72, 320
Massin, Brigitte, 272
Maxwell, Elsa, 87
Maynor, Dorothy, 184
Maysles, Albert, 306
Media conferences. *See* Press
conferences
Medtner, Nicolai, 61, 104, 158–
159, 194
Mehta, Zubin, 255–56, 284
Melba, Nellie, 240
Mendelssohn, Felix, 325, 348
Mendelssohn, Francesco, 70, 83
Mengelberg, Willem, 124, 125, 135
Menuhin, Yehudi, 248
Merö, Yolanda, 128
Merovitch, Alexander, 68, 96,
119–20
concerts managed by
Berlin, 74, 75, 77, 79, 125
Dortmund, 123–24
Europe, 81
Hamburg, 79, 99
New York, 102–3, 109, 110
Paris, 101
Sonia Horowitz and, 235
Milstein and, 64–66, 100
Piatigorsky and, 99
Schnabel and, 71
Zereteli and, 87–88
Messenger (B'nai B'rith), 256
Metropolitan Museum of Art, 307
Metropolitan Opera House
performances of Horowitz,
228–31, 260, 263–64,
287–88, 345
Miaskovsky, Nikolai, 60–61
Michaelson, Vera, 238
Michelangeli, Arturo Benedetti, 15
Milhaud, Darius, 60, 87
Milstein, Nathan
depression of Horowitz and,
179, 199
From Russia to the West, 57, 274

Gradova and, 123
in Gstaad, 151–52
Wanda Horowitz and, 181
marriage of Horowitz and, 137, 138
Merovitch and, 100
on Berdichev, 37
on Brahms D minor Concerto performances, 143
on practicing, 27
on Rubinstein/Horowitz relationship, 189
painting and, 118
Piatigorsky and, 99
in Soviet Union, 56–62, 64–65
Mirovitch, Alfred, 120
Mitropoulos, Dmitri, 173
Mitterand, François, 272
Mlynarski, Emil, 189
Mohr, Franz
in Berlin, 282–83
Halim and, 293, 299
The Last Romantic and, 269
in Moscow, 25
John Steinway and, 187
Steinway piano CD 186 and, 210, 251–52
in Tokyo, 265
Molinari, Bernardino, 138
Monteux, Pierre, 125, 126, 140, 142, 349
Morrison, Bryce, 353
Moscheles, Ignaz, 325, 348
Moscow Conservatory, 31, 43, 51, 52
Moszkowski, Moritz, 212, 217
Mozart, Wolfgang Amadeus, 53, 138, 197, 286, 287, 295–296, 346–52
Adagio, B minor, 351–52
Concerto No. 23, K. 488, A major, 13, 302–6, 351
Sonata, K. 281, B flat major, 351
Sonata, K. 330, C major, 282, 350

Sonata, K. 331, A major, 340
Sonata, K. 333, B flat major, 350–51
Muck, Karl, 91, 97–98
Munch, Charles, 349
Munz, Mieczyslaw, 189
Music-Hall (New York), 247
Musicians Emergency Fund, 99
Musikvereinsaal (Vienna), 289
Musik-Zeitung (Berlin), 74
Mussorgsky, Modest
Boris Godunov, 51
Pictures at an Exhibition, 39, 326–27
Muzo-Narkompros, 59
Myers, Paul, 223
My Many Years (Arthur Rubinstein), 93

N

Nachrichten (Hamburg), 80–81
Nansen passports, 153
National Foundation for Infantile Paralysis, 158
NBC Symphony, 154–55, 158, 161, 323
Neuhaus, Heinrich, 51–52, 61, 64, 93
New Grove Dictionary of Music and Musicians, 167
New Statesman (periodical), 167
New York blackout (1965), 219, 220
New York critics, 107–9, 165–68, 218
New York Philharmonic
Barbirolli and, 156, 331
Beecham and, 102
Judson and, 101
Mehta and, 255–56
Ormandy and, 250–51, 344
Szell and, 173, 324
Toscanini and, 134–35, 142–143
Walter and, 325

New York *Times*
  Carnegie Hall recital (1965)
    and, 211, 217, 218–20
  Clementi recording and, 197–
    198
  Peter Gelb and, 229
  Halim and, 300
  influence of, 107
  Judson and, 102
  on Carnegie Hall 85th
    anniversary concert, 248–
    249
  on mannerisms of Horowitz,
    251
Nijdam, Oene W., 287
Noailles, Anna de, 87
Norrington, Roger, 348–49
Novaes, Guiomar, 128, 186
N. W. Ayer (firm), 252

O

Octave passages, 106–7, 207, 269
Ohlsson, Garrick, 168
Oistrakh, David, 58
Opera, 15, 36, 43, 73–74
Oratorio Society (New York), 248
Orchestre Symphonique de Paris,
  142
Ormandy, Eugene, 111, 126, 205,
  250–51, 253, 344
Österreichische Musik Zeitschrift,
  290

P

Pabst, Eugen, 80
Paderewski, Ignacy, 44, 117–18,
  128, 188, 240
Paganini, Niccolò, 93, 327
Paolo, Enrico, 137
Paris Conservatoire, 69, 83, 186
Paris critics, 85, 272–73
Het Parool (Amsterdam), 314
Patti, Adelina, 196, 240

Pavarotti, Luciano, 222, 228
Peck, Seymour, 229
Pedal technique, 34, 193–94, 208,
  298
Perahia, Murray, 168–69, 306–7,
  311
Performance practice, 346–47
*Performance Practices in Classic
  Music* (Rosenblum), 348
Performances of Horowitz. *See*
  Concert performances of
  Horowitz; Recorded
  performances of Horowitz
Persimfans (First Symphonic
  Ensemble), 60
Pfeiffer, John F. ("Jack"), 266,
  307
  at Carnegie Hall recital (1965),
    215, 216
  Columbia Records and, 202,
    205
  Wanda Horowitz and, 184, 267
  in *The Last Romantic*, 181–82,
    269
  meets Horowitz, 170–71
  Moscow trip (1986) and, 25–
    26, 32
  on Clementi repertoire, 197
  on health of Horowitz, 174,
    178, 225
  on Marek, 201
  records Horowitz at home, 196
  Silver Jubilee Concert recording
    and, 324
  spliced recordings and, 244
  Steiner and, 252
Philadelphia Orchestra, 101, 140,
  205
Philharmonic Hall (Leningrad),
  32–33
Philharmonic Hall (New York),
  250
Philharmonie (Berlin), 280, 289
Philipp, Isidor, 186
Pianists, 68–70
  American, 122–23
  German, 73, 86

Horowitz on, 14–15
Neuhaus on, 52
on Horowitz, 168–69
Russian, 15, 31, 70, 86, 206
Piano benches, 129–30
Piano regulation, 251
Piano rolls, 79, 90, 320–21
Pianos
Bechstein, 20, 72, 83
Gaveau, 83, 84, 85
Knabe, 139
Pleyel, 83, 350
Steinway. *See* Steinway pianos
Piano tuners, 129
Piatigorsky, Gregor, 99–100, 123, 137, 138
Picasso paintings, 119
Pirated recordings, 324–25
Pittsburgh Symphony, 161
Pleasants, Henry, 15–16, 116
Pleyel pianos, 83, 350
Polignac, Charles de, 90
Polignac, Princesse de, 87
Polivideo (firm), 26
Post (New York), 161
Poston, Gretchen, 252–53
Poulenc, Francis, 89, 90
Power failure (New York, 1965), 219, 220
Press conferences, 181, 229–30, 240, 277–78
Die Presse (Vienna), 290
Previn, André, 112
Pringsheim, Heinz, 76, 77–78
Private recordings, 208, 331–332
Probst, Richard, 25, 28, 263, 264, 267, 273–74
Prodigies, child, 40–42
Project X, 223–24
Prokofiev, Sergei, 88–89, 90
Concerto for Piano No. 3 V.H. on, 89
Concerto for Violin No. 1, 60–61
Sonata No. 6, 171
Sonata No. 7, 326

Sonata No. 8, 121
Sonatas, 157
Promotions, record-signing, 249, 306
Prostitutes, 123–24
Prunières, Henry, 84
Psychiatry, 178
Puchalsky, Vladimir, 44–46, 92

Q

Quantz, Johann Joachim, 348

R

Rabinovich, (accompanist), 110
Rachmaninoff, Sergei
Brahms C major Trio and, 99–100
Brahms D minor Piano Concerto and, 144
Concerto No. 2, Op. 18, C minor, 63–64, 112, 125, 161, 344
Concerto No. 3, Op. 30, D minor, performances of,
1927: 97
1928: 116
1930: 124, 321–22
1932: 92
1940: 111
1942: 156, 331–32
1951: 173, 331
1978: 250–51, 256
on Cortot, 90–91
death of, 156–57, 199
Firkusny on, 86
Friedman and, 94
German pianism and, 68
Sonia Horowitz and, 233
Vladimir Horowitz and, 111–113, 149–50, 152, 155–57
Iturbi and, 93
in Kiev, 48–49
Koshetz and, 58

Rachmaninoff, Sergei, *continued*
  Koussevitzky and, 115–16
  Miaskovsky on, 61
  Milstein on, 58
  Moment Musical, E flat minor,
      344
  in New York, 55, 102, 103–4
  New York debut of Horowitz
      and, 106, 109, 110
  performance of Concerto No. 3
      by (1940), 111
  Polka de W. R., 344
  Prelude, A minor, 194
  Prelude, C sharp minor, 116
  Prelude, G sharp minor, 28
  Prokofiev and, 88–89
  Puchalsky and, 45
  Rhapsody on a Theme of
      Paganini, 208
  Arthur Rubinstein on, 188
  Schubert and, 69
  Sonata, cello and piano, Op. 19,
      G minor, 343
  Sonata, No. 2, Op. 36, B flat
      minor, 262, 345
  Steinway & Sons and, 128, 129
  Symphonic Dances, 155–56
  Toscanini and, 141
  on World War II, 153
Rachmaninoff Competition, 192
Ragtime music, 89
Ramey, Philip, 60, 111
Ravel, Maurice, 88
RCA Victor (firm), 171, 198,
      201, 243–44, 268, 327–
      328, 336
RCA Victor Symphony Orchestra,
      331, 332
Reagan, Ronald, 22, 23, 25, 26,
      284
Reagan, Mrs. Ronald, 284
Recital performances of Horowitz.
      See Concert performances
      of Horowitz
Recorded performances of
      Horowitz, 209, 319–45,
      355–405

early, 90, 124, 143
for
  CBS/Sony, 308–9
  Columbia Records, 202–5,
      218–20, 225, 243–44,
      284–85, 336
  Deutsche Grammophon, 268,
      269–71, 290, 291
  RCA Victor, 171, 198, 201,
      243–44, 336
  pirated, 324–25
  private, 208, 331–32
Record-signing promotions, 249,
      306
Red Seal Records (RCA Victor),
      171
Regulation, piano, 251
Reinecke, Karl, 116
Reiner, Fritz, 136, 140, 251, 331,
      332
Repeats, 351
Respighi, Ottorino, 138
*The Return of Horowitz to Carnegie
      Hall* (recording), 339–40
La revue musicale, 84
Rich, Alan, 218
Richter, Sviatoslav, 15, 52, 206,
      217, 327
Rimsky-Korsakov, Nikolai, 51
Der Ring des Nibelungen (Wagner),
      61
Robin Hood Dell concerts, 101,
      142
Rodzinski, Artur, 102
Rodzinski, Halina, 137
Rolland, Romain, 91
Rolls Royce automobiles, 95
Romantic style, 69, 71
Roschitz, Karlheinz, 289
Rosen, Charles, 331
Rosenblum, Sandra P., 348
Rosenthal, Moriz, 73, 118
Rostropovich, Mstislav, 248, 253,
      343
Rothschild, Baron de, 83
Rothstein, Edward, 259
Royal Opera, 260, 261

Royal Philharmonic Orchestra, 173

Rubato, 70, 339, 349

Rubin, David, 225, 252

Rubini, Giovanni Battista, 43

Rubinstein, Aniela, 186, 189

Rubinstein, Anton, 31
  Blumenfeld and, 44, 51
  Devries and, 117
  Gunn and, 116
  hands of, 233
  Horowitz style and, 34, 47
  influence of, 43–44
  Villoing and, 197

Rubinstein, Arthur, 345
  Horowitz's relations with, 93–94, 186–89, 217
  Kapell and, 123
  Liszt B minor Sonata and, 322
  memoirs of, 274
  on Horowitz, 82, 281
  on Parisian salons, 87
  Paganini-Liszt-Busoni E flat Etude and, 327
  Toscanini and, 141

Rubinstein, Nicholas, 43

Russian Encyclopedia, 38

Russian Musical Society, 104

Russian pianists, 15, 31, 70, 86, 206

Russian piano music, 157–58

Russian refugees, 87–88

Russian Revolution, 50, 54–55, 59–60

Russian War Relief (organization), 158

Rutgers students, 219

S

St. Petersburg Conservatory, 43, 63

St. Petersburg Imperial Opera, 51

Saint-Saëns, Camille, 15, 95, 198

Saitzoff, Natasha
  Sonia Horowitz and, 234, 237

on Dombrowski, 45

on Horowitz family, 39–40, 66

on Samuel Horowitz, 145

on Vladimir Horowitz's birth, 37–38, 39

Salle des Agriculteurs (Paris), 84–85

Salome (Strauss), 73–74

Samaroff, Olga, 116, 122, 128

Sam Goody record store, 306

Samuel, Harold E., 285

Samuels, Jon M., 355

Sanborn, Pitts, 108–9, 136

Saperton, David, 116

Sauer, Emil, 73

Scala Orchestra, 13, 305–6, 351

Scarlatti, Domenico, 194, 279, 287, 337–38

Sch., S. (German critic), 80–81

Scharoun, Hans, 280

Schindler, Anton, 167

Schlesische Zeitung (Breslau), 97

Schliepe (critic), 77

Schmidt, Paul, 119

Schmieg and Kotzian (firm), 129–130

Schmitz, E. Robert, 167

Schnabel, Artur
  Fleisher and, 192
  Horowitz and, 65, 67, 71–72
  individuality of, 68–69
  on Rachmaninoff, 111–12
  piano rolls and, 321
  Schubert B flat Impromptu and, 352

Schneider, Edouard, 83–84, 85

Schnittke, Alfred, 31

Schön, Max Broesecke-. *See* Broesecke-Schön, Max

Schreiber, Wolfgang, 290–91

Schubert, Franz, 69, 352
  Impromptu, G flat major, 290, 337
  Impromptu, Op. 142, No. 3, B flat major, 352
  Piano Sonata, D. 960, B flat major, 174, 177, 225, 333

Schubert, Franz, *continued*
 Ständchen, 29, 208
 Die Winterreise, 58
Schumach, Murray, 213
Schumann, Karl, 279
Schumann, Robert, 90, 182
 Arabesque, 245–46, 282, 326
 Dichterliebe, 343
 Etudes symphoniques, 173
 Fantasy, Op. 17, C major, 71,
   216, 218, 219, 340
 Humoresque, 344
 Kinderscenen, 261, 262, 295,
   330, 336–37
 Kinderscenen. Träumerei, 172–
   173, 337
 Kreisleriana, 16, 271
   concert performances, 33,
     272, 279, 280, 281
   recorded performances, 205,
     341–42, 352
 Sonata No. 1, Op. 11, F sharp
   minor, 44
 Sonata No. 3, Op. 14, F minor
   (*Concerto without
   Orchestra*), 245, 343
 Sonata No. 3, Op. 14, F minor
   (*Concerto without
   Orchestra*). Variations on a
   Theme by Clara Wieck,
   331, 342
 Toccata, Op. 7, C major, 53,
   327–28
Scionti, Silvio, 207
Scriabin, Alexander, 19–20, 88–
   89, 198, 334, 342–43
 Etude, Op. 2, No. 1, C sharp
   minor, 24–25, 28
 Sonata No. 5, 343
 Sonata No. 6, 194
 Sonata No. 9, 174, 216–17,
   340
 Sonata No. 10, 219, 341
Scriabin, Yelena, 20
Scriabin Museum, 19–21
Seidl, Anton, 348
Serkin, Peter, 208

Serkin, Rudolf
 death of, 307
 Graffman and, 193
 Horowitz and, 70–71, 151,
   152, 177
 Istomin and, 192
 Marlboro Festival and, 244
 Peter Serkin and, 208
Sert, Misia, 87
Shaw, Harold, 225–27
 concert fees and, 228
 Drucker and, 241
 Peter Gelb and, 229, 258, 259–
   260
 Halim and, 293
 on artistic temperament, 242–
   243
 White House performance
   (1978) and, 252–54
Shehori, Mordecai, 303–5
Sheppard, Craig, 262
Shultz, George P., 284
Sibelius, Jean, 166
Siloti, Alexander, 73
Silver Jubilee Concert, 173–74,
   333, 340
Singers, 43
Siskind, Jacob, 328
Les Six (French composers), 87
60 Minutes (television program),
   249
Sketches from a Life (Kennan), 86–
   87
Slavic pianists, 69–70
Slonimsky, Nicolas, 37
Smart, George, 351
Smith, Ileene, 274
Sobinov, Leonid, 51, 58–59
Sofronitzky, Vladimir, 85
Sole (fish), 24, 241
Solomon (Solomon Cutner), 15
Sony/CBS Records (firm), 269,
   308–9
Sousa, John Philip, 158, 198
Soviet-American cultural
   exchange, 22, 284
"Special attractions," 120

Spellman, Francis, 188
Der Spiegel (Hamburg), 277, 279
Stadlen, Peter, 262
Städtische Oper (Berlin), 67
Stalin, Joseph, 153
The Star-Spangled Banner, 98
Steinberg, Michael, 167, 224–25
Steinberg, William, 156
Steiner, Christian, 252, 270
Steinert, Alexander, 87
Steinway & Sons (firm), 110–11,
    119–20, 126–29
Steinway, Henry Z., 127
Steinway, John, 187
Steinway pianos, 72, 74, 83, 97,
    126–27
  CD 186, 210, 251–52, 299
  CD 279 503, 25, 137, 252
  CD 314 503, 137
  CD 443, 252
Stereo recordings, 329–38
Stern, Isaac, 217, 248, 284, 343
Stern, Vera, 254
Stevens, Risë, 249
Stock, Frederick, 135
Stokowski, Leopold, 140
Stolyarsky, Peter, 56
Straram, Walter, 84
Strauss, Johann (the younger),
    297
Strauss, Richard, 73–74
Stravinsky, Igor, 87, 327
Süddeutsche Zeitung (Munich),
    278–79
Sulungan, Stephan, 293, 296
Sunday Morning (television
    program), 30
Susskind, Walter, 173
Szell, George, 140–41, 173, 324
Szymanowski, Karol, 60, 90

T

Tageblatt (Berlin), 97
Tarnowsky, Sergei
  Blumenfeld and, 51

Blumfield and, 195
Sophie Horowitz and, 48
Leschetizky and, 44
Milstein and, 57
on Vladimir Horowitz, 41–42
at Pasadena concert (1976),
    245–46
as teacher, 46
in World War I, 50
Taruskin, Richard, 348
Tatum, Art, 16
Taubman, Howard, 197, 222, 223
Taubman, Philip, 30, 32–35
Tausig, Karl, 44, 352
Tchaikovsky, Piotr, 117–18, 142,
    247
  Concerto No. 1, Op. 23, B flat
    minor
    concert performances of, 65,
      74, 77, 79–80, 85, 105–9,
      125, 158, 166
    Philipp on, 186
    recorded performances of,
      323–25
  Eugene Onegin, 34, 340
  Furtwängler and, 98
  Symphony No. 6 (*Pathétique*),
    34
  Trio, Op. 50, A minor, 343
"Tea for Two" (Youmans), 16
Television concerts
  London, 261
  Moscow, 30–31
  New York, 222–24, 255–56,
    341
  Vienna, 290
  Washington, D.C., 253–54
Television interviews, 249
Television programs, 120
Tempos, 139–40, 290, 348. *See
    also* Rubato
  Beethoven *Emperor* Concerto,
    135–36
  Beethoven Ninth Symphony,
    349
  Brahms D minor Concerto,
    143–44

Tempos, *continued*
  Liszt B minor Sonata, 322
  Mozart A major Concerto, 306
  Rachmaninoff Third Concerto,
    156, 331–32
  Tchaikovsky First Concerto,
    105–6, 323
Thalberg, Sigismond, 9, 54
Thibaudet, Jean-Yves, 14
Thompson, Oscar, 136
Thomson, Virgil, 165–67, 168,
  224
Ticket office mismanagement, 169,
  230–31, 254
Tokyo critics, 264–65, 283
Toscanini, Arturo, 119, 149, 156,
  256, 302
  Battistini and, 59
  Beethoven *Emperor* Concerto
    and, 92, 135–36
  Blumenfeld and, 51
  Brahms B flat major Concerto
    and, 154–55
  Brahms D minor Concerto and,
    142–43
  death of, 157, 188, 199
  Fascism and, 152
  Horowitz marriage and, 132,
    137
  Sonia Horowitz and, 145–46,
    233, 234
  Wanda Horowitz and, 181
  Janis and, 161
  Koussevitzky and, 115
  Muck and, 98
  on Paderewski, 117
  rehearsals of, 126, 140–41
  Arthur Rubinstein on, 189
  Sobinov and, 58
  Tchaikovsky First Concerto and,
    158, 166, 323–24
  Thomson on, 166
Toscanini, Carla, 133
Toscanini, Wally. *See* Castelbarco,
  Wally
Toscanini, Wanda. *See* Horowitz,
  Wanda (wife)

Toscanini family, 132–33
Tosi, Pier Francesco, 349
Tual, Denise, 83
Tuners, piano, 129
Turini, Ronald, 200

U

Urchs, Ernst, 110–11

V

Van der Ven, 287
Variety (periodical), 256
Vengerova, Isabelle, 116,
    191, 192, 194, 195,
    234
Verlinden, Gérard, 287
Vetter, Eddie, 287
Videocassettes, 120
Vienna critics, 290
Vienna Philharmonic, 290
Villoing, Alexander, 197
Vladimir, Prince, 39
*Vladimir Horowitz: A Television
    Concert at Carnegie Hall,*
    223–24
*Vladimir Horowitz: The Last
    Romantic* (film), 181–82,
    267–69, 271, 274, 286,
    306, 350
Vladimir Horowitz in Moscow
    (television program),
    30
Vlasenko, Lev, 31
Vossische Zeitung, 77
Vuillermoz, Emile, 85

W

Wagner, Cosima, 137
Wagner, Richard, 14, 61, 69, 91,
    348
Wallace, Mike, 249

Walter, Bruno, 140, 143, 286, 290, 325
Warnecke, Kläre, 277
Watts, André, 15, 169
Webster, Beveridge, 304
Weissmann, Adolf, 78
Welte-Mignon piano rolls, 78–79, 320
WETA-TV, 253
Wheel of Fortune (television program), 120
Wiesel, Marion, 274
Wilford, Ronald, 258, 259, 265, 266
Wilson, Charlie, 222
Wolff-Sachs agency, 74, 75, 78
Woodside, Lyndon, 248
Woolsey Hall, 285
World War I, 50
World War II, 153, 157
Wozzeck (Berg), 67

Y

Yale University, 285, 314, 354
Yoshida, Hidekazu, 264–65, 283
Youmans, Vincent, "Tea for Two," 16

Z

Zecchi, Carlo, 134, 207
Zeisler, Fannie Bloomfield, 122
Die Zeit (Hamburg), 279
Zeitlin, Lev, 60
Zereteli, Alexis, 87–88
Zimbalist, Efrem, 57, 161
Zimmerman, Pierre, 69
Zimmermann, Helene, 79–80
Zorba the Greek (television program), 224
Zwerin, Charlotte, 306

About the Author

HAROLD C. SCHONBERG, one of the world's leading music critics, was born in New York City. He received his B.A. from Brooklyn College and an M.A. from New York University. He has been conferred the honorary degrees of Doctor of Letters from Temple University and Doctor of Humane Letters from Grinnell College. He joined the New York *Times* in 1950 as music critic, was named senior music critic in 1960, and continued at that post until he became cultural correspondent in 1980. Schonberg was awarded the Pulitzer Prize for Criticism in 1971. The author of thirteen books—including *The Great Pianists, The Great Conductors, Lives of the Great Composers, Facing the Music,* and *The Glorious Ones*—he has served as a juror in many international piano competitions, including the Rubinstein in Tel Aviv and the Liszt in Budapest.